THE NEW BYZANTINES

SEAN MATHEWS

The New Byzantines

The Rise of Greece and Return of the Near East

HURST & COMPANY, LONDON

First published in the United Kingdom in 2025 by
C. Hurst & Co. (Publishers) Ltd.,
New Wing, Somerset House, Strand, London WC2R 1LA

Copyright © Sean Mathews, 2025
All rights reserved.

The right Sean Mathews to be
identified as the author of this publication is asserted
by him in accordance with the Copyright, Designs and
Patents Act, 1988.

Distributed in the United States, Canada and Latin America by Oxford
University Press, 198 Madison Avenue, New York, NY 10016, United
States of America.

A Cataloguing-in-Publication data record for this book
is available from the British Library.

ISBN: 9781805264187

EU GPSR Authorised Representative
Easy Access System Europe Oü, 16879218
Address: Mustamäe tee 50, 10621, Tallinn, Estonia
Contact Details: gpsr.requests@easproject.com, +358 40 500 3575

www.hurstpublishers.com

Printed and bound in Great Britain by Bell and Bain Ltd, Glasgow

For Mark,
My brother and fellow traveler

CONTENTS

Map		ix
1.	Dancing in Piraeus	1
2.	Epirus: Pashas, Communists and Merchants	37
3.	Pearl of the Aegean: Orientalists and Oligarchs	67
4.	The Last Pasha of Kavala	111
5.	Egypt: Greece's Ally or a Ticking Time Bomb?	133
6.	Cairo: Beer in the Greek Club	157
7.	Priests and Crypto-Christians: Intrigue in Jerusalem	179
8.	The Israel–Greece Alliance	211
9.	Thrace: Greek Minarets	229
10.	Istanbul: The Old Byzantines	261
11.	Meze in Kadiköy	285
Epilogue: Sea Captains on the Edge of Asia		307
Notes		317
Selected Bibliography		337
Acknowledgements		339
Index		341

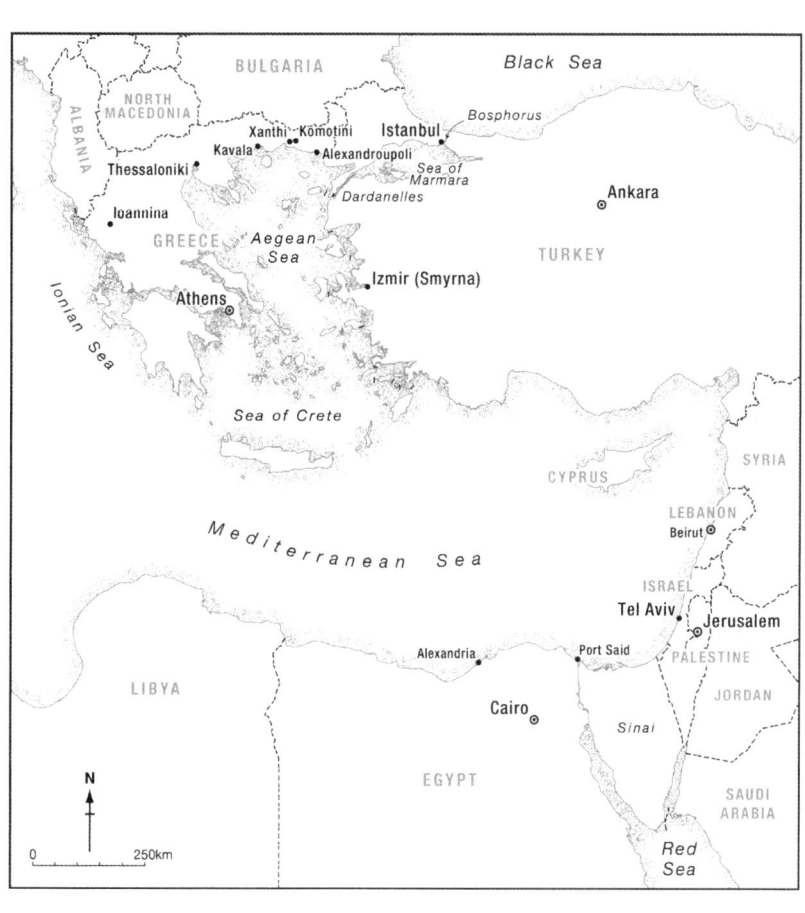

1

DANCING IN PIRAEUS

The hastily built post-war apartments that blanket skylines in the Balkans and the Middle East tend to be depressing eye-sores. In Bulgaria and the former Yugoslavia, they recall a dreary, centrally planned existence. In the Arab world's Mediterranean periphery, the oppressiveness of water-stained concrete is offset by a certain playfulness, usually achieved with a battered red or blue-and-white striped awning. Athens' *polykatoikias* are their own beasts.

Apartments in Athens are tiered, so their balconies increase in size the higher one goes. The fourth and fifth floors are gardens, overflowing with jasmine, palm trees, pointy yuccas and agaves, sticking out of big terracotta pots. Pops of yellow and orange burst out from lemon and kumquat trees. These oases float above an expanse of off-white concrete, among satellite dishes, rusty water tanks and solar panels. What would be third-world urban sprawl in any other city, takes on beauty in Athens. The Acropolis is an afterthought in this skyline.

At ground level, on a narrow street in Neos Kosmos, all I see are shutters. They are drawn down on the buildings around me, perhaps for privacy, but just as likely they are getting scrubbed clean for their next guests. Because of its central location, relatively affordable property prices, and proximity to the subway, Neos Kosmos has one of the highest concentrations of Airbnbs of any neighborhood in the Greek capital. In Athens, where short-term rentals have ferociously mushroomed, that is no small feat.

Neos Kosmos earned its name, New World, welcoming arrivals of a different sort. Greek and Armenian refugees fleeing the persecution of Christians during the Ottoman Empire's implosion settled here during the last years of the First World War and after 1923, when Greece and Turkey agreed to exchange their Christian and Muslim populations, in a round of state-sponsored ethnic cleansing.

Greece was therefore a homeland for refugees from the Middle East before migration became a buzzword in our era. Then, it was Christian refugees. In a twist, the ones who settled in Neos Kosmos faced discrimination from their own religious and ethnic kin. They were seen as a burden on the state's resources. But a deeper battle was at play over Greece's culture. These Christians were viewed as strange, oriental cousins by Athens' European Greeks. There are many shades to the migration debate. The backlash against migration in our era is more complex than the "racist hate" narrative suggests.

A few of the two- and three-story tenements the refugees built still stand, but most were torn down in the decades after the Second World War when Greek migrants flooded into Athens from the countryside. People clawed for every square inch of this city. The Athens that visitors see today was built raw and haphazardly, basically as a sprawling refugee camp, just like other cities that rim the Eastern Mediterranean. But again, its development was unique. There was no forced egalitarianism, government housing program or even private bank-lending. Instead, a totally organic system emerged called *antiparochi*, through which property owners gave developers their land to construct apartments. In exchange, the builders saved some units for the owners and their families.[1]

The result is that Athens is lathered in concrete, and aesthetically closer to Damascus and Alexandria than Rome and Madrid. This turns off most Western tourists who come to hop around whitewashed islands, but I find it delights Middle Easterners. My Lebanese friends who visit play a game called "Guess Where," snapping pictures on the street and asking whether the scene is Athens or Beirut.

I turn down an alley where beauty salon girls smoke cigarettes on their stoops. Going by the smoldering stubs in front of him, Tasos Meneshian appears already to be into his morning pack of cigarettes. He sits on a small second-floor balcony. A garden hose snakes around cheap plastic patio furniture and an awning is pulled low for privacy. A tiny thimble of syrupy Turkish coffee and a copper *briki* lie on the table.

"When I first saw Neos Kosmos, it reminded me of Beirut. I felt right at home," he told me. "I threw away my plan to go to America and put my roots here."

Tasos, whose Armenian name is Harout, speaks Arabic, Armenian, Turkish and Greek. The sixty-three-year-old's life reads like a novel from a bygone era. He would not be out of place in any grimy port city of the Eastern Mediterranean whether it be Muslim or Christian; Arab, Turkish or Greek.

Tasos was born in Aleppo, Syria. His ancestors had fled from Gaziantep in Turkey during the Armenian genocide as the Ottoman Empire collapsed. Thousands of Armenians and other Christians sought refuge in Aleppo, which was then controlled by colonial France. Tasos came of age when Syria was under the grip of Hafez al-Assad, the father of Syria's former leader Bashar, who was toppled by Islamist militants in 2024, ending five decades of Assad family rule. Aged twenty-two, Tasos was drafted into the Syrian army. He fought in the Lebanese Civil

War. Hafez al-Assad deftly manipulated warring Christian and Palestinian sides in that conflict to exert influence over Syria's smaller neighbor. Tasos once pulled up one of his pant legs and showed me a long scar, a wound from the war. He has a full-grey beard and the scraggy body type that is rare in the West but common in the former Ottoman world. When he returned home from Lebanon, Hafez's government tried to draft him again. This time he fled. He drifted around Beirut and the Jordanian port of Aqaba until he made his way to Athens. "We are closer to Jordan and Lebanon than the tourists realize. Greece is a Middle Eastern country," he told me.

Tasos' etched, veined hands bear the marks of a man who has spent a lifetime working as a car-upholsterer. With his son George, we talk about the wars in Gaza and Ukraine.

Tasos has a sharp mind for geopolitics—the kind of understanding that has nothing to do with ideology or university education, but lived experience. It is brutally realist and cynical. You find it among men like Tasos in Greece, which is a frontier state clinging to the West for protection as wars and migration rage just outside its borders.

"We used to drive in the summer from Athens to Aleppo to visit my family," Tasos said. "That was a beautiful drive when my kids were young. I told my family they would destroy Syria. Now, Erdoğan and Israel own it," he said, remarking on the two regional powers who have grabbed territory there in the wake of the Assad dynasty's collapse.

Tasos doesn't need to travel to the Middle East anymore, because it is coming to him. "All the apartment buildings around us have been bought up by Lebanese and Israelis. I have lived here for forty years. I've never heard so much Arabic on the street as I hear now. The traffic and parking are awful."

* * *

DANCING IN PIRAEUS

I first met Tasos' son, George, in 2020 at Athens' Syntagma Square. I was there reporting on a rally held by Greeks and Armenians in front of Parliament to denounce Azerbaijan and Türkiye during the second Nagorno Karabakh war. Greece and Armenia share close ties. Both are small states made up of diaspora Christian communities whose people endured ethnic cleansing in the last days of the Ottoman Empire. The protestors burned an Azeri flag and railed against Turkish President Recep Tayyip Erdoğan.[2] George was the mellow guy in the crowd.

He is big, gregarious, and has an unquenchable thirst for alcohol, but I have yet to see him drunk. We became fast friends. In the span of one drinking session, usually with a *nargile* (water pipe) between us, our conversation bounces from George complaining about Greece's corruption and the difficulties of landing a job here, to politics, women, and history. Like most of my Greek guy friends, George is allergic to calling it an early night. Our winter hangout is a tiny Athenian dive bar called Batman. The earliest we arrive is midnight. For George, the weekend isn't a success unless he drops me at my door, staggering with my keys, as the sun rises.

The Meneshians, like most Greek families I know, are a synthesis of East and West. But because of Tasos' Syrian roots, George is cognizant of the cultural similarities in a way I find other Greeks are not, or are reluctant to admit. In fact, George embraces them.

"We are in the European Union and have European freedoms. I can work in Brussels if I want, but the Greek mentality is Middle Eastern. Our politics is Eastern."

It was George who introduced me to the *nargile* bars and *ouzeris* in Piraeus. Athens' gritty port neighborhood is a warren of traffic-clogged streets, *polykatoikias*, crumbling neoclassical shops and intimidating *kafenios*, where old men sit flicking *kombologia* (worry beads) and sipping Turkish coffee. Piraeus has the veneer of being frozen in time. But it is changing.

American officials and lawmakers I meet as a journalist know Piraeus because China controls the main port. The Chinese COSCO shipping company owns a sixty-seven per cent stake in the Piraeus Port Authority, having bought a majority stake in 2009 and expanded it in 2016 when Greece's cash-strapped government further privatized the port during its economic crisis.

Piraeus Port is one of China's most valuable assets in the Eastern Mediterranean. Despite the Americans hyperventilating about its control, businessmen in Athens credit COSCO with streamlining operations and running the port smoothly. There has been little drama. For me, Piraeus underscores how underwhelming China's influence is, at least in the Eastern Mediterranean. China took over commercial operations at Piraeus Port, as the United States military expanded its influence throughout Greece. Today, Greek diplomats wouldn't dare play China off against the United States. They wake up every morning paranoid that the United States is going to abandon NATO or leave them at the mercy of their increasingly expansionist NATO ally and historic foe, Türkiye.

The development that is more palpable here is the nearby Ellinikon Project. A coastal strip of land that was once Athens' airport is now the biggest urban renewal project in Europe. Next door to gritty Piraeus, a new Dubai is being built, an isolated playground for the uber rich. Greece wants to fill it up with rich investors from the East.

After years of delays, the cranes and trucks on the Athenian coast are working at a rapid, decidedly non-Greek pace to get this project done. Sleek glass-fronted apartments are oversold. Ellinikon is just one project that encapsulates the wave of foreign money flooding into Athens and sending real estate prices soaring.

Turks, Emiratis, Chinese, Israelis, Lebanese, Egyptians, rich Europeans and Americans are buying up the city at a head-spinning rate. The wealth is diffuse, but a lot of it is coming from east and south of Greece. This speaks to the increasing multipolarity of this region. Money and people from smaller countries are sloshing across the Eastern Mediterranean. China and the United States matter less. A wealth divide now pits poorer Greeks against their richer neighbors who aren't from Europe. In sum, to understand this region, look to Ellinikon not COSCO.

Piraeus is a target for foreign real estate speculation because of its proximity to the Ellinikon Project and relatively cheaper prices. Apartment values here rose almost thirty per cent in 2024.[3] The rally is leaving priced-out Greeks awestruck.

One hotel manager in the posh city-center neighborhood of Kolonaki told me about a client from Israel who stays weeks at a time at her hotel, as he scours Piraeus, a twenty-minute cab ride away, for deals.

"He said he was going to buy a whole block of apartments! He made an offer to buy our hotel," the manager said. "They treat Athens like a shopping mall."

The tourists who descend on Piraeus for ferries to the islands don't spend much time here. Despite the rush of foreign investors, Piraeus' bars and clubs still attract a decidedly Greek crowd, which means women with lots of makeup, bearded men with crisp fades in T-shirts, and everyone dressed in black.

Piraeus has always had a seedy, underground identity. The classier bars and pricier tavernas are located around a smaller port in the neighborhood that, until Turkey's 1974 invasion of northern Cyprus, was called Turkolimano. Greeks dropped the prefix alluding to their neighbor's name, and now almost everyone but the oldest Greeks call it Mikrolimano. If you ever wondered, this is how Turkish coffee magically transformed into Greek coffee.

Tasos is under no illusions. "This is the soft Middle East," he said. "It's Alexandria, but with more alcohol and girls."

By 2 am, the clubs in Piraeus switch off American hits in favor of Greek pop music. The tone is unabashedly oriental. I remember going to one party, where George and I descended the steps into the basement of an old warehouse refashioned into a subterranean party venue. It was packed with twenty-something Greeks dancing to a new hit by Greek singer Despina Vandi called, "Ya Habibi." When the lyrics hit the spot where Vandi says *Tsiftefli*, the women toyed with the belly dance, coiling their arms and flexing their midriffs.

"The Arabs stole belly dance from us. It's ours!" Anastasia, a twenty-nine-year-old primary school teacher screamed into my ear above the music. I avoided going down the dangerous rabbit-hole of who has the most righteous claim to belly dance, but said the party in Piraeus put those in New York City and Miami to shame.

"This is why I am not leaving Greece. In the United States, you have a better economy, but you work until you die. We are more like the Lebanese. We know how to have fun," Anastasia said.

Here is another trend simmering in Greece. During the economic crisis, an estimated 500,000 Greeks, mostly young and educated, moved abroad.[4] Now, the diaspora is trying to return—that includes second- and third-generation Greeks. Conservative ones I meet in New York City and London blame "woke culture" in the West and the decay of those cities; those on the Left cite the better work-life-balance in Athens. It's two sides of the same coin. As Greece leaves the financial crisis behind, it's drawing people back, particularly the moneyed who can work remotely.

Only a few Greeks I meet now in their twenties and thirties want to leave. Most are trying to hitch their fortunes to the country's tourism boom, which has been chalking up record numbers since the pandemic. The Greeks are intent on extracting every euro they can out of the arrivals. I have a friend who is a promising political scientist who works for a company handling golden visa investments. Another is a doctor who goes to Mykonos for medical tourism. Riding this sugar high is the surest way to make good money in Greece.

"My salary is €900 a month. It almost doesn't pay for my make-up expenses, but live in the United States or UK? Never," Anastasia said.

She used a new government program that lowers mortgage payments for first-time Greek homebuyers to purchase a bungalow on her home island of Kefalonia for less than a €100,000 at a mortgage rate that would make Americans salivate. Her parents are helping her renovate it.

"I was lucky, because I have a stable salary and I'm from a region where tourists go," she said.

At 5 am, the pop hits die down and "Stin Athina Mou" ("My Athens") comes on. The song was released by a Greek heartthrob singer and has become an end-of-party favorite. In the basement we break into separate groups and crouch in low circles around dancers. Arms extended and faces solemn, they move as if in a trance. Toward the end of the song, some drop to their knees and slap the floor with their hands or take shots of booze.

This dance is called *Zeibekiko*. It has no set moves. The dancer feels where he or she wants to go. *Zeibekiko* originated in Asia Minor, modern-day Türkiye, during the days of the Ottoman Empire. Despite its age, *Zeibekiko* resonates with young Greeks in a way folk music or the Great American Songbook simply don't in the West.

Zeibekiko can also be danced to *rebetiko*, a type of Greek urban blues music. *Rebetiko's* iconic instrument is the bouzouki. This was the music of poor Greeks who plied their trade across ports in the Near East like Beirut, Smyrna (modern-day Turkish Izmir), Alexandria, Istanbul, Piraeus, and Salonica. Their typical haunts were "hashish-smoking dens and waterfront bars, with idle hours spent over the nargileh, and with a dandified trick of flicking those tasseled and time killing amber beads," British travel writer Patrick Leigh Fermor observed.[5]

Fermor first encountered *rebetiko* on the Black Sea coast while walking to Istanbul in the late 1930s. He called the steps to it a "burlesque Turkish belly dance," saying: "Critics of these dances may be right in dubbing them oriental, but they are wrong to call them un-Greek ... To me, they seemed at the time, and they still seem, to be exactly that amalgam of Greece and the Orient which is covered by the word Byzantine."[6]

No topic is taboo for *rebetiko* crooners: the white slave trade, drugs, and prison life all feature. The songs were considered so perverse that they were banned in Greece by the right-wing dictator Ioannis Metaxas in the 1930s. Another military dictatorship, known as the Junta, banned them again in the late 1960s and early 1970s. For these dictators, *rebetiko* was a decadent oriental stain on the Hellenes, heirs of ancient Greece and the founders of the Western world. Of course, the dictators' hatred for *rebetiko* only added to its popularity. Not all Greeks appreciate the genre today, but it is considered a part of Greek DNA.

My favorite is the song "Misirlou," or "Egyptian Girl," which has been recorded in Greek, Arabic, Hebrew and Turkish. For me, *rebetiko* is a knot that links Greece to the Middle East.

* * *

I have lived across Greece and what we popularly call the Middle East since 2019. Although I grew up Greek-American in upstate New York, I had no idea where *rebetiko* originated, any more than I knew about the other similarities between Greece and this region, which Western popular culture has drilled people into associating, almost exclusively, with the Arab world and Islam.

I knew the flavors and rituals of my father's Greek family. I would taste my *YiaYia*'s (grandmother's) bitter Turkish coffee and watch as my dad mixed his Ouzo with ice until it reached a milky white hue. I learned that, unlike us, the few Lebanese families who attended our Greek Orthodox Church sprinkled pistachio on their baklava. But I didn't know they had their own anise alcohol concoction called *arak* or that Turkish coffee could be deliciously flavored with cardamom. All of that came later.

When I was twenty-three years old, I was in medical school. Plowing through the deluge of exams and tests, I had forgotten to ask whether I actually wanted a career in medicine. When I finally asked myself the question, I dropped out and went to Greece without a job or plans. I had been to Greece before, but this was different—a stopover on my way to Amman, Jordan where I had decided to study Arabic. I only had a vague understanding of what made my dad's immigrant Greek family different from those of my friends growing up. It wasn't just the beloved and over-hyped "Mediterranean culture." The staunchest Italian-American families I knew didn't have our traits or historical baggage. Living and traveling across Jordan, Lebanon, Egypt and Türkiye, I realized that Greece is much closer to its Eastern neighbors.

Athens ended up being the perfect base for me to get a foothold as a low-paid, freelance journalist. It is a forgiving city and its airport provides cheap, easy access to the Arab world. Living in Athens and traveling across the region, I discerned a continuum between Greece and its neighbors. It was hard to name. One of the problems is that Greece itself is a notoriously difficult country to pin down.

The British journalist David Holden said Greece "might be defined as not so much a place, as a happening."[7] In Neos Kosmos and Piraeus you sense Greece's fluidity; its people and customs came from lands outside Greece's modern borders. Speaking the

Greek language is a defining feature, but many of the refugees who settled in Neos Kosmos spoke Turkish and even Arabic.

Somewhere on the list of what makes Greece what it is and belong where it does, is religion. Here, Greece is definitely part of the Middle East. Greece might be characterized as the Christian Middle East (as we shall see in our travels, even this description must be taken with a grain of salt because there are Greek Muslims).

Church and state never really separated in Greece. In fact, the 1832 constitution recognizes Orthodoxy as the state's prevailing religion. Greece is an overwhelmingly Eastern Orthodox country. Of course, it does not have a monopoly on the religion. Russia is the most obvious example. There are Arab Greek Orthodox Christians, too. I find that Greece's closest spiritual and cultural neighbors are Lebanese Christians.

Greek Orthodoxy has been weathered by the Eastern Mediterranean and is linked in Greek consciousness to the lands of Byzantium: Constantinople, Antioch, Jerusalem, and Alexandria. In this sense, Orthodoxy is one component of Greek identity, although it is cultural more than religious. I see its influence even in non-observant Greeks, who have a respect and deference for piety that has been lost in the West. This is one reason why Greek diplomats I know are better able to relate to their Muslim Arab counterparts than Western officials. Greece is a European Union and a NATO member. But despite being tethered to these Western institutions for decades, there is a deep cultural chasm between Greeks and Europeans in countries where Catholicism or Protestantism were once the prevailing faiths. In the mid-2000s this was seen as a detriment to Greece, the odd man in Europe. In a world that is becoming more reactionary, and where the West is in retreat across Europe, I believe it is now an asset.

I have to clarify that when it comes to religion I am not referring to the Greek Orthodox Church as a source of Greek identity. There is a difference between the Orthodox faith and the Church. I don't mean the vague concept of spiritualism that has become the fad in an irreligious West, but the mysticism, tradition, and ritual that are the backbone of Eastern Orthodoxy. I had a girlfriend who took a sadistic pleasure in expressing how much she despised priests each time we passed a black-robed father, but whose mother used to prayer over a rock from a monastery to ward off the evil eye. She was the first to request these prayers. Western institutions and technology have clipped these rituals, but not destroyed them. The Orthodox faith still trickles down into everyday life in Greece. That is a Middle Eastern trait.

Pascha, or Easter, sets Greece's national calendar. The names and patterns of the holy days before the resurrection of Christ are drilled into Greek vocabulary, with their specific foods and routines, like *Tsiknopempti* (Smelly Thursday), when platters of meat are grilled, and Clean Monday, for octopus and *taramasalata* (a fish roe dip), to usher in the month of feasting. In the Holy Week before Easter Sunday, some self-declared nonreligious fast, even if it's just a token effort.

Greece also has a rich vocabulary of invocations that remind me of ones my Muslim and Christian Arab friends use. The Greek equivalent of *Alhamdulillah* is *Doxa to Theo*, or glory to God. *Prota O Theos*, which roughly translates to God-willing, is the Greek equivalent of *Inshallah*. In Cyprus and parts of northeastern Greece, *Mashallah* is still thrown out in villages to boost parents' pride when gazing at their new baby and to ward off evil spirits.

Greek last names also tie into the religiosity of the Middle East that the West tends to associate only with Islam. The prefix Haj- on last names, for example Hadjipateras, indicates a family member who once made the Hajj (holy trip) to Jerusalem. For every birthday there is also a name day, the latter being a celebration of one's given Saint's name (ancient Greek names also have their days, so no one is left out of the fun).

The Orthodox faith's brilliance is revealed in Greece. This is a religion that has neither tried to accommodate nor confront modernity. Instead, it rises above it. With its candles, incense, chanting, feast days, godparents, crosses, and saints, it offers the faithful something else: timelessness. Because the Orthodox faith is so conservative, it rises above the cultural conflicts raging in the West. That is one reason why, despite the legacy of the economic crisis and being on the frontlines of migration, Greece is more stable domestically than its Western European peers, and has yet to succumb to populism. Greece's coherence amid an unraveling of the West is part of its relative rise.

* * *

I came to understand more about my family's roots when the old tropes about Greece, Europe, the West and the Middle East were being smashed to bits. This started in 2019. The destruction of these decades-old assumptions has only accelerated at the time of writing.

Athens became my home in 2020. It was a remarkable time to move here. The country was just starting to shake off the memory of the Greek financial crisis. I won't bore you with the intricacies of it, but we need to set the scene to understand Greece's economic recovery since, and where this region is going, so bear with me.

From its economic highpoint in 2007—the era of the now infamous vacation loans—to its lowest point in 2016, Greece's economy shrank by nearly a quarter. One out of every three Greeks became unemployed. Hundreds of thousands of businesses shuttered. Suicides spiked. Greece had capital controls and bank runs that people thought had gone out of fashion with the Great Depression. Between 2010 and 2018, Greece had three bailouts from the European Union and International Monetary Fund, totaling €320 billion euros. They stopped Greece from crashing out of the Eurozone, but dealt a double body-blow to Greeks, who were smacked once by austerity measures mandated by international creditors and again by tax increases.

Most books I came across on Greece when I moved here were something like end-of-times prophecies. Western journalists have a fetish for embedding with anarchists and Greece has lots of them. Their coverage focused, rightly at times, on neoliberalism's worst impacts on Greece and the real suffering Greeks endured. It gets even better. Greece was in economic upheaval just as the 2015–16 migration crisis unfolded, so the coverage was especially gloomy. It seemed like everything wrong with the world was converging on Greece. The lens from which all this was viewed depended on your politics, but they overlapped. On the Left, many rightly noted Greece's history of being treated like a neocolonial statelet, first by European powers who carved out a tiny Greek puppet kingdom from a chunk of the Ottoman Empire, and later by the crusading Americans of the Cold War. Meanwhile, those on the Right seemed to wallow in the fun of labeling Greece a lazy socialist state where no one worked, that was under assault from Muslim migrants.

The Greece I moved to was leaving both those narratives in the dust.

Greeks, it turned out, weren't all communists and protesters. In 2019 and again in 2023 they voted overwhelmingly for a center-right government, which, at the time of writing, is one of the most stable and competent in the European Union. It has cracked down on migration and, by European standards, is pursuing pro-business reforms. Because Greece lives in a tough neighborhood it is security-minded. It is one of the biggest spenders in NATO when measured by percentage of GDP. Having flirted with social collapse and chaos during the financial crisis, Greeks understand the need for stability.

Greece is an economic and political success story compared to the rest of the European Union. Greece's economy is one of the best performing in the bloc, growing at twice the Eurozone average. In 2024, Greece's cost to borrow was lower than France's.

Admittedly, the Greek comeback is deceptive. But this fits into the theme of Greece not really belonging to the West, in the sense that it is difficult to make accurate quantitative measurements here. Greek wages were declining until 2022. A very good salary in Greece is €1,500 per month, but you need double that to raise a family. The middle class has been hollowed out. There is little social and economic mobility. The most viable way to get ahead in Greece is to get a job with a foreign company that doesn't pay pitiful Greek wages. The country has one of the lowest standards of living in the Eurozone and its economy is still about nineteen per cent smaller than it was in 2007. Greeks are more reliant on side hustles and tax evasion to make ends meet than ever. Doctors and lawyers are paid under the table so that it's hard to track their salaries. Greece depends on money from abroad spent on real estate and tourism. Yet, in a world of trade wars, Greece's reliance on these industries is becoming an asset, compared to, say, heavy industrial production.

Athens is booming. Luxury developments are going up at a record pace, and suitcases full of cash are fueling property purchases. Salaries are officially low, but just try getting a table at a semi-popular restaurant on a Thursday night without a reservation. Athens is perhaps the European Union's last great underdeveloped capital, where a city-center apartment can still be had for around $2,000 a square meter, mainly because the financial crisis crushed Greek assets, which are still recovering.

A once cheap and provincial capital city is being gentrified and globalized. My own street, on the fault-line of plush Kolonaki and Exarcheia, a one-time anarchists' den, is at the centre of this trend. As I write on my balcony, I see one neighbor flying a flag that decries the construction of a new metro stop at Exarcheia's only square. They are the minority. Below me, fancy shoe shops, gourmet ice cream stands, wine bars and real estate offices are popping up every month. A decayed neoclassical mansion that faces my home is being restored by a Greek family. Every month, another old apartment building is being renovated, often tastefully and minimally. The Bauhaus curved balconies and wood shutters, which evoke a softer Eastern Mediterranean, are being refreshed with paint and potted plants.

This growth is both real and an illusion. Most Greeks I know believe a huge bubble is ready to burst in their real estate market. But the double-digit rally in prices isn't being financed by debt. Only twenty per cent of houses in Greece are purchased with a mortgage.[8] The crisis scared even the rare Greeks who can qualify for taking out a loan. House hunting is a nightmare here because of foreign buyers with deep pockets. I have had sellers reject offers made at their asking price if the payment is with a mortgage.

Cold cash and shady money from the East are powering Greece's economic turnaround. Most Greeks are priced out. The mismatch in Athens between an average salary and a €150,000 starter apartment is a sick joke. As the Greek economy grows, Athens has earned the worst metric of rent affordability in Europe.[9] Don't blame the investors. The disparity is because Greece does not innovate or create new wealth. Athens is the ultimate rent-seeking capital. In that sense, the boom is a bubble. It is being imported from abroad.

Tourism is a global trade. Americans and Brits are scooping up real estate and coming in droves. They always have. The more interesting trend is the new arrivals. The Chinese came a decade ago for golden visas. They bought thousands of apartments. As the Greek economy recovers, the government has clamped down on giving residency permits in return for property purchases. The price of a ten-year golden visa for a real estate purchase has gone from €250,000 to €800,000. In the future, the program will likely be scrapped all together. But that won't reverse the influx of middle and upper-class people from the East. The boom is being powered by Arabs, Israelis and Turks.

Athens is taking its place among the Eastern Mediterranean's entrepôts. The ones last century, in order of their destruction, were: Smyrna, Alexandria, and Beirut. Just as the Lebanese capital became a magnet for wealthy Arabs fleeing war and socialism in the 1950s and 1960s, Athens has become the region's new bolthole. Turks are seeking refuge from their authoritarian government, secular Israelis are buying back-up homes, and middle-class Arabs are fleeing their inept and corrupt rulers. Such is the fever pitch that once, I just mentioned purchasing a home to my neighborhood bank manager, and a real estate broker at the next table snuck up on me, offering his card—offices in Athens, Limassol and Beirut.

So, the 2016 narrative of austerity and malicious Western capitalism is dead, like the narrow prism through which migration was viewed. The influx of hot money to Greece and migrants are both symptoms of a tectonic shift shrinking the space between Europe and Asia.

Why is the Athens boom important? Because as the historian Fernand Braudel observed, "The story of the Mediterranean has often been determined by the triumph of one route, one city, over another route and another city."[10]

Athens is thriving as Greece's geopolitical importance grows. In part, the capital's growth is because of the upheaval in the wider Middle East. At the same time as investors are rushing in, Greece as a whole is being reabsorbed into the wider Middle East, a region that it historically belonged to, and only half left. That is what I came to recognize as a journalist as I rediscovered my Greek roots and all of those cultural similarities.

Greece is being pulled to the East the same time the West declines. For more than a century, Greece tried to join the West. Now, the alliances that it pinned its hopes on, NATO and the European Union, are less reliable. Greece isn't the only country in Europe facing this issue, but it's in a unique position because it is nestled on the continent's southeastern periphery. Greece is in the crosshairs of a revisionist Türkiye and adjacent to lands that a militant Russia sees as its sphere of influence. Greece's newest allies, Israel and Egypt, could just as easily export instability to Greece as help defend it against Türkiye. Athens is partying within an arc of instability.

* * *

Lumping Greece into the Middle East sounds strange to modern ears. Greeks use the euro; Christianity is the majority religion. Visitors know the country through its white-washed islands like Santorini. None of this jibes with the Middle East, which from a European perspective is usually seen as beginning in Türkiye. But defining the Middle East simply through Islam, or where continents start and end, is too simple for a world where borders are no longer sacrosanct, and great and middle powers are carving out spheres of influence that blur the line between East and West.

One reason I am drawn to an older generation of travel writers, and will lean on them heavily to make sense of the countries and regions I visit, is because they saw Greece as part of the East. The era of neat and tidy regions with clear labels was an anomaly and is now over.

THE NEW BYZANTINES

To orient ourselves, we need to go back a century to the time of British diplomat George Curzon. An explorer, Viceroy of India, and Foreign Secretary, he was a conservative colonial administrator who knew a thing or two about borders. He helped carve a lot of them up after the First World War. He was called "the most traveled man who ever sat on a British cabinet." Incidentally, he was opposed to establishing a Jewish state in historic Palestine because he thought it would destabilize the region.[11]

"The Mediterranean has never in civilized times been the southern frontier of Europe; the latter has in reality been supplied by the Atlas Mountains and the great Desert of the Sahara," he observed in *Frontiers*, a book published in 1907.[12]

During the Cold War, the line between East and West was set in stone. The United States then entered a poorly defined conflict called "The War On Terror." The notion of a strictly Islamic Middle East fit with narratives that followed the 9/11 attacks. In the grand sweep of history, this conflict, and the torrent of memoirs, TV series, and counter-terrorism analysts it churned out, will be remembered as a blip, if at all. Its lessons already seem irrelevant when nuclear armed countries are waging wars and Middle Eastern states are becoming regional powers. "The War On Terror" temporarily solidified a sense of separateness between Asia and Europe. But the immutable facts of geography that Curzon noted more than a century ago are reasserting themselves.

Curzon's observation helps us understand the intractable problem of migration, but doesn't totally explain why the distance between Greece and the so-called Middle East is shrinking. Great Powers like Russia, China and the United States are losing their relative heft in this part of the world to rising regional powers like Israel, Saudi Arabia and Türkiye. Because of its geography, Greece is at the epicenter of this shift. The East, in all its revisionist, rapacious and autocratic glory, is nudging up to Greece.

"The Middle East" is a messy term. It signifies a land of cultural and political gradients. I learned that traveling from Greece to Jordan in 2019 and I am reminded of it every time I depart Athens for Cairo, Tel Aviv, Istanbul, or Beirut. Tasos Meneshian realized the same thing on his road trips to Aleppo.

Patrick Theros, one of the US State Department's most prominent Greek-American diplomats, remembers a time when the United States saw Greece as part of the wider Middle East. "I joined the State Department in 1963. Back then, there were a lot of Greeks in the State Department. We were viewed as guys from the region," he told me.

I caught up with Theros at a Greek diner in Washington, DC in November 2024 during a reporting trip right before the Presidential election. The State Department has something called the Bureau of Near Eastern affairs to handle diplomacy in the Middle East. As late as the 1960s, Greece, Cyprus and Türkiye were included in its purview. In 1974, those countries were moved to the Bureau of European Affairs. But Theros, who is into his eighties, said his Greek roots continued to help him in his career, which spanned over three decades in the Middle East.

"When my Arab counterparts met me, they kinda sensed something was off," he explained. Theros is one of the most fun former diplomats I know, with a mischievous, acerbic tongue.

> The Arabs are great conspiracy theorists. They would look at me intensely and ask, 'Patrick, where are you from?' I would tell them, 'Michigan.' And the reply was something like, 'No, no, no. Where are you *really* from?' When I said 'Greece,' it was an icebreaker. 'Oh. I knew it! You are one of us,' they said. My Greek roots were an advantage. I wasn't seen as an outsider.

The term "Near East" is a throwback to an earlier era when borders and identities were fluid. Admittedly, it is a Western-centric term. It defined the world in terms of its distance and orientation from London, the old imperial capital. The British Empire gets a bad rap today. But this term is the best one I know to describe the region where half of my family is from, which I live in and report from. The Near East stretches like a big scimitar from the Black Sea through the Eastern Mediterranean, down to the Red Sea.

"Where today is the Near East?" asked Laurence Grafftey-Smith in *Bright Levant*, an account of his life as a British consular officer in the waning years of the British Empire from the First World War to the Second World War. "Our parish ran from the Yemen border to the Balkans, from Western Türkiye to eastern Persia," he wrote, "The Levant was a rich mine of political experience."[13]

"Near East" is often used interchangeably with the term "Levant," which is derived from the Italian word for "rising," as in where the sun rises. It was coined by seamen in the fourteenth and fifteenth centuries, when Venice and Genoa competed with the Ottoman Empire for influence in the Eastern Mediterranean.[14]

For the Venetians and Genoese, Greece was in the Near East. The islands of Chios, Rhodes, and Crete were strategic outposts in their trading empires. Later, the French and British would supersede them as the dominant powers angling for influence against the Ottomans.

The French were the first to strike agreements called the Capitulations with the Ottomans. In 1536 France signed the first capitulation treaty with Suleiman the Magnificent. The treaty allowed French subjects to work and trade in the sultan's empire under their own legal code. The Capitulations are viewed as exploitative today, but they were necessary and mutually agreed upon by two powers. Since the Ottoman Empire was an Islamic Caliphate with a different legal code for Christians and Muslims, the Capitulations were an important step to guarantee stability and legal protection for European traders, who the Ottomans wanted in their domains.

Over the years, other European powers agreed to Capitulations with the Sublime Porte. As the Ottoman Empire weakened in the nineteenth century, the Capitulations became a way for the Europeans to exert their dominance over it. But it wasn't just them. Non-Muslim Ottoman subjects fought to get these extra-judicial privileges, including members of the Greek, Armenian and Syrian Christian minorities. By the turn of twentieth century, the Ottomans' legal jurisdiction over port cities like Salonica, Smyrna and Beirut was compromised, stoking resentment among its Muslim subjects.[15]

The Capitulations cleared a path for one of the most unique types of international business dynasties: the Levantines. Purists about the term say that it does not apply to Greeks, because they are indigenous to the region. Technically, the Levantines were Western European transplants to the Near East who carved out trading and finance empires connecting East and West. But for me, the term Levantine captures the spirit of Greek, Armenian, Jewish and Arab traders of the Near East, whose business acumen is legendary.

Levantine had "a pejorative connotation," according to Grafftey-Smith, who said, "It implied the elevation to a principle of mere financial success; a blurring of essential standards; a certain moral suppleness and probably the wrong attitude during shipwreck."[16]

That shiftiness is a feature I've noticed across the Near East. It's why Greek shipping magnates have showed no qualms transporting Russian crude oil that counterparts wouldn't touch amid the war in Ukraine. And it helps explain why Greek businessmen often are more comfortable operating in Russia or even Syria than their Western peers. Like Lebanese, Syrians, and Armenians, entrepreneurialism is a part of Greek diaspora identity. Grafftey-Smith's attributes of a Levantine are ones that my father, a Greek-American businessman, would call assets.

* * *

After meeting Tasos in Neos Kosmos, I walked through the neighborhood of Koukaki, another Airbnb hotspot where tourists and Athenians are already spilled out at cafe tables sipping Freddo coffees. Instead of passing through Plaka, I divert through the Athens National Gardens. I like to kill time here between interviews. With its dirt paths and weeds sprouting between carob and palm trees, it's a park that is not trying too hard. It has the careless, natural elegance Italians call *sprezzatura*. If you try to replicate it, you won't get it.

I exit the park and come out on Vasilissis Sofias Avenue, one of Athens' busiest thoroughfares. Greek taxi drivers have managed to fight off the arrival of private Ubers. This concrete mass of a city teems with yellow Mercedes and battered Škodas. Teenagers in skinny jeans, wrap-around sunglasses and bumbags—a biker style known as *Kagkouras* popular with Greek men—zip by retirees in Panama hats and American college girls in white summer dresses.

I duck through a wrought iron gate into the quiet courtyard of an imposing neoclassical mansion that is home to the Benaki Museum. All the layers of Greek history are here; marble busts of gods and goddesses, icons showing Orthodox saints slaying dragons and, of course, paintings of *Palikares*, the mustachioed fighters who rebelled against the Ottomans, and whose sashes hold long, silver inlaid pistols.

I came here to discuss Antonis Benakis, the man behind the museum, with George Manganis, its Academic Director. Benakis' life is indicative of the Greek tussle between Europe and the Middle East, albeit an elite version of it. His lineage speaks to the ebb and flow of Greeks in the Near East. His father, Emmanuel, was born on the Cycladic island of Syros to a family that fled the Turkish massacre of Greeks on Chios in 1822. He traveled to Alexandria, Egypt in 1863, where he made a fortune as a cotton exporter, earning the title "King of the bourse."

The Benaki family were among the 150,000 Greeks who once called Alexandria home. Along with Italians, Armenians and Jews, they thrived there right up until the early 1960s, when President Gamal Abdel Nasser's socialist and Arab nationalist policies sounded a death knell to their cosmopolitan existence. Emmanuel Benakis left Alexandria well before that. In 1911, he moved to Athens with the fortune he had made in Egyptian cotton, and renovated this villa, which he later endowed as a museum. His son Antonis Benakis would fill it with artifacts and antiques from across the Middle East.

"When the Benaki Museum was founded, the bulk of its collection was Islamic and Asian antiquities," Manganis told me.

> That wasn't random. The Benakis family was deeply aware of the Orient. The first item catalogued in the museum was an Iznik tile from Asia Minor. That is quite interesting when you think that the museum opened less than ten years after Greece and Türkiye came out of a major war. Benakis was a cultured man. He knew that Iznik tiles originated in the Ottoman Empire.

The Benaki family were ardent Greek nationalists and Hellenophiles. Both Antonis and his father espoused the values of European Greece. Emmanuel served as a Minister of Finance and Mayor of Athens. But the Middle East still filtered down to their collecting. "There was a toing-and-froing of fashion and tastes among well off Greeks of that era, who would mix oriental and European tastes. They understood the Orient better than the Europeans because it was all around them and familiar," Manganis told me.

To be sure, the Benakis family never saw themselves as Middle Eastern. Penelope Delta, Benakis' daughter, wrote that the family prized European products and believed they stood above other merchant families in Alexandria, especially those from modern-day Syria and Lebanon. "The Adjective Greek was for us something superior, extraordinary, luminous, adorable," she wrote, adding that they had the "greatest contempt" for Egypt's *fellahin*, the poor Arab farmers who toiled to produce their cotton.[17]

Greek friends would scoff at me for drawing a parallel between Piraeus and upscale Kolonaki, where the Benaki Museum sits. But a common thread unites them. As far as museums go, the Benaki is usually quiet. Tourists, who may squeeze in a trip to the Acropolis before heading to the islands, bypass it. But in Piraeus and Kolonaki we see how the Near East oozes throughout Greece into high and low culture, rich and poor, alike.

I have another interview. I step into Kolonaki. The old cotton trader would be at home here. He could stroll up to Tsakaloff Street where businessmen in slim suits and cutaway collars sip cappuccinos at Da Capo cafe. Cigar smoke wafts through the air and women with lip fillers and noses carved by surgeons' scalpels eye rich husbands. This environment would be more familiar to Benaki than contemporary Alexandria, whose cosmopolitan grandeur is now a distant memory.

"The elegance, corruption and aristocracy of wealth has vanished in an emigrant stampede ... Where [there] was a Greek colony is now the shadow of an Omdurman market, for Africa has engulfed the last bastion of the Mediterranean," Graffey-Smith wrote in *Bright Levant*.[18] Now, the Middle East has nudged up to Greece. Kolonaki's cafes echo with snappy Lebanese Arabic, Hebrew and Turkish.

I find Evangelos Kalpadakis siting at a deserted Kolonaki coffee shop. With his bushy black beard and oversize button-down, he looks more like a chill college professor than a seasoned diplomat. Our conversation is interrupted when a colleague passes by from the foreign ministry to say hello.

Kalpadakis explains that the US State Department wasn't alone in trying to take Greece out of the Near East. "From the 1970s until the 2000s, Greek foreign policy was Westward focused. The goal was integration into the European Union," said Kalpadakis, who was chief foreign policy advisor to Alexis Tsipras, Greece's Prime Minister from 2015 until 2019 and leader of the left-wing Syriza party. "Greek diplomats worked to disconnect the country from the narrative of the Near East and for Greece to be recognized and supported as a European ally in Washington, not as one more piece in the scramble for power in the Near and Middle East," he added. Kalpadakis has a great trait for his profession: likability. When he speaks, you feel he is taking you into his confidence and sharing some intimacy with you:

> After joining the Euro and holding the Olympics, the economy was rockin' and rollin'. Private consumption and big construction projects ruled the day. Germany was the first to benefit because its exports skyrocketed and German companies took over construction projects. This was the era of skyrocketing Porsche sales. Then the collapse came. Greek foreign policy struggled to catch its breath during the crisis. Governments, like people, can only handle so many crises at the same time.

But the migration crisis, the rise of a revisionist Türkiye, and the Muslim Brotherhood rippled across to Greece. It started paying attention to its eastern and southern neighbors, explained Kalpadakis:

> Greece realized it needed to be a strong force in the Eastern Mediterranean. This would strengthen its leverage with the European Union and United States. It is a throwback of sorts to the Near East. On the Left, the narrative is that Greece can be a pillar of peace and

stability and bridge for countries in the region to the West. On the Right, the language focuses on Greece being a strong force in NATO's southeast.

These are two sides of the same coin. Tsipras, a far-left politician in his youth, actually doubled down on Greece's alliance with the United States. With American backing, he sought out new partners in the Middle East, mainly Egypt and Israel, two stalwart American protectorates. The center-right government of Kyriakos Mitsotakis, in power since 2019, has accelerated the trend, particularly with Israel. When foreign policy moves cut across domestic political divides, it represents a paradigm shift for a nation. So Greece is pushing itself toward the East and being pulled in that direction.

* * *

A bias toward ancient Greece and the "birthplace of democracy" in academia, politics and popular culture has long overshadowed Greece's place in the Near East. But the latter is the one in the ascent now. This is Patrick Leigh Fermor's belly dancing Byzantines.

After the fall of Rome in 476 CE, the eastern half of the Roman Empire continued for another thousand years. From its seat in Constantinople, the Byzantine Empire extended Orthodox Christian rule throughout the Eastern Mediterranean, including what is today Israel, Egypt, Syria, Lebanon, and Türkiye.

A whole generation of British writers—eloquent, cosmopolitan and cash-poor—recognized that modern Greece was closer to Byzantium than the ancient Greece of Socrates and Plato. They came to Greece between the First and Second World Wars, and drifted listlessly across the Levant as diplomats, journalists, soldiers, teachers and ne'er-do-wells.

"You English seem to be completely under the spell of the Graeco-Roman period and you judge everything without reference to Byzantium. Nevertheless that is where you find the true source of Greek thinking, Greek *moeurs*. That is what you should all be made to study," British travel writer Lawrence Durrell noted in *Bitter Lemons*. The book is a penetrating account of his time in 1950s Cyprus during the waning years of the island's British occupation, when ethnic tensions were simmering between Greeks and Turks.[19]

The Byzantines were the ultimate survivors. They endured civil wars, an insane level of palace intrigue, and constant conflict with Bulgars and Arab raiders on their borders. They came close to collapse several times but kept bouncing back. By 650 Arab Muslim armies had expelled them from Damascus, Jerusalem and Cairo. Still, in 1025 historians could remark that at his death, Emperor Basil II, left the Byzantine Empire at its "apogee," with Constantinople looked upon as "a unique city of marvels," the capital of the "richest, most powerful, most civilized state on earth."[20]

Turkish raiders coming from Central Asia swept through the Arab lands. One, the tribe of Othman, would settle in northwestern Anatolia and establish one of the greatest empires the world has known by overrunning the Byzantines. But in between, there were years of peace between Greeks and Turks. Even when it was collapsing from all sides, in its final century, Byzantine art and culture showed signs of a renaissance.[21] The lesson to take away from the Byzantines in our era is that empires die slow deaths and national decline is not always obvious to the people living through it.

The greatest shock to the Byzantine Empire came not from Muslim invaders, but European Christian Crusaders, who, instead of liberating Jerusalem from the Muslim Arabs decided to sack Constantinople in 1204. During the Fourth Crusade,

Western Christians slaughtered their Eastern Christian brothers. Like mafia bosses, they proceeded to whack up the Byzantine Empire into little fiefdoms for the leading royal families of the West. This war of Christian colonial conquest against fellow Christians was the ultimate act of strategic folly. By tearing up the Byzantine Empire, the Western Europeans sowed the seeds for the Ottomans' advance because they crushed the Near Eastern buffer state that stood in its path.

> One must execrate the memory of the Fourth Crusade, and the greed and Christian sectarian bias that sacked Constantinople, destroyed the Byzantine Empire and called down the doom of Christendom's eastern half. It is as vain to blame the Turks for spreading Westwards over the wreckage as it would be to arraign the laws of hydrostatics for flood damage,

Leigh Fermor observed, flexing his wordsmith skills.[22]

The final blow to the Byzantines came on 29 May 1453 when Constantinople fell to Sultan Mehmed II's army. By then, the Byzantine Empire had been reduced to a rump state straddling the Bosphorus and Peloponnese. Its collapse is still ingrained in Greek minds as a tragedy. Some older Greek sources I interview still insist on pushing back meetings a day if I suggest a Tuesday, because that is the day that Constantinople fell to the Ottomans, considered the unluckiest day of the week in Greece.

As we shall see in the next chapters, far from spelling the demise of Greeks in the region, the Ottomans ushered in a golden era for Eastern Christians compared to what they had endured under the thumb of Western Europeans. Greeks achieved high positions in the Ottoman court and prospered. In fact, the Greeks in the Constantinople neighborhood of Phanar exercised so much influence over the Sublime Porte that most opposed the war for Greek independence when it broke out in 1821 out of fear of losing their privileged positions. There is, in fact, more of a continuum between the Byzantine and Ottoman empires than both sides like to admit.

This is one reason why modern Greece is better suited to withstand the long-term upheaval of migration than Germany or France, and is more comfortable than northern Europe in courting countries like Saudi Arabia, the United Arab Emirates and Egypt.

Living in Athens, I sense that Greece has been less polarized by migration. This is especially true for migrants from the former Ottoman and Byzantine worlds, although less so for African and South Asian migrants. As a Near Eastern state, Greece is better able to absorb migrants than Germany. It might sound paradoxical, but this is because Greece is more conservative, family-oriented and religious. Orthodox Christianity, a generally conservative religion, shares much with Islam.

I remember one Egyptian carpenter living in Exarcheia telling me he had no interest traveling for a higher paying job in France because Athens was like Egypt and he liked the Greeks. Likewise, I remember going to a house party hosted by an Iranian Kurdish family where the Greek guests kept remarking that they felt "right at home, like a Greek house party," as our hosts piled food on our plates and brought out their grandparents—the behaviors of a middle-class Greek family. Our hosts' son was being drilled in the popular history of the Greek Revolution and spoke Greek with a mastery I envied.

The Byzantines gave the Ottomans a concrete culture, one that, "four centuries after that civilization's [the Byzantine's] extinction, could still enable the most inept of human races to uphold the skeleton of its political idea," British travel writer Robert Byron, clearly no fan of the Ottomans, suggested in *The Byzantine Achievement*. In his words, "The Ottoman Empire was the Byzantine Empire; Constantinople the heart of each."[23]

Byron published *The Byzantine Achievement* in 1929. His jaundiced view of the Ottomans was informed by the Greco-Turkish war. He intended his book be a history of the Byzantines as much as a contemporary critique of the European powers who he believed abandoned Greeks during the 1919–22 conflict with Turkey.

Byron was a witty writer and a sharp cultural observer. He inhabited a golden age of travel. His account of journeying through the Middle East and Central Asia, *The Road to Oxiana*, is considered one of the finest travel books ever written. Greece was his starting point for the Middle East. The Greek people were "poised between East and West, child of neither, yet receptive to both," he wrote, "European neither in fact nor feeling, they talk of 'Europe' as somewhere else."[24]

* * *

The ugly breakup of the Ottoman Empire, and the religious and ethnic bloodletting that preceded it, should not cloud the centuries of economic advancement and stability the Ottomans brought to this region.

The Ottoman Empire was first and foremost an Islamic Caliphate with two different systems for Muslims and non-Muslims. The Ottomans grouped their subjects by religion in *millets*. Non-Muslims paid special taxes, but other rules, such as religious color-coded dress, were implemented more sporadically. The Ottomans' top governing priority was collecting taxes to fund their wars of conquest. Otherwise, their subjects were left to govern their own affairs. Christians and Jews attained great wealth and power in the empire. They dominated the commerce and trade that Muslims wouldn't touch, feeling it was beneath them. Greeks were substantially freer in Ottoman lands than their contemporaries ruled by Europeans.

While the Ottomans were tolerant by the standards of the day, that didn't stop the Christians from occasionally revolting, and hoping for liberation. The Ottomans were colonial overlords; therefore, they had to deal with uprisings. Local Christian leaders told their flocks that they had to endure subjugation, but their salvation would one day come through the resurrection of the Byzantine Empire. The Greek Christians put their faith in the Russian tsar and Europe's Christian monarchs. They had a word for their salvation, the *romeiko*, which came from their understanding of themselves as the descendants of the Eastern Roman Empire. This was based on religion, not ethnicity.

The Greeks were the first people of the wider Middle East to acquire the bug for Western nationalism, but it evolved slowly. What it meant to be "Greek" was not straightforward, except for some elite Greeks in the Western diaspora infused with Western Enlightenment principles. These Greeks, along with Western Europeans, drilled the oriental Greeks into seeing themselves as heirs to an ancient, pagan culture, that gave Western Europe democracy. Eventually, an Orthodox Christian identity transformed into a national, ethnic one.[25]

The Greek revolt began in 1821. It didn't start anywhere near the borders of modern Greece, but in the far off Danubian provinces of Moldova and Wallachia, where the Ottomans had long entrusted the Phanariot Greeks to govern. The man who raised the flag of rebellion was Alexander Ypsilantis, a privileged Phanariot Greek who served as an officer in the Russian Empire. The revolt spread to mainland Greece, the Peloponnese and islands. For the majority of the rebels, their liberation battle was a religious struggle to throw off a colonial, Islamic yoke.

The state the Greeks carved out for themselves in 1832 comprised mainland Attica, the Cycladic islands and the Peloponnese. This new country, which was about as stable as Somalia in our era, only emerged because European powers reluctantly entered the fray. They imposed an end to the war on the Ottomans because they were tired of dealing with anarchy in the Mediterranean. The highpoint of the European intervention was the Battle of Navarino, when the Russian, British and French navies destroyed the Ottoman fleet. Then the Europeans and some elite Greeks began a process common in our era: Western state-building.

Just like in the modern Middle East, outside powers who grudgingly backed the rebels wanted to appoint a pliable client they could control. It was felt to be best if this leader didn't favor one of the main external powers over the others. The Europeans searched the "deep state" of the early nineteenth century—royal families—and dug up Prince Otto of Bavaria, a seventeen-year-old German aristocrat who spoke no Greek and was Roman Catholic. Otto was so alien to Greece, the thinking went, none of its warring chieftains could possibly accuse the Europeans of favoring one over the other. Little did the Europeans or Ottomans know that the schizophrenic, fragile little country they had created, called the Kingdom of Greece, would set a precedent for a century of struggles—from Bosnia to the Arab Gulf—for national independence and self-determination from the Ottomans.

But the Greek story was just beginning. For another eighty years, more Greeks lived outside their fledgling nation-state then inside it. Thessaloniki, Greece's second largest city, remained in Ottoman hands until 1912. Greeks were scattered across the Eastern Mediterranean. In addition to Alexandria, they called the cities of Smyrna, Constantinople, Alexandria, and even Damascus home.

"I was born in Damascus, as was my father, grandfather and great-grandfather. Our Greek citizenship was passed along from father to son," Charles Catinis, a Damascus businessman who is a leading member of the Greek community in the Syrian capital told me during a phone interview.[26] I sought out Catinis on Facebook groups for an article back in 2020. We were last in touch in December 2024, as Islamist rebels stormed into Damascus, toppling Assad's government. "We are fine. We hope the situation gets better each day," Catinis wrote me via email, when I asked how the rebels were treating the few Greeks left in Damascus. They are by far one of the most endangered of all the Greek communities I have interviewed in the Near East. They are also a link between the old and new Near East.

To understand where the Near East is headed, and why Greece is set to play such a pivotal geopolitical role in the coming years, we need to leave Athens and travel to Greece's borderlands and abroad. Athens has all the glitz and glamour, but Greece's distant regions and neighbors are where the effects of evaporating borders and the threats of revisionist powers are most palpable. In sum, we need to go where the "amalgam of Greece and the Orient" is warmest to the touch.

2

EPIRUS

PASHAS, COMMUNISTS AND MERCHANTS

A light rain began to fall and the scent of pine trees mingled with that of damp earth. Droplets pit-patted on the slate roof behind me, but Lake Pamvotida was still. I watched a ferry cut across the water, a smaller model of those that dot Istanbul's Bosporus; it looked like a toy set against the imposing foothills of the Pindus mountains.

There is something about faded, provincial Ottoman cities in Greece, and their cozy coffeehouses and canopy-covered shops with Eastern bric-a-brac in the windows, that makes me feel cocooned.

Ioannina, nestled between the Ionian Sea to the west and the Pindus to the east, is a proper bolthole. It is close to Italy, and just far enough away from the Middle East that you sense its approach, but feel insulated from it. This enviable position is one reason why eighteenth-century Greek merchants stashed their wealth here, and later turned it into a hub of the Greek Enlightenment.

I took shelter from the rain inside the seventeenth-century Aslan Pasha mosque. My eyes adjusted to the stark, whitewashed walls, then lapped up the brilliant folk-art colors decorating them: mint-colored tulips painted above the windows, blood-orange stalactites dangling in the corners like icicles, and floral motifs scrolled on the *minbar* (pulpit). I imagined an old imam clutching this railing to deliver his sermon to the Ottoman *agas* (barons), not all that long ago. I was just seventy miles from the touristic fantasyland of Corfu, but was reassured that I faced the Holy City of Mecca because of the *mihrab* niched into the wall in alternating patterns of red and turquoise.

For centuries, Ioannina faced the East as a trading hub. Could it again?

The imbalance between a young West Asia and a rapidly depopulating Balkans means Ioannina is closer to the East than it realizes. This city may be remote, but it makes concrete-smeared Athens seem backward. On weekends, families take their *volta*, a daily evening stroll, along the lake. They don't carry themselves with the flair of their Italian neighbors across the Ionian. There is nothing dandyish or effeminate about Ioannina. The pot-bellied, underdressed guys with overdressed girlfriends, and the solemness of Greek families out for souvlaki, all remind me of the small prides and rituals of the Middle East, just like the setting. Ioannina's old town is a labyrinth of meze restaurants called *tsipouradika*, and two-story houses with *sachnisi*, those jutting oriel windows that whisper of Ottoman refinement.

Ioannina exemplifies what David Holden called Greece's "fundamental ambiguity." In his excellent book, *Greece Without Columns*, he noted, "If we ask, for example whether Greece is a western or an eastern country we are obliged to admit that it is a bit of both."[1]

Holden was one of the most astute observers of Greece I know, because he was schooled in the culture and politics of the Middle East. As *The Sunday Times*' chief foreign affairs correspondent for the region in the late 1960s, he reported in an era before advocacy journalism, an overabundance of "news-analysis," and government-approved leaks passed off as "scoops" ravaged the trade.

Greece Without Columns has aged so well because it comes from a time when more journalists showed up in foreign lands, studied their history, and talked to people who weren't just part of the think-tank world. Holden was mysteriously killed, execution style, in Cairo in 1977. One old-time journalist who knew him, told me he was likely passing messages to the Soviet Union's KGB and was assassinated by his Egyptian contacts at the behest of the CIA.

"Three thousand years ago, when Greek life evolved from the oriental patterns of Egypt, Mesopotamia, Anatolia and the Levant, [Greece] gradually acquired what we recognize as in some ways a western character ... but one thousand years of Byzantium and four centuries of Turkish rule re-emphasized the oriental heritage," he wrote.[2]

Welcome to Ioannina.

I first traveled here, like many Athenians, for a weekend getaway to Zagorochoria, a Pindus mountain region of little stone villages. This is where in-the-know Greeks come to hike, get their fill of fiery *Tsipouro*, and feast on stewed goat in old tavernas filled with rusty *nargiles* and kilems.

What a contrast to the Cycladics that show up in Instagram reels, where sleek villas and plunge pools are draining the barren islands of water and pricing local teachers and doctors out of the rental market. Zagorochoria sits in a UNESCO world heritage park. Strict building regulations limit new constructions between the forty-six villages, which are linked by treacherous roads. In the plane tree- and trellis-shaded town centers, no one tells you how much you need to spend in order to sit at a cafe like in

Mykonos or Paros. To be sure, these islands represent another eastern instinct in Greece, the trend toward "Dubaization." Like the Emirati city-state, the islands unapologetically embrace lavish displays of wealth. The rich are from everywhere, but increasingly outside of Europe. Rich Indians and Arabs come to Mykonos to gobble up overpriced sushi. Spain and Italy might talk about cracking down on foreign homebuyers and real estate speculation. Greece is too Eastern not to embrace the trend. I suspect the coming years will see a divide emerge in the Mediterranean, where the western half imposes more regulations on foreign investment, while Greece continues to court outsiders.

Epirus didn't stand out to me simply because it had a healthy balance toward tourism. Mercifully, "Dubaization" is absent, but Ioannina is where Lake Como meets the East. The over-touristed islands of Crete and Rhodes give you the same impression. Holden observed:

> At the opening of the nineteenth century, no western traveller could doubt that the Orient, in all its imagined romance and barbarity, was in full command of Greece ... It was not just that the Ottomans were its rulers ... the Greeks themselves appeared to western eyes so thoroughly, and often shockingly oriental.[3]

This feeling still permeates Greece's borderlands, particularly those last conquered by an expanding Greece in the early twentieth century from the Ottomans. This is why despite not leaving Greece when you travel from Corfu to Ioannina, it feels as if you are passing between two different cultures. Holden's assessment applies. The Venetians successfully defended Corfu for 200 years against repeated Ottoman assaults. When that trading republic collapsed, the island was ceded to France, then Britain, and finally Greece in 1864. Whereas Ioannina passed from the Byzantines to the Ottomans and remained under the latter's control until the eve of the First World War. When Greek friends in Athens and Thessaloniki tell me they plan summer vacations to Corfu, they still subconsciously let slip that they want a "more European-style vacation."

Before my last trip to Ioannina, I met Spiros Rizopoulos in Athens. He was born in Ioannina, emigrated to the United States and moved back to Greece in the early 2000s.

Rizopoulos is a Near Eastern wheeler and dealer out of central casting. His desk is decorated with bulky, expensive-looking *kombologia*. Our interview was interrupted by locals in Ioannina calling him up for favors. He made a failed run as an independent candidate to be governor of Epirus. Ioannina is the capital of the Greek region, a historic swath of land that also includes parts of modern-day Albania. Thousands of Greeks still live in southern Albania and roughly ten per cent of Greece's population is Albanian, although statistics are hard to come by. Over 450,000 Albanians have Greek residency, and tens of thousands more have Greek citizenship.[4]

Albanians flooded into Greece destitute after the collapse of their communist government in the 1990s. Many assimilated so fully that they took Greek names and adopted Orthodox Christianity. Second-generation Albanians speak flawless Greek. Tourists don't realize it, but the waiter at your island taverna and the taxi driver at the airport are probably Albanian. Greeks never miss it. They profile Albanians by their physical features. I find that almost everyone in the Near East stereotypes their neighbors, and looks down on them with a sense of haughtiness. Epirus has been at the center of Greece and Albania's acrimonious ties since their nation-states emerged out of the ashes of the Ottoman Empire. Tirana and Athens only established full diplomatic relations in the 1970s.

Rizopoulos ran for governor of this conservative region, vowing to cut corruption, stop the lucrative trade of cannabis smuggling from Albania, and diversify Epirus' economy by boosting the number of foreign workers to support industry. He also wanted to establish new universities to retain young people. It didn't work out that way.

"I call Epirus the Golan Heights of Greece," he says. "I use this metaphorically because the conflict isn't one of militaries, it's one of civilizations and cultures. Epirus is where the traits of the Ottoman Empire, poverty and corruption, seep their way into Europe." His voice booms.

Rizopoulos has a fleshy build, white beard, and a penchant for profanity. He tries to talk me out of going to Ioannina. He argues that reporting from there would hurt my argument that Greece's fortunes are on the upswing.

"Democracy is undervalued there. The politicians pretend to run for office but just horse-trade seats among themselves. It is common knowledge that votes are for sale, by monetary means and otherwise," he says, describing how voters turn up at politicians' offices the day before elections to take voting slips and barter favors.

"You know the newest job the governor's office created?" I admit to not being up to date on the local news. "Paying one guy $37,000 for two years to check his office every night and make sure the lights and air conditioning units are turned off," he continues. "If this would happen in any other country of the European Union it would be considered corruption. Not in Epirus. All the corruption and misuse is covered up with a distorted sense of history. Ioannina never left the Ottoman Empire."

Am I wrong to love this place? Epirus, with its old mosques, *tsipouradika*, goat herders, corruption, Orthodoxy, eastern suspicions and mountain virility. The minarets may no longer call the faithful to prayer, but incantations to God are still heard here. The chants emanate out of Byzantine churches louder in Ioannina than Athens. One friend from Syria and I agreed that the words and languages are different, but the rhythmic, Eastern wail is the same.

Epirus has always been famous for resisting authority. It was the scourge of empires and conquerors. Unlike other parts of Greece, the Ottomans' hold here was tenuous.

"The breath of Asia which is so manifest throughout the Balkans is a legacy of Turkish Islam. It disseminated the gifts it had itself received from the distant East. Through it, town and countryside alike were permeated with oriental culture," the historian Fernand Braudel observed.[5] But the Ottomans' colonial project faced limits: "'The steepest places have been at all times the asylum of liberty' ... A poor thing was Turkish despotism, ruler indeed of the roads, passes, towns and plains, but what can it have meant in ... Epirus ...?"[6]

During Ottoman times, the Pindus mountains were controlled by Christian chieftains called *armatoles*. Their clans were nominally charged with policing the mountain passes for the sultan, but they could just as easily turn into bandits called *klephts*. The line between criminality and policing was razor thin in Ottoman Epirus.[7]

In fact, the gravest challenge to the sultan's authority here came from one of his own lieutenants, a vicious, cunning old pasha who the poet Lord Byron called the "Mahometan Bonaparte."[8] Ali Pasha of Ioannina was by all accounts a remarkable self-made man. This Ottoman despot still looms large in Epirus. One of the locals' favorite stories remains how he ordered the drowning of eighteen women in Lake Pamvotida, officially for adultery, but unofficially because one of the women resisted his advances. Ali Pasha was born in Tepelene, Albania in 1744 to a Christian family of Albanian speakers who converted to Islam when the Ottomans swept across the Balkans. His family were followers of Bektashism, a Sufi mystic order, whose light-touch approach to Islamic tenets might explain why he was a wine drinker and very tolerant of Christianity.⁹ Ali Pasha rose to power in the dirty world of early-nineteenth-century Ottoman politics relying on duplicity and sheer violence.

I came to Epirus as the first stop in my travels to understand the setting of Ali Pasha's rule. I believe he would be right at home in the multipolar Near East of our time, where autocrats are again filling vacuums in the region left by Russia and the United States. He would have been a backstabbing ally of the Arab Gulf rulers who are flush with sovereign-wealth-fund cash. Forget human rights, ideology and superpowers, the new Near East is Ali Pasha's world.

Ali Pasha started his career as a brigand recruited by the Ottomans to guard the Pindus passes. He consolidated power, eventually earning the commission of pasha. His main local rivals were the Souliotes, a group of Christian Albanian tribes. In the late 1780s, Ali Pasha saw an opportunity to expand his power and wealth at their expense when they answered a call by Catherine the Great, Russia's most strident Hellenophile ruler, to revolt against the sultan. Since the Russian-Ottoman Treaty of Kutchuk Kainardji in 1774, Russia had asserted itself as the protector of Orthodox Christians in the Ottoman Empire. Ali Pasha did not crush the Souliotes out of service to the sultan, but to serve his own goals. He was even parlaying with the Russian Empire to undermine the sultan. He was a master intriguer, who courted Napoleon for advantage against the Venetians, then took weapons and money from France's foe, the British. By playing the European powers off against each other, he carved out his own independent statelet, infuriating the sultan.¹⁰

By the turn of the eighteenth century, the Ottoman Empire was already coming apart at the seams. The sultan had lost control of foreign and economic policy in his European heartland. At the peak of his power in 1820, Ali Pasha's rule extended over vast estates and 1.5 million people who lived in land stretching from Albania's modern-day capital of Tirana deep into mainland Greece.

Ali Pasha was a minor celebrity in Europe when Lord Byron arrived in Ioannina in 1809. Byron was so smitten with the city's mosques, snow-capped mountains and warlords, that he started writing his epic poem, "Childe Harold's Pilgrimage," here. Byron came to Ioannina as a tourist, a phenomenon that so puzzled his Ottoman hosts that he noted it in his journal.[11] The Napoleonic wars had made continental Europe a no-go zone for upper-class young travelers like Byron, so they turned to the Ottoman Empire. This rewiring of the elite tourist trade away from France and Italy to the Eastern Mediterranean created a generation of writers who Bryon christened the "Levant Lunatics."[12] They planted the seeds for Patrick Leigh Fermor, and his heirs, like Colin Thubron and William Dalrymple.

Byron was one of the leading romantics who galvanized popular support for the Greek rebels across Europe. But he was also an Orientalist and admirer of Ottoman culture. He went to the exotic East to escape prudish British life and for a chance at homosexual encounters. An ardent defender of the Luddites, the machine-breaking textile workers who would be attacking AI data centers in our own era, he found haven in Greece from the sweeping technological advances ushered in by the industrial revolution. He was besotted with Ali Pasha's harem, which reportedly boasted 300 women slaves and concubines, along with young boys. He described Ali Pasha in the following terms:

> Very fat, and not tall, but with a fine face ... he possesses that dignity which I find universal among the Turks. He has the appearance of anything but his real character, for he is a remorseless tyrant, guilty of the most horrible cruelties, very brave, and so good a general.[13]

Ali Pasha was an autocrat. He stole whatever he wanted and executed his opponents at will. However, like a later generation of authoritarian leaders in the wider Middle East, he facilitated Western education. His iron-fisted rule coincided with a liberal Greek awaking. Ioannina was a center of Greek learning and intellectualism. This is where a wealthy, Western-influenced Greek merchant class began to develop a national identity. Ali Pasha's wife, Kyra Vassiliki, was Greek, and a patron of Orthodox Christian causes. Likewise, his closest advisors were Greeks. Most of them belonged to the Filiki Eteria, or Friendly Society, that originated in the Ukrainian port city of Odessa and lit the spark for the Greek Revolution against the Ottomans.

Without Ali Pasha, the Greek Revolution would probably have been stamped out. Not that he had any sympathy for the Greeks. But the sultan was convinced that the troubles in his rebellious territories were all the work of his mutinous governor. Constantinople couldn't fathom that a crackpot group called the Filiki Eteria spreading rumors of the *romeiko* was a genuine movement. Therefore, the sultan ordered his best general, Khurshid Pasha, from the simmering Peloponnese peninsula to northern Greece with orders to remove Ali Pasha from power just before the Greek revolt broke out. Khurshid Pasha exemplified the early-nineteenth-century Ottoman elite. He was born into a poor Georgian Christian family, and sold as a boy into slavery to a pasha. The Ottoman Empire was a festering slave market for Christian boys and girls. Converting to Islam was one path to power. Khurshid Pasha took it. He rose through the Ottoman ranks, serving in Egypt, Syria and Bosnia. He was a brilliant and obedient servant of the sultan, unlike his foe.[14]

As Khurshid Pasha prepared to attack Ioannina, the Greek insurgents struck in the lightly defended Peloponnese. The Greek Revolution was remarkable because it didn't have a singular figure leading it, but a bevy of Greek chieftains, politicians and warlords, often competing with each other for power and loot. Two of the most famous figures were the *klepht* general,

Theodoros Kolokotronis, and the Ottoman bey of the rugged Mani peninsula, Petros Mavromichalis. At its core, the revolution was a religious conflict that pitted Orthodox Christians in the Peloponnese against outnumbered Muslims. But many Greeks stayed out of the conflict. In Constantinople, the Greeks were reluctant to rise up against the sultan, as were Greeks in cities like Thessaloniki and most of the eastern Aegean islands. The concept of a Greek nation-state was just starting to emerge. The Peloponnese and Attica were the main theaters of battle.

The bloodletting between Christians and Muslims was arguably worse than that seen in modern-day conflicts like Syria's Civil War and the killing fields of Darfur. There were also alliances and counter-alliances. Muslim and Christian warlords back-channeled and cut deals with each other. Christians slaughtered Christians. Plunder and looting were used to pay soldiers' salaries.

The Greek insurgents made an alliance with Ali Pasha as he fought Khurshid Pasha; some even hoped the old Pasha of Ioannina would lead their new independent state. Still, other Greek chieftains joined with the sultan to fight against Ali Pasha. In sum, the Greek Revolution was a nasty Near Eastern war from start to finish.[15]

Khurshid Pasha eventually surrounded Ali Pasha in Ioannina's citadel. The rebellious Albanian was killed in 1822 and his severed head was sent back to Constantinople. Epirus remained in Ottoman hands until 1913. Ioannina went into a period of decline after Ali Pasha's death. But killing Ali Pasha didn't end the Greek Revolution because it was an organic Greek uprising. The Kingdom of Greece was established in 1832, but it would take roughly 100 more years for the borders of Greece that we know to form.

The main takeaway for our purposes is to understand that Greece's modern borders grew by clawing territory away from the crumbling Ottoman Empire piecemeal as Greek partisans and armies fought the Turks and other nascent Balkan nation-states. This informs how most Greeks see themselves as the unloved frontier state of Europe. Therefore, if you want to understand the Greek psyche, don't start by reading mythology, but Nikos Kazantzakis' novel *Freedom and Death*, which tells the story of the Greek Cretan revolt against the Ottomans in 1889.

If Kazantzakis is known abroad at all, it is for his hard-drinking, loafing, music-loving character Zorba in the novel *Zorba the Greek*, later adapted as a movie staring Anthony Quinn. Kazantzakis was born in 1883 on Ottoman-controlled Crete. He modeled the main protagonist of *Freedom and Death*, Captain Michalis, after his father. Captain Michalis is a taciturn and stoic *palikari* (irregular soldier), whose entire being is dedicated to expelling the despised Muslim Turks from his island. When the time comes, he leads his fellow Greeks in revolt against the Ottomans. Captain Michalis' nemesis is his Turkish blood brother, Nuri Bey. In describing Captain Michalis, Nuri Bey gives the quintessential character traits of a Greek *palikari*, which still define manhood in this traditional country: "What a man! What pride and what courage! He never says a superfluous word, he never boasts. He doesn't quarrel with those beneath him. He knows no fraud. He has no respect even for death."[16]

Captain Michalis' comrade in arms, Captain Polyxigis, is more like Zorba. He is a flirtatious Cretan captain who whisks away Nuri Bey's beautiful Circassian slave girl. "When we are at peace, I seduce *hanums*. When we're at war, I kill *agas*. That's what I call being a man," he summarizes his life code to Captain Michalis.[17]

Freedom and Death is a nationalist, blood-and-guns account of the Ottoman Empire's dying days. There is no soft sentimentality here for a lost Levant. Unlike *The Bridge on the Drina*, another excellent novel about the Ottoman Balkans, Kazantzakis' Greeks are in a gloves-off death-match with their Muslim neighbors.

They are imbued with nineteenth-century nationalism and yearn to be united with the "beggar-mother" Greece. Every inch of their island is soaked in Christian blood, where, "For generations and generations, the Pachas had hanged the Christians who had dared to raise their heads."[18]

The Greeks' long, bloody battle with the Ottomans defines how they see themselves on the rim of Europe. Crete only achieved independence from the Ottomans in 1898. When it did, the island was administered by a new phenomenon in the realm of foreign relations at the time, an international peacekeeping force. It comprised the Great Powers: Britain, France, Italy and Russia. For more than ten years, they dithered on whether to allow Crete to join Greece at all. Crete was swept up in the Eastern Question, as the European powers fought over how to divide the territory of the splintering Ottoman Empire. Crete was officially annexed to Greece in 1913, the same year Greek troops conquered Epirus.

* * *

Of course, it would be a mistake to let the bloody, final 100 years of Ottoman rule in Greece completely define Ioannina. The city was a thriving commercial center even two centuries before Ali Pasha came on the scene. It was a nexus for overland trade between the Ottomans and Western Europe. For the historian Traian Stoianovich, Ioannina was the home of the "Conquering Balkan Orthodox Merchant."[19]

This was when the Aslan Pasha mosque was built (1618). Then, the world was multipolar and it was very hard to draw a dividing line between East and West. It sounds familiar. Today, we have a militarized Russia battering Ukraine, revisionist Türkiye expanding, and new Arab powers asserting themselves.

In the early 1600s, Ioannina was on the upswing after 100 years of tumult. The collapse of the Byzantine Empire had left a power vacuum in the Balkans. Control of Ioannina whipsawed from Serbian rulers to Byzantine hangers-on and Italian nobles who governed a crumbling rump-state called the Despotate of Epirus. The Balkans were a fragile house of cards before the Ottomans arrived, which helps explain why Ioannina was voluntarily handed over to them in 1430. In return for their peaceful submission to the sultan, Ioannina's residents were granted the privilege to trade freely. Ioannina thrived because of its ambiguous position between East and West.

The Ottomans' trade and urban policies positively impacted Ioannina. After he conquered Constantinople, Sultan Mehmed II set about restoring the capital's population, which had dwindled under the Byzantines. The fifteenth- and sixteenth-century sultans were unapologetic imperialists. Therefore, they understood the relationship between demographics, economics and power. They coaxed and cajoled people to move to Constantinople. If that didn't work, they used what human rights activists of our era call "forcible displacement." Once Constantinople's population started to grow, it needed to be provisioned. But the Muslim elite didn't want to sully themselves with trade, so the Ottomans turned to a network of Christian merchants across the Balkans. The sultans also tried to shift the silk, sugar and spice trades away from Damascus and Alexandria toward Constantinople. Although they had limited success on that front, their efforts led to the creation of overland trade routes connecting the Black Sea to the Adriatic, passing through places like Ioannina. A rising Ottoman Empire made the Greeks rich.[20] "The victory of the Ottoman Empire symbolized, in the sphere of economics, a victory of Greeks, Turks, renegade Christians, Armenians, Ragusans, and Jews over the two-century-old commercial hegemony of Venice and Genoa," Stoianovich wrote.[21]

Some Greek Orthodox merchants were so eager to capitalize on their new empire's clout that they dressed in Muslim attire on trips to European business centers like Vienna and Lyon because the style, "afforded them the prestige and protection of the new 'Byzantium'."[22]

By the early 1700s, another shift was underway. France, Austria, Germany and Britain were developing industries. The Ottomans tried to foster their own domestic manufacturing sector, but failed, in part because they were bad protectionists. They did not come up with an effective plan to subsidize local manufacturers or apply tariffs. European diplomats in Constantinople shrewdly lobbied against the rise of Ottoman industry to protect their own export market. This was one of the seeds of the Ottoman Empire's decline. But the rise of European manufacturing created new opportunities for Ioanniotes. Soon, Christian merchants from Epirus were scouring the Balkans for raw materials to sell to the West. Merchants from Ioannina captured the trade of exporting Balkan wool and cotton to factories in Austria and Germany. In return, they imported sugar, coffee, and manufactured goods into Adriatic and Ionian ports for the Ottoman landowning elite.

* * *

Does Ioannina have a contemporary equivalent to these traders? Potentially. I made the three-and-a-half-hour journey from Athens to Ioannina to meet its new globalized class of businesspeople: a very small group of Greek technology professionals. Most work remotely for tech companies abroad and others use Ioannina as a base for their startups. They told me Ioannina is an attractive, cost-friendly bolthole.

One of them is Tassos Koutlas. With his bushy beard and ruffled T-shirt, Koutlas has re-adapted to the rhythm of his mountainous hometown. He moved back to Ioannina from the United Kingdom in 2021 after his wife obtained a job at the local university. He kept his tech job and works remotely.

Since moving back, he has founded a co-working space in the old town for other tech professionals. "Working on a UK salary in Ioannina was a no brainer. The quality of life is much better here. You get so much more for your money. And this is home. In a global world, you don't need to be physically in London," he told me.

"Historically, Ioannina fell on the Eastern trade route from Venice to Thessaloniki and Istanbul. In the 1600s, in Venice's chamber of commerce, there were Ioanniotes," he said. "Today's equivalent to those traders are web designers, software developers, product managers, and AI experts. I think we need to learn from our past. We just need to rejig it for the AI and digital world."

The bar is set so low for Ioannina, that it doesn't need to become a Silicon Valley to succeed or build sprawling data centers. It has attracted some middling European tech companies, but it has also emerged as a hub for small Greek startups because of its lower labor and living costs.

Thanasis Navrozoglu is the CEO of Natech, a Greek company that specializes in digital banking platforms. He employs sixty people in Ioannina. The average salary of his developers is €4,500 a month. That is less than one-third what an equivalent hire in Germany would get, Navrozoglu says, but a solidly upper-middle class income by Greek standards. "For the business owner and his employees, Ioannina is a good base," he tells me. "It is a beautiful city to raise a family."

His main concern is that there isn't enough talent to go around. "Usually, I'd expect to see thirty or forty applications for each job opening I put out. Recently, I am getting only twenty," he told me. He blamed a bureaucratic decision by Greece's Ministry of Education that reduced the number of students entering the University of Ioannina's tech departments. "The university is a big reason to be here. If we don't have a steady supply of graduates it will be a problem in the future."

Indeed, Nikolas Dermaris finds himself in high demand. He is a computer science and engineering major at the university, which has 20,000 students. When Dermaris is not in class, he works as a freelance software developer and helps run his father's tech company. They have a program that assesses data to monitor underground construction projects. None of their clients are in Ioannina and only one, the company expanding Athens' subway, is in Greece.

"It's a great time to be a student in Ioannina. My email is flooded with career day announcements. Companies are giving students internships, and hiring them. In Greece, the opportunities are always in Athens and Thessaloniki, but for a career in tech, you can do well for yourself in Ioannina," Dermaris told me.

He struck me as serious and hard working. "A graduate from the University of Ioannina can find an average tech job here for €1,500 a month, net income," he said. "I know that sounds low for the United States, but compared to the €900 a month a lot of young Greeks make, it's night and day."

Greece has a staggering imbalance between low wages and cost of living. The latter has many culprits. One is astronomical energy prices due to the war in Ukraine and reliance on imported LNG when wind and solar energy are not available. There is also the influx of foreign real estate investors, high taxes and Greece's stifling bureaucracy. Because of this cost-of-living crisis, young Greeks aren't buying homes and starting families. This is a problem across Europe, but provincial regions like Epirus are ground-zero for it. Greece's population decline has reached a point that is impossible to arrest.[23] Dismal Greek birthrates combined with migration from the Middle East, mean Greece is being reabsorbed into the Near East in more ways than one.

Visitors to Greece who stay in Athens don't recognize just how old and empty the country is, because the capital is a sponge that soaks up all the money and youth. In 2022, Greece recorded its lowest number of births on record, chalking up a fertility rate of just 1.3 children per woman (2.1 children for every woman is required for a population to replace itself). By 2050, Greece is expected to lose a million citizens, as its population of 10.6 million drops to 9.5 million.[24] This will stress social services and military spending.

Ioannina was the first stop in my travels because it is a rarity: a provincial Greek city that is young, although the countryside around it is graying. In a chaotic, globalized Near East, a positive future for Greece's hinterlands looks something like Ioannina. It relies on good universities turned into hubs, remote workers who can float between cities and dodge the European Union's red tape by working for companies abroad, niche startups, and balanced tourism. It also needs young Greeks who see an attractive cost differential in the countryside compared to Athens. The alternative long-term trajectory for places like Ioannina is that they become depopulated, desolate wastelands.

* * *

Practically everywhere I traveled in this book, Greeks I met asked me whether the United States would abandon NATO. To be frank, Greeks I met didn't care much about Ukraine's demands to retain the Crimean Peninsula or its eastern borderlands. They were eager for the war to end quickly in the hope it would lower energy prices. What the Greeks cared about was whether the United States would cut a similar deal for a zone of influence with an expansionist Türkiye as with Russia.

I believe that Greece will be where American power dies hardest in Europe, but in the end it will diminish. If Greece remains relevant in Washington, it is not because it's a member of NATO, but because it belongs to the wider Middle East.

EPIRUS

Asia is creeping up to Europe. Greece is on the frontlines of the end of the post-war order. Epirus is the perfect place to stop to understand how Greece became a member of NATO in the first place, and why I suspect it will remain in the United States' sphere of influence in a reduced way. After all, this was the first country were the United States replaced the British as the Western world's superpower.

We have to go back to the Second World War, when Greek troops inflicted what is considered to be the first major defeat against the Axis powers in Epirus. In 1940, Benito Mussolini had staged his army in Albania. With his troops massed on the border, he gave Athens an ultimatum to surrender. The one-word response of dictator Ioannis Metaxas' government, which ruled Greece from 1936 to 1941, *Oxi*, or no, is still celebrated every 28 October in Greece and among the diaspora.

The Greeks fought the Italians to a standstill in Epirus, forcing Hitler to divert troops he needed for the invasion of the Soviet Union to support his Italian ally. The Greeks' last stand was the beginning of a decade-long saga from which Greece emerged as the tip of the spear for the United States in the Eastern Mediterranean.

The 1941–44 Axis occupation of Greece is one of the most underreported horrors of the Second World War. The Nazis ravaged Greece. They emptied it of foodstuffs, entrenched themselves in Athens' finest hotels and then divided the rest of the country up among their allies; Bulgaria was given control of northeastern Greece and Italy ruled the Dodecanese islands and Western Greece. According to one American government assessment, Greece suffered more severely during the war than any other Allied country except the Soviet Union. The Greeks were tortured, beaten and literally starved to death in a famine. It is estimated that eight per cent of the entire country—over 500,000 people—were killed in the war or died under the occupation. Hundreds of villages were razed to the ground and wholesale executions were common.[25]

The Greeks resisted the Nazis, but to what end is a matter of dispute. The resistance conducted sporadic sabotage operations that succeeded in forcing Hitler to divert 300,000 troops from other fronts to chase the Greeks in the mountains. Right through 1944, partly because of the Greek resistance's attacks, Hitler believed that the Allies would invade Greece and the Balkans, which British Prime Minister Winston Churchill famously referred to as Europe's "soft underbelly."

But the Greeks mainly focused their energies on killing each other. Militias loosely affiliated with the Left and Right fought turf wars. Familial and clan feuds took route amid the chaos of the occupation. As C.M. Woodhouse, the British commander of the Allied Military Mission to Greek guerrillas, observed, the resistance was subsumed into the Greeks' "tradition of anarchy and vendetta."[26] The Greeks treated the Axis occupation like a return to Ottoman times. They reverted to the brigand ways of the *armatoles*. Notably, the resistance stayed united only in Crete. One Greek diplomat I know with roots on the island attributed this unity, not unreasonably, to Cretan society resembling North African tribal politics. Because clan and family are so supreme there, he argued, no Cretan wanted to be the first to fire a shot that risked mutually assured self-destruction.

The most effective Greek resistance movement was by far the leftist Hellenic Popular Mobilization Army, known by its acronym ELAS. This was the military offshoot of the Greek Communist Party's National Liberation Front, or EAM. Among the Allied Powers, support for the Greek resistance was the domain of the British. They sent arms and supplies to ELAS and its rivals, including royalists and the anti-communist National Republican Greek League (EDES). The British also embedded commandos with the Greeks. Woodhouse knew the communist resistance very well, and like another British commando, Patrick Leigh Fermor, developed a genuine love for Greece, its culture and his Greek comrades in arms. However, politicians in London viewed Greece as an oriental client state. In keeping with that theme, the Special Operations Executive's (SOE) Greek mission was run out of Cairo along with the rest of the Middle East and Balkans. SOE oversaw Britain's covert operations against the Nazis. Cairo was also home to Greece's royalist government-in-exile. The British manipulated the exiled government at every turn to ensure they had an obedient client that could be sent back to Athens the day the Nazis were defeated.

The Axis occupation ended in November 1944. Germany withdrew from Greece after the Soviet Union occupied Romania. But Greece's troubles were just beginning. The country's social fabric was obliterated. As the Germans withdrew, Greece's simmering social and political tensions erupted into an all-out civil war that lasted six years. Greece was food-poor, but rich in weapons and young men bent on revenge against Nazi collaborators, political rivals and petty foes alike.

Simmering tensions between EAM and a newly arrived British-backed government in Athens came to a head. With the Nazis gone, Britain wanted to sideline the leftists it had backed with arms and reinstall a monarchy. Winston Churchill, who never saw a Near Eastern state he didn't want to meddle in or carve up, personally oversaw the maneuvering. As one British minister quipped at the time, Greece was "Egypt without Cromer," a reference to the British diplomat who lorded over colonial Egypt for twenty years. On 3 December 1944, a mass demonstration in Athens' Syntagma Square organized by EAM erupted in gunfire. Historians still dispute whether Greek police or protesters supporting EAM fired the first shot. Regardless of who did, Greece was primed to explode. ELAS and EAM were the most powerful, and genuinely popular, movements in the country, but the British were still tied to their colonial ways.

Woodhouse is blunt about Britain's chokehold on Greece, writing, "Up to 1947, the British government appointed and dismissed Greek Prime Ministers with the barest attention to constitutional formalities. British experts dictated economic and financial policy, defence and foreign policy, security and legal policy, trade union and employment policy."[27]

Churchill, quite rightly, saw Greece as the linchpin to power projection in the wider Middle East. Great Powers dominate here when they have a reliable foothold in Greece. Churchill gave ominous orders to British troops backing his besieged client government in Athens: "Do not hesitate to act as if you were in a conquered city where a local rebellion is in progress." With classic Churchillian flair, he even made a surprise Christmas Day visit to Athens in 1944, packing his own pistol to mediate a truce between EAM and the government.[28] The agreement was a band-aid. Fighting erupted again in 1946 between the Greek Army and communist guerrillas ensconced in the mountains. The conflict only ended in late 1949 when the last communists fled behind the Iron Curtain.

To most Americans, the Greek Civil War is presented as the first Cold War battleground between the United States and the Soviet Union. This is not the whole truth. First of all, Joseph Stalin was ambivalent toward the Greek communists. In fact, historians wonder why he didn't support ELAS in 1944, given that Soviet military advisors embedded with them could not but have assessed that the communists were the most popular force in Greece. If ELAS had acted quicker after the Nazi withdrawal, Greece would have been behind the Iron Curtain.

Churchill was really enmeshed in a local rebellion driven by intra-Greek squabbling and resentment over colonial rule, not the civilizational fight with godless communism he made it out to be. In fact, Stalin had already relegated Greece to the sphere of British influence. In October 1944, he reached a secret "Percentages Agreement" with Churchill that granted the British ninety per cent influence over Greek affairs in exchange for the Soviet Union dominating the rest of the Balkans. Stalin reaffirmed his commitment to non-interference in Greece in exchange for mastery of the rest of Eastern Europe at the 1945 Yalta conference when the British, Americans and Soviets carved up their spheres of influence.[29] In a new Yalta era, Greece is likely to be preserved within the American sphere of influence, even as the United States steps away from Eastern Europe and, potentially, the Baltic states.

Standard Western perceptions of the Greek Civil War are a classic case of the West injecting ideology into conflicts fueled, at first, by local politics and grievances. Until its last years, the war was a Greek-on-Greek conflict best summarized by Nikos Kazantzakis as a fratricide.

The Greek Left relied on Josip Broz Tito, the communist leader of Yugoslavia, for support. He aided them with arms and training not out of ideological fervor, but what he viewed as Yugoslav national interest to have a stake in historic Macedonia and boost his influence in the Balkans. In fact, one of the signs that the tide was beginning to turn against the Greek communists by late 1948, was that their new recruits were increasingly ethnic Slavo-Macedonians and not Greeks.

For its part, the United States had only a passing interest in Greece during the early days of the war. Nevertheless, Britain's 1944 clash with ELAS enraged the American public, which saw Churchill pursuing his imperial ambitions at the expense of the democratic ideals that Americans believed their sons were fighting and dying for.

The United States developed an interest in Greece gradually. This was less because of Greece itself than because every country around Greece—Bulgaria, Yugoslavia, Romania and Albania—had fallen to the communists. Greece is where America's "domino theory" was born. The Americans were determined not to let Greece fall to the communists, whether they were backed by Tito or Stalin, or homegrown, for fear that other "third world" countries could be toppled next.

American intervention in Greece marked the symbolic passing of the torch from one Western superpower to another. The British were folding up their imperial holdings, in Greece, India and then Palestine. The British told the Americans they no longer had the will or money to support Greece's government. In 1947, President Harry S. Truman gave his now famous speech to Congress asking it to pass the Truman Doctrine, which pledged massive quantities of American military and economic aid to countries faced with a communist takeover. The Americans were determined to hold Greece at all costs. Military and economic aid, along with American intelligence officers and advisors, flooded in.

Woodhouse gives an enduring description of these new arrivals, who were hustled and fleeced by Greeks in the bars and brothels of Piraeus and Athens. His remarks could apply to Americans in more recent foreign interventions in Afghanistan and Iraq.

"They were apt to assume that history began when they first came to the scene," he wrote. Compared to the British, the Greeks found the Americans, "more inflexible, less adaptable ... more inclined to impose American methods regardless of national characteristics [but] they were vigorous, resourceful, and immensely efficient."[30]

The Americans were certainly vigorous in giving the Greeks napalm to bomb the communists in their mountain hideouts. Between 1947 and 1949, the US gave hundreds of millions of dollars to Greece's right-wing government, which sent thousands of political prisoners to barren Aegean islands, the most notorious of which was Makronisos, to be tortured and "indoctrinated" against communism. It is generally believed that Greece's right-wing government was behind the murder in 1948 of American journalist George Polk, who was critical of the US intervention in Greece. His assassination is believed to have been covered up with the help of American intelligence officers and embassy employees.[31]

But when the Americans arrived in 1947, the Greek government was in real danger of falling to the communists. Both sides used torture, forced conscription and massacres to achieve their war aims. If the Greek Civil War was a local power struggle in the mid-1940s, by 1947 it had morphed into an intra-Greek ideological war. The United States' intervention, which dispersed American advisors and culture across Greece, probably accelerated the hardening of Greek positions. But the fault-lines had existed for at least a century.

This was not a simple rich capitalists versus poor workers battle, or one that fits neatly with stereotypes about Cold War communism and dictatorship. Some Greek Orthodox priests fought on the side of the communists. Traveling throughout Greece's borderlands, I met communists who were more conservative than center-right voters.

As Woodhouse explained, "all classes were equally represented on both sides ... the conflict was genuinely ideological, between two conceptions of society, one traditional and one revolutionary, but both Greek in character."[32]

A deeper battle was playing out for the soul of Greece during the war—one that is important to keep in mind as Russia reasserts itself in Europe today. This was a fight between a part of Greece whose ancestors saw themselves as aligned with Tsarist Russia, and loathed Western interference, and another who embraced the seafaring, trading British Empire.

One side saw Greece as the Near Eastern outpost of the West, and the other, as the Mediterranean extension of Eurasia. Some historians argue that Greece's fate was probably pre-ordained despite the communists' close brushes with victory because of the very essence of its modern creation. Greece was the first nation-state in the Near East fashioned by Great Powers, and the dominant one was Britain. The factors that made Greece dependent on sea powers two centuries ago haven't changed. Greece is a resource-poor country that relies on trade, shipping, and remittances. Today, add in tourism. Greece's natural patrons are globalized sea powers who control international finance.

Stalin understood the Greek Civil War better than most and his geopolitical analysis reflects why Russia sometimes reaches into Greece, but then wobbles. Stalin knew the Greeks were fickle communists. He rejected a zone of influence here and focused his energy on consolidating Soviet control of Eastern and Central Europe. It sounds familiar to our era. Now, Russia wants to reassert itself in Eastern Europe. This time around, it is the United States passing on extending NATO membership to Ukraine and considering withdrawing from Eastern Europe.

By 1948, Stalin was urging the communist governments of Yugoslavia and Bulgaria to end their support for the Greek rebels, saying, "The uprising has to fold up. What do you think, that Great Britain and the United States—the most powerful state in the world—will permit you to break their line of communication in the Mediterranean Sea! Nonsense. And we have no navy."[33]

The Cold War left Greece safely isolated. Five years after the American intervention, Greece, along with Turkey, joined NATO. Both were developed with American tax-dollars under the Marshall Plan. The United States transformed Greece's impoverished countryside and war-ravaged cities for the better. In return, it surpassed the British Empire's wildest dreams of exerting naval and air dominance across the Eastern Mediterranean. The

Near East—as a geopolitical concept—ceased to exist. Likewise, there were no regional powers in the Arab world or West Asia to angle for influence in the Eastern Mediterranean. This bipolar world was an aberration. The ideological battlelines of the Cold War are not relevant to the new Near East, but Greece's geography is.

Building on Stalin's analysis, the civil war reaffirmed Greece's status as a linchpin for sea powers against Eurasian land powers. This battle has raged in the Mediterranean since at least 1571, when the Christian Holy League sunk most of the Ottoman navy in the Battle of Lepanto. The Ottomans, who swept across the steppes of Asia, were literally grounded. When the European powers carved out a fledgling Kingdom of Greece in 1832, it was Britain who dominated, even though a wide swath of Greeks believed their Orthodox Christian cousins were in the Russian Empire.

How could the British Empire, with its mighty navy, not take Mediterranean Greece under its wing? Likewise, what were the Nazis but a Central European land power? During their final days, the communist guerrillas were reduced to fighters of the mountain passes.

As the United States' superpower status diminishes, a new, loose network of seafaring and trading states are looking for a foothold in Greece: India, Israel and the United Arab Emirates. The first is a flawed democracy. The second's leader, Israeli Prime Minister Benjamin Netanyahu, has an outstanding arrest warrant with the International Criminal Court for alleged crimes against humanity in Gaza. The third is ruled by an autocratic Arab royal family that brooks no dissent. India is shopping around for a Greek port. And Israel and the United Arab Emirates don't need American coaxing in order to deepen their foothold here as they look to compete with Türkiye and find a cheap backdoor into Europe. Greece's security and growing importance to regional powers is tied to geoeconomics and geopolitics, not democracy and human rights. As a journalist, it's been entertaining to watch the Greeks respond to this change. They desperately want these new allies, but are still playing a part for the Brussels bureaucrats and Washington think tanks. I spoke at one high-powered Greek policy forum in a beautiful mountain resort, where an Emirati analyst asked me, quite perplexed, why the Greeks kept talking about being the birthplace of democracy. As if the United Arab Emirates cares. They also made the largest single foreign direct investment in Greece in 2024.

Because Greeks live in such an unstable neighborhood, the United States' flirtation with territorial expansion in the Western hemisphere and abandonment of NATO unnerves them. They fear it will set a precedent for Türkiye to make a land or sea grab. Even serious Greek analysts I know, at the most moderate and liberal think tanks, quietly ask what Greece could do if Türkiye occupied an islet in the Eastern Aegean in the coming decade and the United States did nothing.

Türkiye is one of the Near East's two revisionist powers. It is not accidental that Greece's new closest ally is the second: Israel, which, besides Cyprus, is the only other non-Muslim-majority country in the Eastern Mediterranean. Greece is betting its relationship with Israel will keep the United States here, too.

Leave aside that Greece's conservative, Orthodox Christian culture has a certain appeal to the ascendent right in global politics; Greece's importance to the United States for projecting power will endure. It is a low-cost, one-stop-shop for reduced American power projection into Europe and Asia. It checks all the boxes for a power that is downsizing. Like a good post-colonial state, Greece bends with the breeze. The United States is becoming more mercantilist toward the European Union. Enter Greece, where American Liquified Natural Gas (LNG) destined for Ukraine is arriving. Greeks, the ultimate Levantines, are well placed to navigate a ruthless and more transactional new world.

Although Greece is more exposed to conflict than Western European states, I suspect it will withstand the coming upheaval better than, say, the Baltic states and Central Europe. I'm not arguing that Greece can flourish if Europe burns. If Eastern Europe becomes a Russian sphere of influence again, that will put Greece on the frontline of Eurasia. Potentially, with little American backing.

Greece needs a strong European Union. It is a net recipient of transfers from the bloc. In fact, Greece's economic success since the coronavirus pandemic is due to a goldilocks situation. A windfall in tourism revenue and real estate investment has been augmented by payments from the European Union's Next Generation investment program. Greece is its third largest recipient, taking in nearly €40 billion worth of grants and favorable loans, in return for making basic, structural economic reforms.

And what of Russia? With its dwindling and aging population, Russia is much weaker than it's made out to be. In fact, in the next chapter, Greece provides an example of how bungling and inept Russia's foreign policy is in the Eastern Mediterranean.

Putin's interest in Greece has withered as he pursues territorial expansion in Ukraine. But there is nothing remarkable about Putin's decisions in the Near East. His approach to the region recalls that of the tsars and Stalin. To understand Russia's retreat from the Eastern Mediterranean, look no further than how it passed up an opportunity to fill a vacuum in Greece after the financial crisis.

3

PEARL OF THE AEGEAN

ORIENTALISTS AND OLIGARCHS

Locals call the seaside corniche in Thessaloniki, *paralia*, or beach. It is the central artery of Greece's second largest city, where every visitor ends up. From here, you can spot the White Tower, a stone fortress constructed after Thessaloniki fell to Sultan Murad II's army in 1430. The rest of Thessaloniki's Ottoman gems are tucked into Ano Poli, the old hilltop Muslim quarter of the city that withstood a devastating 1917 fire and, later, Greece's post-war apartment building craze. Rows of ugly *polikatoikies* face *paralia*. Their million-dollar price tags (a staggering sum for northern Greece) are justified by their one and only attribute—that they have a view of the Aegean and not other ugly *polikatoikies*.

Thessaloniki offers a different kind of Mediterranean vista; one I honestly prefer.

Container ships sit on the Thermaic Gulf's placid waters, waiting to be unloaded at Thessaloniki's port, the main maritime access point for central Europe and the Balkans. To find the port, just look for the phalanx of unloading cranes in the sky. Far from spoiling the view, the cranes and vessels add to Thessaloniki's edgy charm, reminding residents each day of the utilitarian, inner workings of the global economy.

The port is owned by Ivan Savvidis, otherwise known as "the Kremlin's man in Greece," and the "Tsar of Thessaloniki."[1] He is the type of character loathed and misunderstood in equal measure by diplomats and officials in the West. Savvidis is one of the most popular men between Thessaloniki and the Turkish border. The pistol-packing, prayer-bead-strumming businessman epitomizes that heady mix of populist conservatism, nationalism and distain for liberal culture that is rising across Europe. It is indigenous to northeastern Greece.

Savvidis was born in 1959 a long way from the Aegean, in a little town called Santa in Soviet Georgia, to a family of Pontiac Greek peasants. Pontians come from the southern shores of the Black Sea, in what is today northern Türkiye. During Catherine the Great's rule, some migrated to the Russian Empire for trade and business opportunities. The Ottomans began killing Pontians in a genocide alongside Armenians as they lost ground during the First World War. Tens of thousands fled the emerging nation-state of Türkiye for Greece, the Caucasus and Russia.

There are two categories of Pontians in Greece today. The first are those who arrived during the 1920s wave of Asia Minor refugees. They faced discrimination, but eventually assimilated into the great refugee mother that is the Greek nation-state. Savvidis hails from the second category, who came after the collapse of the Soviet Union. Besides their Orthodox faith, they shared little in common with Greeks, who still derisively call them "Russo-Pontians." Adding to their sense of isolation, they speak Greek with a Slavic accent and their own language, a distant Greek dialect, is influenced by Russian and Turkish. Russo-Pontians I met in northern Greece, by and large, hated so-called woke culture, sympathized with Putin, and despised

Türkiye even more than is usual for Greeks. They ended up in northern Greece through nothing short of a great replacement program.

In the 1990s, Greece's socialist government, PASOK, encouraged the migration of Pontians to the regions of Macedonia, and especially, neighboring Thrace, using housing subsidies, social welfare and jobs programs to resettle them. This wasn't to create some Greek socialist nirvana. The uber nationalist Pontians made good allies, and like other refugees, would make a reliable voting block for the government that welcomed them, or so at least the thinking went. But PASOK really wanted to use the Pontian refugees to boost the Christian demographics in Thrace, which is home to a sizable Muslim minority. They were unnerved by fighting in Yugoslavia, were Christians and Muslims were butchering each other.[2]

Savvidis lived in Georgia until he was fourteen. He moved to the southern Russian city Rostov-on-Don, where he worked at a state tobacco factory rolling cigarettes. He arrived in Greece in the early 1990s, but later returned to Rostov-on-Don, which had become a mafia and smugglers paradise. Savvidis cut his teeth in the free-wheeling and violent world of post-Soviet capitalism. He turned Donskoy Tabak, a middling tobacco company he acquired under murky circumstances, into one of the largest cigarette manufacturers in Russia. He earned allies in Moscow by gifting a billion cigarettes a year to the Russian army. In 2003, he entered Russia's Duma as a member of United Russia, Putin's political party. Savvidis, who Forbes estimates has a net worth of $1.5 billion, is a small-time oligarch compared to Roman Abramovich and Alisher Usmanov, but he is a player in northern Greece, where he started buying up assets during the Greek financial crisis.[3]

Suddenly, a man no one had heard of, a Russo-Pontian who barely spoke Greek, had catapulted into the Greek tabloids. One minute he was partying at Athenian nightclubs surrounded by models and Greek crooners, and next he was huddling with monks at Mount Athos where he made donations to Orthodox monasteries. He purchased, and later sold, a Greek tobacco company, and took stakes in prominent Greek media companies. He bought a share of Mega Channel and acquired left-leaning Greek media outlets, including Greece's Open TV and Ethnos. But what made Savvidis a hero in Thessaloniki was his decision in 2012 to rescue the indebted football club PAOK.

"PAOK's debts are now also my debts. I don't owe anything and soon PAOK won't either," Savvidis announced after personally going to the Greek tax office, in a symbolic move to pay off the endangered club's debts. In acquiring PAOK, Savvidis gained a diehard fan club.[4]

The Super League club is neo-Byzantium in a nutshell. It was founded in 1926 by Greek refugees from Constantinople. During match days, Thessaloniki's Toumba neighborhood, where PAOK's stadium is located, is awash in Byzantine-double eagle flags (the club's emblem) and fans sporting white and black colors, which represent mourning for the loss of Constantinople to the Ottomans. PAOK fans are more than soccer hooligans. As a group, they wield political power. Their wrath can unnerve governments and shut down city streets.

PAOK's fans cut across social and class divides, but it is a working man's team. One time when I had a car accident in Thessaloniki, I hitched a ride in the front seat of the tow-truck. The pot-bellied, crucifix-wearing driver had two decorations on the windshield: an icon of Saint Demetrius, Thessaloniki's patron saint, and a PAOK emblem.

The religious-like zeal of PAOK fans is felt most strongly in Thessaloniki's poorer west side. I remember sitting in a cafe in its Evosmos suburb with a friend's twin eighteen-year-old cousins to watch a PAOK match. The Greece around me would have been almost unrecognizable to island-hopping tourists.

"We are all *kágkouras* in this place," Angelos, one of my hosts, told me. He was referring to the Greek biker-style. He and his friends sported the classic look: black T-shirts, black jeans and short cut hair. We drank Alpha beer. None of the guys had girlfriends and they wore their crucifixes over their T-shirts. "PAOK fans will die for our club. We will fuck up anyone who stands in its way. We love Savvidis. He saved our club," Angelos said.

No one in the cafe was above twenty-five years old, but each one traced their origins back to Asia Minor or Pontus. A working-class cosmopolitanism was alive here. Two of the kids were born after their parents arrived in Thessaloniki from post-Soviet Georgia, another from Russia and one from Armenia. Savvidis was their cultural icon. Unlike Greece's Western-leaning shipping elite, with apartments and charitable foundations in New York and London, Savvidis is a dyed-in-the-wool man of the East who appears to PAOK fans in social media videos against a backdrop of Orthodox icons. My hosts' favorite story was how in 2018, Savvidis rushed onto the pitch, grabbing a holstered pistol, to protest a penalty decision against PAOK.

I lived in Thessaloniki for months. The port city was a convenient base to report in Greece's borderlands near Türkiye. During that time, one of the best descriptions of the city I heard came from Thouli Misiroglou, the director of Thessaloniki's Museum of Contemporary Art. Misiroglou has stylishly ruffled hair and bohemian, artsy vibes. She is the antithesis of a classic PAOK fan. Running a contemporary art museum in a conservative town, she is also skilled at tip-toeing around political and cultural minefields.

"Contemporary art focuses on sub-groups and how they interact with society," she conditioned her remarks to me. "But if you ask me, 'what is the hard center of Thessaloniki, its core?' I have to say, 'PAOK.'" She thought for a moment. "PAOK is Thessaloniki."

Savvidis' growing sway in Thessaloniki irked American diplomats and intelligence officials. They saw him as an agent of the Kremlin and worried that Putin was reassessing Stalin's old commitment to a zone of Western influence in Greece. Regional developments added to those concerns. In 2017, Türkiye announced it would buy Russian air-defense systems. Russia had already intervened in Syria's Civil War on the side of former President Bashar al-Assad. For a moment, it seemed like Russia was back in the Eastern Mediterranean.

Savvidis liked Putin, but it wasn't clear that he had a political agenda. He purchased trophy assets in Thessaloniki like historic mansions and beach-front real estate. He took over the defunct Makedonia Palace on Thessaloniki's waterfront and carried out a massive renovation, making it the city's top hotel. By 2016, he had cemented himself as northern Greece's most powerful businessman. In 2018, he acquired his most strategic asset when his Cyprus-based firm Belterra Investments joined a consortium of German and French companies to take a twenty per cent stake in Thessaloniki's port. In 2021, he boosted his share an additional forty-seven per cent, making him the port's majority owner. At the time of writing, Savvidis has a lock on the port. There are signs Russia's European foes are trying to kick him out. In 2025, he defended his majority stake by purchasing shares above a surprise public offer by French group Louis-Dreyfus. CMA CGM, one of the world's largest shipping companies, with close links to the French government, was part of the effort to oust Savvidis, Greek media reported.[5]

I found that senior American diplomats I met over the years underestimated Savvidis' cultural relevance and overinflated his geopolitical importance. Ukraine sanctioned Savvidis in 2023.

After that, one senior American diplomat I met dismissed Savvidis to me as "irrelevant," boasting that "his world had been turned upside down" and that Thessaloniki had turned against him because of the war in Ukraine. This was delusional.

Greeks oppose Putin's invasion of Ukraine. Support for Russia has plunged here. According to a 2023 poll, just thirty per cent of Greeks held a favorable view of Russia compared to seventy per cent before the war in Ukraine.[6] Savvidis has stayed away from Greece since the war started, but he still owns PAOK and all of his other Greek assets. His popularity hasn't dropped. In northern Greece, I sensed frustration with the war in 2024 and 2025. Greek farmers complained about high fertilizer costs and everyone was angry about sky-high energy prices.

The roots of Savvidis' popularity in northern Greece go back centuries before Putin came on the scene. After Greece was established as a client state of the Great Powers in 1832, three Greek parties dominated its politics. They didn't even try to hide their sympathies. Each one was literally named after its foreign patron: Russia, France, and Britain. Savvidis is part of an old Greek tradition that respects Moscow as a modern, Orthodox metropolis, yet despises the Slavs and when push comes to shove rejects the Kremlin.

Russia's last, half-hearted attempt to assert itself in Greece underscores its failed foreign policy in the Near East. Despite Savvidis' buying spree, the Kremlin did not swoop in on Greece in the wake of the financial crisis. Putin de facto reaffirmed Greece as an American zone of influence.

For all the reasons discussed earlier, Thessaloniki should have been the soft underbelly for Russia into Greece. In fact, just as Savvidis was at the pinnacle of his power, the Syriza government was begging the Russians to invest in the country. "We went to the Russians and said, 'We are privatizing state assets. Why don't you show your good ties to Greece and buy a port. We want Russia to be a player here to create competition with the Americans,'" a senior Greek diplomat involved in the discussions at the time, told me. "We told them to come up with an offer and business plan for the ports of Kavala or Alexandroupoli. We wanted Russia here for healthy competition with the Americans. The door was wide open," the diplomat continued:

> The response from the Russian ambassador in Athens was something like "My hundred-thousand-dollar Mercedes in Moscow is worth more than your port of Kavala." That summed up Russian diplomacy toward Greece; arrogance and lack of strategic vision. The Russians treated Greece like it was some African country. Moscow thought it could come with a suitcase full of cash and Greeks would roll over for them because they bribed some priests. They totally misread Greece.

In the summer of 2018, Greece's government released details about an intelligence operation in which Russian agents tried to bribe Greek military officers, Orthodox priests, and government officials in northern Greece. Russia was trying to exert influence over nationalists and Orthodox clergy through the Imperial Orthodox Palestine Society, a nineteenth-century organization created to expand Tsarist Russia's influence in the Near East.[7] Russia's ultimate goal was to provoke protests that would prevent the expansion of NATO in the Balkans. It failed miserably. The meddling infuriated Syriza, which until then had refused to join other NATO allies in expelling Russian diplomats in retaliation for Moscow's poisoning of former Russian double-agent Sergei Skripal and his daughter in the United Kingdom. Overnight, Athens went from soliciting investments from the Kremlin to expelling Russian diplomats. This is where Savvidis comes in.

Russia's operations were intended to derail an agreement between Greece and North Macedonia that facilitated the latter's entry into NATO. The two neighbors had been locked in an obscure feud since the breakup of Yugoslavia in 1991, when the

Republic of Macedonia declared its independence. The move provoked a firestorm in Greece, because the name Macedonia is associated with the ancient Kingdom of Philip of Macedon, father of Alexander the Great. Thessaloniki is the capital of the Greek region called Macedonia. The Greeks felt their history was being pulled out from under them by the upstart Slavs, while the Macedonians felt dictated to by the arrogant Greeks. For years, Greeks and Macedonians bickered over the name. Their stubborn Balkan nationalisms left outside observers befuddled.

Then, in 2017, a window of opportunity opened to settle the spat while pulling the Republic of Macedonia into the West. Zoran Zaev, a center-left politician, was elected prime minister. He wanted to move his country toward European Union membership, which requires Greece's consent. NATO was used as a stepping-stone. Syriza was willing to negotiate on a new name—North Macedonia—and drop Greece's veto against the renamed North Macedonia joining the military alliance. The first Trump administration and the European Union backed the talks, but the main drivers were Greek and Macedonian politicians. Russia, as expected, talked a big game to stop the deal.

The United States accused Savvidis of working with the Kremlin to derail the agreement. It turned out that the American intelligence services were snooping on Savvidis' emails, texts, and phone calls. They claimed the Russian-Greek billionaire was funneling payments to protesters in North Macedonia to disrupt a referendum on the name change. Savvidis reportedly gave $350,000 to soccer hooligans, nationalist parties, and politicians to protest against the vote, according to the Organized Crime and Corruption Reporting Project.[8] Savvidis denied the allegations.

The Prespa Agreement, which ended the dispute between Greece and its neighbor with the compromise name of North Macedonia was signed on 17 June 2018. Despite the Kremlin's angry rhetoric and clumsy covert operations, it was powerless to stop it. The Prespa spat is interesting for a few reasons. It shows that the right-wing populism that is on the rise in Europe does not, by itself, equate to more political influence for Vladimir Putin's Russia. In fact, these nationalisms are hollow. Senior Greek diplomats tell me the United States over-emphasized Savvidis' importance. "The Americans wanted to make Savvidis the bogeyman because he was once in Putin's party," one of them told me.

The truth is that Savvidis didn't need to pay protesters for there to be genuine opposition to the compromise. Pontian Greeks have been mobilized by successive governments on the Left and Right in Athens to oppose the name "Macedonia" for decades. Greece's neighbor entered NATO. Yet, almost every Greek I know still refers to the country by the name of its capital, Skopje. Greek customs guards, glaringly, even refuse to stamp the passports of people coming across the land border from North Macedonia. I have a cosmopolitan, liberal Greek friend whose girlfriend is from North Macedonia, which he calls Skopje. For their part, Greece's neighbors call their homeland Macedonia and some politicians continue to whip up revisionist claims against Greece.

The lesson to draw from this episode is that Russia offers no alternative to the European Union and NATO. Despite having an ally on the ground like Savvidis, the Kremlin's efforts to derail the deal were pathetic. Russia could not even be a spoiler. The Kremlin's hybrid culture war barely moved Greeks and Macedonians, despite their decades of animosity over the name.

Perhaps the greatest irony of Prespa is that the Trump administration facilitated the entry of an obscure, post-Ottoman Balkan country into NATO. The reality is that membership in the alliance matters little to North Macedonia. This aging, depopulating state is more of a burden to the alliance than a strategic asset, too. North Macedonia is not Sweden or

Finland—wealthy, strategic countries that joined the alliance after Russia's invasion of Ukraine. The more important step is for North Macedonia to join the European Union. That's the real prize, and what North Macedonians crave. The European Union would be more transformative than NATO membership. North Macedonia's politicians continue to refer to their country without the geographic adjective that it now written into their constitution. Greece warns that Skopje's refusal to abide by Prespa risks derailing its support. Complicating matters, Bulgaria has also come out in opposition to its neighbor's accession into the EU, citing its own beef over a Bulgarian minority there.

What about Savvidis? He is definitely waiting to pop up again in Thessaloniki. While living here, friends often pointed out his son and daughter-in-law to me at the family's plush restaurant and bar, Avenue, on *paralia*. Despite what the Americans said, their world was not turned upside down by the war in Ukraine. If the drinking habits of Thessaloniki's locals are any measure, the Savvidis family is one of the most popular in town.

A rumor floating around political circles in Athens is that Savvidis could sell his majority stake in the port, if induced with the right price. Yet, his efforts to bolster his ownership in 2025 and fend off a French takeover underscore how he, and his friends in the Kremlin, continue to see the port as a strategic chip on the board as European security is rearranged. Another, less likely, option is that a Russian-American rapprochement could see Washington more comfortable using the Savvidis-owned port as a link in an infrastructure corridor that the United States wants to run from India through the Arab Gulf and Israel into Europe. The so-called IMEC corridor is confined to power-point slides for now, but it's not unthinkable that the Russians and Americans could cut a deal to use the port. If IMEC is to become a reality with US backing, it would have to avoid Piraeus

Port, which is majority owned by China's COSCO. The port has also seen interest from India and Arab countries.

But we have to go more local to find the Prespa Agreement's lasting legacy. That is in the overlooked role Thessaloniki played as a hub for regional diplomacy when the city's former firebrand mayor, Giannis Boutaris, hosted North Macedonia's Zaev and got the ball rolling on negotiations.

As I write in a coffee shop in downtown Thessaloniki, I have spotted several license plates from North Macedonia. I ask the waitress about the visitors. "They keep coming," she tells me, "They are taking over Thessaloniki."

* * *

"A beautiful May day, a beautiful sun, a clear sky ... When the foreign boats arrived, the executioners on the quays put the finishing touches to their work: six hanged men performed the horrible final contortion ... the Turkish authorities smiled at this familiar sight." So the novel *Aziyadé* begins.[9]

Even by today's standards for romance novels, a writer has to go out on a limb to begin their story with a hanging, but that is how Pierre Loti chose to introduce readers to Thessaloniki, called Salonica during Ottoman times. *Aziyadé* is best remembered for its setting in Istanbul, but Thessaloniki is where Loti began what is perhaps the most iconic Orientalist novel ever written.

In Salonica, Loti's protagonist is a world-weary European naval officer, who hatches a plan to begin an affair with a Circassian harem girl. When Columbia professor Edward Said wrote his scathing book *Orientalism*, he had Loti in his sights. Of course, Western readers devoured Loti's fanciful and erotic description of Salonica. *Aziyadé* propelled Loti to literary stardom when the novel was published in 1879.

Loti's account of Salonica is full of the tropes that European writers of his time used to describe their interactions with the Near East. But Loti, whose real name was Louis Marie-Julien Viaud, was a descriptive writer who provided a rich, first-hand account of Thessaloniki in the 1870s when he was stationed here as a French naval officer. Loti's Thessaloniki resembles Jerusalem or Cairo more than any European metropolis. Thessaloniki is a "crazy city of oriental bazaars and mosques," and Loti describes nighttime scenes that could come straight out of Lawrence Durrell's *Alexandria Quartet*: underground bars offer "bizarre prostitution" and port-side cafes bustle with patrons ordering "hookahs, Skyros wine, Turkish delight, and Raki."[10]

The Ottoman Empire anchored Thessaloniki to the Near East during Loti's time, but the city was a transition zone between East and West before Islam's advance into the Balkans. Paul the Apostle stopped in Thessaloniki to proselytize during his journey to bring Christianity from Asia to Europe. Thessaloniki was founded in 315 BCE, taking its name from the sister of Alexander the Great. After the fall of Rome, Thessaloniki enjoyed a golden era in the Byzantine Empire as the second imperial city after Constantinople.

It was first conquered by the Ottomans in 1387. Because it surrendered peacefully, agreeing to pay a head tax to the sultan, it was granted autonomy and spared destruction. Byzantine Emperor Manuel II wrested back control in 1403 during a time of tension in the Ottoman court. In 1423, the Byzantines ceded Thessaloniki to the Venetians in a bid to bolster its defenses, but seven years later it was reconquered by the Ottomans after an unrelenting siege by Sultan Murad II's forces. This time, the Ottomans slaughtered and enslaved its Byzantine inhabitants. After its fall, merchants recalled seeing chain gangs of Greek women and boys throughout Macedonia and Thrace. Murad II then colonized Salonica with Muslim settlers.[11]

Thessaloniki's transformation into an Ottoman city was completed by Sultan Bayezid II, who decided to welcome Jews to his territories who were being persecuted in Western Europe. The city had no Jews in its 1478 census. They came after 1492 when King Ferdinand of Spain expelled Sephardic Jews from the Iberian Peninsula during the Inquisition. The Ottomans jumped at the chance to welcome this educated, skilled race of artisans and financiers. "You venture to call Ferdinand a wise ruler," Bayezid II was reported to have said after instructing his officials to welcome Jews. "He who has impoverished his own country and enriched mine!"

In Thessaloniki, the Jews' wealth and numbers multiplied. They were so much a part of the local fabric that by the seventeenth century, Ottoman travel writer Evliya Chelebi noted "the city is full of Jews." So ubiquitous were they, that he sensationally claimed that "Hebrew Kings" had battled the Byzantines there and that Jews were in the city when the Ottomans conquered it.[12]

In Salonica, the Sublime Porte gave Sephardic Jews, who spoke a Judaeo-Spanish language called Ladino, a monopoly to produce uniforms for the Janissary corps, the elite military unit made up of enslaved boys from Christian families forcibly converted to Islam. The Greek Orthodox Christians saw their demographic and economic heft diminish in early Ottoman Salonica as the city was revived, and resented the newcomers. In 1700, there is a record of Greeks asking the Ottoman authorities to stop Jews from mocking them and throwing trash in a church courtyard. By 1520, Thessaloniki was a Jewish majority city.[13] The city's Muslim, Christian and Jewish inhabitants lived more or less harmoniously until the advent of nineteenth century nationalisms.

Loti came to the city when it was in transition. Thessaloniki was dotted with minarets. It was an Aegean entrepôt where

Turkish, Greek, Ladino, French and Slavic languages could all be heard on a single street. The city's hodgepodge of religions and ethnicities included those like the vanished Donme, ostensible Jewish converts to Islam who continued to practice Judaism in secret. Ottoman Salonica was dubbed "Jerusalem of the Balkans."

Jews continued to make up the majority of the city's population until the early twentieth century, followed by Muslims and lastly Greeks. They were not just an elite business class, but embedded in the city as artisans, laborers and port workers. The death knell to Thessaloniki's thriving Jewish community came during the Second World War when the Nazis murdered ninety-six per cent of the Jewish population in the Holocaust. Still, businessmen in their fifties and sixties I met here remembered the names of the few surviving Jewish families active in local commerce until the 1960s. Many prominent Thessaloniki Jews joined the Zionist movement in the British Mandate of Palestine a decade before the Holocaust. One of the most active Zionists was Abraham Recanati, who facilitated the migration of skilled Jewish longshoremen in Thessaloniki to Israel's Haifa port in the 1930s.[14]

Thessaloniki's Muslim population that did not flee after Greece's 1912 conquest of the city was expelled during the 1923 population exchange. On the surface, Thessaloniki bares little resemblance to how Loti found it in the late twentieth century. Besides one survivor, the minarets were demolished by the Greeks. The city is not preserved like Ioannina. Until recently, Thessaloniki's main draw was cheap *bouzoukia* nightclubs for Greek tourists. But the Cold War borders that cut Thessaloniki off from its Balkan hinterlands are long gone. More recently, political and economic changes are bringing the old ethnicities that Loti encountered back. It's not just the Macedonians, but Bulgarians, Albanians, Turks and Israelis, who are coming in droves to shop on the waterfront and buy apartments.

Old Near Eastern nationalisms are still here, but they are the sideshow. Thessaloniki is a seedy entrepôt again.

"The Slavs come in big SUVs and pay in cash. They said that Greek merchants would conquer the Balkans when Yugoslavia broke up. What happened instead is Thessaloniki became a playground for Slavs with black money," one fine rug dealer in Thessaloniki's well-healed Mitropoleos Street told me. "If it wasn't for Turks and Bulgarians, I wouldn't be in business."

The whole city seems for sale. A prominent Greek lawyer I met for coffee one afternoon spent the first ten minutes of our interview pointing out gorgeous surviving art deco buildings that have been purchased by Israeli clients from his fifth-floor office window. "You are a journalist in the Middle East. Find me rich Israelis and Arabs! We can make a fortune selling properties," he said.

Another lawyer friend whispered to me how Israelis were now opening their own law offices in the city. "They already bought the hotels. Now they are bringing their own lawyers, too," she said.

Property prices in Thessaloniki have risen at an even faster clip than Athens. Because of Thessaloniki's chronically bad economy, there has been less pushback to Airbnbs and foreign real estate speculation, I notice. Gentrification has yet to sweep the city. Despite the alloy of new Near Eastern wealth here, the nickname that still sticks is *Ftokhomana*, or mother of the poor, a legacy of the hundreds of thousands of impoverished Christian refugees who settled here after the Greco-Turkish war.

Thessaloniki exists in a sliver of the northeastern Balkans where the United States' interests have become transactional at best and Russia is in retreat. It's the absence of American and Russian power that is felt here. Thessaloniki, a socially conservative city, has become a party port for a globalized, Near Eastern middle class that is untethered to ideology and underwritten by the European Union.

Thessaloniki was historically more sophisticated than Athens. That legacy survives in its cuisine, which is the envy of Greece. Salonica was an Ottoman metropolis thanks to the modernizing Tanzimat reforms of 1839–76. But the introduction of streetlights and European architecture in the late nineteenth century did little to address the problem of competing nationalisms as Greek, Bulgarian and Turkish identities took root in the city. The Macedonian name dispute is one of its legacies.

After the First World War, no other city in Greece underwent such a swift transformation from being the pride of an oriental empire in Europe, to a monolithic Greek metropolis as Thessaloniki.

The jaw-dropping speed of change plays out in real time as one drives along Vasilissis Olgas Avenue, where nineteenth-century mansions built in eclectic styles by wealthy Jewish, Christian and Muslim residents are sandwiched between interminable rows of seven- and eight-story apartment blocks built by Greek migrants. The jumble of architectural traditions squeezed onto the Mediterranean shore makes Thessaloniki feel like a cross between Belgrade and Beirut. There is a strong whiff of the decayed Near East here.

I put my theory about Thessaloniki's revival to Misiroglou. To begin with, she took aim at my assumption that Thessaloniki had left the Near East. "After the First World War there was a movement to promote 'Greekness,' to expunge the oriental identity within Greece. This included promoting Greek folk art because it was seen as more purely Greek as opposed to Ottoman. Yet, Thessaloniki retained its oriental character through the 1930s," Misiroglou said. "Thessaloniki never chose between East and West. This is partly what makes it such a neurotic city."

Thessaloniki's guiding force is Byzantium and its beating heart is Aristotelous Square, which was constructed in the 1950s from the plans of French architect Ernest Hebrard. The square was a pre-planned architectural project intended to impose

European order on top of the ashes of oriental Salonica after the devastating 1917 fire.

Aristotelous Square runs from the ruins of the Roman Forum right down to *paralia*. It is flanked by large cream buildings that remind me of French-colonial parts of Marrakech and Casablanca. But the architecture stakes its claim to a different empire. The pealing facades, long colonnades, and arches are modeled on Byzantium. And to the left and right of Aristotelous Square, the sprawling, maze-like Near East—Loti's Salonica—rears its head.

Tucked behind Aristotelous Square's western edge is a warren of two-story shops with little arched windows called Kapani Market, whose history goes back to the fifteenth century when it was founded as a flour market. In these dilapidated cafes and tavernas, old men sit sipping Turkish coffee and ouzo. The shops and stalls are stocked with spices, meat carcasses, cheap cloths, and Orthodox icons. The market sprawls out like a slum in defiance of deliberately laid out Aristotelous Square. On the opposite side is Athonos Market, where carpenters and basket weavers work alongside tiny ouzeris. The ten-minute walk through Kapani across Aristotelous Square to Athonos encapsulates Greece's ambiguity.

"This is why I would never leave Thessaloniki. If I want Bouzouki music, ouzo and cheap seafood I can sit at Athonos. Can you think of another big city in the European Union where carpenters actually work in the center at a tiny shop anymore? Where they haven't been kicked out by developers," Maria, a twenty-eight-year-old Greek friend told me over a night of mezze in Athonos. I couldn't think of one.

* * *

One of the grandest villas on Vassilisis Olgas Avenue still standing once belonged to the Allatini family, Levantine Jews whose business monopoly extended from shipping to tobacco. The red-brick palace, which is now a government office, was the gilded prison of Ottoman Sultan Abdul Hamid II after he was overthrown in 1908 by the Young Turks.

Thessaloniki was the power base of the Young Turks, a motley crew of secular, liberal, revolutionary, and nationalist Ottoman officers. They sprang up in opposition to the sultan after his decision in 1878 to suspend the Ottoman Constitution. The spot in 1908 where the officers launched their putsch in Salonica still bears the name Platia Eleftherias, or freedom square. Today, it's a car park cluttered with empty liquor bottles. The initial lofty ideals of the Young Turks' revolution fared about as well as the square.

The Young Turks wanted to reverse the Ottoman Empire's decline and reinvigorate its brief flirtation with constitutional government. Underpinning their vision was finding a way to reconcile the demands of the empire's various ethnic and religious communities, which were tearing it apart. Their initial vision was summed up by Enver Pasha, one of the leaders of the movement, in a proclamation he read out in Salonica following Abdul Hamid II's overthrow. "Today, the arbitrary ruler is gone, bad government no longer exists, we are all brothers. There are no longer Bulgarians, Greeks, Serbs, Romanians, Jews, Muslims—under the same blue sky we are all equal, we are all proud to be Ottomans," he said.[15]

While it sounds delusional to talk about "Ottomanism" as an identity today, it wasn't farfetched at the time. Indeed, the promise of European-style liberty and egalitarianism under an Ottoman constitutional government was welcomed by many Jews, Muslims and Christians across the empire in the aftermath of Abdul Hamid II's autocratic rule. The bourgeois Greek Orthodox communities in Constantinople and the eastern Aegean islands were particularly receptive to the Young Turks' early promises. The historian Roderick Beaton dubbed this "Hellenic Ottomanism." Their thinking was somewhat logical. If the Islamic caliphate could give way to a constitutional government with equal rights for citizens, the Greek Orthodox may be able to claim political leadership at the highest levels of government. They already controlled much of the empire's trade with the outside world and the sultan's finances. If a true constitutional government was achieved, perhaps, they could hoist the flag of Byzantium over Constantinople by taking power from within.

In his 2022 novel, *On the Back of the Tiger*, Turkish dissident writer Zulfu Livaneli described the mood in the "freest and most cosmopolitan city of the empire," when Abdul Hamid II was ousted. Muslim, Jewish and Christian patrons at Salonica's nightclubs and bars erupted in cheers. This was expected in the decadent port, which "smelled of sea, fish, raki, ouzo and sometimes revolution and gunpowder."[16]

For the liberally minded residents of Salonica, it was a just retribution that the sultan who squashed dissent, ordered massacres against Armenians and promoted pan-Islamism, should wither away at the Villa Allatini with his harem in tow.

What is obvious to us in hindsight, soon became apparent. Ottomanism didn't have a fighting chance. The fissures among Christians and Muslims; and between Turks, Greeks, Bulgarians, Arabs and Armenians, were, by the early twentieth century, irreparable. The demand for self-determination only grew among these various ethnicities. In October 1908, three months after the Young Turk Revolution, Bulgaria declared its full independence. Meanwhile, the Turkish-speaking Muslim population seethed with anger at the upstart Christian minorities, who they believed had gained too much power as a result of the Tanzimat reforms and Westernization.

Ottomanism was attacked from both sides: by the Christian minorities whose religious faiths were now consolidated along nationalist lines, and Turkish-speaking Muslims who believed their privileges were threatened. The Young Turk movement became increasingly associated with Islam and Turkish nationalism. A triumvirate of three military officers, Talat Pasha, Cemal Pasha, and Enver Pasha (the same Enver who proclaimed equality between Muslims and Christians) led the Ottoman Empire into the First World War on the side of the Germans. Enver was chiefly responsible for the Armenian genocide and the Ottomans' military failures in the Caucasus. He was killed in Central Asia in 1922, leading a Turkic revolt during the Russian Civil War.

* * *

The Thessaloniki that I lived in was more linked to the Near East than at any time since 1922, when it was run by Osman Sait Bey, its last Muslim mayor. While living in the city, I thought it would be a good idea to talk with the former mayor, who was elected ninety years after Sait Bey.

Giannis Boutaris was many things: an award-winning wine producer, recovering alcoholic, and firebrand former mayor of Thessaloniki. We met at his lawyer's 1970s-style office in the city center in the late summer of 2024. The eighty-two-year-old Boutaris was in frail health, but his eyes had a mischievous sparkle. As we sat, he smacked down two packs of cigarettes and a take-away black coffee on the table between us. A lizard tattoo crawled down one of his wrinkled hands. The other was busy ripping the filter off a cigarette before he lit up.

Boutaris, who died in November 2024, had a touch of *mangas* about him. The word was first used to describe thugs and working-class Greeks who frequented *rebetiko* bars and brothels like those that once dotted Thessaloniki's port. The *mangas* were members of a hookah-smoking, card-playing, drug-using counterculture. Their habitués were Levantine ports and their most important traits were (and remain) swagger, nonconformity, and old-school chivalry. Greeks still use the word to describe their vision of an alpha male. A guy who juggles five girlfriends at once and can drink from morning till night without a hangover is *mangas*. So too is a man who gives up his seat at a crowded bar for a woman.

"I had a lot of affairs, did a lot of drugs, and partied. But the best years of my life were after I got sober and moved back in with my wife," Boutaris explained to me. He lifted his other shirt sleeve to reveal a tattoo of the winged horse Pegasus. "I got this when my wife died, to commemorate her, because Pegasus is a fairytale and our life was like a fairy tale," he said. Classic *mangas*.

Boutaris started dabbling in politics after his wife told him to stop meddling in his sons' management of the family's famous wine business. He first ran in municipal elections with the communist party. "I'm not a communist. I'm pro-business. I just ran with their party," he told me. Boutaris was elected mayor by a slim margin in 2011 as an independent candidate on a platform that could only spring up in a city like Thessaloniki: he pledged to revive its economy by promoting its old cosmopolitan identity. Putting a spotlight on Thessaloniki's Muslim and Jewish history was (and remains) very controversial. At a time when Thessaloniki was battered by the financial crisis, Boutaris made the pitch that embracing its Ottoman past would open up more investment and tourism opportunities.

"The Jews gave Thessaloniki its wealth. This was a rich city during the Ottoman times," Boutaris told me. "We didn't promote Thessaloniki's history just for economic reasons. It was the right thing to do. But there was untapped potential."

To be sure, much of Boutaris' work as mayor between 2011 and 2019 involved the unglamorous job of reforming a city plagued by corruption and mismanagement. "Thessaloniki was an example of the worst of the Greek system. That is the Balkan and Middle East mentality: corruption, too much bureaucracy, and laziness," he told me.

Underscoring the point, Boutaris' predecessor was sentenced to twelve years in prison for embezzlement. When Boutaris took office, his first job was to change City Hall's mentality. He eschewed sleek cars and the other trappings of power that politicians all over, but especially in the Eastern Mediterranean, like to flaunt. He rarely wore a tie. When it came to the local economy, his entrepreneurial side won out over his social leftism. He cut taxes on businesses and ran the city like his wine business, watching costs and attacking waste. He was shortlisted several times for an international award for best mayor while in office.

I ask what he thinks about the surge in Airbnbs and foreign real estate speculation. He was not concerned it was driving up housing costs. "It will even out," he said, dismissing critics. "Our model was that you don't revive a city by tearing down or building out. You revive it from the inside. In Thessaloniki, we had a bunch of abandoned apartments. Foreign investors liked the city center. The investment has been good for Thessaloniki," he said.

Boutaris remains a controversial figure among many in Thessaloniki, but he is widely credited with improving its urban spaces and giving it fresh life. He oversaw the expansion of its waterfront promenade, fixed a backlog in rubbish collection, and boosted the number of pedestrian streets and squares. His gold stud earring won him the nickname "The Pirate" at City Hall. He shot to international fame for his unconventional and outspoken style of governing. Socially on the Left and strongly anti-nationalist, he clashed with Thessaloniki's conservative culture. To this day, many in Thessaloniki resent that Boutaris allowed its first gay pride parade in 2012.

The fault-lines of Boutaris' mayorship were evident before he was elected. He had antagonized the city's powerful Orthodox

Church leaders when he called Thessaloniki's Bishop "a mujahedin," mocking his conservative social views. In a hot-mic incident, the Bishop was caught scolding Boutaris. "He told me, 'You will never be mayor in this city.' I think that helped me win the election. People didn't want our bishop saying who the mayor would be," Boutaris said.

Boutaris' decision to promote Thessaloniki's Ottoman past was loathed by many in the Church, as well as by locals. Orthodox religiosity runs deep in Thessaloniki, which is linked socially and politically to Mount Athos, the center of Orthodox monastic life. Many locals trace their ancestry back to Asia Minor and view the Ottoman period as an occupation.

Boutaris reopened the historic Yeni Mosque as an exhibition space and, more daringly, allowed it to be used for prayer by Greece's Muslim minority. Boutaris proved to be ahead of his time. The tradition he created has held. In 2024, Ramadan Eid prayers were conducted in the mosque under Thessaloniki's center-right mayor. "As cynical as it sounds, the possibility for Muslims to carry out their religious obligations when they come to the city would boost tourism, which the city is in dire need of," Boutaris said at the time.[17]

Whereas previous mayors tried to brush aside Thessaloniki's Islamic past, Boutaris integrated it into the rhythm of the city as a strength. Not content with starting the contemporary art biennial, he backed the move to sprinkle pieces of art across abandoned Ottoman monuments, including Yeni Mosque, the city's old Hammam, and the fifteenth-century Alaca Imaret mosque. Boutaris' focus on reviving Ottoman monuments and places of worship put Thessaloniki on the map as an avant-garde Aegean city.

"Look what Erdoğan did with Hagia Sophia," one well-healed Greek art collector told me over drinks at Thessaloniki's port, referring to Erdoğan's 2020 decision to reconvert the Byzantine

Orthodox Cathedral from a museum back into a mosque. He continued:

> What did Boutaris do? He opened a mosque for prayer and then put art inside it. This is what Greeks who want to forget the Ottoman past get wrong. These monuments are our treasures. Greece is open. Erdoğan is killing the creative space in Türkiye. Thessaloniki could be an art hub for the former Ottoman world. We have freedoms that Dubai and Doha don't have, but we need another Boutaris. We need a vision.

Boutaris was an amateur historian. His own family is a case in point of Greece's often overlooked diversity. He was Vlach, an ethnic group that was once scattered across the mountainous Balkans. They assimilated into Greece centuries ago, but traditionally spoke an eastern Romance language called Aromanian. To call someone a Vlach today still smacks of poking fun at their shepherd roots. Boutaris' father came from modern-day North Macedonia. His family settled in Naoussa, a wine producing region in Greece's western Macedonia, before his grandfather opened a wine shop in Thessaloniki. His mother's family arrived in Thessaloniki from modern-day Albania on the eve of the Second World War.

"The problem with Thessaloniki is that we still have locals who were born here, put down roots and raised families here, but too many of them don't think of the city as home, even today after all these generations. For them, home is Smyrna or the Black Sea," he said.

Boutaris courted investment from Savvidis and was invited to his parties, but the two fell out after Boutaris positioned himself as an early mediator between Greece and North Macedonia over the name change. In 2018, Boutaris was assaulted by a Pontic mob when he attended an event marking the Pontic genocide.

"For too long we have been obscured by this nationalistic foolishness and populist propaganda," Boutaris told *The Guardian* newspaper when he hosted North Macedonia's former prime minister for talks. "I will take Zaev to the best fish taverna, and no doubt Alexander the Great will be part of the conversation, but my priority will be to ensure that, as my guest, he has a great time too."

One of Boutaris' most controversial moves was the decision to support the renovation of Mustafa Kemal Atatürk's childhood home. Mustafa Kemal, who founded the Turkish Republic in the aftermath of the Ottoman Empire's collapse, was born in Thessaloniki in 1881. His early life underscores Salonica's then-seamless integration into the wider Middle East, when the empire's middle- and upper-class elite hopped across territory now bisected by modern borders.

After a short stint of schooling in modern-day North Macedonia, Mustafa Kemal moved to Constantinople to attend military academy. He served a posting in Damascus and saw combat in the Italo-Turkish War in Tobruk, Libya. Like other young Ottoman military officers, he became disillusioned with the sultan and associated with the Young Turks.

Upon hearing the news that his birthplace, Salonica, had been conquered by Greece in 1912, a shaken Mustafa Kemal replied to a friend in Türkiye, "How could you leave Salonica, that beautiful home-town of ours? Why did you hand it to the enemy and come here?"[18]

I stopped at Atatürk's house before meeting Boutaris. The handsome Ottoman home sits at the intersection of the city center and Ano Poli. It is attached to Türkiye's consulate and is replete with a wax figure of the "Father of the Turks." As the homes of founders of republics go, Atatürk's is quite humble, but it is one of the best preserved examples of Ottoman architecture in Thessaloniki. The upper story juts out on big wooden beams and the *sachnisi* are surrounded on three sides by fine windows trimmed with wooden shutters. Turkish tourists loll around snapping pictures in front of souvenir stalls that sell tote bags adorned with Atatürk's piercing gaze.

"We love Thessaloniki," one Turkish tourist I met at a coffee shop across the street told me. "I feel more at home here than in Istanbul now. Thessaloniki is what Istanbul should be," he said. His family was wearing Balenciaga T-shirts and designer sneakers. His wife and teenage daughter had long silken hair. The family oozed the social mores of Türkiye's Republican People's Party, or CHP, the secular, nationalist party founded by Atatürk. For this half of Türkiye, Atatürk is not only the national hero who vanquished foreign armies from Anatolia. He also put the Islamists in their box, replacing the backward caliphate with a secular, modern republic.

I told the Turkish tourist about Boutaris. "I'm glad he restored this house. My great-grandmother came to Istanbul from Thessaloniki. There was violence on both sides. That's history. This is my fifth time in Thessaloniki. I always feel welcome here. I love Greece," he said.

Boutaris' decision to promote Salonica's Ottoman history came at an opportune time. President Recep Tayyip Erdoğan's populist, Islamist politics were ramping up and the country was about to enter an economic crisis. For liberal Turks, Boutaris's take on neo-Ottomanism, a softer, gentler kind, was a breath of fresh air.

Turks are powering Thessaloniki's service-sector economy. More Turks started eyeing a proper bolthole in Greece after the failed 2016 coup against Erdoğan, which prompted the Turkish leader's violent crackdown on opponents. Real estate agents in Thessaloniki started seeing a surge in demand from Turks wanting second homes. Not all of them settled permanently in Greece. Turks are the second highest number of applicants for Greece's golden visa after Chinese, although the Chinese far outstrip them. But more Turks are choosing to spend their time and money in Greece instead of their homeland. Thessaloniki is one of the most popular destinations. The number of Turkish flights to Thessaloniki increased 226 per cent during his first term in office, as a result of lobbying for more direct routes, Boutaris told me. The trend has outlasted Boutaris.

In 2023, the number of Turkish visitors to Greece jumped ninety per cent from 478,000 to 877,000.[19] It keeps rising. Türkiye used to be the place where Greeks near the border went for cheaper groceries and dining. Because of Erdoğan's economic mismanagement, Greece is now more affordable for Turks than their home. Türkiye's runaway inflation hovered at seventy-five per cent at one point in 2024. It has since fallen to around forty per cent, but the price gains are not going away.

The Turkish family I met outside Atatürk's house was impressed by how well they were eating in Thessaloniki. "We had fish, calamari, and Ouzo for lunch. It cost sixty euros. In Istanbul lunch at the same style restaurant would cost me at least 100 euros," the father told me. "And we aren't in the European Union. The lira is supposed to make things cheaper, not more expensive. Thessaloniki is more reasonable than Istanbul."

Would he consider buying an apartment in Thessaloniki? "I live on Spitogatos," he said. This is one Greece's most popular real estate websites.

I asked Boutaris about the new arrivals. "It makes sense that the Turks who don't like the Islamists want to come to Thessaloniki for our nightlife and lifestyle. I feel similar to the Turks. We have the same culture. I said when we unveiled Atatürk's house, 'Greeks and Turks are brothers.'"

Thessaloniki's locals by and large welcome the influx of Turkish tourists. Notably, most of them are secular. Turks are such regular visitors to the city now that I know shopkeepers who have become friends with their clients and pay reciprocal visits. For perspective, the drive from Istanbul to Thessaloniki is just two hours longer than that between New York City and Washington, DC. The Near East is small.

While secular Turks lionize Atatürk, the two groups who may loath him the most are Turkish Islamists and Greeks, albeit for different reasons. For the former, Atatürk was a traitor to Islam who aggressively pushed to secularize Turkish society, ripping apart the vestiges of the centuries old Islamic caliphate. He banned the fez, promoted raki (Türkiye's anise flavored answer to ouzo), outlawed the call to prayer in Arabic and stigmatized wearing the veil. Among Greeks, he is remembered as the general who drove their ancestors out of Asia Minor and oversaw the destruction of Greek Orthodox Christianity in Anatolia.

Again, we return to Thessaloniki. During the First World War, the city was the scene for a showdown in Greek domestic politics that culminated in a brutal war in Anatolia which opened a path for Atatürk's meteoric rise to power.

* * *

By 1914, Greece had conquered vast new territories from the Ottomans, including most of Epirus, Macedonia and the eastern Aegean islands. When the First World War broke out in July 1914 between the main European powers—Britain, France and Russia on one side, as the Allied Powers, and Germany and Austria-Hungary on the other, as the Central Powers—both Greece and the Ottoman Empire initially remained neutral. But by October that year, the Ottomans joined the conflict on the side of the Central Powers.

This presented Greece with a dilemma: whether or not to enter the fray, too, as part of the Allied Powers. The choice seemed obvious. The Austrians had been hostile to Greece, with its dangerous liberal and nationalist ideals, since its founding in 1832. Meanwhile, Russia, France, and Britain were Greece's "protecting powers." Joining the Allies would give Greece the chance to push its borders further east against the Ottomans and bring the remaining Greek Orthodox populations there into an expanded Kingdom of Hellenes. Some sensed the most tantalizing prize of all, to hoist the flag of Byzantium over Constantinople, was within reach. This vision blended twentieth-century nationalism and the older, immutable promise of a Greek Orthodox Christian Empire. Greece, the advocates of this vision argued, should naturally stretch as far as Greeks lived.

A smooth-talking, tenacious and shrewd political operator from the violent world of Cretan politics emerged as this movement's standard barrier. Greek Prime Minister Elefterious Venizelos shot to prominence by leading Crete's struggle for independence from the Ottomans in the 1890s. He then lobbied for Crete's *enosis*, or union, with Greece. He crashed into the Greek Prime Ministership in 1910. Venizelos dreamed of a Greece spread over "two continents and five seas," extending from the Aegean to the Black Sea. This *Megali Idea*, or Great Idea, had been a galvanizing force in Greek politics since 1832. Venizelos had the wind at his back. A liberal reformer, he favored an alliance with the Allies and forged a particularly close partnership with Britain's Liberal Prime Minister Lloyd George.

On the other side of the debate were the cautious, traditional Greek conservatives. They warned that Greece risked overstretching its thin military resources in the name of uncertain territorial expansion in Asia if it joined the Allies. The conservatives had well-founded concerns that a war against the Ottomans would leave Greece vulnerable to a potential invasion by Bulgaria, which Greece was competing with, at times in open war, for a greater slice of Macedonia and Thrace. There was logic to their caution, too. At the time, the Central Powers' defeat wasn't guaranteed. Should Greece join the Allies and lose, their argument went, millions of Greek Orthodox Christians in the

Ottoman Empire—many of whom didn't even speak Greek—would be vulnerable to retribution. Although the Allies did not lose, this retribution is exactly what happened.

A cultural division also lurked behind this split, one that can still be detected in Greece today. The lands of New Greece, recently liberated from the Ottomans, were as strange and backward for the Greeks from the Peloponnese and Attica, or Old Greece, as they were for Pierre Loti. Athenians, then and somewhat still today, looked at the Greeks of Macedonia and Thrace as annoying oriental cousins. Demographics were also at play. Why should Athenians risk a clash with the Central Powers on the chance that it might gain them more territory with sizable Muslim populations? In Macedonia, Greek Orthodox Christians had just a slight majority over local Muslims and were a minority when set against Bulgarians, Jews and Muslims combined.[20] Greece's Germanophile ruler at the time, King Constantine, was the standard barrier of this strain of thought. He favored neutrality, giving his supporters the name Royalists.

The showdown between Venizelists and Royalists is known as the National Schism. It played out in revolutionary Thessaloniki. In 1915, Bulgaria declared war on the Allies. In flagrant violation of Greece's neutrality, France and Britain deployed the Allied Army of the Orient under French General Maurice Paul Sarrail to Salonica. By 1916, Greek soldiers loyal to Venizelos were in open defiance of their king and fighting alongside them. When Greek army officers declared a new government in Thessaloniki, Venizelos seized his chance. He fled Athens and traveled to Thessaloniki where he headed the government with the aim of bringing Greece into the war on the side of the Allies. Greece was split in two. One government was in Athens, or Old Greece, on the side of neutrality, and the other in New Greece, Thessaloniki, champing at the bit to push Greece's borders further east. The royalists were fighting a losing battle. Since its founding, Greece had been dependent on the Allied powers. Venizelos's revisionist dream had the support of Greece's colonial patrons. In 1917, King Constantine was expelled from power and Greece formally joined the Allies.[21]

The lack of serious fighting in Greece earned the Army of the Orient the title "the Gardeners of Salonika." The Macedonian front may be one of the most forgotten battlefields of the First World War. It gave rise to one of the most lyrical books written about the region I know. *Macedonia: A Plea for the Primitive* was published in 1921 by two long-forgotten British authors who trekked all over wartime northeastern Greece when it was occupied by the Army of the Orient. The result is a first-hand account of Thessaloniki and its countryside when they were on the cusp of astonishing changes. In its pages, old, oriental Greece is dying, but modern, nationalist Greece has yet to emerge. For example, despite being part of Greece, the region of Macedonia still held large Muslim communities before the population exchange. *A Plea for the Primitive* is an Orientalist love fest with lots of opinions that some would deem politically incorrect today, but buried inside are some timeless truths about geopolitics. The authors write, "[Macedonia] marks the spot where Westernisation, baulked by the proud obstinacy and racial intolerance of the Turk, has reached its limit. For years Macedonia was the buffer state of East and West."[22]

The authors are obsessed with the aesthetics of Ottoman Macedonia. It is noteworthy because as late as 1921, this part of Greece clearly belonged to the Orient. Walking the alleys of Ano Poli in Thessaloniki, they write: "Is not the East one huge fairytale? Are not the white minarets and the mysterious old houses, the storks on the roof, the beggar at the fountain, the very cobble-stones and, above all, the deep blue sky and the star-strewn night the very essentials of magic and romance?"[23]

Like *A Plea for the Primitive*, the Macedonian front has faded into obscurity. But the blow that precipitated the Central Powers' collapse was struck here. In the summer of 1918, a force of Serbian, French and Greek soldiers unexpectedly smashed through Bulgaria's front lines in the battle of Dobro Pole. The blitz sparked a crisis in the Bulgarian army's ranks. It sued for peace, signing an Armistice in Salonica on 29 September 1918. Bulgaria's defeat left the Central Powers' southern flank exposed. Little more than a month later the wartime bloc collapsed with the surrender of Germany, Austria-Hungary and the Ottomans.

* * *

Greece was on the winning side. Venizelos was in the perfect position to ask for a large portion of the Ottoman Empire at the 1919 Paris Peace Conference, where the so-called Big Four—British Prime Minister Lloyd George, Italian Prime Minister Vittorio Emanuele Orlando, French Prime Minister Georges Clemenceau, and American President Woodrow Wilson—convened to decide the fate of the post-war world.

The "Sick Man of Europe" was finally dead. France, Britain and Italy maneuvered to see how much of the corpse they could grab. The mood of the victorious European leaders was captured by British foreign secretary Arthur James Balfour, who was quoted by diplomat Harold Nicolson in his excellent book *Peacemaking 1919*, "Those three, all powerful, all ignorant men sitting there and carving continents with only a child to lead them."[24]

Balfour and Nicolson were in the thick of negotiations at the Paris conference. Balfour himself is best remembered for the 1917 declaration bearing his name that promised Britain would support a Jewish state in Palestine, despite previous pledges that the land would go to the Arabs who revolted under the British officer T.E. Lawrence. One of the more interesting aspects of the peace conference is how new nationalist leaders from across the Near East traveled to Paris to make their case for national homelands in front of the Great Powers. Prince Faisal, who led the Arab revolt, attended, as did Zionist leader Chaim Weizmann. Egyptian politician Saad Zaghlou, who made a failed bid for the British to leave Egypt, was there too. Some of these emissaries were members of the old Ottoman elite themselves, now representing their respective ethnic communities, like Sherif Pasha, the Ottoman ambassador to Sweden, who represented the Kurds, and Boghos Nubar Pasha, who lobbied in vain for a sizable Armenian state. The Kurds' case for a homeland was ignored by the Europeans and the Armenians were given a barely defensible rump state. None of these Near Eastern politicians could hold a candle to Venizelos.

"Venizelos quickly won a reputation for moderation, wisdom and statesmanship. This reputation, founded on passionate sincerity and strength of will coupled with charm of manner and political tact, enabled him to press Greece's claims to the utmost," Michael Llewellyn-Smith observed in his deeply researched book *Ionian Vision: Greece in Asia Minor 1919–1922*.[25] Venizelos used a diplomatic formula that successive Greek governments continue to deploy with richer and more powerful Western states right through our era with only minor alterations. He hammered home the fact that Greece, the cherished birthplace of Western democracy, belonged to Europe, even as its geography and people lay in the East. By that logic, how could the Great Powers deprive their Greek allies of their ancestral lands? Venizelos made the case that it was in Britain's self-interest to back Greece's territorial expansion. Greece was a steady, familiar and reliable friend in a turbulent region. The argument resonates because it's true. Unlike Egypt, Greece, a pseudo-colonial country at the time, would not confront the European powers to achieve its aims in the Near East. The colonial client brilliantly exploited the patron. This is the Levantine killer instinct.

Greek interests clashed with those of the French and Italians, who had their own territorial ambitions in Asia Minor and the Dodecanese islands, but Venizelos had British backing. In May 1919, Greek troops landed in Smyrna, nominally to administer the city, although no one was fooled that Venizelos' plan was anything less than to bring Smyrna, and as much of Asia Minor as he could grab, into an enlarged Greece. The next year, the Treaty of Sevres was signed. It massively expanded the borders of Greece to include all of Thrace, and almost guaranteed that Smyrna and most of Asia Minor's coastline would be incorporated into Greece.

Atatürk made Sevres a paper-tiger. He had distinguished himself as a frontline Ottoman commander during the First World War, repelling Allied troops in the Battle of Gallipoli. He had no intention of letting Anatolia slip away like his beloved birthplace Salonica. He rallied Turkish nationalists and remnants of the Ottoman army to his side. The deployment of Greek troops to Asia Minor sparked a Turkish nationalist backlash. The Greek-Turkish war raged from 1919 to 1922. Like the Greek War of Independence, this was a bloody conflict that pitted Turkish Muslims against Greek Orthodox Christians. The Greeks of Smyrna welcomed the Greek Army, but the Turks saw them as foreign invaders. As the war dragged on, Greek troops pushed deeper into Anatolia and found themselves stuck in indefensible positions, with no natural barrier between them and their enemy, and their supply lines stretched thin and vulnerable to attack. This was exactly what the Royalists had warned about. Meanwhile, the European powers who had backed Greece's deployment to Smyrna, were showing no appetite for a prolonged war of attrition. Their populations were clamoring for demobilization and peace.

The British refused to let the Greeks march on Constantinople, which was lightly guarded by a small contingent of allied troops. Had Greek troops moved from Thrace into their old Byzantine capital, it would have dealt a huge blow to Turkish morale and Atatürk's war effort. But the British had declared the city part of a neutral zone. Constantinople was too tantalizing a prize to allow the Greeks to take, because it would have upset the balance of power in the Black Sea and jeopardized navigation through the Bosporus. Meanwhile, Atatürk checked Greece diplomatically. He signed the Treaty of Moscow in 1921 with the Soviet Union, which allowed him to move resources from Turkey's eastern borders to engage the Greeks in the west. He also started receiving military supplies from the Soviets.[26] The Italians, who were always wary of an expanded Greece in the Eastern Mediterranean, ceded their claim to Turkey's southern coastline, consoling themselves with acquiring the Dodecanese islands. At the same time, the French decided their interests were best served cutting a deal with Atatürk, who had proven on the battlefield that the Turks could not be brushed aside so easily by diplomats in Europe.

On 9 September 1922, Turkish troops broke through the exhausted Greek frontlines, and descended on *Ghiaour* Izmir, or infidel Smyrna. Thousands of Greek refugees were gathered on the magnificent quayside looking out at the European warships in the bay. By evening, Smyrna was ravaged by the Turkish army's looting and killing. The European warships were ordered not to interfere. Greece's commissioner in Smyrna, Aristeidis Stergiadis, reportedly said, when asked why he didn't do more to help the native Greeks flee, "Better they stay here and be massacred by Kemal, because if they go to Athens they'll turn everything upside down."[27]

Turkish soldiers and Muslim residents attacked the Greeks in their homes. Smyrna's archbishop was mutilated by a mob of

Muslims. The massacres and rapes went on for days. It was the crescendo to a war that saw hundreds of thousands of Greeks and Christians killed. On 13 September, a fire broke out in the Armenian quarter. Historians still dispute who started the blaze, but the Armenians suffered some of the greatest brutalities at the hands of the Turkish nationalists. The fire soon spread throughout the Christian and European sections of Smyrna. In a few days, the blaze engulfed one of the richest and most cosmopolitan ports of the Levant, the epicenter of Greeks in Asia Minor. Türkiye marks the taking of Smyrna as a high point in its war of independence and liberation. For Greeks, it is "The Catastrophe."

In 1923, the Treaty of Lausanne was signed, which mandated a forced population exchange of Greeks and Turks. It was mutually agreed, state sanctioned ethnic cleansing. The determining factor for who went where was not ethnicity or language, but religion. Turkish-speaking Christians were sent to Greece and Muslims who spoke Cretan Greek to Turkey. About 1.2 million Greek Orthodox who called modern-day Türkiye home were forcibly displaced, along with 400,000 Muslims. Thessaloniki's population changed overnight. At least 88,000 refugees arrived in the first year, not counting the thousands more in surrounding villages.

* * *

Floorboards creak beneath my feet. Long-handled *briki* for brewing Turkish coffee balance precariously on cheap Victorian furniture. I soak up the smell of musty *kilims*, battered leather-bound books and incense. I have weaved my way through Bit Bazaar in the center of Thessaloniki. The name comes from the Turkish word for lice. The bazaar was built by Asia Minor refugees after 1923. Decades ago, it was overtaken by antique shops and ouzeris where university students go to drink and eat cheaply. My destination is a shop called Platon Antiques.

My eyes adjust to the darkness inside, then fall on a splendidly colored steel engraving of two Greek fighters in traditional *fustanella* clutching bejeweled muskets. Next to it, I spot a map titled "Graecia." The tag dates it 1595. Attica, the Aegean islands, Asia Minor and the Peloponnese are sketched out in soft pink and yellow hues. There are dozens more eighteenth- and nineteenth-century maps of the Eastern Mediterranean. They recall a time of seamless travel, and identities older than nation-states. The names of Morea, Cappadocia, Thrace, Arabia, Palestine, Assyrie, and Armenia are written across terrains where borders fall today. An imitation painting, titled *The Battle of Navarino*, is tucked into a dusty shelf.

Bit Bazaar is an oasis in Thessaloniki. I scored a mother-of-pearl inlaid table made in Syria here and big copper trays called *sini*, the kind once used to bake spinach-filled phyllo pies. They were taken out of an old Turkish house in Ano Poli. The bric-a-brac and mementos at Bit Bazaar leave little doubt that Greece belongs to the Near East.

The highlight of Platon Antiques is what's not for sale. From floor to ceiling, the narrow shop is wallpapered in old yellow slips of paper: brittle and oxidizing reminders of a vanished Greek past. They unfurl like rolls of freshly printed dollar bills: teachers' diplomas from Greek towns on the Black Sea, report cards from primary schools in Cairo, marriage licenses from Alexandria, business registrations from Smyrna. They are written in Greek, Arabic and Ottoman Turkish. There are hundreds of ID cards from Salonica and old birth certificates. Some are emblazoned with Ottoman seals, others with Greek or Egyptian. In grainy black and white photos, dandyish men in Western suits and jaunty fezzes stare proudly at the camera. The collection starts on the ground floor, flows down a rickety staircase to the basement and continues. At the stairs, I peruse dozens of children's identity papers; orphans who arrived in Thessaloniki in 1923. There are creased and stained refugee papers of Greeks who landed at Piraeus Port, held together by the tiniest yellow fibers. In another corner, photographs speak to a bourgeois Greek past of tennis, fencing and rotary clubs in Levantine cities. In one photo, boys in military uniform stand at a school in Constantinople holding Ottoman flags on an athletic field. Andreas Vavatsis, who runs the shop, told me,

> My father started this collection twenty years ago. He started buying from walk-in customers. My brother and I keep it going. We buy most of the documents from online shops and auctions. We have IDs and licenses from every spot Greeks once called home. The hardest to find date before 1930. The rarest come from the Black Sea because the genocide against the Pontic Greeks there was the worst. The Ottomans didn't want to leave a trace of paper.

Andreas and I met at a mutual friend's birthday party when I relocated to Thessaloniki. He struck a chord the moment he started telling me, a new arrival to the city, which neighborhood to live in.

"If you gave me the choice between a modern villa in Panorama, or an old apartment around Bit Bazaar, I'd take the city center. It feels a little like Constantinople here," Andreas said. I agreed. Like many Thessaloniki natives, the Vavatsis family's origins are a mix between Macedonia and Asia Minor. Andreas's great-grandparents came from Bursa and Cappadocia in modern-day Türkiye.

"My grandfather spoke fluent Turkish. And my dad's grandmother on his mom's side never learned Greek. They settled originally in Serres," he told me, tracing his family roots. "Our dream is to find a proper museum for this collection, but it's expensive. Even rich collectors can't afford it. This is the type of museum that Thessaloniki should be building. These are our roots."

Andreas is a conservative guy. His politics clashed with Boutaris' leftism, but he voted for him in his second term. "Thessaloniki experienced no development before Boutaris. I am on the Right, but I believe Thessaloniki needs a progressive mayor. Only a progressive mayor would open Thessaloniki up to Israelis and Turks for tourism. Who else is going to come here? Brits and French will go to Athens and the islands," he said.

Andreas is a young, dedicated collector. He is frustrated that Thessaloniki is not living up to its full potential as a crossroads for the region. "Thessaloniki was called the Pearl of the Aegean, it should be a hub for the Balkans and Middle East. But Athens sucks up all the energy," he said.

I heard similar complaints across age and class levels. For decades, locals have complained that Thessaloniki gets short shrift compared to Athens. It is true. That's the way the centralized Greek political system works. This is an old story that is not going away. But the return of the Near East adds a new layer to the question of Thessaloniki's development.

In dozens of interviews, I sensed that locals here struggle to reconcile the fact that Thessaloniki's former glory, which they want to tap into today, requires a certain cosmopolitanism that many are uncomfortable with. Because of its geography and culture, Thessaloniki is a natural magnet for Israelis, Turks, Albanians, North Macedonians, and Bulgarians. Its surviving Ottoman monuments are what make it unique and edgy. Not all Greeks in this nationalistic town are able to see cosmopolitanism like Andreas. Others joke about the city's transformation.

"My friends were telling me about a bunch of mob shootings in Halkidiki blamed on the Bulgarians and Albanians," a Greek official visiting Thessaloniki from Athens told me over a coffee. He was referring to Thessaloniki's nearby seaside resort peninsula.

He added: "I told them, 'you said you wanted to be a hub for the Balkans, who did you expect to come here, Swedes?'" The jab is based on longstanding Greek antipathy for their northern neighbors.

The more legitimate frustration was summed up to me eloquently by an orthopedic surgeon I met at a house party. "We need a vision. The businessmen here just wait for handouts from Athens. It's a mafia economy. And once we sell off all our cheap properties, then what?" He had a point. His family arrived in Thessaloniki as refugees from Cappadocia after the population exchange. "Thessaloniki's port should dominate trade in all the Balkans," he said.

"Türkiye doesn't want trade with Israel because of the war in Gaza, fine. We should take that business." But he resisted Boutaris' cosmopolitanism. "He was too close to Skopje," he said.

* * *

Andreas and I walked up to Ano Poli, where his family has an Airbnb in a house built after the population exchange. Greeks and Turks didn't just gain new citizenships; they swapped homes, businesses and land. Thousands of Greek refuges settled in the abandoned Muslim town. Business has been good at the Airbnb: Ano Poli, while not popular with all the locals, is dynamite with tourists.

"You know this area was for the Muslims before the liberation. The Greek refugees settled here after the Catastrophe. In recent years, it was one of the cheaper places to live and attracted poorer people and students," he said, referring to Greece's 1912 conquest of the city.

We have lunch at Tsinari, a glass-paned cafe from the Ottoman era. It was operating in Ano Poli before *Macedonia: A Plea for the Primitive* was published. Business at the antique shop is doing well, too. Turkish tourists are big buyers of the Ottoman documents and prints that Andreas finds online. "The Israelis and the Bulgarians don't come shopping for antiques. They don't care about the history. They come to Thessaloniki to party," he said.

When the topic of East and West came up, Andreas went down a path similar to many Greeks I have interviewed. "Greece is an American ally. The United States will always be a superpower. This idea of America leaving Europe is fake. It wants to command Europe. We are a true NATO ally. Unlike Türkiye, Greece is a democracy," he said.

Andreas told me he was pro-American, but he roasted Greece's political class, saying they do the bidding of the United States too easily. He points to the increase in American military bases across Greece in recent years, and asked, "What have we gotten out of this?" It's the same populist rhetoric you will hear in the United States, but the flip side of it. Ordinary people I met in Greece's borderlands wanted the United States engaged here, but then complained that their country was hamstrung by Washington, mainly against Türkiye.

I asked him who he believed the most successful leader in the world is.

"It pains me to say this, but objectively speaking, Erdoğan is the best. I didn't like watching Hagia Sophia turned into a mosque, but Erdoğan has made Türkiye a power. His armies are everywhere and he doesn't ask anyone's permission."

Boutaris falls on the opposite political spectrum as Andreas, but I heard the same from him. "Thessaloniki is not West and never will be. The West is boring. There is no flavor or color in the West. I don't strive to be like the Germans. And I don't want to be an ancient Greek, so stop telling me to be one. I want to be a Byzantine. That sounds about right," he said. "Greece benefits from NATO. The United States is a great country. But the smartest leader in the world right now is Erdoğan. Think about it, he is in NATO, does what he wants, and has the Americans and Russians wanting a piece of him," he told me.

This sense of independence was what Greeks admired most about Erdoğan, not unlike American and European populist voters. I lingered longer on the ground in Thessaloniki than Athens. You sense Byzantium more intently here, but it is mostly a city adrift.

The Turks, Bulgarians and Israelis keep coming. Thessaloniki needs a holistic Near Eastern vision to channel the flow of capital and people better in order to position itself as a bridge between Islamic, Orthodox Christian, and Jewish worlds. Thessaloniki can be successful in a multipolar world and competitive, but it can only do so by building on the early diplomacy of the Prespa Agreement. It needs another creative leader like Boutaris.

There is a huge disparity between income and lifestyle here, too. I felt this in Greece, Türkiye, Egypt, and Israel. Comparing salaries with the exorbitant cost of living you feel something has to give. It's remarkable how much people can absorb. Thessaloniki is such a condensed party city, the mismatch was glaring. I still can't figure out how locals afford the lavish spending on display in the city center, even with money from abroad. Of course, Thessaloniki is falling farther behind Athens, the super city-state.

Thessaloniki's future rests in taking the best the European Union has to offer and attracting all the creatives, tourists and investments it can from the East—in effect, milking the best of both worlds. It's already doing it, up to a point. For example, Pfizer has a digital center in Thessaloniki that employs over 500 people.

I dwelled longer in Thessaloniki because it is a getaway, where the wider Middle East starts to win over European Greece. From here, we push further east, into Greece's borderlands and abroad, where Greece becomes subsumed into the Near East.

4

THE LAST PASHA OF KAVALA

Visitors descend into Kavala. Driving east from Thessaloniki, you turn off the Egnatia Odos highway onto a road that weaves through the pine-studded foothills of Mount Simvolo. Gradually, the Aegean Sea pokes out behind the bends of the road and ugly apartment blocks. The first sign welcoming arrivals to this northern Greek port is drenched in blood: "Remember Cyprus," says a billboard, with the Turkish occupied half of the island dripping in red.

When British traveler John Fraser arrived in Kavala in 1906 he described it as "hot and slothful. It is just the place for a Turk. It makes even an infidel feel like a Turk."[1]

Contemporary Kavala is Balkan kitsch to the core. Its crescent shaped port is a departure point for Greece's less traveled eastern Aegean islands. You are more likely to see migrant fishermen here with a day's catch and Greek pensioners sipping Turkish coffee than tourists. Kavala's cheap seafood and decaying merchants' villas still ooze the lazy rhythm of the Levant that attracted writers like Lawrence Durrell and spy novelist Eric Ambler to Greece. The port hasn't developed much since then. It is not too far off from how it appeared in the classic 1964 Jules Dassin crime film, *Topkapi*, based on Ambler's Istanbul heist novel, *The Light of Day*.

I have an appointment to keep and cruise through the quayside to reach Panagia, the old Muslim quarter of the city which juts out on a rocky, hilltop peninsula into the bay.

Kavala's old town is defined by two landmarks. There is the sprawling fortress, first erected during Byzantine times when the city was called Christoupolis and rebuilt after the Ottomans conquered it in 1387. And there is a fine Ottoman baroque compound built about 420 years after the fortress. This compound is my destination. Its soft ochre walls run along the western edge of Panagia and it literally bubbles up among the old Turkish houses: its distinct lead roof comprises dozens of small cupolas that resemble a cross between a mosque and a turtle's shell. It reminds me of Ottoman artist Osman Hamdi Bey's painting, *The Tortoise Trainer*.

In its former life, this complex was an Ottoman soup kitchen, charity house and Islamic school. It was built by Muhammad Ali Pasha, a Turkish-speaking tobacco merchant born in Kavala in 1770. Although his family roots go back to the Central Anatolian city of Konya, Muhammad Ali left his mark on Egypt. He could easily have passed through life as an unknown, illiterate Ottoman merchant and tax collector. Instead, he was recruited into a force of Ottoman irregular soldiers by Sultan Selim III to oust Napoleon Bonaparte's army from Egypt. Muhammad Ali was lucky. His temperament was well suited for warfare and politics. The Kavala native is responsible for founding the modern state of Egypt.

Napoleon tried to conquer Egypt in a daring bid to crush the Ottoman Empire and sever the British Empire's link to India. Egypt, nominally a province, or *pashalik*, within the Ottoman Empire, was a stepping-stone to the Far East for Napoleon via the Red Sea. Like in Epirus, the sultan's authority in Egypt was tenuous at best. Its ruling elite were rebellious Mamluks, a class of slave soldiers descended from Christian converts to Islam who were recruited from across the Caucasus, Anatolia and the Balkans. Although the Ottomans conquered Egypt by the early sixteenth century, the Mamluks continued to exert influence, controlling the military and finances. By the time of Napoleon's invasion, they barely recognized the sultan's authority.

The Ottoman Empire extended a blanket of stability over its territory, but by the nature of its founding, it was in a permanent state of war. The Ottomans divided the world into two parts: The House of Islam, or *Dar al-Islam*, and The House of War, or *Dar al-Harb*. Their overarching goal was to extend the former, which they ruled, over the latter. Therefore, the empire's frontiers were constantly changing as its armies advanced. Hence the lack of distinction between military affairs and civil governance. Local pashas were first and foremost army commanders. The sultan faced constant revolts. Even before the rise of ethnic nationalisms, by the mid-1700s the empire was riven by insurrections and pashas gone rogue. This was the case in Egypt.

Napoleon's modern and well-trained army easily conquered Cairo, defeating the Mamluks at the Battle of the Pyramids in 1798. But he had already overreached. The British allied themselves with the Ottomans. Napoleon's fleet was destroyed off Egypt's Mediterranean coast by British Admiral Horatio Nelson in 1798. Instead of counting his losses, Napoleon went on the offensive and launched a disastrous invasion of Syria that further weakened his army. Supply lines stretched, troops decimated by disease and harassed by local rebels, the French army surrendered to British and Ottoman forces in 1801. A power vacuum emerged. The sultan named Muhammed Ali governor of the province. In mafioso fashion, he invited the Mamluk leadership to a reception at Cairo's citadel and slaughtered them. In one swoop, this obscure thirty-year-old Kavala tobacco trader eliminated a warrior class that had lorded over Egypt since the thirteenth century and defied their Ottoman masters. But Muhammed Ali had as much interest in serving the sultan as the Mamluks.

The "Son of Kavala," as Muhammad Ali was called by Egyptian novelist Mahmud Taymur, was similar to his contemporary, the Albanian Ali Pasha, but much cleverer. Like the unruly governor of Ioannina, Muhammad Ali courted European powers and craved the international spotlight. For the well-connected traveler, a stop at his divan was a requisite part of the Levantine tour. Muhammad Ali had a taste for the theatrical. He relished manipulating European callers to foster his own mystique. Arrivals to his court were sent through a prescribed ritual to create a feeling of suspense: first they encountered a loud antechamber filled with courtiers, petitioners and underlings, then they passed through a divan with a single, low sofa where a man sat shrouded in shadows. Only after engaging with them in the dark would Mohammad Ali tip back his turban and flash a sinister gaze upon his visitors. His yarns were ready-made for Western writers in search of the classic oriental despot. "The only books I ever read are men's faces ... and I seldom read them amiss," was one of his regular quips.[2]

Like the Mamluks and Ottomans, Muhammad Ali was a foreign interloper in Egypt who spoke Turkish and Albanian. He had little sympathy for the Arabic-speaking *fellahin*, or peasants, that he ruled over. He pursued an aggressive modernization agenda, imposing Western technology and military order on the Egyptians. He ruthlessly fashioned the *pashalik* of Egypt into his own statelet.

He was a reformer and modernizer who sensed the Ottoman Empire was weakening. In one letter to his nephew, the governor of Mecca in Saudi Arabia, he observed, "It is clear to all who can see that the Ottoman State, although once a strong and powerful state ... is now feeble and rampant with problems because of its vizier's obsession with ceremonies and tradition."[3]

Unlike other Arab states in the Eastern Mediterranean fashioned by colonial powers, Egypt has an ancient identity. Egyptian Christians and Muslims, secular and religious people, know their nation. That is why despite two coups and a crushing economic crisis over the last fifteen years, it hasn't descended into anarchy or fragmented. Muhammad Ali is credited as its founder mainly because he modernized the state and started its institutions. He also imposed a European style bureaucracy and oversaw Egypt's first modern census, one of the hallmarks of basic governance. He introduced new farming methods and enlisted European advisors to build an industrial base to produce textiles and armaments. His construction of a canal linking the backwater port of Alexandria to the Nile laid the foundations for future fortunes to be made by men like Antonis Benakis by turning Alexandria into a cotton trading hub. To be sure, reforms for this Kavala adventurer were about consolidating wealth and power in his hands. But Muhammad Ali wanted to be remembered in posterity. As a military thinker, he considered himself on par with Napoleon and boasted sharing his Macedonian birthplace with Alexander the Great. Kavala was where his philanthropist ambitions ran wild.

In 1813, he commissioned the first wing of the ochre complex that looms over the city's bay today. It housed a library, an Islamic primary school, a lecture hall and rooms for theology students. This sprawling charity complex would expand with the success of Muhammad Ali's army across the wider Middle East. In 1811, Sultan Mahmud II turned to his Egyptian governor with a request to put down a rebellion in the Arabian peninsula, where Bedouin warlord Abdullah bin Saud Al Saud had forged an alliance with the Wahhabis, followers of a puritanical sect of Sunni Islam. Muhammad Ali's army thrashed the Saud family and their Wahhabi allies, wresting back control of Mecca and Medina, the two holiest cities of Islam, for the sultan. It would take another 121 years for the Saud family to gain control over the Holy Cities and much of the Arabian peninsula. In 1932, Ibn Saud, the grandfather of the oil-rich kingdom's current ruler, Crown Prince Mohammad Bin Salman, was declared king of Saudi Arabia.

I came to Kavala because its history is a reminder of how interconnected this region was. For Muhammad Ali, Kavala was part of the wider Ottoman world.

In recognition of Muhammad Ali's impressive military success, the sultan bequeathed his pasha the Greek island of Thasos, which sits across from Kavala. With the tax revenue from this fertile island, Muhammad Ali expanded his endowment. In 1820, he ordered the construction of a second courtyard around which a *muhandasine*, or engineering school, and a *medrese*, or Islamic seminary, were built. The following year, he completed a third courtyard centered around a soup kitchen, to serve Muslim and Christian inhabitants of the city alike. Kavala might seem like a Balkan backwater, but it was once a cosmopolitan port, connected to one of the Near East's most powerful rulers.

The twentieth century was unkind to the city and Muhammad Ali's complex fell into ruin. Control of Kavala whipsawed between Greece and Bulgaria during the Balkan wars. The Islamic school was shuttered. The soup kitchen, or *imaret* in Turkish, closed in 1923 after Greece and Turkey conducted their population exchange. As late as the 1960s, the ruin was still housing Greek refugees from Asia Minor. It would have been forgotten completely if it weren't for one small detail: through all the wars, occupations and upheavals, the compound remained owned by Muhammad Ali's family. The government of Egypt owns it today through its government-controlled *waqf*, an Islamic charitable trust. This is one of the only properties owned by an Arab government's *waqf* in the non-Muslim world.

In the early 2000s, the abandoned building was caught up in a new spat of geopolitical intrigue when both Türkiye and Saudi Arabia quietly approached the Greek and Egyptian governments with plans to renovate it. They floated a plan to restore some of the compound's Islamic educational functions. Greece was wary of giving Ankara such a prized, cultural foothold in its northeastern province, while Saudi Arabia's funding of mosque projects across the Balkans was tainted by their support for Wahhabism in the aftermath of the 9/11 terror attack. The Greek government found a Kavala native with a passion for Ottoman history, eye for oriental antiques and deep pockets, to take on the project. It helped that she enjoyed good ties to the family of Hosni Mubarak, Egypt's ruler at the time.

I came to Kavala to meet Anna Missirian, the visionary behind Imaret, which is the name she gave to her hotel after opening it twenty years ago. Missirian undertook a painstaking, two-year renovation to preserve Imaret's Ottoman architecture. She owns the hotel, but has a fifty-year lease on the property with Egypt. Missirian keeps a steady stream of scholars, academics and discrete celebrities visiting her hotel. Well-traveled Greeks I meet say that Imaret is the finest luxury hotel visitors to their country have never heard of.

The neighborhood was crowded with tourists from Bulgaria and Türkiye when I arrived. I had to battle for a parking space outside Imaret's nondescript wall. It was clear when we met that the rumors I had heard in Athens of Missirian's uncompromising, intimidating reputation were also true. I was told guests who pay upwards of €1,000 a night to stay at Imaret have been evicted on her whims. Others have been yelled at for speaking too loudly by the pool. The Google reviews are spotty. "She throws guests out for dressing a way she doesn't like," one well-informed traveler in

Athens had told me. "Notorious. An eccentric. She treats Imaret as her private home, not a hotel. She doesn't want Greeks there, only rich foreigners," said another.

Missirian greets me wearing a silk scarf and expensive-looking, blue reading glasses. I put the allegations to her. She is unapologetic. "This isn't a hotel, it's sacred ground. None of this was done to turn a profit. I did all of this to save Imaret. I'm not impressed by someone's ability to throw around money, but how they choose to spend their time," she told me.

Missirian married into a wealthy Kavala tobacco family. She clearly is not trying to impress anyone and plays by her own rules. I liked her within five minutes of our meeting. In my mind, I had already christened her the "Last Pasha of Kavala." She was surrounded by a crew of designers, writers and workers when I arrived because she was in the process of transforming Imaret's nineteen rooms into ten luxury suits. She shifted between French, Greek and English with ease.

Missirian has an eye for details. And it shows in every corner of Imaret, a deliberately and carefully curated oasis. The interconnected courtyards are hidden from the bustle of the old town. The hotel's floors are covered in fine Persian carpets. Glimpsing inside the wood-paneled bar with old books and crystal tumblers, I half expected to find T.E. Lawerence and Freya Stark huddled over a map of the Middle East. This was the old Levant. The differences between Kavala, Beirut and Cairo vanished inside Imaret. I was in a rich, post-Ottoman world. We wandered through passageways and stumbled upon pools surrounded by orange trees, marble porticos, and jasmine-scented gardens.

"They killed Mykonos and Santorini," Missirian lamented. "They are amusement parks. There's no history or culture. I want people to live here for long stays. Kavala is a base to explore Thrace and Macedonia. You can't understand a region or city visiting for two nights," she told me, discussing her plans to transform the hotel.

She believes Kavala is as much a transition zone between East and West today as it was during Muhammad Ali's time. To advance her case, she cites the ancient Greek philosopher Thucydides who said that the border of the historic regions of Macedonia and Thrace is the Strymonas river, which places Kavala geographically in the latter. Thrace's modern borders extend between Greece, Bulgaria and Türkiye, and roughly a third of Greek Thrace's 350,000 residents are Muslim.

"Within twenty-five kilometers of Imaret, the Muslim world begins. Kavala is the point where Europe, as we mean in our Western world, actually meets the East," Missirian said. She emits an old-world Levantine *savoir faire*. She offers me Turkish coffee and ushers me on to a terrace with breathtaking views of Kavala. The city's contemporary Middle Eastern ugliness of concrete and satellite dishes is even more pronounced when viewed from the splendor of Imaret.

"They destroyed the city," she said, pointing out at the vista with a hand clutching an electronic cigarette. "Concrete everywhere, no planning. When I was growing up here, do you know I went to a French Lycée?" I admitted that it was hard to believe. Few visitors to Greece could point Kavala out on the map. "Yes," she took a drag on her electronic cigarette. "We are part of the Levant. Greece suffered from the same aliments that afflicted Beirut and Alexandria. They destroyed their cities."

From our terrace perch, Missirian holds court on a medley of topics. One minute we are discussing the spread of Alevism in the Balkans, a mystical offshoot of Shia Islam; next, we are tracing the lineage and marital alliances of Sultan Mehmed II, conqueror of Constantinople.

"His rule was an extension of the Byzantine Empire. He was a great admirer of the Greeks," she said with a penetrating gaze.

Missirian likes talking politics and her views don't jibe easily with popular Greek history, which places all the country's ills at the feet of the Ottomans.

She explained that as the Ottomans swept across the disintegrating Byzantine Empire they absorbed the latter's customs, traditions and governing styles. Both the Byzantines and Ottomans were religious, multi-ethnic empires. The Ottomans relied on Byzantine administration after conquering its territories. The Ottomans were more interested in expanding their empire through conquest then governing. They left management of local affairs to former Byzantine officials and prominent Greek families. So long as taxes were paid on time and in full, the Ottomans left their subjects alone. Greek *kodjabashis*, or notables, and Orthodox bishops ran municipal affairs. The Greek Orthodox were referred to as *rayah*, or cattle, by the Ottomans, underscoring their Muslim rulers' sense of superiority and nomadic roots, but Greek peasants were certainly better off with the sultan then their counterparts in Western Europe. The Ottomans' light touch method of governing their diverse provinces and peoples worked extremely well.

The Ottomans were, by and large, welcomed by the Greeks, who never forgot the betrayal of the Western crusaders who sacked Constantinople in 1204. The only viable Christian alternative to Ottoman rule at the time, seafaring Venice, reinforced the perception among Orthodox Christians that they were better off within an Islamic caliphate. In nearby Cyprus, Crete and the Ionian islands, the Venetians lorded over their Orthodox subjects, imposing high taxes, denying them any form of self-government, restricting the ability of Orthodox Christians to trade, and proselytizing.[4] All of these factors led to the famous line by Lucas Notaras, the last Byzantine Grand Duke, that he would, "rather see the sultan's turban among us than the Cardinal's tiara."[5]

Mehmed II viewed himself as the heir to the Byzantine emperors. He conferred extraordinary powers on Greek Orthodox Patriarch Gennadius, privileges that extended beyond what the Quran stipulated for "people of the book," or followers of the three Abrahamic religions. The Ottomans ruled the Orthodox Christians through their patriarch, who was allowed to levy taxes on both the laity and clergy. He had full religious freedom and unprecedented civil powers.

In the fifteenth century, the Ottomans were also linked to the Orthodox Christian empires they were fighting through intermarriages. Mehmet II's stepmother, and confidant, Mara Brankovic, was a Serbian princess married off to Mehmed II's father, Murad II, in an attempt to forestall an Ottoman invasion of Serbia. Brankovic was the daughter of Irene Kantakouzene, a Greek noblewoman and cousin of the last two Byzantine emperors. Some historians also believe Mehmed II's mother, Huma Hatun, a concubine in Murad II's harem, was likely of Greek descent. Mehmed II appointed two nephews of the late Byzantine Emperor Constantine XI as pashas. Hass Murat Pasha was named ruler of Rumelia, which is today modern Greece and its Balkan neighbors, and was likely Mehmed's lover. His brother, Mesih Pasha, served as Grand Vezir to Mehmed's son and successor, Beyazit II.[6]

Missirian is too good a scholar of history to compare empires in Manichean terms. She has the healthy skepticism and sarcasm of a Levantine. She has also spent years studying the upstart pasha who built her hotel. "He wasn't a cultured man, but he was so very clever," she says. "All the really good historians who want to write a history of the Greek Revolution come to Kavala and Imaret first, because this is our history. Imaret gives you a different frame of reference to understand the creation of the modern Greek state. We were a part of the Ottoman Empire. Our history is tied to the East," she tells me.

* * *

When the Greeks launched their revolt, the sultan turned to his Egyptian governor for help. Instead of crushing unruly Wahhabis, Muhammad Ali's job was to decimate the Greek revolutionaries. In 1822, he dispatched the largest non-European fleet ever to set sail in the Mediterranean for Greece. He had been promised a tantalizing prize in return for putting down the revolution: the *pashalik* of Crete and the Peloponnese. First his forces landed on Crete to put down a revolt there. Then they sailed to the mainland. Muhammad Ali's army was led by his son and top general, Ibrahim Pasha, who waged a brutal, scorched earth campaign against the Greeks. He razed villages to the ground, slaughtered his way through the Peloponnese and shipped thousands of Greeks off to slave markets in Cairo. His offensive was so bloody that his name still evokes brutality in popular Greek history.

One of the most intriguing figures to fight in the Greek War of Independence was a French officer and veteran of the Napoleonic wars. Joseph Anthelme Sève enlisted as a soldier of fortune in Muhammad Ali's army, which was organized along modern, French military lines. Sève converted to Islam before departing for Greece and took the name Soliman. He ended up marrying a Greek woman who he rescued from slavery in the Peloponnese. The Frenchman's descendants became romantically entangled with Muhammad Ali's family: his great-granddaughter, Queen Nazil, was the mother of King Farouk, Muhammad Ali's great-great grandson.

Sève was one of hundreds of unemployed veterans of the Napoleonic wars who fought for the Ottomans. But it was the Greeks who captured popular imagination across the Western world. Around 1,000 Philhellenes left Western Europe and the United States to volunteer for the Greek cause. They were imbued with the ideals of the French and American Revolutions. For Western liberals at the time, the Greek struggle was a liberation war of Christians against a colonial Muslim oppressor, who was backed by the same conservative European monarchs who crushed the upstart Napoleon. These twenty-year-old volunteers were inspired by Lord Byron and the Romantics. They wanted adventure and glory in the Orient. As one French critic put it, "Go to Greece ... this was, for many tired souls, sated with everything, a moral awakening, the healing of unreal passions, of indeterminate boredom; for the old soldier of the great war, it was to find again an assignment worthy of his not yet rusty sword."[7]

Greece is where Western intervention in the wider Middle East started. Just like today's idealistic interlopers, these volunteers got a wakeup call when they arrived. The Peloponnese was in a state of anarchy. Greek peasants killed and robbed the "rich Franks" who wanted to fight on their behalf. The volunteers who did manage to embed with the Greek fighters realized that their comrades weren't the Plato-citing descendants of Ancient Athens they had been made out to be back home, but oriental Christians who had more in common with their Muslim enemies than the rich kids of Paris and London. These turbaned and mustachioed fighters saw the war as an opportunity for plunder and pillaging. The Ottomans had been massacring and enslaving Christians wholesale and the Greeks wanted revenge. Amid the fighting, the Europeans ended up looking at the slayed naked bodies of Muslim women and children "with compassion and horror," while the Greeks saw it as settling ancient scores.[8]

The irony is that Muhammad Ali was reluctant to enter the Greek Revolution in the first place. He had his mind set on putting his modernized, well-trained troops up against his boss, the sultan, and conquering Syria, which he craved for its resources and population. The Peloponnesian war was a distraction, and as the years went by, he saw it as a liability. He believed the war was a lost cause and resented the sultan for dragging him into it. When asked by a British diplomat whether he could convince the Porte to reach a political settlement in Greece he replied that the sultan was, "too much a bigot and too much in the hands of the Ulemas [Islamic scholars] ever to consent to such a proposition."[9]

Ibrahim Pasha waged a classic counter-insurgency campaign against the Greeks, similar to that of the French in Algeria in the 1950s and Israel in the Gaza Strip at the time of writing. The premise is to use overwhelming force so locals turn on the rebels. It is collective punishment. It takes a moment to wrap your head around just how convoluted, and international, the Greek Revolution's battle lines were. Greek rebels and chieftains waged an independence struggle against an enslaved Arab army, led by the son of a Kavala native, serving on behalf of the sultan, who his father planned to attack later. Ibrahim Pasha's brutal tactics were incredibly effective. He crushed the Greeks at the third siege of Mesolonghi and by 1827 he had largely subdued the Peloponnese by destroying every living thing in his path.

But times were changing. Ibrahim Pasha was probably the first military commander in history to see his brutal battlefield tactics spark a strange new phenomenon: public opinion advocating for foreign intervention to stop a war. In Western Europe, the Egyptian army's rampaging through Greece and wholesale slave trading was met with a furious reaction from people freshly imbued with liberal, Enlightenment principles. Of course, their compassion for the Greeks was laced with hypocrisy by the standards of our day. They could tolerate a black slave trade and European colonialism, but what shocked an emerging middle and upper class in France and Britain was that the lands of ancient Greece were being overrun by a Muslim army, whose chattel were Christians. To be sure, the Ottoman slave trade in Greece was unprecedented in terms of volume even by the standards of the 1800s when slavery was rampant in the United

States. On the island of Chios alone, the Ottomans took 50,000 Greeks into slavery.[10] Abolitionists also took up the Greek cause.

To make matters worse, Soliman Pasha wasn't the only European serving in Ibrahim's army. European soldiers-of-fortune were buying Greeks as slaves as well. A leaked cable even alleged (falsely) that Ibrahim intended to deport the entire Greek population of the Peloponnese and replace them with Muslim inhabitants. It sparked an outcry in Paris and London. The big European powers eventually intervened out of self-interest. They did not want Greece to become a failed state on the Mediterranean. But their actions were also informed by public anger over the Greek slave trade.[11]

Despite his army's advances against the Greek revolutionaries, Muhammad Ali was perceptive enough to see that Britain, France and Russia were gradually shedding their reservations about supporting the upstart Greeks. British financiers had already stepped in to provide loans to the fledgling Greek government. Ibrahim hoped to inflict one final blow against the Greeks by attacking their stronghold islands of Hydra and Spetses, the two bases of Greek naval power that had tormented shipping in the Eastern Mediterranean. However, his assaults on Greek villages enraged the European admirals stationed off the Peloponnese coast. They believed they had extracted a promise from Ibrahim to rein in his troops while diplomats in Constantinople negotiated a political settlement. The blow to the Ottomans that Muhammad Ali foresaw, but was unable to prevent, came in 1827 at the Battle of Navarino, when the combined Egyptian and Ottoman fleet was destroyed by the British, French and Russian navies.

The Greek War of Independence barely touched Imaret. Kavala remained under Ottoman control, prospering as a port for the tobacco-producing hinterlands of Thrace and Macedonia. It was a small version of Salonica. In the twilight of the

Ottoman Empire, Muslim, Christian and Jewish merchants were building eclectic villas in Kavala attesting to the city's wealth and cosmopolitanism. The finest of these, built by Hungarian tobacco trader Baron Peter Herzog in 1895, is now the city's town hall.

Muhammad Ali never had a grudge against the Greeks. It was all geopolitics and business for him. In fact, Egypt was quick to establish diplomatic relations with Greece in 1833. In diplomacy, proximity is a good judge of relations. Egypt's embassy in Athens is literally a stone's throw from the Greek parliament. Muhammad Ali's milieu was the cosmopolitan trading world of Kavala. Even as he waged war on the Greeks, he welcomed Greek traders, artisans, merchants and sailors into Egypt. He turned a blind eye to their funding the Greek revolutionaries he was fighting. One of Muhammad Ali's closest advisors, Michalis Tositsas, was a Greek merchant from the town of Metsovo. He was a staunch Hellenist and the first patron of Egypt's Greek community. The Tositsas family's connections to Muhammad Ali went back to the Pasha's days as a merchant in Kavala. They supposedly loaned him money when he was a provincial trader. The Tositsas commercial empire extended across Alexandria, Damascus, Livorno and Malta.[12]

I suspect Muhammad Ali and his contemporary Ali Pasha in Ioannina would thrive in the transactional, hard-power, and multipolar Near East that is emerging in our era. Muhammad Ali was the kind of leader who benefited from exploiting different powers. The ebb and flow of people and capital in the Near East is surely something he would have found a way to profit from. Missirian's eyes sharpen when I ask how she believes the builder of her hotel would see the wider Middle East today: "He wouldn't tolerate the anarchy we see in the Middle East." She also sits on the board of the Mohammed Ali Research Center (MOHA), which studies the strategic thinking of its namesake. "I think he would have run circles around all of the rulers in the region," she tells me.

I replied that the rulers of the United Arab Emirates may come closest to resembling Muhammad Ali. Like him, they lack any clear ideology. They are motivated by commercial interests and preserving their power. Their main priority is ensuring Dubai and Abu Dhabi attract global wealth and, increasingly, artificial intelligence technology. They have also supported militias and strongmen in wars in Yemen, Libya and Sudan. Dubai's zero-income-tax regime and business friendly policies attract Russian oligarchs, Western tech entrepreneurs and India's nouveau rich.

Missirian agrees, to a point. "I don't think he would like Dubai. It's an international city, but it's manufactured. People are transient," she said. Muhammad Ali had foreigners put down roots in Egypt.

Missirian doesn't just talk the talk on cosmopolitanism. She has carved out a niche for herself preserving the legacy of the city's most famous Muslim native. Yet Kavala is another city where old nationalisms run deep. The memory of ethnic cleansing against Greeks in the Middle East is warm to the touch here. Many of the city's inhabitants are the descendants of Asia Minor refugees. Missirian's own family hails from Constantinople.

In recent years, an influx of Bulgarian home buyers has stoked new resentments among some locals, including Missirian. "I am cosmopolitan, but that doesn't mean you surrender your identity or your heritage. And Kavala has a problem. It has too many Bulgarians. I dislike the Bulgarisation of Kavala," she told me. Bulgaria and Greece have been foes since the Ottoman Empire started unraveling. They share more similarities than differences, yet still harbor old Balkan grudges. In the Ottoman Empire's final days, they both laid claim to Thrace and Macedonia. Greek and Bulgarian partisans killed each other during the conflicts that preceded the First World War. The violence unleashed by their nationalism was summarized by Nikos Kazantzakis' protagonist in *Zorba the Greek*.

> There was a time when I used to say: that man's a Turk, or a Bulgar, or a Greek. I've done things for my country that would make your hair stand on end, boss. I've cut people's throats, burned villages, robbed and raped women, wiped out entire families. Why? Because they were Bulgars, or Turks.[13]

Bulgaria coveted Kavala as an outlet to the Aegean and seized the city three times: in 1912 during the first Balkan War, again in 1916 during the First World War, and during the Second World War when Bulgaria fought alongside Nazi Germany. During the Cold War, Bulgaria was behind the Iron Curtain, but Greece continued to fear a land grab. The collapse of the Soviet Union laid to rest concerns about territorial expansion. Now, Kavala is once again Bulgarians' outlet to the Aegean, although a totally benign one for beachgoers. In 2025, Bulgaria joined the European Union's Schengen Zone. The future of a depopulating northeastern Greece lies with more Bulgarian and Turkish investment, not less. Bulgaria's GDP per capita is catching up to Greece's and will likely surpass it. I sense a hint of resentment among Greeks, who are still used to sniping about their poor Communist neighbors. Now, the latter are scooping up prized seaside properties and taverna tables.

Our talk turns to the war between Israel and Hamas in the Gaza Strip. Missirian has no sympathy for Hamas, but says, "Israel is trying to make a Manhattan in the Middle East. It can't ignore the Palestinians." She is concerned about the socioeconomic and cultural chasm between the Israelis and Palestinians. The best outcome for them would be to have the problems Greeks and Bulgarians have, bickering over vacation houses. We discussed the Nova music festival, held just three miles from the border of the impoverished, besieged Gaza Strip, which the UN dubbed an "open air prison" years before 7 October 2023. The raucous celebration was attacked by Hamas militants, who slaughtered Israeli teenagers and dragged them back into captivity. The competing Palestinian and Israeli nationalisms would have been foreign to Muhammad Ali. But he had a keen interest in historic Palestine. The fallout of Greece's revolution gave Muhammad Ali the push he needed to invade historic Syria, which encompassed all of today's Arab Levant. For the Kavala-native, the Greeks' victory, enabled by the European powers, was a turning point in how he viewed the balance of power in the Near East.

Muhammad Ali redoubled his efforts to orient Egyptian foreign policy toward Europe. He saw Egypt's future as linked to Mediterranean trade, and recognized its importance as the link between Europe and India. As a result, he bolstered ties with the French and British. With his son Ibrahim once again in command, Muhammad Ali's modernized troops invaded Syria and inflicted a humiliating defeat on the Ottomans. They swept across the region and in 1832 Ibrahim won a decisive battle at Konya, deep in Central Anatolia. But the European powers weren't ready to let this upstart pasha deliver the final blow to the sultan. In order to prevent the Ottoman Empire's collapse, they intervened and negotiated a settlement. The 1840 Convention of London guaranteed Muhammad Ali's family heredity rule over Egypt in return for him withdrawing his troops. Although Egypt remained nominally a part of the Ottoman Empire, the agreement effectively made Muhammad Ali and his family independent rulers. His heirs would squander that independence and become colonial vassals when Britain occupied Egypt in 1882. However, the family remained on the throne until General Gamal Abdel Nasser ousted Muhammad Ali's great-great grandson, King Farouk, in 1952.

Missirian and I jump to a tour of Imaret. The hotel rooms are where religious and engineering students once boarded. The soft, unadorned walls contrast with the deep red Persian carpets and oriental lamps that scatter the light into hexagons and triangles. I remember a line from Lawrence Durrell's novel *Justine*, set in Muhammad Ali's cherished city of Alexandria, "It was all of a controlled simplicity, which is the best sort of magnificence."[14]

At night, Imaret's corridors glow in dim candlelight. Missirian invited me to dinner to observe the hotel in action. It has the feel of her private salon. At the oak bar, a group of well-heeled tourists crack open a bottle of Prosecco. Missirian makes the rounds. She shakes the hands of each guest and chats with them. The food is succulent and sourced from Macedonia and Thrace, Greek provinces Missirian knows like the back of her hand. I felt I could happily ensconce myself in Kavala for years.

In the morning, I made my way through the old town to the Halil Bey Mosque. The town is a more decayed version of Ioannina. After 1923, it became a refugee camp. Many of the old houses covered in terracotta tile from Marseille were destroyed to build apartments for the descendants of Asia Minor Greeks. I try to imagine this route when Imaret's soup kitchen was still functioning, as it was described in *Macedonia: A Plea for the Primitive*. I still detect some of this old grandeur:

> [W]e gaze down upon the gallery of a minaret or into some narrow cobbled street sunk between ancient wooden houses, winding its way in and out, up and down. ... [M]ysterious passages and archways ... half-hidden faces behind latticed windows—a kaleidoscopic scene enacted amidst the mystic glamour of the East.[15]

Kavala's contemporary port is less romantic, but it is original. Besides the Bulgarian and Turkish visitors, it has evaded Greece's tourism boom and resembles a real working harbor. I walk along the quayside where fishermen are mending nets and scrubbing their boats clean. Greek cafes that sit side by side have a way of filtering patrons by age and gender. Everyone knows their place.

The old men wielding *kombologia* have their designated hangout. Next door, a trendy cafe blares Greek pop music where twenty-something Greeks sip frozen coffees.

I spot a group of fishermen who have just finished prayer. For a surreal moment Imaret towers behind them as they bow on their knees and face Mecca. Their Arabic dialect marks them as Egyptian. They are surprised when I approach, stumbling my way through Arabic greetings. One man introduces himself and tells me he has been working in Kavala's port for ten years.

I point to Imaret and ask him if he knows the complex built by Muhammad Ali. He tells me the city once had *Masryeen*, Egyptians, then returns to mending his net. I don't know if he is referring to Muhammad Ali or the local lore that the pasha had imported Egyptian peasants to Kavala to manage his real estate empire. Archival Ottoman-era records mention one neighborhood in Kavala settled by Egyptian Coptic Christians.[16] "Kavala is home," the Egyptian fisherman told me.

5

EGYPT

GREECE'S ALLY OR A TICKING TIME BOMB?

Cairo and Kavala. The latter has old mosques and seafood pilaf, but aren't these just remnants of a Near Eastern past? The pine-scented port where Bulgarians frolic in bikinis feels a world away from Cairo's traffic-filled, polluted streets. But is it?

In the fall of 2024, I was on an Aegean Airlines flight from Athens bound for the Egyptian capital. My goal was to meet the last remnants of the Greek community whose ancestors started arriving in Egypt during Muhammad Ali's rein. But I don't want to reduce Egypt and Greece's ties in the new Near East merely to this diaspora. In 1938, Egyptian scholar Taha Hussein argued in *The Future of Culture in Egypt* that the two were cultural cousins long before the Ottomans arrived. He said the ancient Greeks, "before and during their golden age," considered themselves "the pupils of the ancient Egyptians," while the Egyptians "had regular, peaceful, and mutually beneficial relations only with the Near East and Greece." He continued,

> The ancient Egyptian mind is not an Eastern mind, if we understand by the East China, Japan, India, and the adjoining regions. It developed in Egypt as a result of the conditions, natural and human, that prevailed there. It only exerted influence on and was in turn influenced by the neighboring non-Egyptian peoples, principally the Greeks.[1]

Hussein was writing at a time when Egypt was in a state of flux, not unlike what Thessaloniki experienced during the population exchange. In 1938, Egypt was in the early stages of shaking off Muhammad Ali's dynasty and the British who lorded over it. By the late 1930s, Egypt's ruling family was a Levantine anachronism in an age of growing anti-colonialism and rabid nationalisms. The governing elite was an outdated Ottoman hodgepodge of men descending from relations between Circassian harem women and Turkish and Albanian pashas over a century. With the exception of King Farouk, whose Arabic was excellent, Egypt's pashas spoke French and Turkish. Meanwhile, Egypt's business elite were Greeks, Jews, Armenians and some Copts. For 100 years, the elite floated above the peasants in a pseudo-Ottoman statelet, enjoying oriental opulence and the benefits of Western technology, while most Egyptians toiled in poverty.

Muhammad Ali's son and successor, Said Pasha, wanted to turn Egypt into Europe's highway to Asia. He awarded a contract to a French diplomat and businessman named Ferdinand de Lesseps to build the Suez Canal. Its construction was a tectonic shift for geopolitics and trade. It was the 1870s equivalent of artificial intelligence. The canal rapidly reduced communication time between Europe and Asia. It also made control of Egypt a strategic priority for the British Empire, as it was now the quickest route to colonial India.

Said's nephew and successor, Ismail Pasha, oversaw the completion of the Suez Canal and left his own distinct mark on

Egypt. He was so enamored with French architecture during a visit to the 1867 Paris exposition that he ordered the building of his own rendition of the city, famously declaring, "My country is no longer in Africa. I have made it part of Europe."[2]

He pulled Cairo's center of gravity out of the warren of old lanes and Mamluk palaces arranged around the Citadel of Saladin. His "Paris of the East" brought Cairo into the light of day with airy squares and boulevards laid out near the placid banks of the Nile. First came European-style mansions and gardens, followed by Haussmannian and Art Deco apartments.

Muhammad Ali's descendants were aesthetes, but they didn't have the cunning of their old Kavala patriarch. They failed miserably at geopolitics. Their gluttonous and womanizing ways made them playthings for the British. By 1882, Egypt, then as now, was in serious debt, which Britain used as a pretext to occupy it. The British kept Muhammad Ali's family in power, pulling strings behind the scenes when they needed to, or commanding them outright like during the First World War, when they declared Egypt a protectorate.

It took Egypt a few decades to get the Greeks' bug for nationalism, but by the First World War, they were seething at their British overlords and, like the Greeks, wanted an independent state. Leading the charge was the Wafd, a nationalist party headed by Saad Zaghloul, who attended the 1919 Paris Peace conference. The Wafd was secular and attracted Muslims and Christians. Its motto was "Religion belongs to God. The homeland to everyone."[3] But this mustachioed Egyptian politician wasn't as savvy as his contemporary, the Greek Prime Minister Elefterious Venizelos. In 1922, the British gave the Egyptians a semblance of autonomy, but kept the real mechanisms of a state in their hands, like control of the Suez Canal, foreign policy, the military, and protection of foreign minorities. Britain only delayed the inevitable. Their colonial days were numbered. Within twelve years, the Capitulations were abolished.[4] Full independence didn't really come until British troops left after the 1956 Suez Crisis. It was in the early stage of these heady developments that Taha Hussein was trying to figure out his homeland's place in the world and make sense of a very messy identity. He believed Greece and Egypt belonged together in the Near East.

Hussein would have been shocked at how quickly Egyptian society Islamized after the Muhammad Ali family was run out. The scholar who saw Egypt tied to the Mediterranean, probably would have been unnerved by the political and cultural dominance that oil-rich Bedouins in the Gulf exert over his pharaonic homeland.

It's a stretch to say that contemporary Egyptians and Greeks are closely related. It's true that many of Egypt's upper-middle class, both Coptic Christians and Sunni Muslims, have more in common with Greek families in posh Athenian suburbs like Glyfada and Kifisia, than their religious and ethnic kin in Cairo's polluted, garbage-filled, red-brick slums. But that says more about globalization, and how unevenly wealth is divided in Egypt. Cairo's upper-class lifestyle is based on mimicking the gated housing compounds and gleaming towers of Dubai. The cloistered Sheikh Zayed City, named after the founder of the United Arab Emirates, is the ultimate repudiation of Hussein's thought. For good measure, the United Arab Emirates paid $35bn in March 2024 for the right to develop a stretch of Egypt's northern coast as part of an economic bailout program for Egypt's cash-strapped government.[5] The bling Gulf is buying up Hussein's Mediterranean, lock, stock and barrel.

But if you tease out Hussein's premise and look at the new Near East, you realize Egypt and Greece are linked again. They belong on the same scimitar of instability stretching from the Black Sea to the Red Sea. They have the same revisionist neighbors, Israel and Türkiye, and both are vulnerable to the

United States tearing up the post-war order it created that made them Western protectorates.

First, there is a human aspect to all of this. More Egyptians are crossing the Mediterranean than ever. On the one hand, there are middle- and upper-class Egyptians buying apartments in Athens to escape a slow-rolling economic trainwreck in their own country. On the other hand, there are poor migrants. The existence of the latter was lethally underscored by the June 2023 Messenia migrant boat disaster. More than 600 people, mainly from Pakistan, Egypt and Syria, died when their overcrowded boat, launched from Egypt, capsized in Greek waters off the coast of the Peloponnese. A BBC investigation suggested that the vessel sank after Greek special forces tried to tow it outside Greece's maritime waters and that the Greek Coast Guard's search-and-rescue responses were, perhaps conveniently, delayed.[6]

The Europe Union is pouring billions of dollars into Egypt in a bid to stop migrants from coming to its shores. The latest plan, unveiled in March 2024, gives about $8bn to Egypt in loans and grants.[7] These plans are just bandaids. The money is gobbled up by Egypt's governing military elite. No amount of European taxpayer funds can reverse the fact that faraway Kavala is becoming less and less cocooned in its Balkan bliss every year. And the safety net provided by the European Union and NATO is frailer than ever.

One reason I enjoy speaking with Greek diplomats as a journalist is because they understand this trend better than their American and northern European counterparts. The good ones sense that their country is rejoining the wider Middle East.

One of Greece's responses has been to look around the Near East for friends. Over the last decade, they forged a mini alliance with Egypt. I have reported on this partnership for years. Their militaries drill together and their diplomats huddle closely on the world stage. If I want to get a line on Egyptian diplomacy in Libya for example, but can't reach an Egyptian diplomat, their Greek counterparts usually have a good idea about Egypt's maneuvering.[8]

Both countries see that the Mediterranean separating them is shrinking. Migration is just a side effect. The Greeks and Egyptians are wary of the new sultan in Türkiye, President Recep Tayyip Erdoğan. Egypt gives Greece a Muslim and Arab ally to counter Erdoğan. Greece can't give Egypt what it needs most, money, but it has become a staunch defender of Cairo in the European Union and United Nations, working to stamp out criticism of Egyptian President Abdel Fattah-Sisi's horrendous human rights record. Greece's former leftist government was the first to embrace Sisi.

"Tsipras ran a lot of interference for Sisi. We needed an ally in the Mediterranean and [Sisi] needed someone to be his eyes and ears in Western institutions. Not at the United States or France's level, but a partner," one senior Greek diplomat told me, recalling the first years of Sisi's rule. For example, in 2017, a leaked memo showed that Greek diplomats worked with Egyptian officials to remove Egypt from a list of countries criticized by the European Union at the United Nations over human rights abuses.[9]

These diplomatic dealings grate with human rights activists, but the reality is that Egypt and Greece have good geopolitical reasons to team up. They are united by their fear of a revisionist Türkiye. Greece is worried that the chaos that plagued Egypt following the Arab Spring could return if Sisi's secular, military regime crumbles.

For Sisi, the feud with Erdoğan is more dicey. A former general and spy chief, Sisi took power in 2013 by leading a popularly backed coup that ousted Egypt's democratically elected, Islamist President, Mohammad Morsi. An American-trained engineer, Morsi was an ally of Erdoğan, whose own political party is based on populist Sunni Islam. Morsi, a member of the

Muslim Brotherhood, was elected president of Egypt after Hosni Mubarak was toppled in the Arab Spring uprisings. His ascent to power was a political earthquake for the Middle East.

The Muslim Brotherhood was founded in Egypt in 1928 by Hassan al-Banna, a schoolteacher who worked in Ismailia, near the Suez Canal. He believed only an Islamic revival would help the Muslim world end Western colonial rule. After the British were kicked out, the Muslim Brotherhood turned its fury on the United States, Israel, Christian minorities, and secular Muslims. While the Muslim Brotherhood comprises different factions across the Islamic world (and bases its call for political change on democratic elections), its broad goal is to establish government based on Sharia and Islamic law. The Brotherhood is a menace to secular Egyptians.

Morsi was elected by razor slim margins in 2012. He was an inept president. The old secular elite undermined him at every turn, and he played into their hands, doubling down on Islamism and authoritarianism. By 2013, Egyptians were clamoring for his ouster. The military gleefully obliged. Sisi, the then defense minister, led the putsch. His government went to work arresting and killing thousands of Brotherhood members and sympathizers. Those who escaped made their way to Türkiye where they ran media campaigns against Sisi.[10] Erdoğan made no secret of how he felt about Sisi, slamming the leader of the Arab world's most populous state as an "illegitimate tyrant." Although tensions have eased recently, as late as 2019 Erdoğan threatened, "I will never talk to someone like him [Sisi]."

If the Muslim Brotherhood rose to power in Egypt and aligned with Türkiye, Greece would face a pro-Erdoğan front in the Mediterranean. At this point, we need to explain the decades old dispute between Türkiye and Greece in the Aegean to understand why Egypt is a critical partner for Athens. In the West, where anti-Erdoğanism borders on hysteria, Türkiye's feuds with its neighbors are all thrown on Erdoğan's lap. The reality is that Türkiye's rivalry with Greece in the Mediterranean is half a century old and was championed by Türkiye's secular, pro-NATO military rulers. Erdoğan infuses the spat with Ottoman revisionism and has been more adept at pushing Türkiye's objectives.

The crux of the dispute is Greece's insistence that its thousands of islands are entitled to Exclusive Economic Zones (EEZs). According to the United Nation's Convention on the Law of the Sea (UNCLOS), countries have a right to stake a claim to a maritime zone up to 200 miles from their coastlines and islands. Once a state establishes an EEZ it can exploit subsea resources there like natural gas. Türkiye rejects Greece's claim that islands have EEZs, and cites some cases in international rulings to support its argument. But in general, international law and norms accept that islands have EEZs. Türkiye's legal challenge is complicated by the fact that it has not signed on to UNCLOS. The two also have a series of disputes over uninhabited Greek islands and what Türkiye claims is Greece's militarization of the Eastern Aegean. Türkiye wants to bundle all these disputes into one grand negotiation. Greece refuses and says the EEZ dispute should be taken to the International Court of Justice.[11]

Both sides are entrenched in their positions. In 1996, they almost went to war over an uninhabited island, but the United States intervened to pull them apart. Until about a decade ago, the maritime feud was more evenly balanced. Both countries could ramp up tensions, knowing they would have little price to pay because the United States would come in to deescalate. In the 1980s, the left-wing Greek government of Andreas Papandreou threatened to expel American troops from Greek bases if the Americans didn't take Athens' side. Now, Greek diplomacy hugs the United States as tightly as possible, hoping the Americans will stay at those bases. This reflects Greek concerns that the

United States could agree to a Turkish zone of influence in the Eastern Mediterranean as Ankara's power increases. Rejoining the Near East is scary. The maritime dispute could escalate if the United States abandons NATO or normalizes territorial expansion in say, Ukraine.

> In the old days, Türkiye and Greece used to step back from the brink. They still do, but what has happened the last few years is that the envelope keeps getting pushed further. Greece clings stubbornly to the UN Law of the Sea and lobbies the West against the Turks. Erdoğan could give a damn. This is a dispute between 10 million Greeks and 90 million Turks. You think the UN law of the sea matters?

That is how one Arab diplomat explained the feud to me in Athens in September 2022. I reached out to him because he was monitoring the latest flareup after Türkiye accused Greece of harassing one of its F-16 fighter jets. Erdoğan did not miss the opportunity to rile up his nationalist base. He warned that Türkiye could "come suddenly one night" and invade Greece, prompting Athens to give its own hyperbolic warning of a Ukraine-style war breaking out in the Mediterranean.[12]

The dispute over EEZs isn't the most serious matter. Türkiye has also denied Greece's right under international law to extend its territorial waters. Unlike EEZs, these waters are considered sovereign territories. Under international law, Greece reserves the right to expand its islands' territorial waters from six to twelve nautical miles. Türkiye has declared that if Greece exercises that right in the Eastern Aegean it would be a *casus belli*, or a reason for war.

The seeds of this dispute were planted when the Ottoman Empire was being carved up, leaving dozens of Greek islands a short swim from Türkiye's coast. At the time, ironically, both Greece and Türkiye argued that islands like Chios, Samos, Rhodes and Lesbos are logical appendages of Türkiye's mainland to advance their opposing positions: Greece to reinforce its claim to Asia Minor and Türkiye to argue against the cession of the islands to Greece.[13]

If you look at the map of the Aegean, you can see why Greece's claims rattle a revisionist Türkiye that sniffs a power vacuum in the region. A tiny island like Kastellorizo would give Greece a 200-nautical mile wide EEZ, per Athens' argument. If Greece were to extend its territorial waters in the Eastern Aegean, Turkish ships would have to cross sovereign Greek territory. The Greeks could box the Turks into narrow safe-passage zones and drastically reduce the continental shelf they could claim. The two countries' nationalist-tinged medias take a sadistic pleasure in the fight and each clings to maximalist positions.

The maritime dispute usually stays confined to endless technical talks, campaign slogans and maritime law journals. That changed ten years ago when massive natural-gas fields were discovered in the Eastern Mediterranean. Egypt developed its Zohr gas field in 2017, generating billions of dollars in revenue. The biggest winner so far has been Israel, whose Leviathan gas field went into production in 2019, catapulting Israel into the ranks of a regional gas powerhouse. The ethnically divided island of Cyprus has potentially lucrative gas reserves, but has been unable to develop them, in part because there is no lasting settlement over the island's fate between Greeks and Turks. The irony is that neither Greece nor Türkiye have yet found commercially viable natural gas deposits. Energy executives in the region say behind closed doors that developing a find, unless it were massive, may not even make business sense.

But gas is just the proxy in a battle over who writes the rules in the Eastern Mediterranean. I sense that the old balance of power that kept Greece and Türkiye in check is tipping out of Greece's favor. Türkiye is bigger, better armed and less dependent on the West. So Greece, now very much a part of the Near East, needs friends like Egypt.

While Greece can sound intransigent, it faces an expansionist Türkiye whose views on the Mediterranean can be traced back to the so-called Mavi Vatan, or Blue Homeland. The doctrine was drafted by a nationalist Turkish admiral two decades ago. Under Erdoğan it has become the "covenant" of Türkiye's Defense Ministry. Blue Homeland envisions Türkiye controlling waters Greece sees as its sovereign territory and eventually taking over several islands inhabited by Greeks.[14]

Now, enter Egypt and Libya.

Libya has been riven by chaos since an American-led NATO bombing campaign helped a motley assortment of rebels and Islamists topple Muammar Qaddafi. Since 2014, it has been divided into two rival administrations fighting over the largest oil reserves in Africa. Eastern Libya is controlled by a warlord called Khalifa Haftar, a former Qaddafi general turned onetime CIA asset. Haftar has carved out something akin to an eighteenth-century Ottoman *pashalik* in eastern Libya, which he rules with an iron fist. Meanwhile, western Libya is controlled by corrupt politicians in the capital city of Tripoli who are backed by an array of nasty militias.

Haftar's forces are filled with Islamist fighters called Salafists. His money and guns come from Russia, the United Arab Emirates, and Egypt.[15] His rivals in the west of the country include Islamist militias and politicians linked to the Muslim Brotherhood. The Tripoli government is backed by Türkiye.[16] But ideology means little in Libya, which is a real-life version of *Game of Thrones*. In 2019, Haftar launched a months-long offensive to take Tripoli with Emirati and Russian backing. Türkiye successfully intervened to defend its ally, sending mercenaries, soldiers and drones.

In 2019, Türkiye saw an opportunity to put Mavi Vatan into practice. It signed a maritime demarcation agreement with the government in Tripoli that ignored Greece's claims to the Aegean via small islands like Kastellorizo, and large ones including Crete and Rhodes.

The Türkiye-Tripoli deal was partly motivated by Ankara's desire to squash talk of a theoretical pipeline that would run between Israel, Greece and Cyprus, bringing Mediterranean gas to Europe. The three countries have talked about building the world's largest and deepest underwater pipeline since 2017. They are still talking about it because the pipeline is a pipe dream. Energy majors have shown little interest in the plan because of meager gas supplies and construction costs. It makes more business sense for Israel and even Cyprus to export gas to nearby Egypt and Jordan on the cheap. But it rattled the Turks because it threatened their bid for hegemony in the Eastern Mediterranean. Greece wanted to show Türkiye that it could checkmate the Tripoli deal and signed its own maritime demarcation agreement with Egypt. The conflict is semi-stuck but is bound to erupt again.

Greece, Egypt and Türkiye are playing Mediterranean chess. One reason Türkiye needs to protect the government in Tripoli, and why Turkish troops are stationed there, is to defend its Mediterranean interests. Egypt is the linchpin. If an Islamist president like Morsi sympathetic to Erdoğan returns to power, he could leave the Greeks high and dry. Greek diplomats are already concerned that Türkiye could cut another maritime deal with the new leaders of Syria. In sum, an arcane maritime dispute between Greece and Türkiye is now tangled up in a proxy-battle between warlords in the Libyan desert. Greece's ability to counter Türkiye diplomatically in the Aegean is tethered to who rules Cairo. Yes. Kavala and Cairo are very much linked, in this interconnected, multipolar Near East.

* * *

EGYPT

The Eastern Mediterranean is Greece's obsession, but comes fourth on the list for Egypt, Mohammad Anwar al-Sadat told me.

I arranged to meet the nephew of Egypt's former president, Anwar Sadat, in Cairo. I took a taxi from my hotel in one of the downtown's freshly painted, Belle Époque buildings, to the leafy, upscale suburb of Heliopolis. The highway was clogged with morning traffic. We passed government ministry buildings where bureaucrats in baggy suits plodded into work. Roadside billboards advertised mobile banking apps and luxury villas with splashing, crystal-clear water that few Egyptians can afford amid a years-long economic crisis.

Sadat is an Egyptian politician. His office is situated inside a mid-century apartment with potted plants in the foyer that reminded me of upscale, 1970s buildings in Athens. He wore a blue suit and led me into a large room with conference tables and old printers that I thought was his office, but actually belonged to his secretary. His was even larger. We sat in chrome chairs upholstered in leather and surrounded by family photos, awards, and relics of the 1990s.

"In Egypt's mind, Libya will be settled. A frozen conflict there and this maritime business is manageable," Sadat explained. "The main priority for Egypt is the horn of Africa and Red Sea."

Sadat said that Erdoğan and Sisi have worked to patch up ties. They made reciprocal visits to each other's countries in 2024.

"Sisi crushed the Muslim Brotherhood here. He won. Erdoğan and Sisi needed to engage one another," he said. Although they are on opposite sides of the war in Libya, they are backing the same general in Sudan's civil war. "No one talks about that war, but it is worse than Gaza, and our ally, the UAE, is supporting the opposite side from us," Sadat said. Egypt wants Sudan's government to take its side in a dispute with Ethiopia over the Renaissance Dam, which Cairo fears could reduce its flow of Nile water. "No water means our agricultural sector dies.

More poverty, hunger, social unrest and migration. This is Sisi's top worry," Sadat said.

"We lost fifty per cent of our revenue from the Suez Canal because of the Houthis," he said, moving on to the Red Sea. The Houthis are Yemeni militants supported by Iran who started attacking Israel and ships in the Red Sea after Hamas' 7 October attack. The Houthis say they are acting in solidarity with besieged Palestinians in Gaza and have won sympathy across the Arab world for withstanding ferocious American and Israeli counterstrikes. Egypt cares because transfer fees through the Suez Canal are a key source of foreign currency for the cash-strapped government. The drop in traffic cost Egypt $7bn in 2024.

But I really want to talk with Sadat about Israel, which has been the third spoke in the wheel of a tripartite alliance with Egypt and Greece. Sadat's uncle reopened the Suez Canal in 1975 after launching a surprise attack on Israel in the 1973 Yom Kippur War. The elder Sadat was Egypt's most visionary leader since Muhammad Ali Pasha. He took over a broke, hollowed-out state when former President Gamal Nasser died in 1970. The canal had been closed since Nasser led Egypt into the disastrous 1967 Six-Day War which lost Egypt the Sinai Peninsula to Israel.

Anwar Sadat ditched his old army friend's crumbling bid to expand Egypt's power in the Middle East through Arab nationalism. He kicked out the Soviet Union military advisors his predecessor welcomed, flipping Egypt into an American ally. To this day, Egypt remains a bedrock of the United States' power projection in the Middle East. It is crucial for Israel's security. After all, the Egyptians have the only massive, organized Arab army on Israel's land border. Israel joins Greece and Egypt in military drills. All of this security cooperation is underwritten by the United States. But cooperation here has been frozen because of Gaza.

Anwar Sadat remains the only leader of an Arab state to shake Israel's aura of invincibility on the battlefield and then make peace with it. That is one reason the Islamists hate him. He was a statesman who tried to consolidate Egypt's fragile military gains through diplomacy, a lesson Israel has yet to learn, Sadat's nephew told me. Anwar Sadat paid for his peacemaking with his life. He was assassinated in 1981 by Islamist Egyptian military officers.

The sixty-nine-year-old Sadat is a well-placed member of Egypt's old guard. He is gracious and circumspect. As we chat, he chain-smokes cigarettes and sips a Turkish coffee. Sadat was an on-and-off member of Egypt's parliament between 2005 and 2017. He fashions himself as a human rights activist. But Egypt's legislature is a rubber-stamp assembly. Sadat is really a Middle Eastern player. One of the many figures in the region who has no official title, but an ear to the ground in the backroom corridors of power. Despite coups and revolutions, he has preserved some access to the Egyptian military and intelligence officials who know the inner workings of the state. In Egypt, you learn what is happening from guys like Sadat.

He tells me he is concerned about his uncle's legacy and the status of Egypt's cooperation with Israel, including in the Eastern Mediterranean. Since 1979, Egypt and Israel have been peace partners. In return, Israel has refrained from altering Egypt's territorial integrity. An unspoken part of their peace is that Egypt will not have to worry about an influx of Palestinian refugees. That changed once Israel began pummeling Gaza in response to Hamas' 7 October attack. Israel reduced the enclave to rubble and killed at least 54,000 people as of May 2025. Israel and the United States have pressed Egypt hard to accept Palestinian refugees during the war. Sadat says the military and intelligence elite who run the country are petrified over this. They fear accepting refugees would spark an uproar among the Egyptian masses, who sympathize with the Palestinians. The street would view the move as Egypt's leaders participating in the ethnic cleansing of fellow Arabs from Gaza. The military also fears Palestinian refugees could use Egypt as a base for guerrilla attacks against Israel, like they did in 1970s Lebanon.

"200,000 Palestinians have entered Egypt from Gaza since the war started. It has been made uninhabitable. Israel would like the Palestinians to come here. Sisi's military advisors are resisting it. They know that would mean a Palestinian insurgency on our soil," Sadat told me. "The Israelis want to expel them badly." Sadat's estimate is higher than the more than 120,000 arrivals reported in Arabic media.[17] The number is hard to quantify because most Palestinians have escaped by paying bribes to companies linked to Egypt's military at the border.[18] As of May 2025, the latest plan floated by Israel was to send Palestinians to the part of neighboring Sudan controlled by the warlord Egypt opposes. A not-too-subtle message to Cairo.

Egypt and Israel's peace has always been a cold one. The vast majority of Egyptians are hostile to the Jewish state. Relations are managed behind the scenes by spy chiefs and emissaries. Sadat regrets it.

"Israel never shared anything with Egypt before the war in Gaza. In terms of economics, we buy gas from Israel. But Europe bought gas from Russia too, and that didn't stop the war in Ukraine. In fields that could impact our economy, technology and agriculture, Israel shares nothing," Sadat said. He added that if the relationship isn't revamped, it could face a crisis in the coming decades.

"There is no room for peace voices anymore. I am silenced. I can't say anything in Egypt or I am labelled a traitor. The Israeli voices for peace are not the ones in power in government. The Israeli government wants to reoccupy Gaza with settlements," Sadat said. "Israel is running high right now because it has destroyed Hamas and Hezbollah. It is drunk on power and doesn't want to compromise to be integrated in the region," he continued.

Sadat told me Egypt's elite are worried that what happens in Gaza and the occupied West Bank won't stay there. "Sisi didn't ban protests in solidarity with Palestine because he doesn't like Palestinians," he explained. "He did it because he knows that a movement in support of Palestinians could snowball into a mass display of popular unrest."

Sadat's family name and connections give him a little protection to speak out. Sisi has jailed around 60,000 political prisoners. He tolerates no dissent.

"The level of repression is unimaginable," Sadat told me. He believes Sisi has effectively crushed the Muslim Brotherhood, and should now be reaching out to the opposition. "We need some reconciliation, including with Brotherhood sympathizers," he said. "Egypt is sick. In fact, it's on life support."

Egypt's economic woes go back to Nasser, who created a state-led economy where the military pulled the strings behind the scenes. When Sadat assumed power in 1970 he curtailed some of the state's influence. His liberalization program was dubbed *infitah*, or "open door." Sadat opened Egypt to foreign markets, but never did away with Nasser's centrally planned economic system. He stood down when the military balked at serious reforms. After Hosni Mubarak took power in 1981, he created the illusion of free-market reforms over the next two decades. But his idea of privatization and deregulation was the post-Soviet kind, selling valuable state assets off to cronies.[19] In Egypt, the worst forces of neoliberalism and a state-run economy combined to create a dystopian nightmare.

Sisi entered office distrustful of the private sector. He pushed a government-led infrastructure building spree that has saddled Egypt with massive levels of debt and catapulted his military allies to head the economy. The military's tentacles extend throughout every facet of life here. Generals and their buddies control construction firms, concrete manufacturers, media companies, and telecoms. No one with a right mind in the private sector wants to challenge the guys with all the guns. So there is no real competition in Egypt.[20] One of Sisi's responses to Egypt's inflation crisis has been to open military-run grocery stores, where his moon-shaped face smiles down on piles of discounted tomatoes and cucumbers. I suspect Sisi actually sees the economic crisis as an opportunity to expand the military's chokehold over Egypt and snuff out the private sector. Revolutions, after all, come from people who have the time and money to think about politics, not the dreadfully poor. Sadat says,

> We are in an economic crisis with no way out. The main problem is that the military, empowered by Sisi, controls the economy. We are spending too much money and have double digit inflation. There is no outside investment. Why would international businesses come here and compete with military companies that don't pay taxes or customs?

Arab and Western diplomats characterize Egypt as "too big too fail." The implication is that the United States, European Union and oil-rich Gulf states will always come to Sisi's aid because none of them have an interest in a 116 million Egyptians overthrowing Sisi and this country descending into anarchy.

I met Sadat a month before Islamist rebels took control of Syria. Egyptian officials I spoke with during my travels were aghast, saying that Islamist group Hay'at Tahrir al-Sham's (HTS) takeover of Damascus was a bigger setback for Egypt than any of Türkiye's gains in Libya. Türkiye was the main regional power to support HTS when it was in opposition. Ankara provided it weapons and an economic lifeline in trade via its border with HTS's former rebel stronghold in northeast Syria.[21] Now that HTS is in power, Egypt, Saudi Arabia and the United Arab Emirates are all courting the new government, in part to reduce

Türkiye's influence. Saudi Arabia and Türkiye both lobbied the United States to lift sanctions on Syria in May 2025. But Ankara is primed to be the main external power in Syria and is negotiating a defense pact with Damascus. "Türkiye's power is on the rise, clearly," an Egyptian diplomat told me.

I called Sadat when I was back in Athens for his opinion. "It raises concerns about political Islamists which Egypt thought they had beat," he told me. "That is why a national reconciliation is important." But unlike in Libya, Egypt won't confront Türkiye in Syria, he said. "Sisi will try to make an agreement with Erdoğan."

* * *

Back in downtown Cairo, or Wust el-Balad, I met a Western diplomat friend at the Estoril, one of Egypt's last great dive bars. The whitewashed exterior is meant to resemble the facades of buildings in the Portuguese seaside town that is the bar's namesake. Estoril was opened by a Greek couple in the late 1950s. Its dim, bare bones interior and lattice-grill windows give it a cavernous feel, perfect for dissecting the sordid alliances of the Near East.

"Erdoğan talks about giving an 'Ottoman slap' to his neighbors. Cairo wants to work with Greece to offset Türkiye's power in the Aegean, but what Sisi cares about is regime survival. The Greeks can't count on the Egyptians," the diplomat said. "If Türkiye and Greece get into an Aegean shooting match, the Egyptians are going to stand down. They are good at bombing the Sinai desert, but a high stakes naval engagement? The Egyptians would drown."

The diplomat and I ordered Stella, Egypt's cheap local beer, and plates of hummus and *kibbeh*, a fried Levantine dish of ground meat and bulgar.

Estoril was only a stone's throw from my hotel, but to get there I had to cut though Cairo's traffic. The city has few crosswalks. Instead, pedestrians play a version of the 1980s arcade game *Frogger*. You walk head-first into the oncoming traffic. Usually, the cars stop. If they don't, you find yourself standing in the middle of the road as they whizz by, inches from your face. You need to sniff out an opening to zig-zag between them. This sounds fearless until you see little kids and old ladies doing it without flinching.

"People get hit all the time. They die. It's no big deal. We don't have lawsuits like you in the US," I remember one Egyptian friend telling me as we darted across a street in Cairo's Dokki neighborhood during rush-hour.

"You see the economic situation. Awful, can't begin to describe it," the diplomat said. "The military controls everything. The threat here for Greece is the same as it is for Israel, Italy, and Saudi Arabia. All these countries that have bet on Sisi ensuring stability. If Sisi is toppled, everyone is fucked. Does the Brotherhood, or some other populist Islamist group come back?" the diplomat asked. "It's easy to see an Islamist government turning on Egypt's current allies and making common cause with Erdoğan."

I left the meetings with Sadat and my diplomat friend pessimistic about Egypt's prospects. To be clear, Greece has made the smartest alliance it can. As bad as Sisi is at home, he has kept Egypt generally on the course the elder Sadat set out, which means that the Arab world's most populous country is not an expansionist power trying to fill vacuums, but a status quo state.

"Egypt does not move fast and break things," as an Egyptian diplomat once explained to me. This is a slow-moving country, whose bureaucracy is something like the old Soviet politburo. Very cautious and conservative.

The problem is that Sisi's style of governing and his economic mismanagement are jeopardizing the very stability that he has told his partners they can count on. Egyptians are poorer, hungrier, and more oppressed than any time in the last six decades. Sisi, to his credit, pulled Egypt out of its post-Arab Spring chaos. But for twenty-five-year-old Egyptians who can't find jobs or afford to get married, the past is a foreign country. The more distant the memory of the Arab Spring, the more demanding Egyptians will become and the more vulnerable Sisi's position.

* * *

One of the first friends I caught up with when I landed in Cairo was Christos, a twenty-seven-year-old Greek Egyptian. All Christos wanted to talk to me about was Egypt's failing economy.

"Prices are crushing us," he told me. "We can't save. The economic mess is killing people. *Wallah*, we are dead inside. The government expects us to pay European prices on an Egyptian salary."

Egypt's inflation rate hovers at over twenty per cent and its currency, the pound, has plunged in value, losing two-thirds of its worth against the dollar. Rising prices and a currency crisis have been a double gut-punch to Egyptians. Back in 2019, the World Bank estimated that sixty per cent of Egyptians were poor. Although the official poverty rate is thirty per cent, most Egyptians I spoke with said the number could be double that. Cairo is faring worse than the countryside, I was told. As the price of imported goods rises, some Egyptians are moving back to their villages, which are less reliant on imports and more self-sufficient.

The pool of once solidly upper-middle-class urban people like Christos is shrinking. "Everyone is aggressive. Our society has changed. People are at each other's throats. You can feel the tension. Even the rich are cutting back. I am so glad I have a Greek passport."

Christos didn't need a lot of money to be a dapper dresser. He came to coffee in Zamalek sporting a stealth-wealth look in various tones of beige. Zamalek is an island of old-money Cairenes on the Nile next to downtown. Its eclectic mansions and hazy streets with overgrown trees recall colonial India. This is where Patrick Leigh Fermor rented the Villa Tara and hosted raucous parties when he wasn't kidnapping a German general in Crete during the Second World War.

Christos' Egyptian genes are stronger than the Greek. He has a pharaoh's good looks: almond eyes, high cheekbones and a strong jaw. It had been four years since I was last in Cairo. Christos had married his Coptic sweetheart. Now he had a young daughter.

"She's not going to spend her adulthood here. I promised myself that. She will go to the Greek school until she turns eighteen and then university in Athens."

Christos isn't the only Egyptian I met looking for an exit. Moneyed Egyptians are parking their wealth outside the country in a bid to stay one step ahead of the currency devaluation. "All of my friends have bought apartments in Athens," one Egyptian friend told me. "Because of inflation, property prices are mad here. The value for money in Egypt is shit," she continued. "To get a middle-class quality of life with some fresh air and no traffic you need to pay UK home prices. An apartment in Heliopolis or a beach house on the north coast costs more than an apartment on the Athenian Riviera."

I connected with Villy Politi, a Greek Cairene, before arriving in Egypt. I had been tracking the influx of Egyptians into Athens' real estate market. Her family law firm facilitates overseas property purchases in Greece.

"Business has increased 1,000 per cent the last two years. We have more clients than we know what to do with. Greece is familiar to Egyptians," she said. "Egyptians don't want to keep their money in pounds."

Every apartment purchased in Athens by an Egyptian is a hedge against Egypt's future. People who can't vote with their pocketbooks are doing so with their feet. The Messenia boat disaster was not a one-off. Egypt is now one of the top sources of migrants to Europe. Greece is on the front lines. The number of Egyptians seeking asylum in Europe has hit its highest level since 2014 and Egyptians are the third highest nationality arriving by sea in Greece and the fourth highest in Italy.[22] Greece's Migration and Asylum Minister, Dimitris Keridis, characterized this as a "massive flight" in March 2024.[23]

6

CAIRO

BEER IN THE GREEK CLUB

Walking out of my hotel, Cairo hit me like one of its downtown street hustlers—noisy and desperate. They were less noticeable in 2024 than when I lived here four years earlier. The government is trying to clean up downtown. The Haussmanian and Art Deco buildings are getting a facelift with fresh coats of banana yellow paint. But the grime and smog seem to find their way back. Downtown Cairo, once a haven for the Near East's rich, is like a decomposing version of Paris, with cheap Chinese goods instead of luxury brands. The decay is enticing. I could walk here for hours gazing up at the sweeping curved balconies of crumbling Bauhaus apartments and flaking baroque facades.

For me, downtown Cairo is a slideshow of doorways glimpsed out of the corner of my eye. These aren't just any thresholds. They're big double doors, with glass fronts framed in Art Deco wrought iron, guarded by turbaned *bawabs* (doorkeepers) and flanked by yuccas in clay pots. Peeking inside, under thick layers of dust, you can spot the soft-hued, patterned *cemento* tiles that the late, great, journalist Anthony Shadid obsessed over, "Vestiges of the irretrievable Levant, a word that, to many, calls to mind an older, more tolerant, more indulgent Middle East."[1]

I came to know downtown through the juxtaposition of two worlds. First, the polluted, trash-filled streets I walked as a freelance journalist. The other was Shadid's delicious Levant. This was the Cairo of Groppi's and Cafe Riche, which I discovered reading Olivia Manning's Second World War novel series, *The Fortunes of War*. In semi-autobiographical fashion, Manning tells the story of a young British couple, Guy and Harriet Pringle, who travel from Bucharest to Athens and Cairo, staying one step ahead of the Nazis' blitzkrieg.

Manning takes her characters through a twentieth-century version of what Braudel called the Mediterranean's "concentric rings ... hundreds of frontiers, some political, some economic and some cultural."[2] The Pringles' Near East stretched as far north as Bucharest, where their friend's Romanian landlady sipped Turkish coffee and played with tarot cards, "doing everything an oriental woman should do."[3]

Where you read a book determines how you commune with it. The twenty-something Pringles' cash-strapped, itinerant existence struck a chord with me living in Cairo during the Coronavirus pandemic. At the time, I had no steady job, girlfriend, or permanent address. I was emailing news editors at a feverish pace in the hope of scoring pitiful $300 commissions per article. I hadn't escaped war-torn Europe, but I was in Cairo as a refugee of sorts, albeit a privileged one with an American passport.

I was based in Athens when Greece went into its second pandemic lockdown in fall 2020. I had exhausted the number of articles I could write about Greeks sneaking out to drink in *plateias* at night to sidestep curfews. An Egyptian friend mentioned that Egypt had taken a brilliant, or suicidal, approach to the pandemic, depending on which side of the lockdown debate you fell on.

Sisi assumed his fragile economy would collapse if he imposed a lockdown. Cairo was wide open. It sounded like the best place for me, a healthy, footloose, freelance journalist to go. Covid Cairo reminded me of the WWII-era city that the Pringles washed ashore on. Europe was boarded up, but Cairo was full of life. Not with soldiers, spies and exiled European governments, but Egyptian expats and eccentric foreigners waiting out lockdowns. I spent my first few weeks here driving around in a Land Cruiser with moneyed Egyptian friends who chatted in French and played Amr Diab hits. Cairo's traffic is so horrendous, and Egyptian labor so cheap for the rich, that anyone who can afford it has a driver. I have friends in consulting who sit through hours-long Zoom meetings getting from one end of the city to the other.

These friends brought me to nightclubs in Zamalek. The Brits and European royals pulled out when King Farouk was ousted, but Zamalek is still a decadent island. We partied at clubs like Moon Deck where belly dancers flexed their bare midriffs and clubbers swayed in pseudo-oriental dance moves. The music was *mahraganat*, a raw, scratchy street music that is a cross between rap and techno. Egypt was the first Arab country I visited that reminded me of India because of its size and youth. Except here, the poverty was increasing and economy regressing. Egyptians are rightly known for their humor and friendliness, but their society is also rigid and divided by social, religious and class codes. For example, despite the girls' suggestive dance moves and scanty outfits, none of my friends ever hooked up at these clubs. Egypt's Western-educated elite kids can be insular and standoffish. My group rarely considered the world outside their circle of friends. They looked at me like an alien if I so much as talked to a stranger. When I returned to Egypt in 2024

I found people had become more distrustful. In 2020, friends would whisper the names of families they knew whose fathers' businesses had been taken over by the military. Now, they talked about rich kids whose dads' companies worked on military-run construction projects and were not getting paid. Another sign of economic distress.

These kids aren't indicative of the mass of Egyptian society, but they held their own conservative social views. Across the Arab world, sex before marriage is still generally considered taboo and in Egypt, female virginity is put on a pedestal among upper-class Muslims and Christians. "We are sex deprived, but Americans are sex obsessed. It's the opposite extreme. I think you have too much sexual freedom in the United States," one Coptic Christian friend who attended the University of Pennsylvania told me. She was glad to be studying remotely in Cairo during the lockdown, she said, because she struggled to adjust to the ease with which fellow students in the United States slept around.

The street in Cairo is always watching, and judging. There are two sides to this. I felt safer living in Cairo than anywhere in the United States, but also more spied on. I remember one landlord, Shafik, a "Westernized" Egyptian who split his time between Cairo and Toronto, accusing my female friends of being prostitutes for visiting my apartment in the middle of the day. He came up with his own policy to "protect the reputation of his building." Every female guest had to show a passport to prove they were not Egyptian nationals to the *bawab*. Old apartments in Cairo come with these requisite robed gatekeepers. Egyptians truly love their *bawabs*, but to me they are spies. If my *bawab* had to step away from his plastic chair to make tea or run an errand, no worries, he simply banged on my door to request the papers of any female guests afterwards. I soon found a new apartment with a less committed *bawab*.

CAIRO

My male Egyptian friends insisted that for those who can afford it, prostitutes are there for one-night-stands. Many families in the Near East still approach marriage strategically and transactionally. As a result, old-school prostitution is rampant, and awkwardly acknowledged, in cities like Istanbul, Athens and Cairo, in ways that sexually liberated but prudish Westerners can't fathom. Covid-era Cairo was ground-zero for prostitutes from Russia and Ukraine who were locked out of their usual stops in Europe. The girls set up shop in the Sofitel, Intercontinental, and Four Seasons hotels downtown. These behemoth international hotel chains are about the creepiest places I have visited (not that I ever indulged). The lobby bars are filled with Sphinx-obsessed Western tourists and glaring businessmen waiting for their rendezvous. To enter these monstrosities you need to pass barriers and police checkpoints, a tacit admission of how detached they are from Egypt's impoverished reality.

Eventually I got tired of the rich kids and found a bohemian circle of Egyptian friends whose Cairo was reminiscent of Waguih Ghali's 1964 novel *Beer in the Snooker Club*. Set in the aftermath of the 1956 Suez crisis, the novel is about a Coptic Christian, Ram Bey, who struggles to reconcile his leftist anti-colonialism with his British colonial upbringing. Ram Bey pines for Egypt's vanishing cosmopolitanism, but hates the imperial West. He is the quintessential "champagne socialist" with a taste for custom suits and whisky, nonetheless enamored with "resistance" to British and Israeli aggression against the Third-World. As he says, "I would not like to go to prison, but I'd like to have been."[4]

Beer in the Snooker Club challenges many of the easy assumptions about the Middle East that the "West-is-evil-Left" and the "Israel-can-do-no-wrong-Right" beat home. The reality is messier. For example, Ram Bey is an English-educated Copt in love with a Jewish Egyptian who sides with Nasser against Israel during the 1956 Suez Crisis, even as she is harassed by his regime.⁵ Remarkably, a few characters like Ram Bey have survived Egypt's decades of military rule, revolutions and Islamization. I love these loafers, who make downtown Cairo what it is. They lack any of the skills needed to be competitive in a hyper-capitalized, technology-dominated global economy. They have no debt and no net worth. They just exist and drink Stella beer. At some point in time, I suspect, they will be swallowed up by the world. For now, they cling on. The Ram Beys I knew were a mix of Coptic Christians and Sunni Muslims, who hosted booze filled parties on double-decker Nile boats with louche expats. Quite a few of the Egyptians still lived in crumbling Art Deco apartments downtown, paying around $1 a month in rent. This is a legacy of Nasser-era rent control, which destroyed the city center by discouraging investment and building maintenance.

When no one felt like going home at night, we went to dive bars in Wust el-Balad to drink Stella, or Khan Khalili bazaar to smoke *nargile*. "I am a good Muslim. I don't fear Covid. Allah will protect me," I still remember one cafe worker in the bazaar assuring me as he stoked the coals atop our water-pipes.

In my four-year absence, downtown Cairo had become cleaner and more tourist friendly while Egyptians got poorer. Sisi also became edgier. After the collapse of Bashar Assad's government in Syria, he gave a bizarre press conference where he seemed to preempt expectations that his toppling might be next. "My hands are not stained with blood, nor have I taken anyone's money," he said to a group of stone-faced onlookers.⁶

Sisi has learned many lessons from the Arab Spring. I remember an afternoon in 2020 when an old girlfriend and I stopped to take a photo at Tahrir Square. The blond guy and girl with long, silky black hair weren't agitating for an Islamist rebellion. But in no time, a police officer was there admonishing my former girlfriend to put her iPhone away.

Tahrir ("Freedom") Square was the center of the 2011 Arab Spring protests. For eighteen days, Egyptians gathered there in the thousands to demand Mubarak's ouster. They had the ultimate symbol of Egypt's parasitic bureaucracy and deep state looming behind them, the colossal, twelve-story Mogamma Complex, which was the home of dozens of government ministries. Sisi emptied Mogamma of state workers and earmarked it to become a luxury housing development. Admittedly, a great improvement. Tahrir Square is now green and swept clean. But it is also bisected by barriers, fences and raised curbs to stifle any organized form of protest.[7]

As I learned in 2020, Tahrir Square is under twenty-four-hour surveillance.

* * *

Sisi is moving the seat of Egypt's government to a new city, forty-five kilometers into the desert, far away from the Egyptian masses. Egypt's sprawling New Administrative Capital is estimated to cost $59bn. It is the most pharaonic and dazzling in a slew of mega-projects Sisi has ordered to remake Egypt. The government started relocating there in 2023. Sisi has ensured it boasts the biggest of everything in Africa: mosque, church and skyscraper.[8]

What is far from clear is whether it will have any people. Few Egyptians can afford the exorbitant apartment prices. Sisi is building on a dystopian level across Cairo, stacking sprawling overpasses three and four on top of each other, erecting eight-lane highways and new bridges. All of this is contributing to Egypt's economic crisis. The building blowout is being fueled by borrowing, while Egyptians sink deeper into poverty.[9] But Egypt was an economic basket case before Sisi came to power. We have to go back to the 1950s to understand why Egypt failed to develop. The history of the Greeks' exodus from the country is part of the story.

Greeks started arriving during Muhammad Ali's time. Then, Egypt wasn't a place people tried to emigrate from, but immigrate to. Migration has become such a dirty political word in the West that we forget how natural it is to the Near East. The migration crisis is a return to the norm. For 100 years, Greeks left their islands and villages (many of which were still a part of the Ottoman Empire) for Egypt, which offered more opportunities than the fledgling Kingdom of Greece. Remember, mid-nineteenth-century Greece was lawless and impoverished. Up until the 1950s it was wracked by war. In another WWII trilogy, *Drifting Cities*, sums up the flight of Greeks to Egypt:

> Those boys were brought over on warships after Leros fell to the Germans. ... Back in 1922 we had the Asia Minor refugees, in 1897 another bunch. In 1881, there were the people from Chios, who escaped the earthquake, in 1826 the prisoners of Ibrahim Pasha, in 1822 refugees from Chios again, this time escaping the massacre ...We come in waves—wave after wave. The great refugee mother.[10]

The Greek presence in Egypt peaked around the Second World War, when the community numbered 200,000. One popular misconception about the Greeks of Egypt is that they were all like the Benaki family, rich cotton traders and merchants. To be sure, Greeks were financial powerbrokers who built trading firms linking colonial Egypt to the global economy. They were the ultimate fixers. Their playground was Alexandria. I first came to Alexandria through the pages of Lawrence Durrell's *Alexandria Quartet*. Durrell's 1930s Alexandria was a seductive, multi-ethnic playground of "five races, five languages, a dozen creeds, five fleets ... and more than five sexes."[11] In Durrell's world, Jewish socialites sipped cocktails with pashas, Levantine bankers cut deals in the lobby bar of the Cecil Hotel, and the Western expats wallowed in breaking sexual taboos. Well-off Greeks and Levantines might as well have lived in a different city than the Arabs.

The Greeks of Tsirkas' *Drifting Cities* are rawer and less sensational than Durrell's characters. While *Alexandria Quartet* is the more delectable read, *Drifting Cities* is where to go to understand how most Greeks experienced Egypt. Tsirkas' pages evoke a street-level cosmopolitanism. Most Greek Egyptians were lower-middle class shopkeepers, waiters, grocers, factory workers, and tradesmen; a far cry from the world of Durrell's bankers and bohemians. The Greeks were the backbone of industrial Egypt. "You don't have to be particularly smart to know that all the skilled services are held by boys from our schools ... radio communications, interpreters, clerks, engineers, gunners, drivers and so on," one Greek recounts, describing the Greeks' skills in wartime terms.[12] Greeks pop up in every street corner of Jerusalem, Cairo and Alexandria, through where the plot in *Drifting Cities* moves. The protagonist, Manos, is a leftist fighter and hero of the Albanian front. He travels through the Levant, navigating a labyrinth of alliances within the Greek resistance, as Britain attempts to control Greece's government-in-exile.

Scholars still debate to what extent Greeks assimilated into Egypt. In *Drifting Cities*, even lower-middle-class Greeks come across as feeling themselves superior to the Egyptians. Although they are embedded into every fiber of Egyptian society, most Greeks who Manos meets see themselves apart from the country they call home. One of Manos's allies is a Cairene matriarch from the island of Naxos. In one passage, Manos gets into an argument with her husband over the history of Egypt's labor movement. Manos says Greek and Egyptian strikers achieved better working conditions when they acted in solidarity, "Wasn't it back in 1899 that the cigarette workers in the Vafiadis and Melachrino came down on strike, both Arabs and whites together ... didn't the cigarette worker of Alexandria also get what they wanted, because they refused to split the strikers into locals and Europeans?"

But the husband dismisses Manos, "It's obvious you haven't been here long ... This isn't Greece. These local boys need the whip. They've got to fear you, or else you're sunk."[13] The truth about Greek-Egyptian relations in twentieth-century Egypt is somewhere between these views, but probably skews toward the latter.

During Egypt's struggle for independence, the Greeks were caught between colonial Britain, their homeland's patron, and their Egyptian neighbors. In 1919, dozens of Greek shops were burned by Egyptians protesting against foreign communities and the Capitulations. The historian Alexander Kitroeff, who has published an in-depth book on the Greeks of Egypt, said the violence was not specifically anti-Greek. In fact, after the riot, Egyptian nationalists visited the Greek consulate in Cairo to apologize that Greeks were caught in the crossfire. They invoked the Greek Revolution against the Ottomans as a model for Egypt's freedom fight. When Britain exiled Egyptian nationalist leader Saad Zaghlul in 1919, Greeks in the Egyptian countryside protested the move directly to General Edmund Allenby, Britain's high commissioner.[14]

As the nationalist movement gained pace in the 1920s and 1930s, many Greeks tried to accommodate the Egyptians' aspirations. Leading Greek intellectuals like Evgenios Michaelidis, a Greek Jerusalemite, emphasized Greeks' positive role in developing Egyptian commerce and industry. He argued that Greeks had been living in Egypt since pharaonic times. Another thinker, Georgios Arvanitakis, highlighted Greeks and Egyptians as indigenous to Egypt, saying that the ancient Greek presence there was almost snuffed out by Arab invaders and saved by Muhammad Ali. Later, left-wing Greeks made common cause with the nationalists in part to preserve the Greek presence in Egypt.[15]

Tsirkas was a Greek Egyptian who published *Drifting Cities* as the Greek exodus from Egypt was taking place in the early 1960s. He peppers his novel with harbingers of the Greeks' downfall. "This war [the Second World War] is merely paving the way for the return of Beduin culture," one character in Alexandria warns the Greeks.[16]

Tsirkas's Greek matriarch is repulsed by her husband's contempt for the Egyptians. She believes attitudes like his will spell the end for the Greeks, saying, "Why do you dig this ditch between you and them … Why do you keep apart? … The day will come. I can see the crowds jostling on the pier, surrounded by mountains of suitcases and piles of mattresses."[17]

Manos, the protagonist, is electrified when he detects traces of Greece in Egypt. In one passage he realizes Egyptian vegetable sellers are hawking their produce in the Greek language, and reflects, "Suddenly it occurred to me they were Greek words and I was in Egypt … [E]arlier vegetable men must surely have been Greeks … [T]he street call remained in the trade, and was now being used by the Egyptian vendors who had replaced the Greeks." But he inhabits a world of twentieth-century nationalisms. He wants to drive the Nazis out of Greece and make it a socialist haven for the diaspora after the war, not preserve the Greek presence in Egypt:

> When the Greeks grew scarcer, would the produce men of Alexandria still hawk their celery and marrow in Greek? They would grow scarcer … they would disappear in the end. In the new Greece we were about to build, there would be bread for all and this age-old diaspora, this hemorrhage would end at last.[18]

Egypt ended the system of Capitulations in 1937, but by then the Greeks had assimilated so deeply into the economy that they didn't need special protection. They also wanted to stay. Egypt's economy was booming in the 1940s. It's hard to imagine now, but right up until the mid-1950s Egypt was an international destination. It boasted architecture like the Immobilia building, a streamlined Art Deco skyscraper that was the largest tower in the Middle East. Cairo was the cultural capital of the Arab world with a powerful cinema industry that drew visits from Western stars like Rita Hayworth.

Nasser and the Free Officers who ousted King Farouk in the 1952 coup did not set about to destroy this world. They wanted in on it. Dubbed "effendis in uniform," they were young, middle-class army officers who lunched at Cafe Riche. They tapped into the populist demand of an "Egypt for Egyptians." The coup was led by Nasser and General Mohammad Naguib. It is often framed as the end of the Greek presence in Egypt. What I find most poignant, however, is how the Greeks tried to stay. Naguib initially reassured the Greeks and other foreign communities they had nothing to fear. Greek newspapers in Egypt welcomed the Free Officers to power. Later, when Nasser swept Naguib aside and nationalized the Suez Canal, the Greeks of Egypt (and the Greek government) publicly supported the move. Although, as Kitroeff wrote, "privately many Greeks hoped the Anglo-French would force Egypt to reverse the nationalization."[19]

By 1957, the Greeks were under serious economic pressure because of the steady stream of Egyptianization measures. These laws restricted companies' ability to hire non-Egyptians, forced them to fire foreigners, and curtailed which businesses Greeks could run. That in turn put pressure on the schools, hospitals and charitable institutions that the Greeks used to support the community. Still, as late as 1961, at least 40,000 Greeks remained in Egypt. That year was pivotal because Nasser embraced a socialist economy head-on. In the end, there was no reconciling the Greeks' enterprising, cosmopolitan existence with Nasser's toxic blend of socialism and Arab nationalism. The final blow to the Greeks came when Nasser ordered the nationalization of practically the entire Egyptian economy. Greek business owners were locked out of their shops and factories. The Greeks became foreigners in cities they had called homes for generations. Only a few fled to Greece. Most ended up going to South Africa, Australia or the United States.

"We were never expelled from Egypt outright like the Greeks of Istanbul, so we don't have the political trauma, but it was a sort of de facto expulsion," Giannis Melachrinoudis, a Greek Cairene told me. Melachrinoudis is one of the less than 2,000 Greeks who remain in Egypt. I arranged to meet him and half a dozen other Greek Egyptians at the Greek Club in downtown Cairo. I went to our dinner assuming the community would be bitter and stale, absorbed in grievance-driven politics like so many people in the Middle East who share a similar history of displacement. Instead, my Greek hosts were wise, charming, funny, and perceptive observers. They made wonderful drinking companions.

"Look, the Egyptians needed to have a say in their country. It wasn't fair," Melachrinoudis explained. "The Greeks were business people and foreign, they didn't jibe with Nasser's vision of the country. What can we do?"

"Overnight, Greeks who ran factories and banks, or worked as electricians and mechanics were told they no longer had their businesses and jobs. The Greeks were replaced by Army officers and Nasserists with no knowledge of what they were taking over. Egyptian industry was ruined," Alexandros, one of the Greeks at our table, explained to me. "Egypt never fully recovered."

He motioned at the bottles of Stella beer and Gianaclis wine on our table.

"Both of these were owned by Greek businessmen. The Egyptian on the street doesn't know that. At one time, Gianaclis wine was so esteemed that France, the nation of wine, actually imported it. After the nationalizations, the quality dropped. Finally, in the 1990s the government brought in French experts to advise Gianaclis and middle-class locals drink it again," he explained.

Greeks, Italians, Levantines, Jews and Armenians were the juggernaut of Egypt's economy. Nasser effectively kicked out all these skilled workers, financiers and manufacturers. His popularity soared by redistributing the wealth foreign communities had accumulated. But by the mid-1960s, he had run out of riches to recycle.

"There is no talk of pie in the sky and a glorious socialistic future just around the corner. Instead, the masses are being told to tighten their belts today and that tomorrow may be grimmer, not better," the *New York Times* reported in December 1965.[20]

The same article could be written today.

Then, as now, Egypt's economy faced food shortages, soaring inflation and a currency crunch. Sisi even channeled his inner Nasser in October 2023, when he gave a rambling speech that echoed, almost word for word, one Nasser delivered sixty years earlier:

> Listen, if the price of building, development and progress is hunger and deprivation, don't you dare not progress, Egyptians! Don't you dare say, "It's better that we eat!" By God almighty, if the price of the nation's progressing and prospering is that it doesn't eat and drink as others do, then we won't eat and drink.[21]

Is it any wonder that my Greek hosts say their generation will be the last Greeks in Egypt? The Greeks came here for economic opportunity and Egypt's cratering economy will drive the last of them out.

* * *

One of the Greeks at our table was Angelo Athanassoulis. "I'm in the garment business," he said by way of introducing himself.

In fact, he was a third-generation manufacturer. I was surprised. At the time, I thought he must be the last Greek industrialist left in Egypt.

"I am an expert on polo shirts," he said with the flare of a connoisseur. "My polos were so good all the boutiques in Cannes and Nice ordered from me. They said 'don't even ship to our warehouse. Send them directly to the store.'"

Athanassoulis sports a long mane of black hair. He exuded an aging playboy, disco-star style. He wore a high, cutaway collar shirt that rakishly popped out over his tan sports jacket. When he spoke, his wrists jingled with bracelets and a fine watch.

"When I was a teenager, they used to wash downtown's streets at night. Back then, we could still race sports cars here. Look around now, trash everywhere, incessant traffic. They destroyed it," he told me.

The Greek Club is located above the storied Groppi Cafe at Talaat Harb Square. It was one of the most privileged addresses in Cairo. Talaat Harb is a gem, encircled by Haussmanian buildings. The square is one of the better kept parts of Wust el-Balad.

Athanassoulis caught the tail-end of Egypt's glamorous era. He had his own run-ins with the country's elite over the years. He clearly enjoyed growing up here.

"I don't judge a man's wealth by how much money he has in the bank, but by how much he spends. Because that's where his experiences come from. Experiences make you rich," he said.

He told me about a time when Gamal Nasser's son, Khalid Abdel Nasser, discovered that he had imported a rare vintage Corvette into Egypt. The younger Nasser had a fearsome reputation and at one point stood trial for being part of a leftist revolutionary group that assassinated two Israeli diplomats. He was later acquitted.

> Khalid Abdel Nasser came to my factory surrounded by men with submachine guns. He wanted my car as a gift for his son. I loved that car, but my mother told me "you can't refuse Gamal Nasser's son." I agreed to sell, and he gave me a bag full of cash which I never opened. Some days later, Khalid called me and said he couldn't give the Corvette to his son because it was too fast.

Athanassoulis was smiling. By now, he had the attention of our table. "I went to pick up my car and return his bag of money at his house in Heliopolis," he said. "As I was about to leave, Khalid called me over and said, 'you never opened the bag. I see you are an honest man.'" Athanassoulis continued, "Nasser showed me a note that he had placed on top of the money which said, and I quote: 'I promise to help you do anything legal or illegal in Egypt.' It was his gift in return for me selling the car. That's the governing mentality here."

I was curious how Athanassoulis managed to keep his family's garment factory. Hadn't all the Greek firms from that era been nationalized? It turned out the Corvette incident wasn't his family's first encounter with the Nassers.

> My grandfather started the factory in Port Said when the British were here. In 1911, Queen Mary docked at the port. All the business owners were expected to fly the Union Jack. My grandfather was lazy and didn't feel like waking up in the morning to put up the flag. The British arrested him. Nasser heard this story when he came to power and asked to meet the Greek who refused to fly the British flag. He gave my grandfather a medal and when the nationalizations happened, excluded our factory.

Despite its grand interior and formal setting, the Greek Club emitted all the easy charm and unpretentiousness of the Near East at its finest. It is an oasis. Decaying Levantine cities do oases well. You can't quite define what makes an oasis. But the place has a certain rhythm. It can be an austere Mediterranean garden or bustling cafe.

At the Greek Club, waiters shuffled around with trays of mezze and Stella beer bottles. Conversations echoed from the parquetry wood floors to the high ceilings. But it had a dignity missing in Egypt. The club opened in 1893. At first, it was only for elite Greek men.

"Working class Greeks had to cross to the other side of street as a sign of respect to their bosses when they passed by," one of my hosts explained. Now, the board is Greek (Athanassoulis is the treasurer), but since 1952 the club has been open for everyone.

The Greek Club is one of the few spots in Cairo where you can find foreign ambassadors and old-money Zamalek families sitting next to ordinary Egyptians. The Greeks of Egypt have managed to keep the Levantine charm of Waguih Ghali's Cairo going, despite their near extinction. The club has none of the Dubai-like iciness and oppressive sleekness that most Cairo restaurants serving alcohol (a cultural and class divider in the Muslim world) try to replicate. Anyone can walk into the Greek Club and sip a beer, or not. The restaurant has two outdoor patios, which is practically unheard of for downtown, where bars are hidden. On a Tuesday night, the tables were packed with young Egyptians. I spotted one pious looking Muslim couple walk in, curiously look around and sit down with menus. I sensed that Cairo's stifling cultural and class fault-lines had been left at the door. Egypt desperately needs more Greek Clubs.

"It has been a big success. Ten years ago, the club felt like it was dying. Our board turned it around and made it trendy to hang out here. We have a lot of fun with it, too. The Greek food is good," Christos Cavallis, the Greek Community's President told me. "I think Egyptians craved a place like this, but no one was giving it to them."

Like Athanassoulis, Cavallis is an industrialist. He owns a paper mill. As we tucked into our *saganaki* and *keftedes*, he showed me videos from his factory of raw paper being pulverized and turned into fluffy tissues.

"On the one hand, the community is stronger than it has been in decades. Our finances are in good shape and culturally we are very powerful. The government likes the community. But our numbers are shrinking. The people around this table are the last pure Greeks of Egypt you will meet," he said, explaining that mixed marriages with Coptic Egyptians had become more common. Young people are also leaving.

I was curious what the last Greek businessmen in Egypt made of the economic crisis. My Greek hosts understood the sweep of Egyptian history because their families had lived so much of it. There was a surreal quality about sitting in the Greek Club with them discussing the implosion of Egypt's economy. I could almost sense the old cotton traders and financiers smoking their cigars here, plotting their exit in the early 1950s. My hosts painted a bleak picture.

"In the 1980s we had good times. You could make serious money as a manufacturer. Things started going downhill in the 1990s after the first Gulf War, then the 2011 revolution. The last four years killed any hope the economy would improve. Egypt is just limping along. It is unfixable," Athanassoulis told me matter of factly. "A lost cause."

Cavallis chimed in. "I am in a position now that I never imagined I would be, sitting with a customer and not knowing how to price my product because inflation just keeps rising. I don't know where the currency will be tomorrow."

Egypt started a series of currency devaluations in 2016 as part of the requirements for an IMF loan. Egypt first turned to the international lender in 1991. It has become a repeat customer. Over the last thirty years, the IMF loans have multiplied, while

Egypt's economic prospects keep getting worse. Egypt is the IMF's second largest debtor.

The devaluations were not enough to restore investor confidence. Admittedly, Egypt had some bad breaks. Russia's invasion of Ukraine scared international creditors. Foreign investors who had bought billions of dollars of Egyptian debt lured by high interest rates suddenly got cold feet and pulled their money. The war also pitted Egypt's two top suppliers of wheat, Ukraine and Russia, against each other, driving up prices of the commodity and further stretching the government's budget.

By 2024, Egypt's lingering support for its currency was becoming untenable, with the IMF and the Gulf states who back Egypt demanding the government allow the pound to float freely on the market. So in March 2024, the Egyptian government stopped supporting the currency. Overnight the pound leaped in trading from thirty to the dollar to fifty. Egypt secured an additional $8bn loan from the IMF. The UAE's $35bn purchase of rights to develop a slice of its Mediterranean coast was also part of the rescue plan.[22]

"They are all just storing up trouble. Financial gimmicks because everyone is scared to see Egypt go bankrupt," one of the Greeks down the table shouted across to us. "It would be anarchy on Israel's borders and the Mediterranean."

Egypt was vulnerable to external shocks because of deep-seated structural issues. When all is said and done, it creates very little value for the global economy in terms of services or manufactured goods. Its main sources of foreign currency are all based on rent-seeking behavior, despite being a country of more than 100 million. So the devaluations, which were supposed to make exports more competitive and wean the country off expensive imports, created poverty. Meanwhile, Sisi has kept spending lavishly on mega-projects.

"I remember during the Greek Crisis, we had austerity. It upset a lot of people, but it worked to get the finances back in shape. Prices dropped. Here we have the opposite. A debt crisis and more spending and higher prices," one of the Greeks said.

For Egyptians, whose wages are in pounds, life is brutally expensive.

"Egypt is becoming more third-world," one of my Greek hosts said.

For manufacturers who need to import raw materials, like cotton for garments or wood for paper, the currency's crash has been disastrous. Still, why couldn't Egypt become an export hub for Europe? Aren't its low wages and proximity to the continent competitive advantages?

"If it could have, it's too late now," Athanassoulis told me. Egypt needs to create 800,000 jobs every year for young people entering its labor market, but is failing to do so. One reason, the Greeks told me, is a cultural aversion to manufacturing. "Egyptians who leave the country are hardworking, but those who stay want a government job or a desk position. They don't respect manufacturing," one said.

Athanassoulis' wife is from Thessaloniki. She left Egypt for her hometown and is raising their two daughters there. "I stayed for my work. I visit when I can. When I retire, that will be the end of our family in Egypt. My daughters have zero future in this country."

Cavallis told me that with Egypt's pound floating freely and little trust in the currency, Egypt is undergoing a de-facto dollarization. "My wife went out to buy a packet of pens last week and came home sticker-shocked, but I knew what she paid right away. 'It is simple,' I said, 'just assume the price for imported pens is the same you would pay in Athens.' Watch, the next years Egypt will price everything in dollars."

But the Greek community is flourishing. The club's board isn't paid. Profits go to supporting the community's 2,000 members and maintaining properties it owns. Demand for the Greek Club experience is so high that the board is now building a second club in Dahab, a Red Sea scuba diving town. "The idea was that we are generating a lot of profit off the club, but if we keep it in the bank, it will be worthless because of inflation, so we might as well invest it," Cavallis told me. "What can we do, cry in a corner and hide? If this is the end, we might as well have fun."

7

PRIESTS AND CRYPTO-CHRISTIANS

INTRIGUE IN JERUSALEM

I traveled alone in Greece's borderlands and Egypt. I ate dinner for one outside shabby gyro and shawarma stands, then washed down the aftertaste of onion and grilled meat with cheap local beer. Most nights, I listened to underemployed, inherently conservative young men, ramble about sex, inflation, and immigration. The Egyptians all wanted to leave their homeland and their Greek counterparts wanted to stop them from coming to theirs. Otherwise, the guys were the same. Prices were too high for everyone. The Greeks bragged about how many girls they had bedded and the Egyptians asked if I was married. These were the crude exchanges that a single male traveler conjures up in the Near East. I desperately needed a break.

Direct flights from Cairo to Tel Aviv were on hold during the Gaza war. So, from Egypt I flew back to Athens and jumped on a cheap flight to Israel. Less than three months had passed since my younger brother landed in Jerusalem for his first posting as a junior American diplomat. Our parents had birthed two sons, two years apart in age, who had both absconded to the Near East. Neither of us could shake our Greek roots.

After months of traveling, in November 2024, I savored plopping myself down at my brother's apartment, already decorated for Christmas by his fiancé. Their plush State Department-provided housing was in the leafy and upscale Jewish neighborhood of Arnona, which reminded me of the mind-numbing, perfectly laid-out suburbs in the United States. We spent little time there. My brother, who speaks Arabic and Greek with accents I envy, had already burrowed his way into Jerusalem's Palestinian and shrinking Greek communities in the Old City's Christian quarter. Its limestone alleys became our haunt.

I have spent years reporting on the budding alliance between Greece and Israel. The 2020 Abraham Accords, in which Israel established diplomatic relations with the United Arab Emirates, Bahrain, and Morocco, overshadowed this Mediterranean alliance, but their ties are just as strategic and transformative for the region. Afterall, the United Arab Emirates and Morocco's royal families covertly partnered with Israel for decades, whereas Greece was cool, and at times downright hostile, to Zionism after Israel's founding. Today, their partnership is built on three key ingredients that keep this region spinning: tourism, cheap sunny real estate, and geopolitics.

Israelis are one of the main drivers of Greece's rip-roaring property market. The war unleashed by Hamas's 7 October attack turbocharged a buying spree that has been underway for the last ten years. It is impossible to walk around gentrifying Athenian neighborhoods today and not hear Hebrew. Israelis are drawn to Greece by its substantially cheaper prices compared to back home, and convenience: Tel Aviv and Athens are just a two-hour flight apart. White collar Israeli tech workers are flexing their Tel Aviv salaries while living in substantially cheaper Athens. This trend is reshaping Greece's capital and stoking a certain amount of resentment among ordinary Greeks who are getting priced out.

Benjamin Netanyahu has been the mastermind of the alliance on the Israeli side, but Israeli home buyers tend to be the secular, beach-going ones who loathe the powerful, extreme religious Zionists and ultranationalists in his government. Most Israelis I know in Athens hate Netanyahu.[1] Despite the war, my November flight from Athens to Tel Aviv was fully booked with Israelis crisscrossing the Mediterranean.

At its core, the Greek-Israel alliance is based on raw geopolitics. It partly reflects the United States diminishing interest in this region. The Greek-Israel alliance reminds me vaguely of the Coptic-Jewish one imagined by Durrell in the *Alexandria Quartet*. Durrell conjured up a world where Coptic Christian Egyptians covertly allied with the Zionists because of Britain's retreat from the Middle East. Greece and Israel, along with Cyprus, are the only non-Muslim-majority countries in the Eastern Mediterranean. Israel, Greece and Cyprus are joining forces to check the ambitions of Türkiye's new sultan, Erdoğan, as the United States pulls back.

Yet, American retreat has become such a throwaway line, it is now over-emphasized. In the Eastern Mediterranean at least, the United States still enjoys unprecedented hegemony when measured against its rivals, of whom only China can be called a peer competitor. In fact, the United States' relative influence in the region compared to its foes has increased since 7 October. The devastating wars and bombings Israel unleashed on Gaza, Lebanon and Syria after the Hamas attack strengthened the United States and Israel's dual domination of the Levant. Besides their toehold in Piraeus, the Chinese are practically absent in the Eastern Mediterranean. Russia buried its chances for soft power in Greece by invading Ukraine, and more importantly, is sidelined in post-Assad Syria. Putin, like Stalin, ceded the Eastern Mediterranean as a sphere of influence in order to make a rearguard action pushing back against NATO expansion in far Eastern Europe. Israel's strategic takedown of Hezbollah and the collapse of the Assad dynasty were brutal body blows to Iran. The Islamic Republic is at its weakest point since its founding. But just because its foes are degraded, doesn't mean the United States is stepping in more. Look to Syria: having won the long war to oust Iran and Russia, the United States is willingly ceding Türkiye and Qatar a greater zone of influence. Ankara's rising power, and the United States' indifference to it, is what unites the Greeks and Israelis.

This makes sense when you understand the basics of Israel and Greece's modern founding. The two are alike in more ways than one. Both owe their existence to the military, economic, and political backing of Western superpowers, whose steady hand they can no longer take for granted. First it was the British Empire that became exhausted, and now the United States.

What journalist David Holden rightly pinned as "the manifest destiny of modern Greece as a western protectorate," applies equally to Israel.[2] At their core, Greece and Israel are Western-backed nation-states in the Near East for non-Muslim diasporas. Holden observed that,

> A Greek need never cease to be a Greek even unto an infinity of generations, so long as he is Christened in the Greek church and registered with an appropriate official ... [W]here he is born or where he lives, what passport he may hold or what foreign causes he may serve are immaterial ... Like a Jew who "returns" to Israel from anywhere in the world.[3]

Both are vulnerable neo-protectorates used for American power-projection in the wider Middle East. They could wobble if they lose the American security umbrella. For now, the Israel-

Greece alliance is underwritten by Washington. A case in point is the Americans' pet project, however fanciful, to fashion a trade corridor from India through the Arab Gulf to Greece to challenge China.

Arriving in Israel at wartime, it was impossible not to talk about the Israeli-Palestinian conflict. The Greeks have a part in it, which makes the alliance with Israel all the more ironic. At the same time that Greece and Israel have strengthened ties, the Greek Orthodox Church is coming under relentless attacks from emboldened Jewish settlers and ultranationalists who want to take its land.

Before 7 October, I spent little time as a journalist reporting directly on the Israel-Palestine conflict. I never pitched a story on it. My Greek roots drew me to this region. They shaped my concept of a wider Middle East, certainly one much bigger than just the Israeli and Palestinian peoples. Despite their bloody conflict, both are united in believing that their cause should have a monopoly of sorts on the region. That is their right. Living overseas, it was the American media's coverage of this conflict that caused my gut-reflex move away from it. The obsession with Israel in American political life is tiresome and fawning, detached from the ugly realities on the ground of the Israeli occupation. At the same time, the Palestinians struck me, tragically, as their own worst enemies. Their cause was too easy for Israel to isolate because its mantle was picked up, first, by bankrupt Leftist-Marxist movements and later Islamists. The Palestinians needed a Venizelos but never got one. The sclerotic Palestinian secular leaders who emerged from the 1990s Oslo Peace Process are viewed by many Palestinians as corrupt and as no more than collaborators for the Israeli occupation of the West Bank. They failed to deliver on their pledge of ushering in a sovereign, viable Palestinian state through peaceful negotiations. Israel, through its relentless expansion of settlements, sabotaged them.

During my stay, besides a sojourn to Bethlehem and meetings in Tel Aviv, I based myself in Jerusalem, home to a small Greek community and the Orthodox Patriarchate. Make no mistake about it, Jerusalem is the crucible of the Israeli-Palestinian conflict. Not only is occupied East Jerusalem the envisioned capital of a future Palestinian state, but it is the most likely spot for the conflict to become international, because it is home to more sacred places of the three Abrahamic religions—Islam, Judaism and Christianity—than anywhere else in the world. The most combustible piece of real estate here is Al-Aqsa compound, home to Al-Aqsa Mosque and the golden Dome of the Rock, a shrine that Muslim tradition says is the spot where the Prophet Muhammad ascended to heaven. It is also considered by Jews to be the site of the First and Second Temples—the latter destroyed by the Romans in 70 CE. Israeli extremists have the fanatical, messianic goal of demolishing Al-Aqsa and rebuilding a synagogue on the site. Just initiating this step would be the final blow to a delicate balance of religious power that is being degraded by the Jewish settler movement. Less well known, but equally important to the distribution of influence in Jerusalem, is the Greek Orthodox Patriarchate. The Greek Orthodox Church is the second largest landowner in Israel after the Israeli government. In fact, it leases the government the land the Knesset, or parliament, is built on, and holds title to about thirty per cent of real estate within Jerusalem's walled Old City. The settlers want the land.

"If the Orthodox Church sells one spot of land in Jerusalem, it can upend the entire chessboard," a Greek diplomat here explained to me.

The Greeks I met in Jerusalem said the latest effort to undermine the Christian presence here is a push by the Jerusalem municipality to get the Greek Orthodox Church and other Christian churches to pay property taxes on their commercial real estate holdings. This would destroy a longtime status quo that has exempted churches from taxes on the grounds that they use the revenue to fund their operations and run schools, charities and hospitals. The plan threatens the churches with retroactive taxes going back to 1996.

The senior Greek diplomat I met called the Israeli move an effort to "bankrupt the churches." The Greek Church acquired most of its properties during the nineteenth century when Jerusalem was part of the Ottoman Empire. Although land rich, it is cash poor. Its real estate is tied up in ninety-nine-year leases signed with Israeli institutions after Israel's founding. These generate little income, and some Jewish tenants can extend them indefinitely.[4] As a result, the church—deeply in debt—has turned to selling off its properties, often at cut-rate prices to Israeli settler groups. In 2005, a scandal over one sale led to an international incident that dragged in the King of Jordan and the George W. Bush administration.

The Petra Hotel affair erupted in 2004 after the Greek Church sold two iconic buildings housing hotels next to Jerusalem's Jaffa Gate to the American Jewish settler group Ateret Cohanim. At the time, the Petra Hotel alone was valued at a minimum of $10 million, but was sold for a mere $500,000. The deal had everything for a sordid tabloid story: corrupt Greek priests, backstabbing in the Patriarchate, and blackmail linked to sex scandals, including among the clergy.[5] The head of Ateret Cohanim was caught in recordings openly discussing bribing a bishop and offering prostitutes to the Church's Palestinian tenant.[6] It took another twist when the former Greek patriarch, Eirinaios I, blamed his accountant for the sale, alleging the Greek bookkeeper forged documents to seal the deal.[7]

The Palestinian Christians were furious at the Greek priests for selling two crown jewels in Jerusalem's geopolitical monopoly board to their enemies. Protests erupted. The Palestinians wanted Eirinaios' head. But the former Greek monk barricaded himself inside the Patriarchate and refused to leave. That's when Patriarch Bartholomew of Constantinople got involved. He called a meeting of all the heads of the Orthodox Churches in Istanbul, an unprecedented council, where the majority voted to withdraw recognition of Eirinaios over the deal.

The governments of Israel, the Palestinian Authority and Jordan are all required to agree to who the Greek Patriarch of Jerusalem should be. Jordan's role goes back to the British Mandate era, when its Hashemite royal family was awarded custodianship of the Muslim and Christian holy sites in Jerusalem. Because the patriarch is always a Greek, Athens also has some influence over who is selected. The process is obscured behind layers of byzantine intrigue, money and politics. In the past, Greek factions have used savage media campaigns to attack rivals for the seat. During Eirinaios' first election, some Greek newspapers ran photos allegedly showing his rival engaging in a homosexual orgy. The latter's supporters said the photos were doctored.

In 2005, Jordan, Greece and the Palestinian Authority pulled their support for Eirinaios over the Petra Hotel scandal, but Israel dug in. Before agreeing to the current patriarch, Theophilos III, Israel allegedly sought assurances he would not dispute the sale of the hotels and would in fact sell more properties to settler groups.[8] Although the church challenged the validity of the sale, several well-placed sources I met in Jerusalem familiar with the proceedings believe the Patriarchate withheld evidence that could have advanced its case in court.

Intrigue wafts around Jerusalem's Greek Church like a pungent incense from the city's old souk. The deepest sore point is the fact that the patriarch is Greek, as are nearly all the Church leadership, including the Brotherhood of the Holy Sepulchre (the mysterious body of monks from which the patriarch is chosen), while its flock is Palestinian.

PRIESTS AND CRYPTO-CHRISTIANS

These tensions predate the Israeli-Palestinian conflict by about 100 years. It is mainly an elite dispute. Since at least the nineteenth century, the Palestinians and Greeks in the Holy Land have fought over the Church's revenues and properties. The feud is a legacy of how European nationalisms seeped into the cosmopolitan Near East.

After all, during Ottoman times, one's *millet*, the legal community through which the sultan's subjects governed their affairs, was determined by religion. Language and ethnicity came third or fourth down the rung in shaping identity. Then European nationalisms took hold. The Palestinians started to claim that until the Crusades in 1099, when a Latin patriarch was installed, the Arabs were the ones who wielded power in the Patriarchate. That changed when the Ottomans conquered the city and appointed Patriarch Germanus, a Greek who the Arabs say Hellenized the church. The Palestinians point out that unlike the Bulgarians or Russians, they do not have a national Patriarchate. The Greeks respond by saying that the original leadership of the Church was Greek, going back to the Byzantine Empire.[9]

The spat has historically been fueled by Great Power competition. Anti-Greek sentiment among Palestinians was stirred up by the Russian Empire, whose missionaries and diplomats in the Holy Land encouraged the Arabs to split from the Greek Church to boost the tsar's influence. One of the tsar's chief agents was a Russian Arabophile monk named Antonin Kapustin, who purchased swaths of land in Palestine in the 1860s for the Russian Church. The Imperial Orthodox Palestine Society, the Tsarist-era organization formed to expand Moscow's influence among Eastern Christians, also mobilized against the Greek clergy and built churches and schools in the Holy Land. This is the same group Greece accused of running covert influence operations in its borderlands during the North Macedonia name dispute in 2018.[10]

THE NEW BYZANTINES

The tensions are palpable in Jerusalem. Greek priests I met there lamented how, "we lost Antioch," when describing the only ancient patriarchate in the Near East headed by an Arab and not a Greek. The current patriarch of Antioch is based in Damascus, Syria.

In recent years, Russia has stepped up its efforts to regain its foothold in Jerusalem. Moscow is trying to claw back properties that were divided by competing White and Red Russian Churches after the 1917 Bolshevik Revolution. These chunks of real estate later became Cold War bargaining chips. Russia lost most of them. One man in Moscow personally oversees Russian property matters in Jerusalem, diplomats here told me: his name is Vladimir Putin. For Putin, regaining these properties is a crusade. In 2008 Israel transferred back to Russia part of a complex built in the nineteenth century for Russian Orthodox pilgrims, called the Sergei Courtyard. Russia is still trying to get back more real estate including Alexander's Courtyard and Catherine's Courtyard. Israel famously purchased much of Russia's land in 1964 from the Soviet Union for $3.4 million-worth of Jaffa oranges. After Putin invaded Ukraine, he sent a letter to Israel demanding it hand back ownership of these Tsarist-era properties.[11]

Palestinian Christians like to say that they are biggest Orthodox demographic in the Holy Land, but they have competition. Because they are the most educated and cosmopolitan of Palestinians, the Christians have been the most likely to pack up and leave, instead of enduring the Israeli occupation. As a result, only around 50,000 Palestinian Christians remain in Jerusalem and the occupied West Bank. The vast majority are Greek Orthodox. In addition, roughly seven per cent of the 1.8-million strong Palestinian citizens of Israel are Christian. But Palestinian Orthodox Christians have lost their numerical weight in the Holy Land to Slavic speakers who are citizens of Israel.[12]

PRIESTS AND CRYPTO-CHRISTIANS

Father Petros, a Greek priest who has lived in Jerusalem for more than thirty years, and whose name I have changed so he could speak freely, told me Russians and Ukrainians now comprise the largest demographic attending the Greek Orthodox Church.

Father Petros invited me and my brother to his stone-walled abode tucked deep in the Christian quarter of the Old City. As we sipped sweet Greek red wine, he showed us a collection of furniture that he had custom ordered from Syria, inlaid with mother of pearl. Like most of the Greek priests I met, he was a Greek nationalist down to his bones. He was worried about the future of the Patriarchate. "Mark my words, in ten years we won't have a Greek patriarch. Putin wants it badly," he said. "The Russians are putting down roots here. They pray secretly. There are no Greeks left. The Palestinian Christians are leaving."

These crypto-Christian Russians and Ukrainians started making *Aliyah* ("ascent") to Israel after the collapse of the Soviet Union by claiming Jewish ancestry. The majority of the 1.3 million Russian speakers in Israel are in fact Jewish, but in interviews with church leaders and diplomats, I was told that at least 150,000 of these Slavic speakers are secretly Orthodox Christians. You see them everywhere chatting in Slavic languages; in the Church of the Nativity in Bethlehem and the Church of the Holy Sepulchre. Five months after my first visit, I was back in Jerusalem for Easter. My brother, another American diplomat, and I were stuck between hundreds of Russians and Ukrainians—hardly a Palestinian or Greek in sight besides the priests and Greek Consul General—raising our candles to welcome the resurrection during the Patriarchate's midnight church service.

After the war in Ukraine erupted, an additional 84,000 Russians immigrated to Israel.[13] Officially, 45,000 Ukrainians also came, but a chubby Ukrainian diplomat in Tel Aviv told me he was working overtime to account for at least 120,000 more of his countrymen living illegally in Israel. "They celebrate Christmas and Easter at home, not Hanukah," the diplomat said, laughing. "Some Israeli diplomats in Ukraine got very rich creating new Jews."

In fact, a study released in November 2024 by the Knesset's research office found that nearly three out of every four new immigrants to Israel from the former Soviet Union in 2020 were not Jewish, according to how the Israeli government defines a Jew. The Israeli government considers them to have "no religion" but the Greek priests I met said these Israeli citizens were popping up in their pews.[14]

In sum, the Patriarchate is stuck with an unpopular Greek leadership, a shrinking Palestinian flock, and tens of thousands of Israeli crypto-Christians. It is also under attack from Jewish settlers. No wonder the Greek priests I met in Jerusalem were so prone to worrying about conspiracies involving a Russian power grab. They are on shaky ground.

* * *

Dimitri Diliani grew up with the Greek-Arab Church rift. He was married in an Episcopal Church because of Palestinian hostility to the Greek Patriarchate. His Greek family name, which he shares with an assassinated nineteenth-century Greek prime minister, comes from his grandfather, he told me, a communist who left Greece to join the Palestinians' fight against the British Mandate and Jewish militias.

Diliani was one of the chief architects of the campaign that ousted Eirinaios I. He is also a figure to watch in Palestinian politics. He is the spokesman for Fatah's Democratic Reform Current, a secular Palestinian political party.

Diliani and I met at a cafe in Beit Hanina, an upper-middle-class Palestinian suburb in East Jerusalem. On Saturday mornings, during Shabbat, you can hear a pin drop in Jerusalem. Ultra-Orthodox families stroll the city, the men in black robes, their wives with skirts down to the ankles and legions of little kids. The Palestinian neighborhoods wake up late. Beit Hanina was just starting to come alive when my brother and I arrived.

I asked Diliani about the rift in the church.

"It's a long history. The tsar started it, the communists kept it going and then the Arab nationalists. The Greek patriarch is discredited among the Palestinians," he told me, with a New Jersey drawl. He went to college there and credits his time in the US for "waking him up" to the dangers of socialism.

"I came to the United States a hardcore communist believing in all their shit. Once I saw life in America, how rich it is, it took me one day to drop it," he said. Politics is a side-gig for Diliani, who works in real estate development to "pay the bills."

"The feud with the Greek priests is not something Palestinians wake up with every day, but if you ask them how they feel, the answer you will get is they do not like the Greeks in charge of the church," he explained.

"I led the effort to get rid of Eirinaios I. But what I tell people is that Arabization of the church equals Israelization. One of the only things standing between the destruction of the Orthodox Church and all of its lands in Palestine by Israeli settlers is its link to Greece. This is an EU and NATO country. If the Patriarchate is totally Arabized, the church will have no protection. Two groups want that, the Islamists with Hamas and the Jewish settlers," he said. "They have the same interest to take down the Greek Church."

Diliani hasn't lost his New Jersey swagger. He has just come from his family's regular weekend breakfast at his mom's house. He is wearing beefy black-frame glasses with an Off-White label, a University of Pennsylvania baseball cap and Penn State sweater.

He looks more like a finance executive out for a weekend stroll than a Palestinian political operator.

He is on the side of Palestinian politics which loathes Hamas. "We had radical Islamists, promoting all this Muslim Brotherhood crap for too long," Diliani said. He heads a group trying to get more Christians to understand the threats Palestinian Christians face in the Holy Land from the Israeli government.

I asked if there is a secular alternative within Palestinian politics to Hamas. "Of course," he replied, "Fatah. Arafat was the most secular Palestinian leader I knew."

Fatah is the dominant party in the Palestinian Authority, known as the PA, which emerged out of the 1990s Oslo Peace Process. In 1993, under Yasser Arafat, the Palestinian Liberation Organization renounced armed violence against Israel in return for limited self-governance. Fatah filled out the PA's ranks, which was envisioned to govern a future Palestinian State. But the two-state solution has become a fantasy. Israel rejects it outright and is moving toward annexing the West Bank. Israeli settlements there make a contiguous Palestinian State essentially unworkable.

Like all Palestinians I met—secular and religious, Christian and Muslim—Diliani excoriates Israel. He has no doubt that Israel's assault on the Gaza Strip is "ethnic cleansing and genocide" against his people.

This was the best time to ask him about Greece, which for a generation was a champion of the Palestinians, before it flipped to being a close ally of Israel. He regrets the fact that Greece, his ancestor's homeland, has moved so close to this Israeli government, but he doesn't believe it will last. He tells me that Greece can revive ties with the Palestinians, especially if a competent, secular government emerges out of the ashes of 7 October. I feel this is a long shot. But Diliani says the Greeks are mistaken if they believe they can count on Israel in a future clash with Türkiye.

"Don't listen to the propaganda narrative about Erdoğan and Israel. Under the surface, Türkiye and Israel cooperate," he said. Many Christians in the Middle East believe Erdoğan's anti-Israel rhetoric is cover for the close intelligence cooperation between Israel and Türkiye. Diliani points to Syria, where Türkiye has emerged as the main external backer of President Ahmed Al-Sharaa, the former HTS leader. Israeli strikes on Iranian military assets in Syria weakened the Assad regime before HTS's winter 2024 offensive. Many Palestinian Christians I met believed Israel and Türkiye had a mutual interest in toppling Assad and coordinated behind the scenes. Conspiracy theories are rife in the Middle East. But Türkiye and Israel certainly had mutual interests in toppling Assad. Of course, Israel pummeled Syria with airstrikes between January and April 2025 after Assad's ouster. The strikes targeted Syrian army bases which Türkiye had earmarked for deploying military assets as part of a defense pact with Sharaa's government. Under US pressure, Israel entered deconfliction talks with Türkiye and Syria by the spring of 2025.

"Israel and Türkiye will work together in Syria. They need each other. Türkiye is massively important to Israel. It's a Muslim country and the second biggest army in NATO. The Israelis aren't going to cut Türkiye loose, definitely not for the Greeks," Diliani said.

We left Diliani, hoping for a revival of Greek-Palestinian ties, behind. My next interview was back in Arnona, to discuss the Greek Orthodox Church's real estate fire-sale.

Since Theophilos III became patriarch, the church has unloaded hundreds of acres of land and prime properties across Israel. In one case it sold 240 apartments, a commercial building and open land in the center of Jerusalem for just $3.3 million. This is an exceptionally low sum for Jerusalem's pricey market. More real estate in Jaffa, the Israeli coastal town of Caesarea, and

Jerusalem suburbs was sold to shell companies registered in tax havens like the Virgin Islands in 2017.[15]

In Arnona, I met with Danny Seidemann, a Jerusalem attorney who knows more about real estate transactions involving the city's churches than just about anyone. Seidemann has short-cut grey hair and a grey stubble beard. He greeted me and my brother wearing a bright orange windbreaker and Nike sneakers. He looked like a New Yorker.

"So, how did you guys get into this racket?" he asked, trying to figure out why two blonde-haired brothers—one a journalist, the other a young diplomat—were pumping him for information on murky church property sales. I detected a touch of Seidemann's Syracuse, New York birthplace in him, despite the fact that he has lived in Jerusalem since the 1970s.

"You see that traffic light there," Seidemann told us, pointing out his office window. "Everything past there is a settlement. For me, that is where Israel ends and Occupied East Jerusalem begins."

In 1947, a UN partition plan called for fifty-five per cent of the British mandate of Palestine to become a Jewish state and roughly forty-two per cent a Palestinian one. The plan was accepted by Israel's future leaders but rejected by the Palestinians and their Arab neighbors (it also called for the sister cities of Jerusalem and Bethlehem to be governed as an international zone). Fighting between Palestinians and Jewish militias broke out after. Egypt, Syria, Iraq, Lebanon and Jordan then declared war on Israel on 15 May 1948, a day after Israel declared its independence. The Arabs suffered a stinging defeat. The war left Jerusalem divided, with the Hashemite Kingdom of Jordan controlling the east, including the Old City, and the new state of Israel in the west. In the 1967 Six-Day War, Israel wrested control of East Jerusalem and the West Bank from Jordan, and the Gaza Strip from Egypt. Most countries consider Jerusalem a half-occupied, disputed capital. For decades, East Jerusalem has been the envisioned capital of a future Palestinian state as part of the defunct two-state solution. In July 2024, the UN's top court issued a landmark ruling saying Israel's occupation of East Jerusalem and the West Bank were illegal. On the ground, however, Israel's occupation is so ingrained and seamless that the uninformed visitor wouldn't know where East and West Jerusalem begin and end.

Seidemann knows. In the corner of his office, he keeps a three-dimensional map of Jerusalem's Old City. He has rigged it with different colored lights to show the Muslim, Christian and Jewish quarters, along with new Israeli settlements. He says the construction of settlements, much of it on Greek Orthodox Church land, is part of a concerted effort by the Israeli government to encircle the Old City and squash talk of East Jerusalem being earmarked for a Palestinian state. He is especially concerned about what the Jewish settler movement means for Jerusalem's Christians.

"The Christians are in real jeopardy," he said. "The Middle East war started for many reasons but one of them was the situation in Jerusalem. This Israeli government has attempted to change the status quo at Al-Aqsa Mosque," he said, referring to Hamas' 7 October attack.

"What we have is a conflict driven by extreme faith communities: among Jews, it's the settlers and Temple Mount movement, among Christians it's the American evangelicals, and among Muslims it's various iterations of the Muslim Brotherhood. They have marginalized everyone else, including the Palestinian Christians."

Seidemann has an encyclopedic knowledge of settlements. He is consulted by foreign governments on developments in the city. He was preparing to meet a delegation of Greek diplomats to discuss the threat facing the Orthodox Church, when we met. He knows all the sordid details of the Church's wheeling and dealing.

"The Greek Church oscillates between praising Israel and being anti-Israel with nobody believing either. The Patriarchate is so dependent on Israel, it lives a double life," he explained.

One of the Patriarchate's most controversial land deals with settlers is being done in plain sight. The Patriarchate is jointly developing land it owns between Jerusalem and Bethlehem in an area called Givat Hamatos. The project envisions nearly 5,000 housing units and hotel rooms being built along the Hebron road. The Church says that some of the housing will go to Palestinian Christians.[16]

Experts like Seidemann are not fooled. "The Church is actively joining in the construction of big high-rises, whose purpose is to serve as a buffer between Jerusalem and its sister city of Bethlehem," he told me. He said the settlement will be the final nail in the coffin for Palestinian hopes to include even a sliver of East Jerusalem in a future state in the West Bank.

Seidemann painted such a bleak picture of the city, I asked him if he thought the cosmopolitan Jewish-Christian-Muslim make-up of Jerusalem could survive. "Jerusalem is bigger than all the extremists. It will win in the end," he said.

Will it? Discounting the Crypto-Christian Slavs, the impression I got was that the last ember of Orthodox Christianity is being snuffed out in Jerusalem. The city may have a disputed status in international forums, but practically speaking, it is the undivided capital of an increasingly revisionist Israel. What I saw in Jerusalem was a Greek Orthodox Church selling off the family jewels and the laity grabbing on to scraps.

* * *

Father Matheos is hard to miss in the Old City's cobblestone alleys. He holds his long brown hair the Orthodox way, in a little bun at the back of the head. He has a bulky frame, broad shoulders and stands over two meters tall. He looks like a fighter from *Braveheart*. When we walk together, he is greeted by passersby in Greek, English and Arabic. Few of the Greek priests in Jerusalem speak Arabic well, but Father Matheos is chief Dragoman, or interpreter, of the church. After coffee together one morning, he agreed to take me on a tour of the Greek Orthodox seminary school on Mount Zion where he is also the principal.

Mount Zion lies just outside the Old City. Sultan Suleiman the Magnificent wanted Mount Zion to be included in the city's walls when he had them built in the sixteenth century. Besides the obvious defensive advantages, the hill has religious significance; this is where the Last Supper took place and King David is said to be buried. Later, when the sultan inspected the completed project and saw Mount Zion had been left outside the perimeter, he was so angry that he had his architects executed. In 1948, Mount Zion was taken by Israeli soldiers retreating out of the Old City in the face of Jordan's Arab Legion. During Jerusalem's twenty-year division, this was the closest Israelis could get to the Wailing Wall in the center of the Old City.

Father Matheos and I walked along a trail flanked by olive trees. I breathed in the peppery scent of Mediterranean shrubs in the biting, Jerusalem winter air. The seminary is an imposing rectangle of limestone built in 1911 with dozens of Ottoman-style arched windows. It had intrigued me since the first day I arrived, when I spotted the Greek flag flying atop it from my taxi. The Greek flag is, besides the Israeli flag, by far the most prominent in Jerusalem—a sign of the Church's influence. As we walked, Father Matheos pointed across the valley to the picture-perfect neighborhood of Mishkenot Sha'ananim with its windmill and handsome limestone houses. This was the first neighborhood built outside the Old City walls and the first Jewish settlement. When Sir Moses Montefiore purchased the land from the Ottomans in the 1850s, he struggled to get local

Jews to resettle there. Jerusalem's Jews feared moving outside the Old City's walls because of bandits. Now, it's home to houses whose values rival cities like Miami.

Father Matheos is world-weary. "I am tired," he told me. "I am searching for meaning in my life."

His family roots are in Smyrna, but he was born in Germany. "The daily tension in Jerusalem drains you," he told me, explaining that he travels to Greece for breaks now and then. "In Jerusalem, it's the same people every day, the same faces, the same problems," he says. Indeed, the Old City is like a hypertense, militarized village.

His job as principal is not easy. Mount Zion is a target for Israeli settlers and ultranationalists. The priests here are regularly spat on by Israeli extremists and the Greek students are threatened by settlers wielding knives. A few months before I arrived, settlers broke into the basketball court and chapel behind the school. They painted death threats against the students.

Only boys can attend the seminary. We arrived just as the students were finishing lunch. Father Matheos picked one of the guys, who came from Thessaloniki, to give us a tour. The classrooms were decorated with icons and strung with little Greek flags. The seminary was beautiful and well-furnished, but lacked life. There were no posters for events, lectures or concerts. It felt more like a depressing retirement home than a school.

When Father Matheos took over as principal, the school had just one student. By the time of my visit, he had managed to boost enrollment to eleven. He had expected more students but the Israeli government had rejected additional student visas. The school could easily house one hundred. He explained that it was still called a seminary partly out of tradition, telling me: "We teach the Greek Orthodox religion, but the boys who graduate here can go on to study any subject. They aren't forced to study theology and become priests."

PRIESTS AND CRYPTO-CHRISTIANS

Greece recognizes the seminary's degree like any other Greek high school. The students take Greece's nerve-wracking university exams. The boys, who come from poor families in Greece, don't pay tuition. The church covers room and board. I was impressed. What an opportunity, I thought, to spend one's high-school years in Jerusalem. But the environment was depressing. This school should have to turn away Greek students for a free education in Jerusalem. Instead, it struggles to find them, and those who come are threatened. I asked Father Matheos why more people didn't know about the school.

"The times have changed," he said. "It's materialism and social media. Money is what matters to people and countries. Besides, parents don't want to send their kids away to be educated, even if it's free."

Parents certainly think twice about sending their sons to be educated in a place surrounded by knife-wielding settlers. And there is no sign that the attacks will end. Greek locals and priests told me they don't expect the Israeli government to crack down on them. Quite the opposite, because the settlers and their allies in government want the land on Mount Zion and the closure of the seminary.

We ended our tour in the basement chapel where the students attend service. Father Matheos pointed out bullet holes that riddled a painting of Saint Jacob. He said they were left by Israeli soldiers who occupied the seminary during fighting in the 1967 war.

* * *

To understand the Israeli-Palestinian conflict better, from a neutral perspective, I find it is helpful to turn to the Greeks. They are the ultimate insider-outsiders: Near Eastern but not Arab, Muslim or Jewish. Historic Palestine was home to thousands of them. One book that helped shape my understanding of the conflict is the memoir of Greek Jerusalemite and Middle East scholar P.J. Vatikiotis.

Among Arabs and Jews: A Personal Experience 1936–1990 is illuminating, often searing, and entertaining. Vatikiotis starts by recounting his grandfather's journey from the Greek island of Hydra to the Holy Land in the late nineteenth century. It is the same odyssey through an interconnected, borderless region that the Greeks of Cairo could tell about their ancestors.

Recalling his upbringing in 1930s Haifa, Vatikiotis captures the cosmopolitan milieu there before Israel's founding. For example, his Greek family rented an apartment from a Bahai Muslim landlord who fled persecution in Persia (now the Islamic Republic of Iran) for safety in Mandatory Palestine. "Christians, Muslims, and Jews were scattered all over the neighborhood," Vatikiotis writes. His street was occupied by Italians, Armenians, Assyrians, Christian Arabs, and a Jewish emigre he and his childhood friends dubbed "The Fat One" who ran a "delicatessen-cum-petrol station."[17]

Vatikiotis' book is all the better because he spares no one. Greek education in Mandatory Palestine was designed to drill into pupils a sense of "overinflated greatness" for the Greek homeland, which he described as, at that time, a "small Balkan client state." Meanwhile, Greek students were given the "vague though vicious impression that the Jew was anti-Christian ... that the Muslim followed a phony, mad prophet, and that the Englishman who governed had some mysterious diabolical power."[18]

Among Arabs and Jews offers a Greek take on the arrival of European Jews to Palestine in the 1930s and the rise of what Vatikiotis calls "Jewish terror," the climax of which was the 1946 bombing of the King David Hotel in Jerusalem by the Zionist paramilitary organization Irgun, led at that time by future Israeli Prime Minister Menachem Begin.[19]

PRIESTS AND CRYPTO-CHRISTIANS

As Vatikiotis notes, by this time, the Greeks had a homeland whose borders were generally accepted. They had tried the *Megali Idea* (Great Idea) of an intercontinental Greece, and been burned. The Greeks in Palestine were caught between the rising nationalisms of Arabs and Jews, although their ultimate sympathies rested with the Palestinians. After all, when the 1948 war broke out, it was Palestinians who came to visit Vatikiotis' father asking if he wanted to flee with them to safety from Zionist militias. Vatikiotis also distinguishes between Levantine, Arabic-speaking Jews and insular European Jewish emigres, who he says the Greeks struggled to form bonds with. Instead, the Greeks enjoyed "close and very longstanding" ties to the Palestinians which went back centuries and were especially intimate with Palestinian Christians because of intermarriage.

My first few days in Jerusalem I discovered this bond between Greeks and Palestinians in the Christian Quarter. Indeed, what Patrick Leigh Fermor called the "amalgam of Greece and the Orient" was all around. Turning down one ally, the blue and white Greek flag fluttered over an Orthodox Church building. Twisting down another, I spotted Greek letters on rusty signs for old souvenir shops and tavernas. If you look for signs of the Greeks, they are everywhere in Jerusalem, including Palestinian Christian shopkeepers who blare Greek music. Tensions over the Greek clergy have not impacted the Palestinians' fondness of Greece.

The ones I met latched onto Greece like a favorite cousin. When I told locals I lived in Athens, many recalled old honeymoons on Rhodes and the odd business trip to the Greek capital. Demographically, Christians in Israel are massively outnumbered by Muslims and Jews. Therefore, I sensed the Palestinian Christians I met longed for more people to see Greece as part of their region. A few older Palestinians reminded me that Athens is home to the Consolidated Contractors Company.

Founded by Palestinian Christians, established in Syria, and now headquartered in the sleepy Athenian suburb of Marousi, CCC, as it is known, is one of the largest construction companies in the Middle East. It rivals the better-known Bin Laden group.

Unlike in Cairo and Istanbul, where Greeks marrying non-Greeks appeared to be a newer phenomenon, the degree of intermarriage between Greeks and Palestinian Orthodox Christians clearly went back decades in Jerusalem, as Vatikiotis, whose grandmother was Palestinian, noted in his memoir.

"My mother's family came here from Crete during Ottoman times, for business we think," one Palestinian in the Old City I met outside the Patriarchate recalled to me vaguely. She was not alone. Dozens of Palestinian Christians I interviewed had similar familial links to Greece—a great-grandfather here or a grandmother there.

Dimitri and George Chermantas, who are residents of the Old City, have Palestinian wives, but their family is different. Among locals, they are recognized as "pure Greeks" in part because they still speak the Greek language. The brothers have Greek passports.

"We are Greek—Greek Jerusalemites," Dimitri explained. "Our great-grandfather came from Kavala. He killed some Ottoman soldiers before the first World War. The Turks sent him to prison in Acre. When Allenby liberated Palestine [in 1917] he was freed. He came to Jerusalem and married our great-grandmother," who was also a local Greek. On both their parents' sides, the brothers are descendants of Greeks who have inhabited Jerusalem for more than a century. Their choice of wives was telling.

The brothers explained that for the few remaining Greek Jerusalemites—some of whom are Israeli citizens— marriage to Israeli Jews is virtually unheard of. Close friendships are rare too, despite the newfound alliance between the two countries.

I asked Dimitri what he thought of this new alliance. "Greece isn't the United States. It is a small country, dependent on real estate investment and tourism, so it can't tell Israel what to do. Greece is afraid of Türkiye. They need a strong Israel," he said, continuing:

> There is a paradox here. The best and brightest of Israel, the educated, secular people in tech and finance are buying houses in Greece because of this Israeli government and power of the religious extremists. The smart Jews want back-up plans in case they have to leave. The extremists don't go to Greece. They just want to expand settlements.

Vatikiotis himself said he was most at home with his Arab friends, partially because he was a native Arabic speaker. However, he was loathed by quite a few pro-Palestinian Western academics. His own first-hand recollection of Israel's founding probably did not help endear him to them.

Studying at the American University of Cairo when Israel was proclaimed a state, he recalled congratulating a Jewish coed whose "commitment to her cause, incidentally, was total," whereas that of his bourgeois Palestinian classmates was "spasmodic and largely verbal." He also suggests the root of the Palestinians' defeat in 1948 was that they were too quick to take flight as opposed to stay and fight the determined Jewish militias. After they were bested by the Zionists, the Palestinians lacked, "any ability to analyze or discuss dispassionately why the Arabs had failed to defend let alone retain that country," he argues, and instead drifted into "radical political movements."[20]

More than 700,000 Palestinians were displaced during Israel's creation. Israel's independence day is remembered by Palestinians as the Nakba, an Arabic term meaning catastrophe. It was coined by the Damascus-born Greek Orthodox scholar, Constantine Zurayk, who located the root of the Arabs' 1948 defeat in their factionalized politics and their "distance and hostility" to modern Western life, as opposed to the Israelis' embrace of it.[21]

Vatikiotis earned the scorn of Edward Said, who the Greek scholar later accused of injecting "McCarthyism into Middle East studies."[22] Said resented Vatikiotis' closeness to Bernard Lewis. The Jewish scholar is the popular antithesis to the liberal Said. But Lewis, who became a late-life cheerleader for the 2003 invasion of Iraq, always struck me as too easy a target to pit against the suave, erudite, Palestinian Christian academic. On the other hand, what could the Edward Saids of the world do with Vatikiotis? He was such a burden to their worldview. Here was a Greek Jerusalemite, a native Arabic speaker, who was boyhood friends with the founders of the Palestinian Liberation Organization, including the hijacking mastermind Wadie Haddad. Vatikiotis' family was displaced from Palestine by the Israelis like the Arabs, but he wouldn't tow Said's line. He confounded the academic elite's stark and authoritarian premise of Orientalism.

"I, as a Mediterranean ... was looking at the Arabs as someone who had grown up with them, or at least, alongside them, not as one who was promoting foreign interests through and among them," Vatikiotis summarized.[23]

The new Near East does not belong to Bernard Lewis or Edward Said, but Vatikiotis. The Greeks' dexterity is what gives them the advantage in a world where the rigid line between East and West is evaporating, middle powers are rising and cash from the so-called global south is fueling real estate booms in places like Athens. There is no longer any point to harangue about Western colonialism when powers like Türkiye, China, Russia and Iran make no apologies for their old empires. The former colonial world is as picky about the conflicts it wants to give moral support to as the United States. Meanwhile, the Gulf states have shed Wahhabism for mercantilism, AI and mega-projects.

PRIESTS AND CRYPTO-CHRISTIANS

With Western Europe desperate for buffer states against Eurasia, Greece's Eastern Mediterranean identity and Eastern connections are more valuable than ever. The new Near East belongs, once again, to the shape shifters.

* * *

Walking from the Austrian Hospice in Jerusalem's Muslim Quarter to Jaffa gate, you can spot the flags of Israeli settlers dangling out of windows and above rooftop water-tanks. The hospice was constructed 150 years ago by another empire which was devoured by the First World War, the Austro-Hungarian. Like the Ottoman one, it was of the East and cosmopolitan. The hospice was built for Christian pilgrims to the Holy Land. Its halls are tiled in *cemento* and the gardens are manicured but not overdone. Here is Durrell's "controlled simplicity" again, the scourge of modern minimalism.

The Austrian Hospice is the only place I know in the Muslim Quarter where you can sip a glass of wine, which I needed after being in ideological and suspicion-riven Jerusalem, but some of the customers are also pious Muslims. The takeaway is that no one here cares if you are Jewish, Muslim, or Christian. Even the Israeli settlers haven't gone after the hospice yet. In that sense, it reminds me of Cairo's Greek Club. It is not a coincidence that these Levantine redoubts are where local authorities' oppressive rule and stifling social and religious codes subside. The European powers should not have carved up the Levant, but the hospice makes me think that had they stayed a little longer, instead of brusquely pulling out, maybe they could have propped up a gentler, more competent order than the disastrous local governments that filled their vacuum.

I left this sanctuary after a morning coffee to meet George, the leader of the Greek community in Jerusalem's Old City, at

Samaras Cafe next to Jaffa Gate. The Petra and Imperial Hotels that the settlers had seized were above us. Jaffa Gate is the Old City's meeting point. It was crowded with people, even though tourists were staying away due to the war.

George told me that like the Palestinians, Greek Jerusalemites face the same problem of being non-Jews in an increasingly intolerant Jewish state:

> The Jews have decided they don't want anyone but them left in Jerusalem. Doesn't matter if it's Christians or Muslims. But they especially don't like us Greeks because we aren't Palestinians, but have been here for generations. There were literally thousands of Greeks here. We kept Christianity alive in the Holy Land. The last of us are a thorn in their side.

There are different statistics on the exact number of Greeks who once lived here. Michael Vatikiotis, a journalist and son of the late Greek scholar, who wrote a book about his Greek and Jewish-Italian family in the Levant, said Jerusalem was home to at least 8,000 Greeks, in addition to those in trading ports like Jaffa. The statistics I obtained from the Greek Consulate in Jerusalem put the number higher from 1922, with almost 20,000 Greeks residing here. What can be stated with certainty is that a century ago, Greeks were a part of Jerusalem's cosmopolitan fabric. In fact, by the early twentieth century, the community was blossoming so much that it had outgrown the Old City and established the Greek Colony between the present-day neighborhoods of Katamon and Baqa in upscale West Jerusalem. Fewer than 100 Greeks still live in Jerusalem, George told me.

Since its founding, Israel has been arguably as intolerant as Atatürk's Türkiye toward Christians, and as intolerant as Nasser's Egypt toward the Greeks. In 1922, Christians accounted for twenty-three per cent of Jerusalem's population. That was twenty-six years before the creation of the state of Israel. At the time of writing, they number barely two per cent, despite Jerusalem being home to at least six major churches.[24]

In *Drifting Cities*, Greeks jump off the pages of Manos' sojourn in Jerusalem. This is how one Greek resident of the city described the political maneuverings of Jerusalem's communities during the early days of the Second World War:

> Never mind the local authorities, the Allies, the Arabs and the Beduins, who all have their own organizations; never mind the Knights, the Protestants, the Catholics, the Armenians, the Russians, our own Greeks and all the missions who won't stop at anything when it comes to winning souls ... it's the Jews who are organized best. They've really set their minds to getting Palestine for themselves ... the Hagana, the Irgun, who collect the arms for after the war ... the Hadassah, who scoop up boatfuls of American dollars.[25]

It was a rainy late-November afternoon. Samaras Cafe was drafty and our jackets were damp. The Near East is at its finest during winter when the olive-toned terrain is blanketed in grey and wet-cold. We devoured our hummus, *labne* and *mutabbal*, washing the assortment of mezze down with hot mint tea.

"When the 1948 war started, the inhabitants of the Greek Colony fled the Jewish militias and took refuge at the Church of the Holy Sepulchre. They crowded into the Old City for the Arab Legion to protect them. Everything you see here became part of Jordan," George said, motioning out the window of the cafe to the bustling crowd outside.

George spoke with an American accent. He had spent more than twenty years in the United States, where he told me he worked for Las Vegas star Wayne Newtown. I asked him whether he feels Greece advocates for its few remaining nationals here.

"Athens doesn't care about us. Most Greeks don't even know we exist, so if we get destroyed, it won't matter to the politicians," he said.

George, like many Greeks I met in the Middle East and Greece's borderlands, believed the destruction of Greeks in Jerusalem is part of a subtler, centuries-old effort to Europeanize the Greek state and uproot them from the lands of Byzantium. This might sound far-fetched, but east of Thessaloniki it is widely believed. He told me,

> We were the first nation-state in Europe. But Europe never wanted us to be independent. They were scared of a Greek democracy and our ambitions. The first thing they did was erase thousands of years of Roman and Byzantine history and telling us to be like ancient Greece. The same thing is going on here. Erasing the Greek presence.

George wanted to talk to me about the United States. He was flabbergasted by the Evangelicals' rise within the Republican Party and their messianic support for Israeli settlement-building and annexation. "These people have hijacked the Republicans' foreign policy on Israel," he said. "I don't understand what is going on. American Christians have abandoned the Christians here in Jerusalem: Greeks, Armenians and Palestinians. Do they realize what this Israeli government is allowing to happen to the Christians?"

The Evangelicals' diehard support for Israel's expansion in the occupied Palestinian Territories is tied to their literal interpretation of Bible passages where God promises a homeland for the Jewish people and the so-called end-of-times prophecies. One strand of evangelical theology states that the end of the world will be ushered in when Jews return *en masse* to the Holy Land. After that, an Antichrist will come to earth and rule for seven years until this empire is destroyed in Armageddon. Then, Jesus Christ will return to earth and establish his Kingdom in Jerusalem.

I was curious about the evangelical Christians myself. Tens of thousands come each year to visit the Holy Land. I asked George if they ever meet the Greeks or Palestinian Christians in the Old

City. "They want nothing to do with us. We don't see them at the church or at restaurants in the Christian Quarter. They have Jewish or American tour guides. Besides, the Israelis don't want them to hear from us," he said. "They go to the Jordan River to get baptized and outside the Old City," he added. "Where they think Jesus was buried."

Evangelicals believe Jesus was buried at the Garden Tomb, which has become a major pilgrimage site for them. Other Christian denominations believe Jesus was crucified, buried and resurrected where the Church of the Holy Sepulchre sits in the Old City. Custodianship of the sprawling, cavernous church is shared among six denominations: Roman Catholics, Armenian Apostolics, Syrian Orthodox, Ethiopian Orthodox, Copts, and the most powerful of all, the Greek Orthodox. Saladin, the Muslim leader who conquered Jerusalem from the Crusaders in 1187, entrusted two prominent Sunni Muslim families with the keys to the church and the duty of opening and closing it each day. That tradition continues. It's a good way to keep the Christians from killing each other. At times, bearded priests at the Holy Sepulchre get into fistfights over who has right of way in small corners of the church. I personally saw a group of Coptic and Greek priests get into a brouhaha over where a candle holder was placed.

My brother and I walked to the Greek Colony a day before meeting George. It is now Greek in name only. It's an oasis where bougainvilla and pine trees spill out of Levantine gardens. The handsome limestone villas and apartment buildings that once housed Greeks were settled by Jewish refugees after 1948. I wanted to find the Lesky. This is the Greek club where the characters in *Drifting Cities* dance late into the night, drinking and listening to tango records.

The club was built in 1902, in the waning years of the Ottoman Empire. It is made of Jerusalem limestone, with a red-tiled roof and painted shutters. It is set back in a verdant garden behind a wrought iron gate. When we arrived, the club was closed. I learned later from a Greek diplomat that the Greek community— fewer than 100 of them— were in a bitter dispute over the club and fighting over the keys. The Lesky's status fit too well with the mood in half-occupied Jerusalem. Shuttered and unapproachable, it symbolized the withering Greek presence here.

Having met Greeks across the Near East in my travels, the community in Jerusalem was the frailest and most dormant of those I encountered between Israel, Türkiye, and Egypt. In Cairo, at least the Greek Club was the pride of downtown, packed with Egyptians. Even in Istanbul, where I traveled later, the Greeks had a busy social agenda. What makes their weakness in Jerusalem so depressing is that it's occurring against the backdrop of this burgeoning alliance. Of course, the damage to the community's numbers was done after 1948 and 1967. But no one seemed to care about promoting what remained of this historic community or bolstering its visibility.

This campaign of intimidation has reached the center of Christianity in the Old City, and the Greek flag is offering less protection in a militant Israel. During the Holy Fire ceremony celebrating Orthodox Easter in 2024, Israeli police stormed into the crowded Church of the Holy Sepulchre and arrested the Greek consul's bodyguard, dragging him out of the place of worship. The blatant raid sent a chill through the Christian Community that people still talked about when I visited.

"The Israelis never want to discuss the fate of Christians with us, let alone the Church and Greeks," one senior Greek diplomat told me. "They compartmentalize everything so that the geopolitics is separate from the Christians and the Church."

8

THE ISRAEL–GREECE ALLIANCE

It wasn't just the Greeks of Palestine who were historically closer to the Arabs than the Israelis. In 1947, Greece joined Arab states to vote against the United Nations' Palestine partition plan. Greek leaders worried that if they supported an Israeli state it would provoke an Arab backlash against Greek communities in places like Egypt. At the time, the Orthodox Church in the Holy Land, which remains deeply entwined with Greek politicians, had even more to lose from the creation of a Jewish interloper state.

Greece's anti-Zionism in the 1950s and 1960s had a business logic, too. In the post-war era, Greek shipping magnates wanted to stay on the good side of energy-rich Gulf states like Saudi Arabia, whose oil they wanted to make a fortune transporting. Aristotle Onassis, the Greek shipping magnate born in Smyrna, was at the center of this oil intrigue.

Onassis' worldview is the mandatory starting point for anyone trying to understand the universally unsavory leaders of the Near East. "There is no right and wrong. There is only what is possible," he famously declared.[1]

Onassis was a brilliant cynic. He sensed that post-colonial sentiment and Arab nationalism, fueled by the creation of Israel, were motivating states like Saudi Arabia to build their own tanker fleets. Greek shipping magnates bet on a big demand for oil in the post-war years and expanded their tanker fleets accordingly. Their interests were at risk. Onassis basically told the United States Department of State as much in 1954, according to a declassified cable:

> Numerous states which had hitherto relied upon such shipping for their necessary trade were driven to the conclusion that they must henceforth have fleets of their own. Other states which did not require merchant fleets but which were emerging as new members of the world community felt the nationalistic urge to have vessels operating under their own flags. Such was the case of Saudi Arabia.[2]

In a clandestine campaign to torpedo an oil deal between Onassis and the Saudis in favor of American energy companies, the CIA planted stories that Onassis was transporting oil to Israel in violation of his pledge to the Saudis to maintain an embargo on the Jewish state. The CIA's efforts against Onassis reached a comical level when the Greek oligarch arrived in Beirut and complained, "There is a campaign in certain Arab newspapers which attempts to present me to the world as a Zionist," whereas, he said, in the United States he was denounced as "a notorious anti-Zionist."[3] Onassis' contract with the Saudis was cancelled in 1955.

But Greek shipping tycoons got rich off the Israel-Palestine conflict. When Nasser closed the Suez Canal in 1956 he inadvertently created a windfall for Greek tanker owners because Gulf oil destined for the West had to be transported on a longer journey around the Cape of Good Hope in southern Africa. Shipping rates are determined by supply and demand. Because tankers had to take a time-consuming journey to get from the

Persian Gulf to the West, the de facto supply of ships dropped and rates soared.

It's not a coincidence that the golden era of Greek shipping occurred in the late 1960s and early 1970s when the Suez Canal was closed. Upheaval in the Near East might spark migration crises, but in general, Greece's elite, true to their Levantine selves, find ways to benefit from war and instability in their neighborhood. Therefore, far from being a menace to Greek shipowners, the Houthis' attacks in the Red Sea over the last few years were a godsend. They created a windfall for ship-owners by putting the Cape of Good Hope route back in vogue. The last thing vessel owners want is to transport cargo on a quick route when they can charge more money to go the long way.[4]

But the high point in Greek-Palestinian relations was the 1980s, when Greece was governed by the PASOK party under Prime Minister Andreas Papandreou. The Greek socialist firebrand was a close ally of PLO leader Yasser Arafat.

Arafat was given a hero's welcome during his 1981 visit to Athens as his forces fought in Lebanon's Civil War. "Greece, this great country, is playing the same role it did in ancient times. It is the link between the Arab world and Europe," Arafat declared to chants of: "Greece, Cyprus, Palestine, every American must go!"[5] Arafat was feted in Athens, where he was ferried around by helicopter to crowds chanting, "Revolution until victory!" and "Down with Zionism, victory to the PLO!" Two years later, when the Israelis succeeded in driving the PLO out of Beirut, Greek ships, sailing under the flag of the United Nations, ferried Arafat's forces to safety.[6]

Papandreou's support for the Palestinians was not merely Third Worldist virtue signaling. He wanted Muammar Qaddafi's oil-rich Libya and Saddam Hussein's Iraq to invest in Greece, and aligning with the PLO was useful to this end. The investments never materialized. In 1982, Greece even helped a member the

Palestinian militant group Abu Nidal avoid extradition to Italy for an attack on a Rome Synagogue by sending him to Libya.[7] The Arab world's rulers are now so close to Israel that Papandreou's diplomacy based on Arab solidarity with the Palestinians seems naive and quaint. The United Arab Emirates and Saudi Arabia want Israeli technology and intelligence. Meanwhile, Jordan, and to a point Egypt's government, are propped up by Israel as buffer states, despite all the very public lecturing by their toothless foreign ministries about Gaza.

But let's try this. The speed with which Arab leaders flipped from attacking Israel to partnering with it raises the question, could they flip again? It seems far-fetched, but imagine a decade from now when the Islamic Republic of Iran, which is very weak, potentially collapses, or transforms into less of a threat to the Arab monarchs in the Gulf. Tehran is already in the midst of a fragile rapprochement with Saudi Arabia and the UAE. Indeed, Israel's takedown of Hezbollah and the collapse of the Assad dynasty in Syria have given Iran and the Sunni Gulf states two fewer hotspots to fight over. If Iran undergoes a transformation, the common foe uniting Israel and the Arab Gulf monarchies would be gone. There are already whiffs of this. In the spring of 2025, Israel was lobbying the US to launch preemptive attacks on Iran, while Saudi Arabia, the United Arab Emirates and Qatar lobbied for a nuclear deal. The Gulf states are moving in the direction of Türkiye in terms of how they view themselves on the world stage: as independent powers that don't bend to the United States or Israel.

A few things could stir the pot between the Gulf and Israel. A decrease in oil demand in the coming decade would hit Gulf states' coffers and burden their societies. An easy way for Arab leaders to gain support on the street will be to position themselves against Israel, given their young populations whose views on their Jewish neighbors are now shaped by Israel's obliteration of Gaza. A prime example: Saudi Arabian Crown Prince Mohammed Bin Salman has publicly accused Israel of committing a genocide in the Gaza Strip. Even if Gulf leaders don't care about the Palestinians deep down, they do care what an Israel bent on territorial expansion means for the regional balance of power. A revisionist Israel could also compete with the Gulf states over the carcass of the Islamic Republic. Let's even assume that Saudi Arabia normalizes ties with Israel, an obsession in the United States. So what? Egypt and Israel signed a peace treaty in 1979, but ordinary Egyptians are still livid at Israel for its occupation of Palestinian lands. The fear of a coup d'état or revolt in Egypt is nestled in the back of every Israeli spy chief's mind.

Greece's anti-Americanism and anti-Zionism in the 1980s were also gut reactions to the memory of the disastrous right-wing military dictatorship that governed the country from 1967–74. The CIA and State Department supported Greece's Junta as an anticommunist bulwark, but "The Regime of the Colonels," as it was known, also developed covert ties to Israel, striking deals to purchase Israeli small arms and mortars.[8] The State Department said in a declassified memo at the time that despite the Junta's "pro-Arab posture," it accommodated the United States during the 1973 Yom Kippur War. Operation Nickel Grass, the United States' airlift of supplies to Israel during the conflict, relied on Crete's Souda Bay and Greek airfields to resupply the American Sixth Fleet in the Eastern Mediterranean.[9]

The Yom Kippur War showed Greece to be a stepping-stone to the Arab Levant and crucial fallback for the United States when there is a big war. As Elmo Zumwalt, the Chief of US Naval Operations, reflected three years after the war, "In the course of the Middle East war, Türkiye permitted Soviet aircraft to use its airspace and created obstacles for us. To the contrary, Greece permitted the Sixth Fleet to continue to launch from its bases and this is the major difference between Greece and Türkiye at critical moments."[10]

The United States' decision in recent years to beef up its portfolio of military bases in Greece has its roots in Zumwalt's speech. In fact, there are parallels between Greece's strategic position in the Yom Kippur War and the Middle East war sparked on 7 October 2023. After 7 October, Greece and Cyprus were again backstops to resupply Israel. In June 2024, the assassinated leader of Hezbollah, Hassan Nasrallah, was so unnerved by this new alliance that he even threatened to attack the island of Cyprus if Israel used bases there to strike the Shiite militant group.

Cyprus' role in the conflict was the culmination of its place as the third link in the chain of the alliance between Greece and Israel (I am referring to the internationally recognized government of Cyprus and not the Turkish-occupied north). Before Israeli troops launched their ground invasion of southern Lebanon in October 2024, they trained for it in Cyprus where the terrain resembles Lebanon's mountains. As Israel waged war against Iran's proxies—Hezbollah, Hamas and the Houthis—it was being supplied with arms and munitions airlifted via Cyprus. Britain's Royal Air Force has a base in Akrotiri, Cyprus, a holdover of British colonial control of the island. In addition, Israel was able to tap a steady stream of signals intelligence on Hezbollah thanks to a listening post it accesses in Cyprus' Troodos Mountains. When most airlines cancelled their flights to Israel amid the war, Greek and Cypriot airports kept Israelis connected to the West.[11]

In 1990, Greece became the last European state to establish full diplomatic relations with Israel. The decision was made by Prime Minister Konstantinos Mitsotakis, father of Greece's Prime Minister at the time of writing. But it would take another twenty years for their alliance to get hashed out. The big storm cloud uniting them—a revisionist, populist, Islamist Türkiye—was just starting to brew, but the spark, as often happens in geopolitics, was accidental. The unlikely venue was the Pushkin Cafe in Moscow, a haunt favored by Russian oligarchs and their super-model hangers-on. In February 2010, the then-leaders of Israel and Greece, Netanyahu and George Papandreou, son of the anti-Zionist, US critic, happened to be dining at Pushkin on the same night. Both American-educated and fluent English speakers, they hit it off. As Netanyahu recalled in a 2017 interview with Greece's Kathimerini news,

> I was sitting with my wife and a waiter came over and said, "the prime minister of Greece would like to talk to you." I said, "by all means," and we started having a conversation. We were the last people in the restaurant—we kept them open—and immediately following that there was every reason to form this bond ... every conceivable reason to do so and no reason not to do so.[12]

At the time, Israel's partnership with Türkiye was coming apart at the seams. Previously, Türkiye had been Israel's closest Muslim ally. But the year before the Pushkin meeting, Erdoğan appeared at the 2009 Davos Summit and raged at Israeli President Shimon Peres over Israel's invasion of Gaza. When the moderator tried to silence him, Erdoğan stormed out. His lecturing rattled the Western establishment but instantly endeared him to millions of Muslims and Arabs.

The next year, a flotilla carrying hundreds of pro-Palestinian activists and thousands of tons of supplies for the Gaza Strip set sail from Türkiye. Its goal was to break the devastating blockade Israel has exercised over the impoverished strip since Hamas took control in 2007. Israeli naval commandos stormed the Turkish aid ship, *Mavi Marmara*, killing eight Turkish activists and sending relations with Ankara into a tailspin.[13]

In 2011, the Gaza freedom flotilla was back, this time at Greek ports. Israel reaped the benefits of an accommodating Greece. Papandreou banned all the ships in the flotilla from leaving Greece's ports. When American and Canadian ships tried to depart Piraeus, they were boarded by the Greek Coast Guard and turned back at gunpoint. The Israeli newspaper *Haaretz* reported that, concurrently, Netanyahu was lobbying the European Union to throw Greece a financial lifeline amid its debt crisis.[14]

"To be frank, there is nothing like killing a few Turks to make you popular with the Greeks. But in all seriousness, we had common interests," Eran Lerman, Benjamin Netanyahu's former deputy national security advisor, told me. He identified exactly seven points of commonality between Greece and Israel, and they all began with the letter "E."

I have known Lerman for more than half-a-dozen years. He advised Netanyahu from 2009–2015. He was one of the chief architects of the Greek-Israel alliance. "I had a little something to do with it," he said with a grin. He has the sort of lustrous English accent that belongs to another era. He agreed to meet me at Luciana restaurant in Jerusalem's upscale Mamilla mall for lunch to assess the relationship since 7 October.

"It has held up well during the war. We will need Greece in the European Union as our eyes and ears more now," he said, noting the censure Israel has received from Spain, Ireland and even France over its offensive on Gaza. "The Greeks have been helpful in Brussels, keeping us abreast of the situation in the European Union," he added. But the European Union is a sideshow. Lerman said uniting Greece and Israel was part of his wider vision:

> I have always been a big advocate for a Mediterranean Israeli identity. Talk about the Middle East and Israel together, and we stick out like a sore thumb. Basically all Muslim and Arab. But when you think about

the Eastern Mediterranean, you get a mosaic: Greeks, Turks, Jews, and Arabs. I wanted Israel to look toward the Mediterranean for friends.

With his snow-white hair, wire-rimmed glasses and striped wool jumper, Lerman is like an old Jewish mandarin out of John le Carre's *The Little Drummer Girl*. His Arabic accent, when a word pops up now and then, is good. A twenty-year member of Israeli military intelligence, his grandfatherly appearance and professor vibes mask a security-conscious, hawkish instinct. He tells me:

> I hope they don't annex the whole West Bank, it would be a stupid thing to do because we would have to account for two million Palestinians. But the Jordan Valley, we could make a good case we need to keep that for our defense. We could never allow a full Palestinian state after what happened on 7 October.

I steered the conversation back to Greece and Israel. "Before 2010, it was clear to me that Erdoğan was taking Türkiye to a place beyond our reach and that the Greeks would be more important to us. They could be a substitute," he said.

"Erdoğan," he said with emphasis. "That was the first 'E'."

The Papandreou-Netanyahu meeting occurred just before the Arab Spring created another. "Egypt," he added at a clip.

Lerman's doctorate at the London School of Economics focused on colonial Britain's control of Israel's neighbor during the Second World War. He explained, "A Muslim Brotherhood regime in Cairo linked to Erdoğan was a nightmare for Greeks and Israelis." Then he rattled off the rest of his list: "Energy, military exercises, emergencies, the environment, and economy."

"I told Netanyahu to issue a statement of trust in the Greek economy during the [2015] debt crisis. It cost us nothing, but was appreciated by the Greeks," Lerman said.

What Netanyahu's support did do was make Greece a darling of the powerful pro-Israel lobby in Washington, DC. Jewish

American lobbyists who once went to the mat for Türkiye's secular generals in the 1990s, pushing the United States to sell Greece's arch foe military hardware, and even advising Ankara on ways to fight congressional attempts to pass an Armenian Genocide bill, had a new friend.[15] The switch was head spinning.

The Greeks were now allied with the undisputed masters of the lobbying sport. As a journalist covering the region with sources in the lobbying business, I constantly see the Greeks latching on to the Israelis. Greek Americans never had the deep pockets and instinct for what makes American lawmakers tick. Greece's compelling and truthful case, that it is a stable, democratic, pro-American outpost in the Near East, got more attention in Washington because of the Jewish American lobby.

But this could leave the Greeks vulnerable in the future. Since 7 October, more Americans are becoming disillusioned the tremendous amount of influence the Zionist lobby has in Washington. The ascendent left wing of the Democratic Party and "America First" wing of the Republican Party are speaking out about the billions of dollars in US taxpayer money flowing to Israel. A poll released in April 2025 by Pew showed that fifty-three per cent of Americans have a negative view of Israel—an eleven per cent increase since 7 October. The shift in negative sentiment has been especially big among young Republicans.[16] For the foreseeable future the Israeli lobby remains a force to reckon with, but in the long term Greece would be wise to spread its bets.

The big test for the Greece-Israel alliance came in 2015, when Alexis Tsipras stormed into Greece's premiership on a wave of popular anger at anti-austerity measures imposed on Greece by its international creditors. A former member of Greece's communist youth movement, the tie-averse Tsipras fashioned himself as an anti-American and anti-Zionist politician. But just as leftist Tsipras would surprise the West with his commitment to Greece's international creditors and NATO, he doubled down on Greece's alliance with Israel.

During the Tsipras-era, Greece, Israel and Cyprus began holding regular trilateral summits. Military drills became more frequent. Israeli investors charged into Greece's real estate market. This is when talk of the fanciful EastMed gas pipeline, envisioned to run between Israel and Greece, reached its apex.[17]

"We were worried about Tsipras at first because he had these radical left roots. But he did a lot to bring the partnership forward. It was one of the more pleasant surprises," Lerman said.

Just as Erdoğan's revisionism was threatening Greece, the Turkish leader had deprived Israel of the strategic depth it needed to train its air force. Israel is a small country boxed in by Arab populations who despise their governments' peace treaties with it. The fact that Türkiye's skies became no-go zones for Israel after 2009 was no small matter. Greece stepped in and allowed Israel to train its pilots for long-distance missions over its airspace. That has led to a flurry of military drills over the last fifteen years. Greece has effectively moved into a loose security bloc comprising Israel and the United Arab Emirates, the most pro-Israel Arab state. Since 2012, the Greek and Israeli navies and air forces have joined in military exercises called Noble Dina backed by the United States. These focus on defending Mediterranean gas-drilling installations, simulating air-to-air combat, and anti-submarine warfare.[18] Greek airspace has also become a hub for Israel to train with Emirati pilots. During the 2020 spike in Greek-Turkish tensions over maritime zones, the United Arab Emirates dispatched F-16 jet fighters to Crete to drill alongside the Greeks and Israelis. Just a month before the Hamas attack on 7 October, the Israeli Air Force staged a major long-range strike drill in Greece designed to practice taking out Iranian nuclear facilities.

THE NEW BYZANTINES

In 2021, Israel and Greece signed a $1.68bn defense agreement, their largest ever. That deal created a flight training school run by Israeli defense contractor Elbit Systems that opened in 2022 in Kalamata Greece. In absolute dollar terms, Greece is a small defense market compared to other members of NATO, but when measured against its GDP, it is one of the alliance's highest spenders, mainly because of its rivalry with Türkiye.[19]

Greece has purchased Israel's Rafael Systems' Drone Dome. It could deploy it against Turkish drones in its borderlands should a conflict erupt. It has also purchased Orbiter 3 UAVs and anti-tank missiles from Rafael.[20] The Greeks are making a strategic calculation that reflects the tectonic shifts in Europe and the Middle East. The United States is moving away from NATO. Türkiye's relative power is growing. Even before Donald Trump, the United States' long-term trajectory was disengagement from Europe and downsizing in the Middle East. The single most powerful neighbor Greece can partner with is Israel.

Make no mistake about it, Israel is now the dominant power of the Near East. Israel decimated Hezbollah in Lebanon, where a president bent on disarming the Shiite group was elected in January 2025. Israel contributed to the toppling of Bashar al-Assad in Syria through its airstrikes on Iranian assets there. The Israeli economy suffered from the war, but not nearly as badly as its critics made out. Supported by American arms, Israel smashed Iran's Axis of Resistance in the Near East in a way that made Sunni Gulf States who loathe Tehran secretly salivate.

A former senior Arab diplomat once told me, "In the Middle East, we want to be on the winning, strong side." The Greeks certainly do. The month I arrived in Jerusalem, the Greek government announced plans to develop a $2bn anti-aircraft and missile defense dome with Israel. The timing is not a coincidence. Everyone in the wider Middle East watched Israel's air defenses take out Iran's missiles and drones in 2024.

THE ISRAEL–GREECE ALLIANCE

The critics of Greece's realpolitik alliance with Israel, including many dear friends, say it ran roughshod over Greece's historic ties to the Palestinians—the very relationship I had savored in the Old City of Jerusalem. It is one thing for Greece and Israel to have diplomatic relations, but how can a country like Greece, which trumpets international law in its maritime dispute with Türkiye, cut arms deals with Israel while the UN's top court says it is illegally occupying the Palestinian Territories? While Israel is trampling over the rights of Orthodox Christians and empowering settlers to attack Mount Zion? Others will point to Human Rights Watch and Doctors Without Borders' judgements that Israel is pursuing ethnic cleansing against Palestinians in the Gaza Strip. Israel vehemently denies those allegations, but every Palestinian Christian, Greek, and priest I met in Jerusalem endorsed them. As I write, the International Criminal Court has an outstanding arrest warrant for Netanyahu and his former defense chief, Yoav Gallant, for alleged crimes against humanity and war crimes.

On the one hand, the lesson to draw from the Greece-Israel alliance is not in the Hague. Nor is it in Ramallah or the occupied West Bank's rolling olive groves, which are under vicious attack by settlers. Rather, the lesson lies in the historic rotation forging a new Near East. In sum, as the rimland of Europe becomes absorbed into Asia, human rights, democracy and even ideology, count for less compared to military might. Greece sits at the crossroads of a militarized Russia, a weakened Europe and a revisionist Türkiye. In their return to Ali Pasha's world, the Greeks think they need an ally like Israel.

But in the long term, an alliance with an expansionist, ultranationalist Israel could pose problems for Greece. A word of warning: Greece's fragile maritime claims are based on stringent interpretations of UN law. Athens opposes Türkiye's occupation of Northern Cyprus in the same vein. Those positions are going to be seriously tested.

Many Greek officials I know—including senior ones who work with the Israelis—are already making the case privately that this alliance is out of whack. One of the most obvious examples of this for ordinary Greeks is their government's inability to move the economic side of the relationship beyond Israeli real estate speculation.

Greeks across the political spectrum in Athens and Thessaloniki believe Israelis are pricing them out of their housing markets. Athens' seedy Omonia Square has become the most bizarre hotspot for Israeli investment. The area is home to crumbling neoclassical mansions and filthy brothels. It has become a gentrifying, twenty-first-century version of Lawerence Durrell's Alexandria. Walk through Omonia one afternoon and you will find hipster Israelis crowding into falafel and shawarma shops run by Egyptians and Syrians. In Omonia, which pretentious middle-class Athenians avoid like the plague, migrants fleeing wars in Africa and Asia rub shoulders with Israelis in swim trunks. Greece needs investment in such places. Big Israeli investors were the first to come to Greece, but in recent years the makeup of buyers has shifted to middle-class Israelis priced out of their own country's housing market. They favor Athenian neighborhoods like Exarcheia and Pangrati over edgy Omonia. This is where Greeks say that without a course correction, the relationship is bound to create trouble and tension in future.[21]

Athens' housing prices are a sad joke for Greeks, whose average salary is around $1,000 a month; but they are still affordable for an average Israeli salary of $3,400 a month. All the Greeks I know talk of a bubble that has to burst, but for $250,000 an Israeli family can buy a two-bedroom apartment in the city center, whereas the average price of a home in Israel in 2024 was roughly $606,000. You really can live in Athens and work in Israel. They are that close. One Israeli investor I know in upscale Kolonaki makes a living just flipping Greek real estate among Israelis. Greeks are cut out of the process.

Private investment by itself isn't a problem. Greece needs more private sector, not less. The concerning part is that it is so one-sided. Athens should press Israel hard to diversify the economic relationship. Very few Israelis who buy houses in Greece open businesses or invest in productive enterprises that employ Greeks, despite Israel having a tech sector that is the envy of the world. Well, that is not totally fair.

The most prominent case of an Israeli tech company operating in Greece was Intellexa, the firm behind Predator spyware. Intellexa was founded in 2020 by Tal Dilian, a former Israeli military officer who commanded the IDF's Unit 81, an elite, secret technology unit. First based in Cyprus and then Athens, Dilian established a string of spyware companies, recruiting hackers from the Israeli military's elite units.

In August 2022, a scandal erupted in Greece dubbed "Predatorgate," after an attempt to plant the spyware on the phone of PASOK party leader Nikos Androulakis was exposed. That led to revelations of a massive surveillance campaign by Greece's National Intelligence Service. Dozens of journalists, politicians (including half of the conservative Greek government's cabinet), their family members, and businesspeople were reportedly targeted with Predator spyware.[22] Prime Minister Kyriakos Mitsotakis' office repeatedly dismissed allegations that he had ordered a wiretapping operation. The scandal was conveniently squashed. In 2024, Greece's supreme court quietly closed the case, concluding that no state ministry or agency had used Predator spy software. Dilian also denied any role. Greece's government admitted that it had licensed Predator to be sold to the government of Madagascar. From Athens, the software was also sold to a Sudanese warlord and pitched to the government of Ukraine.[23]

* * *

By the time I returned to Athens from Jerusalem, the map of the Middle East had changed dramatically. Syria was under new leadership and closer than ever to Türkiye. Türkiye already had 20,000 military advisors and troops in northern Syria training and equipping rebels before the new government requested it support. By the spring of 2025, the US itself appeared to de facto recognize a Turkish zone of influence in Syria. Regional officials believed it was only a matter of time before Turkish troops deployed around Damascus. If the Turks go a little further south they could hear the roar of Israeli transport vehicles. Israel took advantage of Assad's downfall to send its forces into, and beyond, a demilitarized zone that had separated its border from Syria since the 1970s. As of 2025, they reached up to roughly twelve miles from the Syrian capital. Israeli troops also sit on Mount Hermon, giving them control of the highest peak in the region.

Türkiye wants to start negotiations with Syria to delineate their maritime boundaries. Among Greek diplomats in Athens I detected a new worry. The Greeks used to ask what Israel would do for them if they clashed with the Turks; now some whispered, "what happens if Israel drags us into a fight with Türkiye?"

Besides abandoning the Palestinians, Greece faces this geopolitical danger. Allying with a strong Israel determined to empower Palestinian peace partners and contribute to the reconstruction of Syria and Lebanon makes good sense for Greece. But that is not where Israel is. This is not a government issue. Israeli newspaper *Haaretz* published a poll in May 2025 that showed eighty-two per cent of Israelis want to forcibly expel two million Palestinians from Gaza and fifty-six per cent support expelling Palestinian citizens of Israel. The settlers are determined to expand Israel's borders in the West Bank and create buffer zones in Syria and Lebanon.

The main regional power that can oppose Israeli expansionism is Türkiye. A direct clash between NATO's second largest army and the US's most powerful ally in the Middle East may seem far-fetched. But with some imagination it is possible. It could occur accidentally, like when Greek and Turkish warships collided in 2020. Turkish and Israeli troops could come too close in Syria or a Greek-Israeli naval drill could rub Türkiye the wrong way. If tensions with Israel spike, Erdoğan could threaten an islet claimed by Greece in a bid to "escalate to de-escalate."

Israel and Türkiye have a lot in common. Both are revisionist and slipping away from democracy. Türkiye has the Blue Homeland doctrine. For the fanatical settlers, Jerusalem is the God-given capital of a Greater Israel, whose borders they envision stretching from southwestern Syria into the totality of the occupied West Bank. Israel's claim to be a democracy will evaporate unless some kind of Palestinian State is created. Israel will continue its endless occupation over three million Palestinians in the West Bank and East Jerusalem, where they are denied the same rights as their Israeli occupiers, corralled into different highways, deprived of voting and property rights, and denied representative government. To sustain itself, the occupation will need to become more violent.

To glimpse where Israel as a whole is going in the coming decades without a course correction, look to Jerusalem, not Tel Aviv. As secular Israelis grow more queasy over the winner-takes-all ideology of settlers and ultranationalists, more of them are buying homes in Athens. In turn, Israel will rely more on settlers from the United States and Ultra-Orthodox to bolster its population. In the Jewish quarter of the Old City and ritzy Mamilla Mall, the streets echo with American-accented English spoken by soldiers with M-16s slung over their shoulders. Jerusalem is an Ultra-Orthodox city. Haredi make up twenty-eight per cent of its total population and about forty-six per cent of the total Jewish community. Israel's overall number of Haredi is increasing too. They will make up a third of the population by 2065. The Israel of the future will be one of more Ultra-Orthodox and settlers.

The Greek school on Mount Zion has no place in this Israel.

9

THRACE

GREEK MINARETS

Writers who deploy the phrase "crossroads of East and West" must do so with caution. It is an overused term. As one old friend in Cairo told me, "Every school kid in the Eastern Mediterranean is taught their country is the crossroads of civilizations. Lots of crossing going on, but where are the roads?"

The crossroads business of geopolitics is a crowded space. The word's popularity evinces a shrinking world, in addition to the strategic calculations and public relations of more and more states. When Great Powers are carving up zones of influence and you don't want to pick a side, a good reply is to bill yourself as a crossroads, or even better, a mediator. There are standard-bearer cultural crossroads like Lebanon, and ones with political and economic ambitions like the United Arab Emirates, Serbia and Iraq. They are all trying to carve out a niche in this way, and exploit bigger neighbors or Great Powers. Türkiye, the subject of so many crossroads travel writers, has moved beyond its mediator stage, and is now a proper regional power.

The phrase "crossroads of East and West" smacks you in the face in Greece's Thrace. Kavala really is a crossroads, in that its history naturally pulls you south to Egypt, but culturally and geographically it belongs to Thrace, and yes, Istanbul. It is very hard to pick your route from Kavala. Anyway, in late summer 2024 I was on the Egnatia Odos, Greece's modern incarnation of the ancient Via Egnatia, which linked the Adriatic Coast to the Bosporus Straits for the Romans. Tasos Meneshian and his family took Egnatia Odos on their summer trips from Athens to Aleppo. I racked up hundreds of miles on it, driving between Ioannina and the Turkish border.

Outside Kavala, trucks packed with goods made in Türkiye are heading west on the highway to markets in Europe. The Bulgarians that Missirian and other Kavala natives complained about are cruising in their big black SUVs alongside cars with Romanian and Albanian license plates.

There is a point on this highway, somewhere after Kavala, where the popular idea of Greece vanishes. I arrive in the city of Xanthi just in time to hear the faint call of the *Dhuhr* prayer before it's drowned out by a Turkish pop hit on the car radio. Xanthi is thirty-two miles northeast of Kavala, and nestled in the foothills of the Rhodopi mountains. Here, the resinous smell of pine trees replaces the briny Aegean air. Unlike the abandoned mosques in Kavala, in Xanthi, the minarets still work.

Thrace is a historic region that was swallowed up by Bulgaria, Greece and Türkiye after the Ottoman Empire's collapse. In Thrace, Greece's Westernizing tendencies, made-for-Instagram tourist hotspots, and modern Hellenism are filtered out. What's left is a raw Near Eastern hinterland, attached to the West by the barest threads of the European Union and NATO. Because Thrace is a borderland, it is vulnerable to these institutions cracking; yet this fragility makes their anchoring power all the more striking. At a time when the Western alliance and European

Union are being seriously challenged, Thrace reminds you why they are so valuable. When I first visited here in 2022, I felt I had been transplanted to a mountainous corner of Lebanon or the Caucasus, such is the hodgepodge of religions and languages: Greek Orthodox Christians, Sunni Muslims, Roma, Armenians, and Alevis all mix here.

Xanthi was a prosperous trading town a century ago. Like Kavala, fortunes were made here off the tobacco industry. The city is split between a new town of mid-twentieth-century apartment blocks, and a hillside one of old, white-washed Balkan homes and neoclassical mansions that scream faded opulence. Today, Thrace is one of the poorest regions in the European Union—nearly a third of its population is at risk of poverty. Few diplomats or foreign journalists bother coming to Thrace. Athenians avoid it like the plague.

Eleni Diafonidou, the owner of Xanthi's daily newspaper *EMPROS*, summed up the region's economic plight, to me, "Thrace isn't growing, it's shrinking. No one invests here."

Diafonidou and I met at an old Ottoman caravansary-turned-cafe. It was tucked behind the local bazaar, where women in colorful Muslim headscarves jostled aside girls dressed in skimpy jean shorts, their thighs sticky with sweat in the late summer heat. The vendors sold uber cheap clothing under tattered umbrellas and electrical wires.

Diafonidou is one of a vanishing breed: the owner and editor of a local newspaper that still churns out paper copies every morning. Because Thrace's economy is mainly dependent on agriculture, she knows the intricacies of weather patterns, fertilizer prices, farm subsidies and the European Union's agricultural policies. Xanthi may be a provincial rural backwater, but it is a cosmopolitan town, as I saw in the bazaar.

"We have so many origins and cultures: Greeks from Anatolia, Greeks from Albania, Greeks from the Peloponnese, the Muslims, Turks, Pomaks, Armenians. We are a mosaic. In Athens, you can see all the origins of the world, but they aren't locals like here. And Türkiye doesn't let us forget it's next door," she said.

The swirling mix of languages and religions makes Greek Thrace fertile ground for Türkiye's influence operations. More than anywhere else in the European Union, Thrace is where Türkiye's hard power reaches deepest into ordinary people's lives. This unnerves Greece, whose officials simply avoid talking about Western Thrace (the province's official name).

"Türkiye has a big influence here. They always try to stir up tensions with the Muslim locals," Eleni said. "The Americans are the newest arrivals." Since the war in Ukraine, American troops have descended regularly to the port of Alexandroupoli, thirty miles to the southeast of Xanthi. A few months before my visit, the American and Greek armies unloaded 3,000 pieces of military equipment from the port, including dozens of tanks, armored vehicles and Humvees destined for the battlefields of Eastern Europe.

Thrace was always a trampling ground for empires and cultures—Roman, Byzantine and Ottoman. But its current diversity is a legacy of the Treaty of Lausanne. When Greece and Türkiye decided to end their war in 1922 and mandate a forced population exchange the following year, they made a few exceptions. The Greeks on two small islands in the Aegean, Imbros and Tenedos, were exempt, as were about 130,000 Greeks who lived in Constantinople. The Greek community in Constantinople was prosperous. The Greek government knew that finding homes and businesses for them in Greece would stretch their impoverished state's resources. Preserving their presence in Istanbul also made it easier for the Greek Patriarchate to remain there, sidestepping the nasty question of whether the center of Greek Orthodoxy should uproot. So these Greeks got to stay.

In return, Türkiye arranged for the minority Muslim population in Western Thrace to remain on their lands. They were mainly farmers, and their presence on a chunk of territory next to the border helped make Thrace a buffer.

Greece and Türkiye bartered people like poker chips in an internationally approved game of ethnic cleansing.

The Greeks in Constantinople were nearly wiped out by Türkiye's government, which stoked up a pogrom against them in 1955 and expelled tens of thousands in the 1960s. But the Muslims in Western Thrace have maintained their demographic size. While they make up just one per cent of Greece's overall population, these Muslim heirs to the Ottomans number at least one third of Western Thrace's 370,000-strong population. They are Greece's only officially recognized minority. In effect, a modern *millet*.

Traveling in Western Thrace is like stepping back in time. In this poor border region, it's as if the population exchange never happened. Of every country I have traveled to in the Eastern Mediterranean, it is Greece that has best preserved the Ottoman *millet* system and mentality in its purest form, here in Thrace.

The Treaty of Lausanne stipulated that the minorities would be able to live according to their religious and social customs, just as the Ottomans had allowed. So the Muslims of Western Thrace have their own schools. Until a few years ago, this was the only region in Europe where Sharia law was compulsory. Greek courts even deferred inheritance, marriage and divorce cases to Islamic judges. In 2018, Shariah was made optional, so that it is now only used if both parties opt to go before an Islamic judge as opposed to a Greek civil court.

After meeting Eleni, I drove through the outskirts of the city, passing by a local mosque whose minaret had been overshadowed by high-rise concrete apartments. I drove in the direction of the Pomakochoria. The inhabitants of these remote, mountainous villages, Pomaks, are Balkan Muslims who speak a Slavic language very close to Bulgarian. Pomaki is one of the rarest languages in Europe. It's close to the southern dialect of Bulgarian, but has no alphabet or proper grammar. The Pomaks converted to Islam during the Ottomans' conquest of Thrace. They had the zeal of converts and were, therefore, the sultan's fiercest defenders.[1] When the empire collapsed, the Pomaks went from being loyal subjects of a sultan, to citizens of nation-states, scattered across Greece, Türkiye and Bulgaria. Their Islamic faith and Slavic language made them hard to box into new national borders. That fluid identity put them in the crosshairs of these states. Türkiye wanted to coerce the Pomaks into identifying with Atatürk's new nation. Greece was particularly suspicious of them. First, they were Muslim. Secondly, Athens viewed them as potential allies of communist Bulgaria. Greece literally kept the Pomaks under lock and key during the Cold War. From the 1930s until 1996, the Pomak villages above Xanthi were garrisoned by Greek soldiers like open air prisons. Locals needed passes just to visit neighboring villages and leave the mountain.[2] It only became possible for foreigners to travel here without a permit in the 1990s. Eleni remembers traveling with her father through army checkpoints thanks to his journalist pass.

I met Emine and several other Pomak women at Pleteno Koinsep, a weaving cooperative on the edge of Xanthi. Over Turkish delight drenched in powdered-sugar and small cups of Turkish coffee, the women told me what it was like growing up in a country that treated its own citizens like foreign agents. "We were isolated. Cut-off. Imagine being told you can't leave your village after midnight even if there is an emergency. We couldn't communicate between ourselves" Emine told me. "Greece didn't want us. We were forgotten because we wore the headscarf and had different sounding names," one woman said.

The women all wore beautiful floral headscarves, whose significance is cultural as much as religious. We sat along a wooden divan in a cozy room stacked with woven bags and baskets. A cast-iron stove occupied the middle of the room for cold Rhodopi winters. Not long ago, the building had a more sinister purpose. "This was the guardhouse where Greece kept us locked in the villages," Emine said.

The women remember having to show ID cards to the Greek border guards who manned this post. My hosts were in their forties and fifties, and had never finished middle school. As a result of decades of harassment and segregation by the Greek state, the Pomak villages are isolated and desperately poor. The cooperative was set up to give these women a secondary source of income. The Greek government converted the guardhouse into a shop in 2022.

Restrictions on the Pomaks were part of a wider Greek policy dubbed "Administrative Harassment" against the Muslim minority that started in the late 1950s. It's one of the saddest chapters in the nation's recent history. Greece pursued the policy when Türkiye was persecuting the Greek minority. In Western Thrace, the uneasy coexistence between Greeks and Muslims that held immediately after the Lausanne Treaty deteriorated around 1955 as Greece and Türkiye bickered over Cyprus. The Greek minority in Istanbul and Turkish minority in Western Thrace became de facto hostages of their respective governments, who embraced a policy of "reciprocity" in which an abuse inflicted on one minority warranted retaliation against the other.[3]

Athens responded to Türkiye's 1955 pogrom against the Greeks and 1964 expulsions with measures designed to make life unbearable for the Muslim minority. Besides the system of military checkpoints in the mountains, Muslim land was expropriated. They were denied driving licenses and prevented from joining professional associations or obtaining building repair permits. Greece curtailed funding for minority schools. Life was micromanaged by Greek officials to the extent that in 1970 only one Turkish-language movie was allowed to be screened here.[4]

In 1990, the minority's frustration boiled over into social unrest. Greeks and Muslims clashed in a violent riot in the neighboring city of Komotini. Greeks started to worry that Western Thrace could descend into ethnic conflict along religious lines.[5] The specter of internal strife hovered over the region just as Yugoslavia was breaking up. This was another of the close calls in Greece's modern history. Greece could choose to be an outpost for democracy and rule of law in the Near East, or another former Ottoman land that let ethnic and religious tensions thrive in its borderlands. It chose the former, although the scares of past policies are still felt here. Former Prime Minister Konstantinos Mitsotakis lifted the policy of harassment in the early 1990s and pledged the minority "equality before the law and equality of rights."[6]

My hosts chatted in Turkish and Pomak among themselves. When the women address me, it's in Greek or English.

"Language isolated us," Vengyul told me. Like the other women, she has the bright blue eyes, bony face and porcelain white skin that are classic Pomak features. Her grace is accentuated by a colorful headscarf.

Within the Muslim minority, the elite pressed villagers to learn Turkish. "In school, we had one hour of instruction in Greek a day, Pomak at home and Turkish the rest of the time. How can you be part of a country if you don't speak the language?" Vengyul said.

My hosts didn't dwell on past grievances. They evinced the gentler cosmopolitanism of the old Near East. Greece will need more of this going forward as it is absorbed into the wider Middle East through immigration and geopolitics.

THRACE

Türkiye used to be the promised land for this Muslim minority when Greece was harassing them, but Greece's entry into the European Union and slow reforms have reduced its allure. "Western Thrace has Muslims and Christians; some call themselves Turk, others Pomak, others Greek. There are also atheists. No one cares how you identify yourself. Things are better today," Vengyul explained.

The Pomak women offer a unique window into how Greece has changed. Despite the media drumbeating about a new, xenophobic far-right in the European Union, the experiences of these Pomak women, across a longer timeline, point to a more tolerant and open Greece.

"I lived in Athens for three years and remember the stares I would get with my hijab. Now, when I go to Athens, I don't feel tension," Emine told me. She has two children at university, one daughter in Athens and a son studying in Komotini. "My daughter doesn't wear the hijab. My children are proud to be Greek, but they also want the stories of our past."

The big worry here in the foothills of Rhodopi is the economy. My hosts' husbands can't find work in Western Thrace and spend six months of the year working construction and painting jobs in Germany. Many work in shipyards. The push of Thrace's awful economy and pull of the European Union's common market has made these villagers global citizens.

"Six months in Germany, six months in the village. There is a town near Frankfurt with only Pomaks from Rhodopi. They work at the airport. The whole village emptied out. Western Thrace lives off money from abroad," one of the women told me.

I thought of Diafonidou, who hails from the Christian majority. She shared the same mixed emotions about Thrace as my Pomak hosts. Both talked with pride about the respect between Christian and Muslim neighbors after years of tensions, but also painted a depressing picture of Thrace's economic outlook. "No one wants to go back to the time of the 1980s and 1990s. The dynamics between the Muslim and Christian communities are so much better," Diafonidou said. "The problems for the minority are the same for the majority: the economy and standard of living. The minority is farther behind, but the worry is the same."

Diafonidou said successive governments in Athens—on the Left and Right—were suspicious of Thrace, treating it like a foreign land. A case in point is that Greece's foreign ministry assigns a diplomat here, to represent Greece in one of its own provinces. The post has been around for decades in response to Türkiye's widespread meddling in local politics. But for the elite in glitzy Athens, Thrace is just too oriental and old fashioned. Promoting Thrace, with all its political baggage and history, is too complicated when you are trying to turn Athens into Dubai. The irony is that Western Thrace is desperate for tourists and Airbnbs. They don't have any.

"We have mountains, rivers and beautiful villages but no tourists. Imagine that the last two years, the three biggest hotels in Xanthi closed even as Greece has record tourist numbers," Eleni told me. "Every year we have a music festival to commemorate the composer Manos Hadjidakis. Students who come have to stay in Kavala because we don't have enough rooms. There is no interest to promote Thrace. No one talks about us as a cultural destination."

"I don't think it's a priority for the Greek state. Quite the opposite. It's better to have a place you can manipulate easily, because when people get more wealthy, they start asking for things. Look how strong Crete's voice is in Athens," she said, referring to the island that has filled out Greece's political elite over the century. "They speak up," she said.

The lack of interest in Greek Thrace reveals just how hollow the global tourism trade is. I have been to Xanthi in winter and summer. Despite being in a region that faces steep demographic decline and high poverty levels, whenever I visit, this city of 60,000 is always buzzing. In the winter months, the alleys and bars in the old town are filled with students from the engineering school. In the summer, locals who moved elsewhere in Greece or abroad trickle back to their villages. The university here is one of the easiest for Greek students to enroll in. Studying in Thrace is treated like exile to Siberia by Athenian teenagers. Even the Turkish tourists driving to Kavala and Thessaloniki rarely linger here.

For me, Greece's poorest and least-travelled region is its richest. Thrace has an organic cosmopolitism. It's not imported. The food is delicious and the nightlife eerily similar to parts of Beirut because of the university students and religious diversity. I remember leaving a club with a group of off-duty Greek soldiers one winter night in Komotini. We stumbled through the streets reeking of berry-flavored *nargile* smoke just as the early-morning call to prayer sounded.

Of all the regions I travelled to, Thrace is the one that would be most familiar to the authors of *Macedonia: A Plea For the Primitive*. It hasn't changed much. On the hillside of Xanthi's old town, grandmothers in headscarves poke out of white-washed houses to pluck pomegranates and oranges from their gardens. Trellises above the taverna tables drip with big clumps of green grapes and begonia. Food is cheap here, even by Greek standards. Patrons devour Ottoman dishes like *Hunker Begendi*, an eggplant purée topped with stewed lamb meat. I've never paid more than €40 for a delicious dinner for two in Western Thrace. In Xanthi's cobblestone back streets, bereft of tourists, you appreciate how little it takes to live a good life. It doesn't require a fortune.

Despite the sad legacy of harassment in Greek Thrace, the old-school cosmopolitanism of the Levant was never snuffed out here as it was in Cairo or Thessaloniki. The newer Athenian version is powered by hot money and real estate speculation. In Xanthi, you find a gentler cosmopolitanism that is measured in centuries. Thrace's blend is based on coexistence, not multiculturalism. In fact, conservatism and cosmopolitanism go hand in hand here in a way that would baffle the Left in the West, and quite a few people on the populist Right.

You have to fight the initial urge to want to transplant Xanthi to a coastal setting. The rust-colored terra-cotta tiles and neoclassical mansions with ornate lintels and flaking shutters could belong on the Aegean. But walk here for a bit, and the mountain isolation and sea of green pine pulls you in. If there is a Near Eastern fairytale town, old Xanthi is it. A century ago, all of this beauty was underpinned by commerce centered around the cultivation and trade of the local variety of Basmas tobacco. The oldest houses in Xanthi are built in the traditional Balkan style, with *sachnisi*, those jutting Ottoman bay windows that hang precariously over the street. Some jut out so far they almost touch overhead. The newer mansions were built in the late nineteenth and early twentieth century by merchants. Even when Thrace was an unstable battleground between Greece, Bulgaria and the Ottomans, people were making money and placing bets on immovable assets, like luxury houses. It might sound strange for me to argue that Greece's economic boom can continue on the frontlines of instability, but this is what makes relatively safe Athens and Thessaloniki more appealing to Greece's neighbors. One of the oldest trades in the world is betting on which cities will thrive as a result of chaos next door.

Western Thrace was rich, strategically situated, and hotly contested. The Ottomans swept through here in the fourteenth century before they conquered Constantinople in 1453. Thrace was linked geographically, culturally and economically to Istanbul, not Athens. As a region, this is where the European Union ends and Türkiye begins, but there is no natural border here. The Evros river that separates them is relatively small and placid. Keeping Greek Thrace and Istanbul apart is difficult.

As the Ottoman Empire was unraveling, Thrace existed in a hazy limbo, bouncing between nation-states like a ping-pong ball during the First and Second Balkan wars. In 1913, a short-lived Republic of Thrace was established before it was occupied by Bulgaria. By 1918, the Allied army took over administration. It wasn't until 1920 that Western Thrace was ceded to Greece. During the Greco-Turkish War, Greek generals were aching to send troops in Thrace to occupy lightly defended Istanbul. But the Allies stopped them.[7]

In modern times, Erdoğan has shown how easy it is to penetrate Thrace's borders. In February 2020, he unleashed thousands of migrants toward the Evros region of Thrace to blackmail the European Union for financial aid.

"What did we do yesterday?" Erdoğan declared in a speech as Turkish police officers and guards stood by to let refugees pass, "We opened the doors."[8] Since then, Greece has been laser focused on beefing up security at the Evros border with drones, sensors and cameras.

* * *

Thrace's piquant setting is the backdrop for a bitter dispute between Türkiye and Greece over what to call the minority population. Greece officially recognizes it as Muslim, according to the Treaty of Lausanne, whereas Türkiye invokes the cultural and linguistic ties it shares with Greece's citizens to assert they should be recognized as a Turkish minority. To outsiders, this can seem like an eccentric, pointless feud, but both governments, and some locals, take it deadly seriously. Like gas in the Eastern Mediterranean, the minority's name is a vehicle for Türkiye's regional power projection.

Tasos Chatzivasileiou, a Deputy Foreign Minister and close advisor to Greece's Prime Minister, explained to me why Athens is so committed to the Lausanne Treaty's terminology about a Muslim minority. "We have just seen one war erupt in Europe with a country claiming it must protect an ethnic minority," he told me in 2022 when he was an MP, referring to Russia's invasion of Ukraine, which Moscow partly justified in terms of defending ethnic Russians. Lurking behind the fight over the minority's name in Greek minds is Cyprus. Türkiye invaded the north in 1974 on the grounds of protecting the Turkish minority. Privately, Greek officials worry that if Ankara's claim that the minority is Turkish is recognized it will give Türkiye more influence in Western Thrace and an excuse to intervene more in this strategic borderland.

Statistics on the minority are hard to come by. But Greece breaks it down into three subgroups, saying around fifteen per cent are Roma, thirty-five per cent are Pomaks and the remaining fifty per cent are an oddly named group called "Greeks of Turkish descent."

Both countries use the minority to support their claims, promoting cultural associations and clubs that identity with their preferred name. Greece gave Ankara an inside track to the minority during the period of administrative harassment because Türkiye was able to trumpet itself as the Muslims' protector when Athens was harassing them. It is still paying the price for that strategic folly.[9]

Like other issues in Greece and Türkiye's rocky relationship, the fight over the minority pre-dates Erdoğan, but he ratcheted up tensions and infused them regional power ambitions. Western Thrace is a textbook case of how big powers step in to fill vacuums and expand their influence by exploiting genuine local grievances.

The Muslim minority didn't avoid the changes sweeping Türkiye after the Ottoman Empire's collapse. Türkiye worked to impose its ethnic and nationalist identity on the minority, while Greece supported traditional Islamists to counter the Kemalists' narrative. It failed.

"All of them [the minority] today are Turks, being Turkified wholly, due to our indifference," one local Greek official reported as early as 1955.[10]

The feud saw Greece support Islamists to combat Turkish nationalists. Greece's imposition of Sharia law in Western Thrace right up until 2018 was part of its effort to emphasize the minority's Islamic nature in the face of Türkiye's ethnic claims. Greece made common cause with Turkish Islamists in the past. During the Greco-Turkish War, some Greek officials even floated allying with the Ottoman sultan in a bid to win over traditional Islamists opposed to the Kemalists.[11]

By the 1960s, Ankara was bankrolling sympathetic journalists, businessmen, imams and teachers in Western Thrace. At a time when the minority faced severe harassment in Greece, many bought property across the border. Thousands of members of the minority were given scholarships to study at Turkish universities. By the early 2000s, some estimates say that 7,000 members of the minority were on the Turkish state's payroll.[12] That lingers today. In this poor border region, Türkiye wields influence through a vast patronage system that it can use to silence dissent.

Türkiye's influence operations in Western Thrace are the oldest and most sophisticated of its operations in the Balkans. Türkiye started restoring old Ottoman mosques in the Balkans decades ago. Now, it is selling Bayraktar TB2 drones to Albania and howitzer canons to North Macedonia.[13] These deals are small, but because the Balkan states are so poor and neglected by the big superpowers, Türkiye gets a good bang for its buck.

Türkiye wasn't always so interested in the Balkans. It took the breakup of Yugoslavia and Erdoğan's rise to power for Ankara to rediscover the importance of this region to its foreign policy.

THE NEW BYZANTINES

As the United States and Russia carve out their spheres of influence, both seem to be passing on the Balkans. There are good strategic reasons why they shouldn't care about Greece's landlocked northern neighbors. They are poor, have aging populations, immature economies and little purchasing power. Probably the main reason the impoverished and ethnically divided Balkans have been so peaceful the last twenty years is because they are so grey. Young people are needed to fight wars, not pensioners. The Balkans were the deep core of the Ottoman Empire until its final days. It is natural that Türkiye should step back in. The Ottoman elite were Turkish speakers from the Balkans. Bosnia, North Macedonia, Bulgaria, and Kosovo all have Turkish minorities. In 2024, Erdoğan visited Tirana, Albania to inaugurate the largest mosque in the region. More of Türkiye in the Balkans might be a good thing. Just look at the demographics. Türkiye's median age is thirty-three while North Macedonia's is forty-one and rising. A younger and bigger Türkiye invested in this region can help their economies and ghost villages.

The Greek government regularly complains to American and European officials about Türkiye's violations of its airspace and its bellicose rhetoric. But it makes less of Türkiye's meddling in Western Thrace, because it is too sensitive. Athens does not want to draw attention to what is effectively a low-level Turkish fiefdom in its borderlands. If you ask Greeks about Western Thrace, first they will be shocked you know it exists, and then you will hear them filled with alarmism that in the next decades the Muslim minority will be the majority. One friend who is a respected policy analyst in Athens told me with a straight face that Greece should leverage its good ties with Egypt to facilitate the arrival of thousands of Coptic Egyptians to Thrace to dilute the Muslim presence and boost its agricultural production.

"What we call the minority today isn't going to be the minority in twenty years. Both the Christian majority and the Muslim minority are shrinking, but the Muslim minority has more children and its young people are more likely to stay in Western Thrace," Diafonidou told me. "That should not worry Greece. The important thing is that Greek citizens feel they belong to Greece."

* * *

How do members of the minority feel about the dispute? It is sort of like how Greek Orthodox Palestinians view the issue of Greek priests in Jerusalem. They care, but it's not an issue that dominates their everyday lives, unless they can profit from it (as some of the elite are doing). Most members of the minority say Greece is doing most of the harm to itself.

Mustafa Mustafa, a former Syriza member of parliament from Komotini, and now a local doctor, told me that the average member of the minority does not consider the geopolitical tensions when deciding their identity, precisely because Western Thrace is so peaceful. "We are Greek citizens who have lived here for 100 years having no problems with our Greek neighbors," he told me. But he opposed Greece's policy of adhering to the minority's religious label. As he explained it, "I say I am Turkish and want respect. If someone says they are Pomak they should also be respected," he said. "Religion is a personal thing. I don't want it said that I am a Muslim. My surname is Mustafa, but I am an atheist. My grandfather spoke Turkish. In this part of the world it matters what language your grandfather spoke," he told me during an interview in 2022.

The dispute gets more bizarre the deeper you go. I remember interviewing one local doctor who tried to convince me his skull shape proved he was Turkish. He fumed that the Greek government referred to his village as a Pomak one despite what he said were his cranial features clearly proving he was Turkish. When pressed a little, locals here delight in becoming rookie anthropologists, and guessing the ethnicity of passersby.

* * *

In 2017, Erdoğan became the first Turkish head of state to visit Greece in sixty-five years. He made a historic stopover in Western Thrace. The visit was part of the Syriza government's efforts to build bridges with Ankara. It turned into a disaster for Greece when Erdoğan unexpectedly railed against perceived Turkish grievances. He sent a shockwave through the country when he said that Greece and Türkiye should reexamine the Treaty of Lausanne that defines their borders and stipulates the status of the minorities.[14] When he visited Thrace, he was warmly welcomed. For many Greeks, Erdoğan's visit reinforced concerns that Ankara wants a piece of this province, or at the very least, to make it a sphere of influence.

To check Ankara's ambitions, Athens has been accused of favoring Roma and Pomak ethnic identities over Turkish. For example, Greece allows associations and clubs to register as legal entities that contain the word "Pomak," but not those with the word "Turkish," though they operate unofficially. Türkiye backs rival organizations. In this poor region, the best way to make easy money is to open a professional association under one or the other government's preferred names. Western Thrace boasts over 200 such groups.[15]

Xanthi is where Greece's foreign ministry keeps an office and the Pomaks' presence is stronger. The center of Türkiye's power projection in Western Thrace is in Komotini, which is home to its consulate.

THRACE

I took the back road from Xanthi to Komotini. It trailed through little white-washed villages whose approaches are announced by minarets piercing the sky. At the trellis-shaded coffee houses, old men flicked prayer beads; they had mastered the art of engrossing themselves in judging the speed of cars as they sipped iced coffees.

Komotini is a proper trampling ground, laid out on the Thracian plain. Unlike other Greek cities I visited, it's not organized around mountains or a port. Instead, apartment blocks mushroom out from the city's nucleus, the Ottoman-era market. This warren of one- and two-story shops with faded awnings is arranged around the Yeni Mosque, which dates to the sixteenth century.

Komotini is made for passing through. You only need to spend a day here to understand why Thrace's patron is Saint George. In iconography, Saint George is drawn riding atop a horse in the style of ancient Thracian cavalryman while spearing a dragon. I can imagine the *Sipahi*, or Ottoman cavalry, sweeping down across the Thracian plain. Komotini is flat, dusty, and bisected by a two-way offshoot of the Egnatia Odos. Camel caravans trotted down its streets until the 1960s. Komotini still connects East and West.

After Russia invaded Ukraine, it became a cog in the United States' plan to supplant Russia in eastern and central Europe's gas market. In October 2022, a small pipeline was launched here. The 113-mile-long IGB pipeline runs from Komotini deep into Bulgaria. It links Greece's pipeline network with its northern neighbor. Because of IGB, Bulgaria is connected to the Trans Adriatic Pipeline (TAP), which runs from Azerbaijan across Türkiye and into Greece. It is also connected to a new gas import unit in Alexandroupoli. The port city is thirty-five miles southeast of Komotini. Alexandroupoli has a Floating Storage Regasification Unit, or FSRU, that allows Greece to convert liquified natural gas (LNG) carried on tankers back into gas form before moving it via pipeline to northern Europe. The terminal started operating in October 2024 and has already received American LNG.

By December 2024, American LNG had found its way to Ukraine via Greece. The entry point was Greece's larger LNG import facility in Revithoussa, near Athens. The whole point is that Greece envisions its entire coastline as a hub for LNG seeping its way north through a network of pipelines and terminals. Greece is trying to market the facility to energy-rich Arab states too, including Qatar, the world's largest LNG exporter, and Saudi Arabia, whose state-owned energy company, Aramco, is trying to get into the LNG business.

Greece's bid to become a regional energy hub is almost totally dependent on Russia being cut off from European markets. The IGB pipeline is owned by a consortium that includes Bulgarian and Greek state-owned energy companies, and Italy's Edison. The pipeline operator wants to increase capacity in the coming years, but has a demand problem.[16]

The European Union is trying to reduce its reliance on Russian gas. It stopped importing pipeline gas directly from Russia after the Ukraine invasion, and Russian gas stopped flowing to Europe via Ukraine in 2025. However, it still transits to Europe through TurkStream. This pipeline cuts across the Black Sea. It connects Russia with Türkiye's region of Eastern Thrace. Russia has accused Ukraine of trying to attack the pipeline, which effectively allows Türkiye to send Russian gas into Europe. Türkiye also imports gas from Azerbaijan. Gas molecules don't have DNA, but this so-called "Turkish Blend" is made up of at least forty per cent Russian-origin gas. The Turkish blend is cheaper than American LNG and demand for it is high. The Turkish connection has been a godsend to Russia.[17]

In January 2025, Russian gas deliveries to Europe via Turkstream hit an all-time high.[18]

The more European countries import from Turkstream, the more Ankara's influence is boosted and the more difficult it becomes for Greece to make Western Thrace into an energy hub. Türkiye has faced some setbacks. It wanted to establish another gas distribution hub in Eastern Thrace using additional Russian gas, but Russian energy giant Gazprom backed off the plans in early 2025 because the Turks wanted to market the gas alone.

The Greeks' bid to become an energy hub depends on how the US and EU treat Russia. As of May 2025, the EU was weighing a plan to ban all Russian gas imports—that would include through Turkstream. This is easier said than done, but it would be a boon for the Greeks. The United States is the wildcard. President Donald Trump wants to increase American LNG exports to Europe. Greece seems like a natural partner. But he is trying to negotiate an end to the war in Ukraine and is flirting with a rapprochement with the Russians. One sweetener Moscow is holding out to the Americans is a grand bargain to cooperate on sending energy supplies to Europe. In March 2025, Putin said that if "the United States and Russia agree on cooperating in the energy field, then a gas pipeline to Europe can be ensured." He was referencing the Russian undersea pipeline Nord Stream 2 which Germany has halted from operating.[19] In sum, if big volumes of cheap Russian gas find their way back to Europe with the United States' blessing, the Greeks' ambitions are toast.

Xanthi is beautiful. Komotini is ugly and kitsch, but better for journalists. Komotini is one of my favorite cities in Greece. Just mentioning it to Greeks makes them cringe. The ugly apartment blocks give dreary Soviet Union vibes. The Roma slum of Alan Kogioy reaffirms that you are on the very edge of Europe, full of castaways. Komotini's dilapidated Ottoman marketplace is a maze of tiny streets covered by pergolas. Turks, Greeks, North

Macedonians, Armenians and Pomaks all mingle here. With your ears wide open, you hear *inshallah* muttered to seal local business deals at the coffeehouses, and *kalimera*, the Greeks' "good morning."

Ankara's influence operations in Western Thrace are bare-knuckled. They include paying off journalists for favorable coverage, bribing local members of the Christian and Muslim elite, distributing money to the poor and funding newspapers critical of Greece at every turn. Greece is the only NATO member state that has to cope with such a level of meddling by an ally.[20]

The local political party aligned with Türkiye is the Friendship, Equality, and Peace Party, or DEB. I met Cigdem Asafoglu, the party's leader, during a 2022 trip to Komotini. "We as a party advocate that this minority is Turkish," she told me. "I am a Turkish politician, Greek citizen."

Her party has been unable to breach the three per cent electoral threshold needed to enter parliament, but it works as a pressure valve that keeps members of Greece's parliament who are from the minority on the defensive. The Greek parliament doesn't reserve seats for the minority, but because of its size it usually sends around three MPs. They are represented in Greece's center-left and left parties, like PASOK and Syriza, but they are far from ideological. Their main focus is playing the Turkish consulate and Greek political elite off each other to stay in power. In 2023, two minority MPs were attacked in the Greek press for posing behind a sign that declared the minority Turkish.

Ilhan Ahmet is an MP with Greece's center-left PASOK party. When I met him in 2022, he had fallen out with the Turkish consulate. He was ousted from a local minority advisory board which accused him of not being "one of us, but Greek" and losing "all emotional ties to the minority." This is the kind of separatist rhetoric Turkish-backed groups use.[21]

With his short cropped white hair and rimless glasses, Ahmet looks like a provincial banker or accountant. He is a savvy Thracian politician.

"I represent everyone from Rodope, minority and majority alike. I think Türkiye wants to keep the minority separate. It wants conflict." When asked where he fits into the mix he told me, "I have Turkish origins, but a Greek mind."

Some organizations, like the Turkish Union of Xanthi, have taken their claim for official status to the European Court of Human Rights. The court ruled that the organization should be allowed to register with the word Turkish in it, but Greece has refused to abide by the ruling citing national security grounds. Organizations claiming Turkish status operate unofficially and in plain sight, but are not given legal status and the benefits that go with it. The dispute has led to some bizarre hairsplitting.

The Turkish Youth Union of Komotini is a prime example. The long, one-story building sits at a busy intersection of Komotini's old commercial center. Its shaded courtyard is a haven from the bustle of market shoppers. In the late morning, the smells of Anatolian flatbread, *lahmacun* and savory *bougatsa* pastries float into the yard. Officially, the club doesn't exist because it includes "Turkish" in its name, but it operates for everyone to see. The building is owned by the Komotini *waqf*, a religious trust, just like the Egyptian one that owns Imaret.

I asked Selim Isa, the administrator of the *waqf* in Komotini, about the tensions. Isa is a laid back Thracian. He has a 1980s-style full head of hair and a local reputation as a partier. He chatted amiably with me over Turkish coffee. Although the *waqf* is backed by the Greek government, it owns the Turkish Youth Union and mosques where Turkish-backed imams preach. Both sides have reached a de facto agreement not to escalate their respective positions.

"We don't want to cause a conflict with anyone, so we don't force people out. The problem is with the Turkish consulate. It tries to stir up trouble. Not the people," Isa told me when I asked him why the *waqf* allows the Youth Union to operate out of its building even though it uses the word "Turkish" in its name.

The reality is that cracking down on the Turkish-backed groups would be the surest way to spark protests and upset the delicate communal balance.

The *waqf's* office is attached to the Yeni Mosque complex whose minaret competes for the top spot in Komotini's skyline with the town clocktower, which was built in 1884 during the reign of Sultan Abdul Hamid II. In the small city center, shop windows burst in the bright colors of Turkish delight and *sucuk lokum*, the long, sausage version of the former. The antique stores here are filled with even more Near Eastern bric-a-brac than Thessaloniki: old *nargiles*, yellow prayer beads, and furniture inlaid with mother of pearl. The smell of fresh ground coffee and grilled meat fills the back streets.

Türkiye's financial pull is also cemented by the presence of the state-owned Ziraat Bank, which has branches in Komotini and Xanthi. One local Greek official told me Turkish diplomats bring in cash for payments to organizations from across the border. The Turks deny allegations that they meddle in Western Thrace. When I brought it up to Türkiye's former ambassador to Greece in 2022 he shot back, "Trust me, nobody needs to be paid or pressured to be critical of Greece's treatment of its own citizens living in Western Thrace."

The status of the Muslim leadership in Western Thrace is also disputed. Greece officially recognizes two muftis in Xanthi and Komotini. Their role in Greece goes back to Ottoman times. In the 1880s, when Greece was liberating its new lands from the Ottoman Empire, it absorbed thousands of Muslim citizens and granted muftis special legal status. The mufti is one of the most respected figures in an Islamic community. He overseas marriages and appoints imams, who lead prayer at mosques. Muftis also act as judges, applying Islamic Law by interpreting the Quran and a collection of the Prophet's sayings and deeds, known as *hadiths*.

Muftis and Orthodox priests in Greece take their salary from the state and are akin to civil servants. In the late 1980s, Türkiye began backing its own muftis. It argues that Greece should allow Muslims to freely elect their religious leaders without state interference.

The shadow muftis operate much like Turkish-backed organizations; they oversee the minority's religious life and officiate ceremonies, but have no legal power, although they are substantially more popular than the ones the Greek state appoints.

"Türkiye is our kinstate. We are Turks. We are Muslims. Our existence depends on Türkiye's existence," Mustafa Trampa, the shadow mufti of Xanthi told me when I visited him at the city's *Sunne Tzami*, or mosque. He gave me a warm welcome in November 2022, serving hot cups of tea Turkish-style in hour-glass cups resting in colored saucers.

Analysts say that Greece only feeds Türkiye's narrative of mistreatment by refusing to allow a process for the free election of muftis.

Below the surface, however, Türkiye's influence has faded, especially since 2016. The dispute between Greece and Türkiye in Western Thrace is mainly one between local elites who play Athens and Ankara off against each other for gain. Young Muslims are tuning out the constant drumbeat of nationalist propaganda.

Abdul, who spoke to me on condition that I change his name, is one of the rare figures in the minority who has managed at various times to offend both Greece and Türkiye. He is former journalist. He has a bushy grey beard and full belly that he pats contently as we sit for coffee. He asked that I withhold his identity to speak freely. He said he was afraid Türkiye could take retribution for what he says by punishing family members in Türkiye.

"Thirty years ago it was popular for the minority to leave Western Thrace for work and school in Türkiye. But the last fifteen years, very few members of the minority that I can think of moved to Türkiye," he said.

"They see the bad state of politics and the awful economic situation. Edirne is more expensive than Xanthi now," he said, referring to the largest Turkish city just a few hours over the border. He told me that Türkiye's policies in Western Thrace are antagonizing the minority.

"Greece's policy at the moment is not to do anything to address Türkiye because it believes Türkiye is shooting itself in the foot. It's right. Türkiye is destroying its influence here acting like a colonial power," he said.

Greece's move to end the horrible policy of administrative harassment has worked. Türkiye's claim that the Muslim minority is under assault here resonates less each year with young people who, as Greek citizens, enjoy more democratic rights than their Turkish counterparts. They benefit from the European Union's freedom of movement and common market. Western Thrace is proof that institutions like the European Union can reduce ethnic grievances and stem conflict. Cosmopolitan, multi-religious and multi-ethnic Western Thrace is Erdoğan's worst enemy. To spite the populists, it's even a traditional and conservative region.

While NATO and the European Union both hang heavy over Greek Thrace, I feel the latter more. Young people in Western Thrace planning summer vacations, pursuing master's degrees or job hunting, interact with the European Union on a more intimate level. Just paying in euros, they don't have rampant inflation like their Turkish neighbors. Ask a young Muslim of Western Thrace if they would rather live in Ankara or Athens.

THRACE

The younger generation will say Athens. I believe Western Thrace makes the case for Ukraine joining the European Union. At the time of writing, Ukraine's post-war future is up for grabs. Joining NATO is not the be-all-and-end-all. However the war ends, if a wide swath of un-occupied Ukraine is able to join the European Union it would be a major victory. Russia talks a big game about NATO and Ukraine, but I suspect that what most worries Putin is a Slavic Ukraine joining the European Union.

* * *

In Komotini, I met Omer Usta, a twenty-nine-year-old graduate of Democritus University. We were introduced through a mutual Christian friend who studied with Omer. He joked that when students arrive from other parts of Greece to attend Democritus University they come grudgingly because it is a backup school, but when they are ready to graduate, they leave a little reluctantly.

"Komotini is something unique," Omer said.

Omer and I sat down at a taverna for *tzigerosarmas*, a Thracian dish of lamb intestine stuffed with liver, rice and dill. We washed it down with Vergina beer, the local lager, and plates of *tzatziki* loaded with garlic.

"I identify as a Muslim and I love Greece. Growing up, I remember some racism. It created a trauma. It's hard to be a member of a minority. But Türkiye has nothing to offer young people from Thrace," he told me. "The local Turkish party, DEB, for example, is still the strongest, but its power diminishes with every election."

His goal is to be the first member of the minority to become a Greek diplomat. "Kids are thinking differently than their fathers and grandfathers. Being multicultural is valuable now. Komotini was always like that. Komotini is all about balance. We take from the East and West."

He reminded me of another young friend, Ragip, whose name I have changed at his request. He is a Muslim entrepreneur here, doing a brisk business certifying local Greek food exports as halal. That doesn't stop him from drinking. We met for beers in Xanthi.

"We had a big contract from a Greek olive oil producer who had an order from Qatar for olive oil with gold flakes," Ragip told me.

Business is booming thanks in part to Saudi Arabia's drive to diversify its economy. The Saudis have apparently discovered Greek cuisine and want it certified halal. They are especially keen on Greek feta. "They only order the best," Ragip said.

Welcome to the new Near East. Ragip has no interest leaving Xanthi, where he says it's preferable to raise a family compared to Athens because of the lower cost of living and the nature.

The European Union and NATO are going to need a lot Ragips and Omers on their borderlands. Long term, the toughest challenge for Greece in Western Thrace is not reducing Türkiye's influence, but getting more young people to remain here and start families. It's possible, but so far Greece hasn't shown the strategic vision necessary. Thrace faces a paradox. Greece recognizes its geopolitical importance for energy and security, but it is depopulating and becoming poorer.

* * *

Not long ago, Thrace was actually a place where the global rich came to invest. In 1869, Jewish businessman Maurice de Hirsch's company, Chemins de fer Orientaux, was awarded a contract by the Ottoman Empire to build a railroad linking Vienna to Constantinople, called the Orient Express. One line on it attached Alexandroupoli to Edirne, formerly Adrianople.

The Dussaud brothers, whose firm built ports from Smyrna to Port Said, constructed Alexandroupoli's first pier.

During Ottoman times, Alexandroupoli was called Dedeagach, a Turkish word that Patrick Leigh Fermor said commemorated the home of its first inhabitant, a hermit who lived under a tree. The newer name commemorates Russian Tsar Alexander II, who led a victorious war against the Ottomans that saw Serbia, Romania and Montenegro gain independence. For a brief period, Russian troops occupied Alexandroupoli, taking Russian influence all the way down to the Aegean. Patrick Leigh Fermor said Alexandroupoli was once "as full of adventure and mystery as a city in the Arabian Nights."[22]

The United States is the latest power to set its sights on Alexandroupoli. The port was inconsequential when the United States felt it could depend on Türkiye as a pro-American ally. Erdoğan changed that and made Alexandroupoli important again. In 2019, the United States spent a paltry $2.3 million to dislodge a sunken dredger from the port. That marked the beginning of its involvement. The port was used to send military aid to Ukraine. In 2021, the United States and Greece updated their mutual defense pact. The agreement gave the United States priority access to Alexandroupoli's airport, port and military barracks.[23] The basing agreement infuriated Moscow. Remember, only a few years before, Athens had begged the Kremlin to invest in this backwater, but Putin passed on the opportunity. The Kremlin had some remorse.

"The problem is very simple, more and more NATO and US troops are gathering in your territory," Kremlin spokesman Dmitry Peskov told Greek television channel ANT1 in December 2021, just before Russia invaded Ukraine. "Hundreds, thousands of units of military equipment are transported through Alexandroupolis and so on," he said.[24]

The base has also irked Türkiye because its leverage as the powerful guardian of the Bosporus straits has been diluted. The American build-up at Alexandroupoli became such a grating topic in Türkiye that Erdoğan raised it in a 2021 meeting with former President Joe Biden. "What is the issue with Alexandroupoli? Establishing a base there bothers us and our people," Erdoğan told reporters when asked what issues he raised at a G-20 summit meeting with Biden in Rome.[25]

The port's geo-strategic value ballooned once Russia invaded Ukraine. In early 2022, Türkiye used its power under the 1936 Montreux Convention to close the Bosphorus and Dardanelles straits to warships. The move was welcomed by Ukraine, which wanted to prevent Russia from bolstering its naval force with warships from elsewhere. But it also effectively locked American vessels out of the Black Sea.

When I visited Alexandroupoli in 2024, the town was overrun with Turkish tourists. Both the Turkish and Greek media overplay the American role here. Every few months, the American military descends on the port to unload cargo for the frontlines in Ukraine. The American soldiers give a short injection of cash to the local economy, but not much more. Eggs and cigarettes sell out quick, locals told me.

"The conflict between Israel and Hamas and the war in Ukraine revived the role of Alexandroupoli. We have a very fruitful cooperation with the United States' military," Konstantinos Chatzimichail, CEO of the Alexandroupoli Port Authority, told me in July 2024.

"If you study a map, Alexandroupoli is an obvious choice for what the United States military needs," Chatzimichail added, giving me the kind of straightforward, no nonsense geography lesson that only a logistics man or a general can give:

> The train from here reaches the Greek-Bulgarian border without big bridges or tunnels so heavy loads or big items can be moved without

difficulty. The port is connected to Helsinki, Finland by the Pan European corridor IX [a highway and rail system running across Eastern Europe, including Ukraine]. None of these routes are crowded, so you can move quickly without delays. It is ideal.

With the United States pushing to end the war in Ukraine, it seemed to me that this is as far as American military power will go here. I sensed that something had peaked. Could the United States retreat, like Tsar Alexander II's troops?

In July 2024, Chatzimichail was already positioning the port for its next stage: the reconstruction of Ukraine. In Greece's borderlands in 2024, people seemed to believe the war in Ukraine had gone as far as it could. Western Thrace is used to seeing the ebb and flow of Great Powers.

"Huge amounts of goods are going to be needed to rebuild Ukraine. Because of the connection, Alexandroupoli will be a gateway to feed its reconstruction. Big logistics chains are going to be established here," Chatzimichail told me, perhaps hopefully. The Greek government wants to keep the United States invested here. Since the end of the Second World War, the Greeks have latched on to the Americans as valuable allies. But what does the pseudo-proxy do when the patron starts losing interest? Chatzimichail has his work cut out for him.

The port was deemed so valuable that Greece scrapped plans to privatize it in November 2022. Greek Prime Minister Kyriakos Mitsotakis cited "geopolitical developments." But in this distant borderland, the Great Powers of old are lurking. One of the four companies that had planned to bid on the port was a Russian-Chinese group led by none other than Ivan Savvidis.

10

ISTANBUL

THE OLD BYZANTINES

If you happen to find yourself on Istanbul's buzzing İstiklal Street in mid-September, keep your eyes peeled for a troop of school kids carrying balloons. Amid the din of *dondurma* sellers banging on ice-cream carts and Arab tourists ogling at perfume-shop windows, they march down the thoroughfare to Panagia Greek Orthodox Church. The students belong to Zografion Lyceum, one of the few remaining Greek schools in Istanbul. They are the old Byzantines.

I came from Thrace to join the students for the opening school day blessing. To reach Beyoğlu, the beating heart of European Istanbul, I drove through suburbs that are their own metropolises. The contrast with Greece's depopulated Thrace was stark.

In Istanbul's otherworldly sprawl, architectural styles blend so that residential towers that wouldn't be out of place in Cleveland or Pittsburg rise above squat, silty apartments that announce the vastness and harshness of Asia. In Istanbul's endless suburbs, the sensation of personal insignificance sets in.

Driving here, I thought how unnatural the Evros river border with Greece is. In another era, Byzantine emperors or capricious sultans would have dispatched Istanbul's rowdy inhabitants on a whim across the Evros, perhaps with some *firman* (edict) to build industry with a favorable tax regime. The Ottomans, as imperial rulers, had an inherent knack for utilizing what we today call forcible displacement. They moved whole populations to rebuild Istanbul after conquering what had become a decrepit capital. "Mehmed the Conqueror and his successors welcomed, urged, coaxed and bodily transplanted Turks, Christians and Jews to the shores of the Bosporus," Stoianovich wrote.[1]

In our era, it is impossible to determine where this city of sixteen million people starts and ends. One day, I imagine, the distant exurbs of this inflation-riven, overpopulated city could touch the Evros. For now, Neo-Ottoman mosques, cranes and clean highways whisk me toward the center of the European side. By the time I reach the working-class neighborhood of Kasampisa, I am subsumed in the concrete, traffic, and crowds that are Istanbul.

Edmondo De Amicis was right when he described this city in his 1877 travelogue as "[that] rendezvous for miscreants from all over the world ... where the people and merchandise of two hemispheres meet and mingle."[2]

In Beyoğlu, the heart of European Istanbul, I feel back in familiar territory. The art nouveau facades and baroque nineteenth-century apartment buildings were once the abodes of Levantines, Armenians, and Greeks. When they were kicked out, Beyoğlu's meandering alleys became the canvas for Orhan Pamuk's *huzun*-soaked novels. Set in the 1960s and 1970s, Pamuk made the communal melancholy of Istanbul famous. His was a cannibalizing, dreary, grey city, where old-money Istanbulites eyed the nouveau riche, right-wing terrorists duked it out with leftists, and Anatolian migrants clawed with their fingernails to survive, all atop the ashes of a collapsed, cosmopolitan empire.

I have left the European Union and an Orthodox Christian country behind, but in Beyoğlu I don't feel disoriented so much as I do humbled. That is because the Near East is a land of gradients. Thrace and Macedonia were, and remain, Istanbul's natural backyard. The city's two biggest demographic shifts in modern times—the supplanting of its Christian population with Turkish and Kurdish migrants from Anatolia's hinterland in the mid-twentieth century, and the arrival of Arab and other Asian Muslim refugees in the twenty-first—have diluted that bond, but not severed it.

In globalized and tourist-filled Beyoğlu, the obvious difference with Greek Thrace is one of scale. The home-cooked dishes behind the glass windows of *lokantas* on İstiklal differ in magnitude from the hearty, buffet-style meals of stuffed vegetables and stewed meats that Greeks call *Megirefta*, but not in substance. The cacophony of Turkish and Greek in the church courtyard also recalls Western Thrace.

Panagia's dull exterior betrays none of its interior Orthodox splendor. During the service, we stand beside jade-colored marble columns, under starry frescos and crystal chandeliers. The chanters wail away in ancient Greek. The iconostasis, which separates the sanctuary from the nave, is enveloped in gilt, and it glistens.

What a magnificent religion. Without a doubt, the mystical and anarchic Orthodox Church is the Christian faith best placed to survive the onslaught of social media and artificial intelligence. No amount of technology or secularization can overcome something so otherworldly.

I grew up in a mixed Catholic and Orthodox household. At the earliest age, we form our identity through contrast and comparison. Mine was forged in the churches I attended, which helped cement in me a vague sensation that Greece, and the Greek part of my family, belonged to the East.

How could we not? In the Catholic Church, the service is subdued and sanitized, like wide American roads with traffic rules and big crosswalks. It is measured, and in the United States, increasingly, culturally liberal. Catholicism's woes are due in part to the fact that it has become too accommodating to modernity. The priests turn over masses like waiters clear tables in a diner. If you miss one service, no worries, there is always another. Catholic priests even reason with you during the homily. The Greek Church is the opposite. It does not care about your schedule or earthly concerns; but at the same time, it is more tactile. As a child, I went less but absorbed more, breathing in the incense while priests with long, grey beards mumbled in an unintelligible ancient language. And there was so much to do! We lit the candles, kissed the icons, kissed the priest's hand, and took the *antidoron* after the service. The Catholic Church we went to had, long ago, stopped allowing 100 strangers to take Holy Communion from the same spoon. In upstate New York, where I grew up, going to the Orthodox Church felt like a Christian version of *Aladdin*.

After the service at Panagia, the priests sprinkled us with holy water using a bunch of basil, the Orthodox Church's official plant. Like much of Orthodox ritual, basil's use is a holdover from pagan times. The ancient Greeks placed it in the hands of the dead to ensure safety in the afterlife. Saint Helen is said to have followed the herb's scent to uncover the cross that Jesus was crucified on in Jerusalem. Helen was the mother of Emperor Constantine, who was the first Roman leader to convert to Christianity. He bestowed on this city his name, making Constantinople the capital of the Eastern Roman Empire.

I lingered for a while at the church. I wanted to take in all of the day's details because they were precious. You see, Istanbul's Greek minority is going extinct. I watched the students, some of whom wore gold and wood crosses over their T-shirts, filter out. These kids are the most prized members of a community whose average age is easily sixty. Few of the tourists or locals who walk along İstiklal even know Greeks still live in Istanbul. The Treaty of Lausanne exempted them from the population exchange but, 100 years after it was signed, the Greeks have shrunk from a 130,000-strong community to barely 2,000 people.

Zografion's enrollment numbers tell the story of the Greeks' demographic demise. The school was built at the turn of the nineteenth century when demand for education in the Greek community was growing. Then, around twenty per cent of Istanbul's population was Greek Orthodox. On the eve of the First World War, around 200,000 Greeks called Istanbul home. The total Christian population was even higher when the Armenians, Bulgarian Orthodox, Catholics and foreign communities were added, comprising at least thirty per cent of Istanbul's inhabitants.[3] They administered and governed their own educational affairs. Zografion was one of the top schools for middle- and upper-middle-class Greeks to educate their children.

Zografion had over 300 students when the 1923 Treaty of Lausanne was signed. Over one million Greeks were expelled from modern Türkiye during the population exchange. Zografion's enrollment was unscathed because Greek Istanbulites were exempted. Despite discrimination and state-sponsored assaults on the Greek population throughout the next decade, pupil numbers continued to creep up, reaching 721 in the early 1960s, even as other Greek schools closed. But by the time Türkiye invaded northern Cyprus in 1974, Zografion's student body had shriveled to 120. I joined Zografion's seventy-four students to kick off the 2024 school year.[4]

Cihanger, a gentrifying neighborhood just below Zografion, was full of Greeks until the early 1960s. Most of those who remain are elderly. The students are the minority's pride because they are the only ones who can keep it from going extinct.

Lakis Vingas, one of the leading members of the Greek community told me,

> We are the only 2,000 people in the world who carry so much diplomatic baggage; whose deaths and births are tracked on the international stage. This is a herculean weight to carry. A Greek from Greece could move to Istanbul and live a totally normal life here as an expat, but not us.

Many Greeks don't even know the community exists. The political forces that led to its decimation are equally misunderstood. Nikos, a Greek Istanbulite I met at the school's opening-day party, told me a story to illustrate. In 2020, he was having a drink with Turkish friends the day Erdoğan turned Hagia Sophia back into a mosque.

"All the Turks at my friend's house were secular," Nikos said. "They came to console me and said, 'We feel so bad for you. We have been thinking about you all day.' Then I was asked, 'How many of you Greeks are left in Istanbul?' I said, 'About 2,000 of us.'"

"Their faces dropped," Nikos continued. "Someone replied, 'Two-thousand! It can't be true. It's a tragedy what Erdoğan has done to you people. We thought there were at least ten thousand.' I said, 'Actually, Erdoğan has been the best. It was your government who did this to us.'" Nikos was referring to the Kemalist, social democratic Republic People's Party (CHP), while prodding, somewhat ironically, at the secular Turks' hatred of Erdoğan.

After the Treaty of Lausanne, Greece and Türkiye experienced a brief golden period in relations. The former foes Atatürk and Venizelos put the conflict behind them and signed a 1930 Friendship Treaty, effectively becoming allies. The bonhomie went so far that Venizelos later nominated Atatürk for the Nobel Peace Prize. This is the kind of whiplash diplomacy that is returning to our world—a diplomacy of strongmen, who rule above entrenched interest groups, lawmakers, and bureaucracies.

As the Kemalists erased the Ottoman past, the Greeks went about their lives. By the 1940s, the Greeks and other minorities were clearly becoming a nuisance to the secular, ethnonationalists. After Atatürk's death, his successor in the CHP, İsmet İnönü, imposed discriminatory wealth taxes on Greeks, Jews and Armenians. During the Second World War, the Greeks were forcibly conscripted into labor battalions.

In 1955, the Turkish government organized a pogrom against the Greeks. Police officers, who the Greeks had trusted to protect them, marked their shops and apartments so that rampaging mobs backed by the government knew which properties to pillage. Some Turks protected their Greek neighbors; others settled scores. The government sensed how hard it would be to get Istanbul's cosmopolitan citizens to turn on each other, so they bused in migrants from the Anatolian countryside and fired them up with propaganda against the rich *giaours* (infidels).[5]

Nektaria Anastasiadou, a Greek Istanbulite author, captures how the pogrom, known as Septemvriana for the month it occurred, haunts survivors to this day. It was a betrayal, the worst crime. In one passage of her novel, *A Recipe for Daphne*, one of the aging Greek characters confronts a Turkish man who he (incorrectly) believes was responsible for the rape and death of his lover more than fifty years earlier. When asked by the suspect why he came, the old Greek replies:

To ask you why you didn't help people who treated you so well. To ask how you could stand by and do nothing when your neighbor's shops were being destroyed and their homes invaded. To ask you what gives you more of a right to this place than we have?[6]

Before the pogrom, Turkish news falsely reported that Greeks had attacked Atatürk's house in Thessaloniki. The bombing was staged and the story planted by the Turkish government.[7] Ankara was pumping out anti-Christian and anti-Greek propaganda in response to tensions in British-controlled Cyprus, which was riven by communal Greek-Turkish violence. This time, it wasn't the CHP, but Türkiye's first democratically elected Prime Minister Adnan Menderes, who had the Greeks in his crosshairs.

Menderes was leader of Türkiye from 1950 to 1960. It is hard to fit him into any one box today. He was a pro-American anticommunist who brought Türkiye into NATO in 1952. He rode a wave of popularity during a brief economic boom that the United States' Marshall Plan investments spurred in Türkiye. Menderes introduced free-market reforms that helped Türkiye's economy grow, but he also overspent. Like Sadat in Egypt, he opened Türkiye's immature market to foreign imports too quickly. By the end of the 1950s, his policies had sparked inflation and a debt crisis. But Menderes is best remembered as a populist who energized Türkiye's Muslim masses. He reopened mosques and restored the call to prayer in Arabic, endearing him to Islamists resentful of the CHP's secularizing ways. Of course, Menderes himself turned into an autocrat after winning elections in 1954 and 1957.

In 1960, Menderes became the first in a long line of Turkish leaders to be ousted in a military coup. When he was hanged, the military referenced the pogrom in his sham trial, but its real motivation was that Menderes challenged their hold on power and Atatürk's secular legacy. Erdoğan, another populist

Islamist, is a great admirer of Menderes. Reportedly, the one time Erdoğan saw his conservative, working-class father cry was when the military hung Menderes.

"We are realizing Menderes' dream. They may have executed him, but he is not forgotten. He is in our hearts," Erdoğan said in a 2014 campaign address.[8]

The pogrom didn't lead to a mass Greek exodus. Instead, the Greeks rebuilt their lives and properties. After all, Istanbul, or the City as Greeks simply call it, was home.

The real blow came when İsmet İnönü and the CHP returned to power in 1961 with the military's backing. In response to tensions over Cyprus, İnönü revoked the 1930 Treaty of Friendship between Greece and Türkiye. The CHP ramped up a policy of discriminating against and harassing the Greeks. They were barred from working in careers as varied as medicine, architecture, plumbing and tourism. In 1964, the government began forcible expulsions. Technically, the policy targeted members of the minority who held Greek passports, but because many Greeks had intermarried with Greeks holding Turkish citizenship, tens of thousands of families left in order not be separated. The CHP gave the Greeks two weeks to leave, with a suitcase weighing twenty kilograms, and no more than $22 in cash. By the 1970s over 50,000 Greeks had been kicked out.[9]

When the Greeks left, Cihangir became a refuge for migrants, prostitutes and drug-dealers. By the 2010s, the old Greek neighborhood was gentrified. In half a century it underwent two transformations, the first ethnic and religious, and the second neoliberal. It is now the transient stop for a new global elite, moderately rich, who rent apartments for a few months at rates well below those of Miami or New York, but high enough to support a Turkish family for a few months. Rents and home prices skyrocketed here. Cihangir is more expansive than most Eastern

European capitals. The rally in prices has been turbocharged by Türkiye's double-digit inflation.

Zografion has coped with the demographic changes. Class sizes stabilized in the 1990s. The school made it a point to open up to families of mixed Greek and Turkish marriages. In the past, mixed marriages here were a taboo, unlike the Greeks and Palestinians in Jerusalem. But with the Greeks' numbers shrinking, the pool of Greek spouses has dried up. The community watches births like hawks.

"There are a lot of forces pushing you to get married and have five kids. On top of the pressure because we are traditional, there is an urgency to keep the minority going. But if you want to find a husband or wife within the minority it's very hard," Evridiki, a chemistry teacher at Zografion in her thirties, told me.

"The younger generation is more Turkish than the older. For a child from a mixed marriage, Zografion might be the only place where they speak Greek," she said. Like minority schools in Thrace, instruction here is split, with mathematics and science taught in Greek and literature and history in Turkish.

In recent years, Zografion decided to accept Greek Orthodox Arab students. Türkiye's coastal city of Antakya was known as Antioch in ancient times. The name is still used to describe the roughly one million Arabic-speaking Christians who live across the Near East. Türkiye is home to about 9,000 Antiochian Christians who found themselves citizens of the Turkish Republic after colonial France ceded Syria's Alexandretta province (since called Hatay) to Türkiye in 1939. After a devastating earthquake in February 2023, hundreds of Antiochian Christians settled in Istanbul. Around twenty are enrolled at Zografion.

So, Turkish, Greek, Arabic and the requisite dose of English can all be heard in Zografion's corridors. In effect, the school has reverted to the Ottoman *millet* system. Zografion isn't ideological about religion, although it does recognize the traditions of Eastern

Christianity. But Zografion is really a bastion of cosmopolitanism in an authoritarian and increasingly Islamist Türkiye. At the same time, it is steeped in tradition and permanence.

* * *

Greeks in Istanbul call themselves Rum, a Turkish word derived from the Greek Romaios, which means Romans. The people who we call Byzantines thought of themselves as Romans because they lived in the Eastern Roman Empire. Their primary language was Greek, but the concept of a Greek ethnicity was foreign to them. Rum identity was based on adherence to the Byzantine Empire's official religion, Orthodox Christianity. As the Ottomans gradually overran the Byzantine Empire, they labelled all the Christians in their new territory Rum, regardless of whether they spoke Greek, Arabic, a Slavic language or Albanian. Only in the late nineteenth century would the Ottomans recognize ethnic churches, like the Bulgarian, in a bid to appease their population's nationalist aspirations.

I told Giannis Demirtzoglou, Zografion's president, that I was jealous of his students' cosmopolitanism. It made me reflect on how provincial my education from primary school through university across three Catholic schools in a small American city was. (I'm not complaining. I received a privileged education thanks to the nuns and Jesuits who are these schools' lifeblood.)

I was curious about whether this cosmopolitan Rum minority had lessons for Europe, whose politics are ravaged by debates over migration and identity. I have already said that Greece is better placed to ride out tensions over migration, in part because it belongs to the Near East and has a unifying Eastern Orthodox faith. The world is becoming more Eastern. This is disorienting for those who aren't accustomed to it, like the Greeks.

Demirtzoglou is too genteel, in the old Levantine sense, to descend into the West's culture wars, but he tells me, "Our Rum identity, the essence of who we are as a minority, is not something we question."

Indeed, at Zografion, I saw a shared culture and common faith contribute to a sense of self-worth and cohesiveness that critics, mainly on the political right in the West, bemoan as lacking in their own countries. The local flavor here was Eastern Christianity, but the same solidarity applies to Muslim and Jewish communities in the Near East. Even secular people in this part of the world acknowledge some unwritten cultural and social codes based on their societies' religions.

"The church is the center of our lives. We aren't radical about religion. We go for the tradition and socializing," Demirtzoglou said. After the service, he welcomed me back to his office. I sunk into a plush beige leather chair. Demirtzoglou is in his sixties. I can already tell ten minutes into our chat that he has a conservative sensibility, but not the kind found in the polarized West. There isn't a shred of bitterness or grievance-driven politics in his body. That includes toward Türkiye. He proudly reminded me that he did his military service in Türkiye, not Greece. When he finished, he said, he was given a sendoff by his Turkish comrades.

"If we lose our culture and traditions, who are we?" he asked.

He doesn't go in for minimalism. The walls in his office are covered with black-and-white photos of graduating classes, trinkets, books and school documents written in Greek and Ottoman Turkish. He points to a photo of a young Patriarch Bartholomew, the spiritual leader of the Orthodox world. This is the sort of eclecticism that the best interior designers can't replicate; the embellishments of a man who has lived a full life.

Demirtzoglou married twice. His current wife is the director of one of Thessaloniki's most prestigious private schools. "I live on the Asian side of Istanbul and she lives in Thessaloniki. We joke that the secret to our marital success is living on two different continents," he said, smiling at what I sense is a well-worn line of his. He sees his wife four months out of the year, usually on weekends.

"I could retire if I wanted and move to Thessaloniki, but here, in Istanbul, I am needed. I have friends and a purpose," he told me. He is tall, balding and relentless. My Turkish friends in Beyoğlu know Zografion for its regular line-up of Greek musical performances open to the public.

"We say that this is the most social school in Istanbul. Today, we showed Istanbul that we are here and we aren't going anywhere," he said.

* * *

The longer I spent with Istanbul's Rum the more the question of identity tugged at me. These people are the descendants of trailblazing globalists—the merchants and traders of the Ottoman Empire. Their descendants' views defied easy political stereotypes. This is an Orthodox Christian minority that saw their city turned upside down, first by ethno-nationalism and then political Islam.

To a certain extent, they live in a bubble. Evridiki told me her friends growing up in the early 2000s were Armenians, Jews, Greeks and some Turks:

> In Beyoğlu it wasn't weird for me to say my name at a restaurant or store. We Rum are small in number, but in this area, our presence is still felt. When I leave Beyoğlu, people hear my name and say "Oh you speak Turkish well for a tourist," and I say, "Yes, I was born here."

"The biggest shock was when I went to university and met the students from the center of Türkiye. They are very Islamic, every girl wears the hijab. They had no idea Christians—Greeks—lived in Istanbul. No one taught them about us," she said.

One of my guides in Istanbul was Yvonne Vingas, the young, glamorous scion of one of the minority's most powerful families. Her father, Lakis, who helped me arrange several interviews, is close to Patriarch Bartholomew and an unofficial emissary of the minority. The Vingas family are as close as you can get to the old Phanariots, wealthy Greek merchants and courtiers who held unprecedented power in the Ottoman Empire. I have to be careful here. I don't mean that as an insult. The Phanariots, who lorded over the Ottoman provinces of modern-day Romania on behalf of the sultan, get a bad rap among Greeks. They are, unfairly in my opinion, remembered contemptuously in popular Greek history because of their hesitancy to join the 1821 Revolution. Not all of them hesitated. Alexandros Ypsilantis was a Phanariot and leader of the Filiki Eteria; but in general they saw their interests as entwined with the Ottoman Empire. But the Vingas family is the living embodiment of the old Greek elite who once ran the Near East: more European than Europeans, international, but with a toehold in the Middle East.

Yvonne worked for the United Nations before returning to Istanbul to join the family's chemical company. She has the sharp chin and turned-up nose of an aristocrat. She showed me around Beyoğlu in a tweed jacket and knit sweater. I suspect she is being groomed to succeed her father for a role as the minority's next unofficial emissary. So our interview was good practice.

"We grew up speaking German in the house and Turkish in the street. I went to a French school. Now we only speak Greek at home," she told me, describing her polyglot childhood with a half-German mother and Greek-Levantine father.

Yvonne is polished. She would be among her own with the dragomans, I thought, the elite class of Christian translators and diplomats who wielded power behind the scenes in the Ottoman

Empire. The dragomans and Levantines have undergone a popular comeback in history as more people look to the cosmopolitan Ottoman Empire to understand where the Middle East went wrong. Others have examined these Ottoman communities in the context of rising nationalisms and the so-called global elite. Yvonne is one of the youngest Levantines still around, so I was keen to hear her thoughts on identity. While cosmopolitan, the Vingas family is deeply rooted in tradition and a sense of place, she told me. This doesn't jibe with the global elite in Dubai or London.

"Religion is important to us because it's part of our identity. We go to the church for the spirit of it," she said. That word "tradition" popped up again. "I have never once doubted my identity. I always knew I was different than the majority in Türkiye. Istanbul is my home. I introduce myself as a Greek of Istanbul, with European roots." Yvonne tells me she never says she is from Türkiye.

She is more of a realist than her elite peers in the United States and Europe. She was unabashed in defending "traditional Europe" and suspicious of immigration changing the continent. She told me that Western Europe's malaise, and trouble with the far-right, is because it lacks a solid sense of self and has lost its traditions.

"Young people are searching for their identity in order to define themselves because of globalization and immigration. So they are actually becoming more religious and nationalistic. Thankfully, I know who I am, and I am proud of it," she said.

How does the tumult in the region look from her perch, as an insider-outsider to both Greece and Türkiye. She shies away from taking a side in Turkish politics but says, "Türkiye needs a strong ruler. Someone to handle internal pressures and someone who can handle its neighbors." What about Greece?

"Greece is becoming more powerful in the Mediterranean. They want to be meaningfully present and I get the sense that they are trying to become closer to the Greek minorities in the Middle East. More deputy ministers of education and other such officials are visiting Istanbul," she said.

Like the Greeks I met in Thessaloniki, she is suspicious of how Greece is being reabsorbed into the Near East. It was interesting to hear this view from a Levantine of Istanbul.

"Are all these new arrivals and investors from the Middle East looking to impose their culture on Greece?" she asked me. She continued:

> The investment is good. We saw Greece hurt for a long-time after the crisis, but Greece is in a risky position of losing its own culture because of over-tourism, globalization and a low birth rate. Greece was appreciated because of its culture and habits. There are too many hookah shops in Athens now. It's not authentic. Greece needs to protect its European identity and not change just for the sake of a good economy.

So Yvonne, a polyglot, jet-setting Levantine, argued for limits to globalization and immigration. In some ways, she made a sensible case in my mind.

But what I found most interesting was that her argument was loosely based on defending the concept of Hellenic Greece, the ancient Greek identity promoted by European powers, Westernized Greeks, and later, Greece's twentieth-century military rulers. Of course, I heard the same suspicion of globalization from Anna Missirian in Kavala, who espoused the views and values of Byzantium. Others I met, like Giannis Boutaris, embraced the new Near East, invoking the Byzantines and a cosmopolitan Greek identity.

The debate adds a new twist to the question that writers like Lawrence Durrell, Robert Byron and David Holden danced around. Does Greece fit in the East or West? That question is becoming irrelevant today, because the East is winning, but it's interesting to look back at a time when Greece was racing to join the European Union and the West was advancing.

Half a century ago, Patrick Leigh Fermor identified Yvonne's hookahs as one of no less than sixty-four cultural fault-lines in what he called Greece's "Helleno-Romaic Dilemma." The Romios, he said, referring to Byzantine-minded Greeks, had a "fondness for smoking narghiles" while the Hellene disapproved, "for obvious reasons." Fermor believed that "inside every Greek dwell two figures in opposition. Sometimes one is in the ascent, sometimes the other; occasionally they are in concord."[10]

The characteristics he lists are spot on. The Romios, for example, distrust the law and believe Greece lies outside Europe. They have a "semi-pagan attachment" to the Orthodox Church and abhor science. Fermor describes Greeks' oriental traits, not the least of which are "fatalism, dread of boredom, reaching agreements by bargaining, secret sympathy for piracy, belief in quick returns, and determining marriage wholly by dowries." In contrast, the Hellene believes Greece belongs to Europe and longs for the days of Plato. They go through life with "principle and logic, reliance on a long view, settling differences with negotiation," and at least counter the importance of their future spouse's financial credentials by considering "romantic and ascetic factors."[11]

As Fermor says, you find both these traits in Greece. But taking the geopolitical long view, the Romaic identity is in the ascent and the Hellenic one is being left in the dust. Western Europe anchored Greece to the latter, but its political heft is diminishing. In fact, Brussels now depends on Greece for its stability. The United States has abandoned advocating for the European Union's advance. The weight of the global economy, and its population, is also heavily skewed to Greece's south and east. As it rejoins the East, Greeks will weather the storm by relying on their Romaic traits. Those were once detriments when the center of gravity in Europe was France and Germany; now they are invaluable in a brutal, messy Near East.

The tussle between Romaic and Hellenic Greece has played out since 1821. In the mid-twentieth century, the Hellenic side was winning. The pursuit of a monolithic, European Greek identity to mimic the West wasn't molded anywhere near as brutally as the way the Kemalists fashioned a modern Turkish one, but it too had casualties. In Western Thrace, the Muslim minority was harassed, but they weren't the only Greek citizens who didn't fit in. Greeks from Asia Minor, Palestine, Syria and Egypt had to surrender their rich, Eastern cosmopolitanism at the door, along with their valuable Turkish and Arabic language skills, when they washed up as refugees in the Greek nation-state. They were hit twice. Once by the Turkish and Arab nationalists who kicked them out, and again by a Western-oriented elite in Athens who wanted to crush oriental Greece.

In her novel *The Bastard of Istanbul*, Turkish writer Elif Shafak captures how post-Ottoman exiles like the Greeks were de-Middle-Easternized by double blows. One of Shafak's characters, an Armenian-American transplant to Istanbul, groans when her distant Turkish cousin professes a love for Western punk, as opposed to oriental music.

"You are not Western. Turks are Middle Eastern but somehow in constant denial. And if you [Turks] had let us [Armenians] stay in our homes, we too could still be Middle Easterners instead of turning into a diaspora people," the character says. Substitute Greeks in for Turks and Armenians, and you have the internal and external pressures that tried, but never fully managed, to kill oriental Greece.[12]

Nektaria Anastasiadou brilliantly reveals the chasm between Rum and Europeanized Greeks in her novel, *At the Foot of the Eternal Spring*. In one passage, her feisty, aging Rum character is kept waiting by a crowd of Greek tourists at a shop in Beyoğlu's fish-market, Balik Bazaar. She says:

> The Greeks, who seem to consider the shop a free cafe, exit. A bourgeoisie lady with a Louis Vuitton handbag says in English, "Sorry we made you wait."
> "No problem," I reply in Greek.
> "Ah! You're Greeks?"
> "Rums."
> She looks at me as if I were a talking stork. I explain: "Byzantines, madame."
> "Ah, you speak Greek so well!"
> I think to myself: Fuck off, Modern Greeks. Out loud I say, "And your Greek isn't that bad."[13]

I took a ferry to Istanbul's Asian side to meet Anastasiadou. Siting on the top deck, I sipped my *çay* (Turkish tea) from a tulip-shaped cup and saucer. I tried to make out the seven hills that old Istanbul was built on. Napoleon Bonaparte once reportedly said, "If the world was only one country, Istanbul would be its capital." That sinks in on Istanbul's ferries as you chug between continents, soaking up the beautiful diversity of Istanbul's inhabitants; faces and fashion styles that could be at home from Western Europe to the core of Asia. Like in Istanbul's suburbs, I am overcome with a feeling of insignificance, but also a sensation of tranquility.

No matter how many times I visit Istanbul, the staggering amount of glassware here impresses me. I am talking about those teacups. If any form of public transportation in the West had as many breakable cups as these ferries, their floors would be littered with shards and ads for personal injury lawyers. But Istanbul's frenzied pace is checked at the terminal. On these old ferries the only things breaking are sesame rolls that grizzled men in caps throw at seagulls stalking the boat.

Anastasiadou and I agreed to meet at Yesil Mavi, a lazy cafe tucked into a leafy cliff in Üsküdar with views across the Bosporus. It was a short walk from the ferry terminal. Along the Bosporus, Turks were spread out on blankets for the evening. Conservative Muslim families had their dinner in Tupperware containers and sat on blankets. Secular bohemians with frizzy hair lounged in folding camp chairs with their shoes off. The little squares of grass in Üsküdar are greener and cleaner than those in big Western cities.

Anastasiadou might be the only novelist left in the shrinking Greek minority. I learned during our meeting that her books about the Rum have rattled some in Greece's tight-knit publishing world. In turns out, she has exposed entrenched biases in the West about who qualifies as Middle Eastern.

"Greece is part of the Near East, but just can't bring itself to admit it," she reflected in a calm voice. "The neatly packaged version tourists see hides it. I was walking in Plaka with a friend on my last visit to Athens and I told her: 'You know, here we are in Greece, but all around us is *Ellada*. They are like two different countries,'" she said, using the country's Greek name.

A Recipe for Daphne was Anastasiadou's first book. It was published in English in 2020. The plot follows Daphne, the daughter of a mixed Turkish and Rum couple, from Miami to Istanbul. A love story is embedded in the novel, but the book is really a tale of the Rum community in contemporary Istanbul, she told me.

"It was rejected more times than I want to admit," Anastasiadou said. We related over how difficult it is as a writer to cross Western biases challenging where the Middle East starts and ends. The world is moving in this direction, but established industries are far behind.

"Publishers said there was no market for the book because people didn't know Greeks lived in Istanbul. Others wanted a depressing story that showed the minority under attack and Istanbul riddled with violence," she told me.

"A few publishers in the United States actually told me to 'Add more bombs and explosions because that is how we see Istanbul over here.' They wanted a sad story that goes with the Western news agenda. But my story isn't sad, it's funny." She is mellow and speaks in a soft voice. She has natural beauty.

As a fan of her writing, I wasn't surprised that an American publisher would struggle to comprehend her modern Greek characters who shout "Allah, Allah," when they are frustrated, and study Ottoman calligraphy to read the engravings on mosques. The Greeks are supposed to be stuck in Santorini and the Acropolis, right?

Anastasiadou reminds you of the reality in every chapter. In one passage, Daphne's Rum lover breathlessly declares, "You are an Easterner!" after she does an impromptu *tsifteteli*, or belly dance, at a crowded restaurant.

The Middle Eastern publishing world was more accepting of the region's diversity than the West. Her book was published by an imprint of the American University of Cairo Press. It received glowing reviews in English media afterwards.

At the Foot of the Eternal Spring is Anastasiadou's second novel. It is more daring because it is written in Politika, Istanbul's Greek dialect, which is filled with Turkish loan words, that are easier for Greeks from Macedonia and Thrace to understand than Athenians. Not everyone in Greece is on board with her books.

"The buzz word for writing about Istanbul in Greece is 'magical.' Anything that doesn't fit into that box, that doesn't paint the most beautiful picture of the Rum before the expulsion and say how miserable and dangerous it is for them now, is viewed with suspicion," she told me.

> I've been interviewed by Greek news sites and afterwards was told that the sound wasn't good and the interview had to be shelved. On one

occasion, I learned later from a journalist friend that the problem was that I portrayed the status of the community in too positive a light. They have to be under assault and afraid. This isn't a problem with the average Greek reader, but for many news outlets it is.

I asked Anastasiadou what she makes of Istanbul's conservative Islamic drift under Erdoğan. Although, I am not a resident, I travel here often. The city's public spaces are now more patently Islamic than five years ago. I ask: is the Christian minority to which she belongs more isolated?

She replies like a good storyteller. She sets the scene for her answer by reflecting on a recent walk she took behind Suleymaniye Mosque in the historic center of Istanbul. "It was rainy and there were no tourists," she said.

> I felt I was back in Byzantine Constantinople. Not despite the fact that I was surrounded by Ottoman minarets and women in religious Muslim dress, but because I was surrounded by them. The old mosques differ little from the exterior of Byzantine churches; and head coverings are almost identical to the robes and headgear of the women saints in Byzantine icons.

Anastasiadou described a continuum between Byzantium, basically Eastern Greek Orthodoxy, and the Islamic world. This is the counter to Yvonne Vingas' Hellenism. In general, throughout my conversations with the Rum minority, I noticed that they were less unsettled about the Islamization of Türkiye then my secular Turkish friends and the legions of Western pundits I know.

But doesn't the minority feel pressure from Erdoğan's brand of populist Islam? I asked Anastasiadou what she made of the decision to convert Hagia Sophia back into a mosque.

Hagia Sophia was erected by Byzantine Emperor Justinian between 532–7. When Mehmed II's army was laying siege to Constantinople in 1453, women, children and elderly who were not defending the city's outer walls prayed inside for salvation. The cathedral was plundered by Ottoman soldiers, in keeping with the tradition of the time—among Muslims and Christians—of pillaging. Just three days after Constantinople fell, a wooden minaret was constructed on Mehmed II's orders and Friday prayer was conducted. Hagia Sophia remained a mosque until Atatürk converted it into a museum in 1935.

I have to say, the crowds waiting to enter Hagia Sophia are now larger because it is a mosque than when the former Orthodox Cathedral was a museum with the Christian frescos on display. Just as Atatürk's unilateral decision to convert Hagia Sophia into a museum was a high-profile secularizing move, Erdoğan's reversal of it was an immediate and obvious way to reassert Türkiye's place as an Islamic power. The populist Islamist move enraged Christians around the world (and even Greek atheists I know) but it endeared Erdoğan to millions of pious Muslims.

Anastasiadou, a Rum, did not share the outrage that I heard from Greeks—and most vociferously, Greeks in the Western diaspora—over the move. "I didn't mind," she told me, shrugging. "Provided the art and architecture was preserved and displayed. If an active Rum church were converted to a mosque, that would be another matter, but Hagia Sophia had been a mosque for over 500 years before it was made into a museum."

Like the Greeks I met in Cihangir, Anastasiadou had a deep knowledge of Türkiye's history from the perspective of a Christian resident. The Greeks of Istanbul were less outraged about Türkiye's populist Islamist drift under Erdoğan than Western commentators and secular Turks. Most surprisingly, and perhaps counterintuitively for many in the West, the Greeks credited Erdoğan with being the most open Turkish leader they have known.

11

MEZE IN KADIKÖY

The first decade of rule by Erdoğan's Justice and Development Party (AKP) was a breath of fresh air for the Rum, who were once afraid to be heard speaking Greek on the street for fear of being assaulted. Once Erdoğan came to power, churches were renovated and nationalist, extremist attacks on the Greek Orthodox Patriarchate stopped. In 2015, a Greek school on the island of Imbros reopened. Erdoğan created a genuine sense of optimism within the minority during his early years as prime minister, members of the minority told me. Despite his Islamist turn, they still give him credit for those efforts.

"Erdoğan was very good to the minority when he came to power and I would argue, in general, he still is," Nikos Markovitis, a Greek journalist transplant to the city told me.

> You see, the Islamists and Christian minorities were all persecuted by the Kemalists. Erdoğan sees himself as a neo-Ottoman figure. He likes to have minorities around him. Like coins in his pocket. Greeks and Kurds. This was the Ottoman way. If you look carefully at state events, Patriarch Bartholomew is always there in the front.

Erdoğan had an important political motivation to stop Türkiye's deplorable abuse of the Rum when he became prime minister in 2003. Türkiye was serious about joining the European Union. Erdoğan was still a democratic darling of the West. Brussels had made it clear that it would not take Türkiye's application seriously unless it stopped discriminating against its minorities and solved the Cyprus problem.

Greece was, and remains, a full-fledged supporter of Türkiye joining the European Union. Athens rightly sees the economic windfall it would benefit from if 85 million people next door joined the common market. Just look at the eastern Aegean islands to see why. Samos, Chios and Lesvos are barely visited by Western tourists. Upper-middle-class Turks power their service-sector economies. Trade and investment in Thrace would boom, too. When Erdoğan came to power, Greek politicians rightly calculated that a Türkiye inside the European Union would have less of an interest in picking fights in the Aegean. That would help Greece reduce its burdensome military spending, which is one of the highest in NATO when measured in GDP.

As Erdoğan said in 2004 during a thaw in the neighbors' tensions, "If Turco-Greek rapprochement is possible today, it is because we have a common ground through which mutual perceptions are most accurate. That common ground is the EU."[1] Erdoğan's government implemented some economic reforms and took steps to put Türkiye in line with Brussels' human rights standards. Erdoğan expanded political and cultural rights for the abused Kurds, who comprise twenty per cent of Türkiye's population.[2] In 2025, at the time of writing, Kurdish militants were in serious peace talks with the Turkish government, even though Türkiye's road to European Union membership had effectively closed.

The most intractable problem that had to be solved was the Cyprus issue. In 2004, the ethnically divided island of Cyprus voted on the Annan Plan, named after former United Nations Secretary General Kofi Annan. The plan was drafted in a major diplomatic push to reach a compromise to unite the island, which has been divided into a Turkish-occupied north and the official Republic of Cyprus in the south since 1974. Türkiye invaded Cyprus that year after a failed coup attempted to unite the island with Greece. It has facilitated around 115,000 settlers to move to the island to boost the Turkish demographics in the north and deployed at least 30,000 troops.[3]

The Annan Plan called for the island to be split into a Greek and Turkish bi-zonal federation. A single government would represent Cyprus abroad, but the island would have two equally weighted constituent states for Greeks and Turks. It was a genuine attempt at compromise. The chance of Türkiye entering the European Union gave it momentum. Türkiye would never be allowed into the bloc while it occupied Northern Cyprus. The plan failed. While it sounded nice on paper, Greek Cypriots harbored suspicions that it would entrench Türkiye's future role on the island. The Greeks worried about the return of their confiscated properties and the status of Turkish settlers. The Annan Plan gave no hard deadline for the removal of Turkish troops in the north nor any way to enforce their withdrawal. Sixty-five per cent of Turkish Cypriots backed the Annan Plan, but Greek Cypriots rejected it by a wide margin. Since the Republic of Cyprus was guaranteed to join the European Union either way, the Greek Cypriots had no real reason to compromise. The Annan Plan's collapse marked the moment when Türkiye's prospects of joining the European Union started to nosedive.[4]

By 2008, the *Wall Street Journal* opinion section was warning that European Union talks were on the verge of collapse. "Failure to reform and deep political polarization have led to a sense of lost direction in Türkiye. Nationalism and human-rights violations are on the rise again," the article said. Meanwhile, in Europe, it warned presciently, "Populations and politicians are cooler to enlargement than ever before. Sound arguments about Türkiye's long-term contribution to the EU are losing ground to nostalgia for an idealized vision of a homogenous European past, along with fears about radical Islam and the potential loss of jobs to Turkish immigrants."[5]

Two years after the *Wall Street Journal* article appeared, Erdoğan, snubbed by Western Europe, turned his attention south and backed popular protests in the Arab Spring. Since 2011, Türkiye has emerged as an independent power in its own right. Because of Russia's invasion of Ukraine, Türkiye's importance to Brussels has massively increased. The toppling of Bashar al-Assad's government in Damascus was viewed in Ankara as confirmation that Türkiye doesn't need the West in a multipolar world. That is probably right. Türkiye is the dominant power here. Remember, it only took fifteen years for Türkiye's allies to take Damascus—a blink of an eye in the grand sweep of geopolitics.

Most in Western Europe breathed a sigh of relief that Türkiye didn't join the European Union. Erdoğan would have made Hungary's Viktor Orban look like a Brussels-loving mandarin. If Türkiye were to join, it would dominate the bloc because of its sheer size and military strength. Türkiye remains an official applicant to join the bloc, but no one takes its application seriously. However, not everyone is happy with this result.

Istanbul's Rum are one of the underreported victims of Türkiye's collapsed bid to join the European Union. They say that had Türkiye entered, it would have created a viable pathway for first- and second-generation Rum in Greece and abroad to return to Istanbul. Rum exiles would also have had a better chance of getting back their families' expropriated properties. Greeks can buy property in Istanbul but face restrictions in municipalities with seafronts like Beyoğlu. Freedom of movement, a cardinal feature of the European Union, would have saved the Rum minority from extinction.

"There was a lot of positivity within the minority after the AKP came to power, because it did reforms and started the process, genuinely at the time, to join the European Union," Minas Vasiliadis, the editor of *Apoyevmatini*, Türkiye's only Greek-language newspaper, told me. "A Türkiye in the European Union would have changed so much for the minority for the better. First and foremost, it would have countered our demographic decline," Vasiliadis said.

Istanbul's Greek minority has passed the demographic tipping point. It will go extinct in the coming decades. According to Vasiliadis, Erdoğan had a second chance to bolster the Greeks' demographics, but he ignored it. "During the Greek financial crisis, thousands of Rum descendants wanted to move to Türkiye from Greece," he explained. "Unlike today, the economic situation was worse in Greece and Türkiye was growing."

Greeks came to Istanbul and tried to establish themselves, but the government didn't facilitate residence permits, let alone a pathway to citizenship for them, Vasiliadis said. "Percentage wise, that would have been huge blood transfusion for the minority. That was probably the last opportunity we had to turn the tide on the minority's demographic collapse."

Apoyevmatini has been published five days a week since 1925. It is Türkiye's second-oldest paper after Turkish daily *Cumhuriyet*. It has a circulation of around 3,000 between print and digital copies, down from 30,000 in the 1930s. I met Minas in the paper's dank, claustrophobic office in Beyoğlu where old editions are piled to the ceiling. Minas has closed the space. He works from home now, like most journalists, but wanted to show me his old office. *Apoyevmatini* is a one-man show. Minas is editor-in-chief, sole-reporter, social media manager, sales representative and tech guy. The paper is kept alive by ads and donations. It almost closed in 2011, but was saved by a fundraising campaign that saw Turks subscribe just to keep it going.

Minas never planned to be a newspaper man. He was born in Athens to Rum parents who left Türkiye during the height of the secularists' persecution of the Greeks. His father, a longtime journalist, left under political pressure and returned to Istanbul when tensions eased after the AKP came to power. He took over *Apoyevmatini* in 2002. By then, the family who founded the paper had died out and the newspaper was rudderless. "A secretary was printing just eighty copies a day. It was mostly death notices," Vasiliadis told me.

In the early 2000s he came to visit his father. "I wanted to open a tech startup, I never studied journalism," he said. "But my dad was printing the paper by hand with this machine." He pointed to a manually operated printing press in the corner of the room that dated back to the Treaty of Lausanne era. "I said, 'Dad we need to digitize this.' Next thing I knew, I was running the paper."

I asked Vasiliadis about the responses I had heard about Erdoğan's treatment of the minority. "It's true, as a community, we can't complain, we are doing well," he said.

> Are things exponentially better for the minority today than they were twenty-five years ago? Without a doubt, yes. If you ask me, "do I feel threatened?" the answer is "no." But the tolerance we enjoy from the government is without checks and balances. This country is run pyramid-style. Everything is micromanaged at the top. Our freedoms, as a minority, depend on the government's whims.

Vasiliadis added that I needed to put the minority's improved status into perspective:

> Number one: we were small when this government took over, so we didn't pose any political threat. Number two: it's nice to have a polished

teddy-bear like the Rum to show off. You can paint the churches, fix them up, and show people singing inside. You send the camera and take some pictures. It doesn't cost you anything with your constituents and makes the West happy. With that said, Erdoğan's government is the only one in the history of the Turkish Republic that so far, has treated us well, and reached out to the minority. This is because it is Islamic, not in spite of it. Other nationalist parties would like to crush us like a bug.

As Holden wrote in *Greece Without Columns*, "It was not mere generosity or diplomacy ... but strict adherence to the Prophet's law that caused the conqueror of Constantinople, Sultan Mehmet, to confirm the Orthodox Patriarch as head of the Orthodox Christian community and thereby make him responsible for [their] behavior and welfare."[6]

Minas looks more like a tech nerd than a journalist. His boyish face makes me think he is a decade younger than his forty-one years. But he carries himself with the somberness and responsibility of someone decades older than his age. We relate because neither of us studied journalism. We both learned on the job. I ask him how he sees Greek-Turkish relations. At the time of my visit in 2024, the neighbors were enjoying a thaw. Minas doesn't believe it will last. He is skeptical the Eastern Mediterranean will remain stable in the long term:

> The Ottoman Empire was a land-power, not a sea-power. That was one reason it collapsed. This government is trying not to make the same mistake. Türkiye is a big country and can project power in the Aegean. Greece is a small country, so it depends on international law and its alliance with the United States to defend its interests.

We both agree that those pillars are wavering, to say the least. But Vasiliadis has observed another trend that he says is more worrying in Türkiye. "When governments pump their people up with virulent nationalism it is very difficult to walk back those hardline positions," he said, continuing:

> Greece is very Near Eastern this way, but the good thing is that it has the European Union. People in Greece operate the Eastern way, putting human relations above the law; they will scream, fight and enjoy life like they are going to die tomorrow, but because of the European Union, there are some things they can't do, so every generation is a little better. But here in Türkiye, I can't say the younger generation will be better. In fact, if we look at the propaganda being spewed out there, the nationalism and xenophobia, I am not confident.

Minas' paper may have a small circulation, but he has a sagacious take on Turkish politics. Because he is Rum, he doesn't carry the secular-versus-Islamist baggage of many Turkish analysts. I believe he is the ideal source to ask about Türkiye's prospects.

Erdoğan secured a third term as president in 2023. The constitution prevents him from running again, but he could skirt that by having parliament call early elections, which would allow him to run once more before the expiration of his current term. More likely, some Turks say, Erdoğan's allies will push for the constitution to be rewritten, allowing him to run again. Either way, Vasiliadis thinks Erdoğan is set to maintain a chokehold on Turkish politics, which could be storing up long-term instability. "I think the era of the CHP is past. The AKP gave the poor hospitals, cheap money, and more opportunities. It gave religious people Islam. They brought inflation, but we have to admit, Türkiye is stronger on the world stage, it is no longer the West's Yes-man. Turks like that," Vasiliadis said.

I told him about the admiration for Erdoğan's independent approach to foreign policy that I had heard expressed in Greece during my travels from people of wildly different political persuasions. Vasiliadis wasn't impressed. "I would like these people to try and set up a business here in Türkiye and rely on the lira, or speak their mind at a protest. During the crisis I tried to eat some 'independence,' but I couldn't digest it," he told me.

* * *

Nikos Markovitis, my Greek journalist friend, explained Erdoğan's appeal to me over *çay* at his local *börekcisi* in Tarlabaşı. "Erdoğan comes from Kasımpaşa. In Türkiye, we say Tayyip walks like a *kabadayı*," he said, trying to mimic Erdoğan's swagger with his shoulders. *Kabadayı* is the Turkish word for street-tough; a rougher version of the Greeks' *mangas*.

Tarlabaşı is one of the last properly degraded neighborhoods around Taksim Square. It has a reputation for crime, migrants and cheap prostitution, including the transvestite version. Most upper-middle-class Turks wouldn't be caught dead here, but like seedy neighborhoods in central Athens, it is gentrifying fast. A one-bedroom apartment in this working-class neighborhood rents for $500 a month, a level slightly below Athens. The minimum wage in Türkiye is $620 a month. There is Istanbul's cost-of-living crisis in a nutshell. Turks are absorbing even more economic pain than people I met in Greece's borderlands.

Tarlabaşı was once home to lower-middle-class Greeks. They were replaced first by Turkish peasants and Kurds. In the last ten years, Syrians and Afghans became the newest arrivals. Istanbul absorbs them all. It is repository for displaced people across the wider Middle East. A few of the old two-story Greek houses still stand. They are beautiful, slender buildings with flaking plaster, exposed bricks, tall windows and big *sachnisi*, sandwiched between ugly cinderblock tenements.

Tarlabaşı is more edgy than Kasımpaşa, the working-class neighborhood where Erdoğan was raised. One of the Turkish president's first jobs was selling sesame pastry rings, called *simit* in Turkish and *koulouri* in Greek, on a push-cart. He later played semi-professional football. Erdoğan entered politics when he joined an Islamist party modeled on Egypt's Muslim Brotherhood. In 1994, he was elected Istanbul's mayor, as an Islamist who promised to pursue municipal reforms. At a political rally in 1997, he recited some lines from poem that so unnerved Türkiye's secular generals it landed him in jail: "The mosques are our barracks / the domes our helmets / the minarets our bayonets." It didn't matter that the poem was written by Ziya Gokalp, a Turkish intellectual who laid the foundations for Atatürk's nationalism and secularism. The military had just led what analysts in the West dubbed a "postmodern coup," a nonviolent putsch against Islamist Prime Minister Necmettin Erbakan. Erdoğan's recital was seen as a call to action. He served four months in prison. When he got out, he founded the AKP and led it to a landslide election victory in 2002.[7]

"The Middle East will not have another leader like Erdoğan in history," Nikos told me. "Look at Mohammad Bin Salman in Saudi Arabia, Netanyahu in Israel, the King of Jordan; none of them had to come up from the streets like Erdoğan. They are all rich guys or royalty," he said. Nikos and I agreed that Erdoğan, who is seventy years old, will not surrender power easily. One alternative is for him to tap an heir to protect his allies and family.

One of Türkiye's most popular public figures is Selçuk Bayraktar, the husband of Erdoğan's thirty-nine-year-old daughter Sümeyye. They are a modern Muslim-Turkish power-couple. Sümeyye has fair features offset by a snug hijab. Strong-jawed Selçuk sports aviator sunglasses and a red flight jacket. The wardrobe goes with his job. An MIT-trained aerospace engineer, he converted his family's auto-parts company into a manufacturer of the armed drones that have propelled Türkiye to the ranks of the world's top drone exporters. Türkiye first used the Bayraktar TB2 drone against Kurdish militants. Since then, it has deployed them in Libya, Syria and Iraq. Türkiye has sold TB2s to Ukraine and Azerbaijan. Even Türkiye's rivals, like the United Arab Emirates, are buying them. The drones are cheap and easy to operate. Their successes destroying Russian tank columns became so legendary that Ukrainians started naming their kids Bayraktar in honor of them. Selçuk blends the entrepreneurialism, modern Islamism and militarism that befits a successor of Erdoğan.

But leaders like Erdoğan face great difficulty in turning over the keys of the systems they create, even to a son-in-law. Diplomats ask over drinks what a post-Erdoğan Türkiye looks like. I think an internal power struggle is more likely than a peaceful transition because Erdoğan has consolidated so much power in his hands and depleted the bureaucracy.

I had a chance to think about how modern Turkish rulers meet their ends when I was sitting at Yesil Mavi cafe. On the horizon, I traced the distance along the Bosporus from the Dolmabahçe Palace to the 15 July Bridge. The palace's construction started in 1839 under Sultan Abdulmejid I. It was a tremendous project that cost the equivalent of $1.9bn in today's terms. It stretched the Ottoman Empire's finances, contributing to its eventual bankruptcy in the 1870s. Six Ottoman sultans lived out their rule at Dolmabahçe. The last, Sultan Abdulmecid II, left when Atatürk abolished the caliphate on 3 March 1924. Atatürk died a natural death there. Erdoğan has built his own palace—a 1,150-room, Versailles-style complex in Ankara. Whereas Dolmabahçe borrowed from European baroque and neoclassical traditions, Erdoğan's White Palace is an icy, postmodernist ode to Türkiye's Asian steppe roots. A ruler may imagine dying in a palace like that one day, but not giving it up.

Across the horizon is the 15 July Bridge, renamed in honor of the 250 people who were killed by mutineering soldiers during Türkiye's 2016 failed coup. The protestors heeded Erdoğan's famous FaceTime video plea to take to the streets and oppose the putsch.

"They showed no mercy when they pointed their guns at my people," Erdoğan roared to thousands of supporters waving Turkish flags on the bridge in 2017 to mark the failed coup's anniversary. "What did my people have? They had their flags—just as they do today—and something much more important: they had their faith." Erdoğan is a mesmerizing orator. But he was just getting warmed up. He turned it up a notch, "First, we will cut off the heads of those traitors. If parliament gives the decision, let them bring it to me, I will approve it," he boasted.[8] A man like that doesn't leave office to tend tomatoes in his *bahçe*.

The inklings of instability in Türkiye will start after 2028. Erdoğan has hollowed out the bureaucracy and institutions. If his secular opponents even appear close to power, providing a chance for Erdoğan's allies and family to be purged, they will fight back. Türkiye is riding high as a regional power at the time of writing, but its future stability, and that of the region, will depend on how Erdoğan orchestrates his succession.

Nikos was the perfect companion during my time in Istanbul. He is a Greek reporter with no agenda. He doesn't share the nationalism or Western condescension that many Greek journalists channel when covering Türkiye. He is also fluent enough in Turkish to understand what people are saying behind his back. I christened him the "Last Greek of Tarlabaşı" because his love for the neighborhood is unmatched. That said, a dozen or so Rum do still live there. We met one ancient Greek who owned a hardware store, and who told us his family came to Istanbul by way of Syria. Nikos has what the Greeks calls *meraki*. There is no solid English equivalent for the word, but it translates roughly to passion.

Tarlabaşı is a thirty-minute walk from Cihanger and a stone's throw from Taksim Square. But when you cross Tarlabaşı

Boulevard something changes. Anyone who has spent time in the Near East can relate to the transition you experience when you leave the expat and hipster coffee shops behind. Every city has its rough neighborhoods, but in the Near East and especially the Islamic world, the differences between slums and upper-class centers are not necessarily measured in wealth, and certainly not in crime. In fact, in Istanbul's poor and conservative neighborhoods, I feel safer than in New York or Washington. In 1877, Edmondo de Amicis described the sensation of passing through Istanbul's layers best:

> At a certain place you begin to notice fewer and fewer European faces and costumes; then European houses disappear, then pavements ... and the farther you go the more surly the dogs become, the more impudently do the Turkish ragamuffins stare you in the eye, and the common women take pains to conceal their faces; until at last you find yourself in the heart of barbarous Asia, and instead of a two hours walk, you seem to have made a two days journey.[9]

This old Greek neighborhood comes alive at night with Kurdish grandmothers cleaning vegetables on their stoops and children playing under the streetlamps. These are the back alleys Armenian photographer Ara Güler trained his camera on, capturing Pamuk's *huzun* on black-and-white film. "Everyone knows everyone's business here. They watch out for each other," Nikos said. "They love me because I'm Greek."

* * *

Greece's geostrategic importance to Israel, the European Union and the United States is a direct consequence of Türkiye's rise as an independent power. If Türkiye was still these countries' yesman, Alexandroupoli and Souda Bay would be much less critical. Greece now finds itself next to the region's strongest power, which happens to be its oldest foe. Ankara's weight is increasing compared to Brussels, dragging Greece into the Near East.

Onur İşçi, a professor of history and international affairs at Kadir Kas University in Istanbul, believes Türkiye's break with the West is irreversible. He told me that Greece is Türkiye's foil. As Türkiye distances itself from the West, Greece is fighting to remain under the American security umbrella. This is why it is positioning itself as an entry point for American energy into Europe and a port of entry for Ukraine's post-war reconstruction. "It's smart for Greece," İşçi said. "They see a vacuum and are filling it."

Erdoğan infuriates his Western critics because, unlike other Middle Eastern rulers, he wins at the ballot box, in free but unfair elections. Western liberals especially have trouble stomaching the fact that democracy in the Middle East gives them outcomes they do not like. That is why, for example, the Greeks in Egypt told me democracy is not all it's cracked up to be. Erdoğan pulled off an impressive victory in 2023, holding back a challenge from a united opposition, but in April 2024, the AKP had its worst showing in local elections since it was founded more than twenty years ago. It was trounced in all Türkiye's major cities including Istanbul, Ankara, Izmir, Bursa and Antalya. Conservative Muslim voters deserted the party en masse for the secular CHP over anger at Türkiye's staggering cost-of-living crisis and Erdoğan's ham-fisted management of the economy.

One of the CHP's most resounding victories was in Istanbul, where Mayor Ekrem İmamoğlu was reelected by the widest margin in four decades. İmamoğlu, like Erdoğan, has his family roots in Türkiye's conservative Black Sea province of Trabzon. The similarities don't end there. İmamoğlu shot to international prominence by taking Istanbul out of the AKP's control in 2019. Erdoğan himself got his political start as the city's mayor in the 1990s. As he likes to say, "Whoever wins Istanbul wins Türkiye."[10]

İmamoğlu's victory unnerved Erdoğan so much that he leveraged all the power of the state to force a rerun of the 2019 race. İmamoğlu won it handily. He would be the most likely opposition candidate in 2028. He was arrested by Erdoğan in March 2025 and charged with corruption and terrorism. İmamoğlu says the charges are trumped up and his arrest sparked some of the largest anti-government protests in decades. Most Turks I know, even some AKP supporters, see the arrest as a pure power-play by Erdoğan.

İmamoğlu is not your grandfather's Turkish secularist. He appears to have recognized their overreach. His 2019 campaign strategy was to "Ignore Erdoğan and love those who love Erdoğan."[11] He is the man to study to understand how much Erdoğan has changed Türkiye, İşçi told me. "İmamoğlu is Erdoğan's successor," he said.

The secularists' standard-bearer can recite the Quran. His own family is reflective of many urban Turks' nuanced and personal approach to Islam; one that continues to disorient Western visitors when they see women in hijabs walking arm-and-arm with unveiled daughters or sisters. İmamoğlu's wife has cascading blond hair, while his mother wears the hijab. And look at how he deftly maneuvered around the question of Hagia's Sophia's re-conversion into a mosque. He suggested he opposed the move, but explained why: "In my mind and conscience, Hagia Sophia has been a mosque since 1453."[12]

İmamoğlu is trying to find a middle ground in a schism that was gnawing at Türkiye a century before Erdoğan came on the scene. It has less to do with democracy versus autocracy, and more to do with culture. De Amicis noted the tension between Türkiye's pious Muslim masses and a Western-influenced elite, "despising all the ancient traditions of the nation," 150 years ago, when the Ottoman Empire ruled over Greeks, Slavs, Armenians and Arabs. His summary makes much of the analysis written about Erdoğan's Türkiye redundant because it doesn't need much tinkering:

> The government is revolutionary, the people conservative ... That is why all those efforts at reform which have been started during the past fifty years have never penetrated farther than the national skin ... What little has been accomplished has been by force, and at its door the people lay the increasing audacity of the unbelievers.[13]

After two decades of being thrashed by Erdoğan at the polls, the CHP is giving up on revolutionary culture wars and instead talking up economic and governance issues. Municipal minutiae are in, and debates about the hijab are out. Erdoğan is scared. The secularists are stealing his playbook from the early 2000s when his party ran on a platform to fix Türkiye's crippled economy and jumpstart development. As mayor, Erdoğan brought running water and garbage collection to Istanbul's slums. It is not for nothing that AKP's logo is a lightbulb. Then, it was the CHP who had gotten lazy with power and oversaw crippling inflation; now, it's Erdoğan's AKP. İmamoğlu's programs have included opening at least 100 daycare centers for working families and dozens of municipal restaurants where meals are served for about $1 to lessen the sting of Türkiye's blistering inflation. Erdoğan is trying to reverse this trend. He has appointed some capable technocrats and has abandoned his bizarre theory that high interest rates cause inflation. At the same time, he has given nationalists and Islamists alike a foreign policy they can be proud of.

İşçi and I met at a bar in Beyoğlu off İstiklal. He told me that he alternates bringing his university students and girlfriends here. Part of his family came to Türkiye from Romania before the Second World War. Greeks weren't the only ones scattered across the Near East. I tell him about my interviews with the Rum. He insists that I don't leave out another vanishing demographic in Istanbul: the White Turks, who he belongs to. The term is popularly associated with secular, well-off devotees of Atatürk, who embraced his vision of a modern Turkish state. There are lots of tropes about the White Turks. I find that most of them are true. They go to top universities, frequent sleek sushi restaurants on the Bosporus, and jog in tight-fitting workout gear in wealthy suburbs like Bebek.

"White Turks are a social construct. They check the box of drinking alcohol and having sex outside of marriage. But that alone is a misrepresentation of the phrase," İşçi explained. The White Turks' relative wealth compared to the rest of their country has diminished. Old money Turks have been hit hard by inflation, he told me. But it is their culture that is vanishing. "To be a real White Turk you need to have lived abroad and, most importantly, you must have a dose of Western liberalism," he said.

I thought about what Minas Vasiliadis had told me about unhinged Turkish nationalism and the lack of guardrails in Türkiye compared to Greece. İşçi says the Near East is in a state of "permacrisis." It "resembles some kind of fifteenth-century anarchy," he said. "The United States can still dictate terms, but its power is no longer infinite."

If Greece is trying to survive by hugging the United States closer, how is Türkiye asserting itself, I asked. İşçi specializes in Türkiye-Russia relations. He said the defining moment of Türkiye's foreign policy was the war in Ukraine. "During the first year of the war, Türkiye thought that Russia would emerge weaker. Now it sees Russia consolidating. The United States was stretched thin supplying weapons to both Ukraine and Israel. Europe was dithering. Türkiye believes Russia can endure. Don't forget, Türkiye was in a protracted war against the Kurds in the south for decades; it knows how a country can sustain a long war," he explained. Our interview was in September 2024.

He said the war is likely to end in a "goldilocks direction for Türkiye," which supplied Bayraktar drones and armored vehicles to Ukraine, but refused to cut economic or political ties with Russia. For example, in 2023 Türkiye officially inaugurated the Akkuyu Nuclear Power Plant project, to be built by Russia's nuclear energy company ROSATOM. The project is based on a build-own-operate model, meaning ROSATOM is putting up the funds for construction and maintenance of the plant, and in return, Türkiye is obliged to purchase seventy per cent of the electricity generated by the plant for fifteen years at a fixed rate.

At the same time, like Greece, Türkiye wants to profit from Ukraine's reconstruction. In August 2024, the two signed a free-trade agreement. Bayraktar is building a drone factory in Ukraine. "The problem for Greece is that the European Union could use Türkiye to offset Russia in the Black Sea if the United States walks away," he said.

> Türkiye wants to see the war end with a weakened Russia; that would give Türkiye more sway in their bilateral relationship. At the same time, Türkiye does not want a Ukraine that is totally under Russia's thumb. But it does want Ukraine to be more dependent on Türkiye as an economic partner and hedge against Russia.

Russia's unwillingness or inability to intervene when Turkish-backed rebels launched their blitz offensive on Moscow's ally, Bashar al-Assad, was a manifestation of the success of Türkiye's foreign policy. As Russia pulled out of Syria, Türkiye emerged as one of the big winners. But İşçi says economic factors are also at play. "Türkiye is positioning itself to be the China for Europe. Erdoğan wants to make Türkiye an export hub. That is why the lira collapsed. He overdid it by massively devaluing the currency and gorging on debt, but the goal is unchanged," he explained.

By now, İşçi and I have gone through our beers and are in the mood for raki, so we shuffle over to a *meyhane* next door. We order *topik*, a cinnamon-flavored, chickpea tofu, stuffed with onions, nuts and tahini. *Topik* is a dish of Istanbul's Armenian community. For good measure, we throw in *dolma*, stuffed grape leaves, and fried *ciğer*, liver. Turks prepare their raki the same way Lebanese do their arak: alcohol first, then water, and finally ice. If you skip the order, it's bad luck. I still shiver when I watch my Greek friends carelessly plop ice cubes into their empty ouzo glasses.

To be a manufacturing hub, you need cheap energy, lots of it. Türkiye's factories soak up Russian natural gas. Russia is giving favorable payment terms to Türkiye, too. In 2023 Russia allowed Türkiye to defer a $600 million energy bill.[14] Throughout the war in Ukraine, the United States has been trying to get Türkiye to buy more American gas. One very senior American energy official I interviewed in Washington, DC, said in October 2024, it was only a matter of time before Türkiye looked to the United States to reduce its dependence on Russian gas. How the tables turned. Under the Trump administration, the United States is flirting with lifting sanctions on Russian energy.

"You have to understand that Russia is selling Türkiye gas at a really, really good price. So it won't go along and buy American LNG," İşçi said. Türkiye has made some natural gas discoveries in the Black Sea that it wants to develop, but right now it is almost totally dependent on imports. Russia provided forty-two per cent of all Türkiye's imports in 2023.[15] Russia has sold oil to Türkiye at a steep discount in recent years too, slashing around $20 off every barrel.

"Could Türkiye change its energy suppliers? Of course, but it would have to pay a lot more, and on time. Will the Americans give Türkiye the same deal Russia is giving on gas? Türkiye and Russia are trading in local currency. Will the Americans accept Turkish lira for their gas instead of dollars?" İşçi asked, without waiting for my answer. "There is an economic logic to Türkiye's approach to Russia."

Türkiye's break with the West cuts across secular and Islamist political lines, İşçi said. "If İmamoğlu comes to power, he can be more flexible. Maybe he won't use stupid terms like 'Blue Homeland' in the Aegean. He will try to cut a better customs deal with the European Union, but will he change the economic equilibrium with Russia? No."

Greece and Türkiye feed off one another. Türkiye's inflation crisis has been a boon to Greece's service sector with middle-class Turks vacationing in Greece. Where Türkiye leaves a vacuum with respect to the United States and Israel, Greece tries to enter it. But big picture, Türkiye's rise as a regional power is Greece's nightmare. Still, there is a mismatch between Türkiye's foreign policy successes and its economic reality, at the time of writing. And Erdoğan has consolidated an unprecedented amount of power in his own hands. As rulers like Erdoğan age, people start circling in the wings. Greece could be on the border of internal strife in Türkiye in the coming decades.

* * *

The longer I spent in Istanbul, the older and greyer Greece seemed. During my last days, I started to see the Rum as a microcosm of the whole of Greece, being reabsorbed politically and demographically into the Muslim majority Near East. One Friday night, I took a ferry to Kadıköy. Leaving the slithering, blue-grey Bosporus behind, we entered the Sea of Marmara and I looked out at vessels and container ships.

The Kadıköy fish market was bustling on Friday night. People spilled out of *meyhanes* and bars onto the streets. I had to rub shoulders with the crowd just to squeak through. Turkish fishmongers know how to advertise. They display their catch trimmed with green sprigs, on a bed of crushed ice that shimmers like diamonds under bright white lights. What really stood out here compared to Greece was the average age. By Egyptian standards, Türkiye is old, but compared to its Balkan neighbors, Türkiye is a baby. No matter who governs Türkiye, its expansionist policies, to a certain point, go along with the demographic imbalance between it and its Western neighbors. My host, Byron Matarangas, reminded me of this mismatch every chance he got.

"Look! Look! Young people everywhere!" he yelled in a high-pitched voice, his hands flailing. I met Byron with my friend Nikos Markovitis in Kadıköy. Bryon is old and walks with small, tip-toe-like steps. We had to slow our pace with him, but he wanted to visit Kadıköy to, in his words, "show us the young people."

"You don't see them like this in Greece. Türkiye is young and vibrant. Greece is literally dying out. Greeks will be the minority within Greece in twenty years," he said. His comments are a bit outlandish. Greeks are aging and having less children, but they are not becoming a minority. Still, his broader premise holds truths. Matarangas is a Rum who emigrated twice. He admits he is detached from Greece. He prefers it that way.

But he is no country grandfather. He speaks flawless English, along with perfect French and Turkish. He was educated in Paris at the Sorbonne, "The best time in my life," he recalled. Matarangas is one of the few members of the Greek minority who made the circuitous journey back to Istanbul. He left Türkiye during the 1964 expulsions, settling with his family in Athens. From there, he moved to Paris to study. He entered the Greek foreign ministry, working as a diplomat in the Middle East. He remembers Iran during the twilight of the Shah's rule. He is one of the few Rum who moved back to Türkiye during the Greek financial crisis.

"Coming back was the best decision I made. Things have changed tremendously. I remember we used to be afraid to be heard speaking in Greek. Now, no one cares. There is no harassment. This is a golden era for Türkiye's minorities," he said.

I enjoyed talking with Matarangas because, although he was a child of the old Istanbul, he didn't betray a hint of *huzun* for it, like other members of the minority; only a fascination for how much his hometown has changed. He lives above Üsküdur near a primary school. He still has a touch of the diplomat in him, and he observes his city like he is writing diplomatic cables. "The girls are all very young and covered head to toe. They put on the hijab very young," he said.

Matarangas believes the geopolitical winds are shifting in Türkiye's direction. He brushes off the inflation crisis as a hiccup, "They have a high-speed train in the middle of Anatolia. This is a smart and technologically advanced country. It has a bureaucracy much smoother than the European Union's. Definitely smoother than Greece's. Türkiye will become a manufacturing powerhouse," he says.

He adds that Türkiye's brand of political Islamism is on the rise. It concerns him. He thinks Hamas' ability to withstand more than a year of war with Israel in the Gaza Strip has energized Sunni Islamists across the region. Türkiye sees the European Union being weak and the United States abandoning this region. He says this gives Ankara confidence to push its muscular foreign policy, including in the Aegean.

"You know, east of Ankara, Türkiye is a different country. When people in Anatolia introduce friends, they don't say, 'He is a good man,' they say, 'He is a good Muslim.' Türkiye has joined the Ummah," he said, referring to the Muslim world.

EPILOGUE
SEA CAPTAINS ON THE EDGE OF ASIA

Oinousses is a windswept, barren speck of an island sandwiched between Chios and the Turkish coast. Only pastel-colored sea captains' mansions break the monotony of scorched, olive-hued earth. There are no hotels here, few tourists and just two tavernas. This is the Near East. The edge of Europe and Asia. This is where my *pappous*, or grandfather, comes from.

The first time his father, Michail Mathaios, left Oinousses for the United States in 1912 he was marked down in the ship manifest as, "ethnicity, Greek" and "nationality, Turkish," or Ottoman. In the decade he was away, working in the steel mills of Ohio and Buffalo, New York, a world war took place. The second time he left Oinousses for the United States, in 1924, he was a married man with a young family in tow. His nationality and ethnicity were now one in the ship manifest: citizen of Greece. The Ottoman Empire into which he was born had collapsed.

I first came across Oinousses when I was five or six years old, through my *pappous*' stories. He was a self-made man who loved the United States with every fiber of his being. He worked so much that he never went back to Oinousses, although he often talked about it. On trips back, I met wrinkled old Greeks who had worked for his painting company before retiring back to Oinousses.

My *pappous* came from a generation before TV, let alone social media, and he had a fantastic imagination. His tales were about an island of pirates and sailors who visited exotic ports. I became so immersed in his world that on kindergarten career day, I told a packed school auditorium I aspired to become a "Greek Pirate," to his gleaming pride. I became something slightly more productive, a journalist.

My grandfather's extended family was too busy "working, drinking, gambling and womanizing," my dad likes to remind me, to leave a written record of what Oinousses was like at the turn of the twentieth century on the fringes of a dying empire. One uncle was killed in a poker game. Decades later, another's boat was torpedoed in the Second World War. These are classic Oinoussen traits. As Stelios, a *komboskini*-strumming sea captain on the island once told me, "I spend seven months at sea. When I go out, I enjoy myself. I tip everyone and buy my wife whatever she wants." Smyrna was just a short swim away from Oinousses. As seafarers, my ancestors were probably the guys there smoking *nargiles* and boozing it up to *rebetika* tunes.

By far the best written account I have of Oinousses is the unpublished memoir of my other, gentler and more scholarly, great-grandfather. He returned to his homeland in 1959 after forty-nine years living in America. Panayiotis Brouzis came from a tiny village called Tsoukka in central Greece. It is practically deserted today. He titled his unpublished memoir *The Teenager Immigrant from the East Going West*. He had no more than a second-grade education but was able to write—with a seven-year-old's spelling—690 pages detailing his journey from Greece to America and back. When he came to America in 1910, he ate a whole banana, including the skin, in a boxed lunch he was given on the train ride from New York City to Rochester, New

York. He had never seen a banana before and didn't know how to eat it. His memoir gushes with pride and gratefulness for the good life he was able to make in America. He taught himself English and worked his way up from selling coffee on the street to starting a restaurant that supported a thirty-year retirement and two daughters, one of them my grandmother.

When he returned to Greece in 1959, he was a rich Americano. He hadn't seen his sister for forty-nine years. At Piraeus port, he worries that he won't be able to recognize the girl he left behind with "beautiful, long black hair." One theme that stands out to me in the memoir is how much he was thanked by fellow Greeks for the United States' support and reconstruction of their country after the Second World War. He himself was astonished at what his beloved adopted homeland, the United States, did through the Marshall Plan for his native land. "American dollars done wonders for Greece. Uncle Sam saved the country," he wrote. In 1959, he went to visit his son-in-law's family (my *pappous*' aunts and uncles) on Oinousses. There, on the edge of Asia, he was stopped by an eighty-nine-year-old priest, who wanted to thank him—some random Americano—because "Harry S. Truman saved Greece from the communists and Greece would be *kaput* if it weren't for America."

Just as one of my great-grandfathers saw the end of the Ottoman Empire, the era of American hegemony that the other recorded, which rippled across to tiny Oinousses, is finished. I come back to Oinousses because it is often in far off borderlands like this where geopolitical changes can be felt and contextualized. The same goes for all of Greece, which is a frontier state in NATO and the European Union.

In my travels, I was left with the impression that Greece is likely to be where the United States' commitment to its NATO allies dies hardest. But that is because Greece is a valuable Near Eastern protectorate for a superpower, not because it is part of

Europe. For eighty years, Greece was pulled in the direction of the West; now it's rejoining the East. In a twist from the crisis years, while Greece's commitment to the European Union and NATO is firm, those institutions now look shaky. No matter how they endure, the line, which Greece sits on, between East and West is vanishing.

Greece is a crossroads, at a tectonic intersection where great and regional powers are carving out zones of influence. Throughout history, when push came to shove, Greece has always been left outside Russia's zone, whether Tsarist or Soviet. In this new era, Greece will sit on the edge, but not inside, the sphere of influence that a militaristic and unstable Russia is pushing for. This will increase its value to Western Europe. In my travels in northeastern Greece, it was Russia's weakness and ineptness that was most deeply felt, not its strength. Still, Russian influence could become more palpable again in cities like Thessaloniki and potentially Alexandroupoli. Remember, Ivan Savvidis invested in forgotten assets that Western businessmen had no interest in, just like China at Piraeus Port. I suspect in due time, some Greek politicians will go back to courting Russia as they did during the financial crisis. This is only natural. It is part of a two-centuries-old relationship Greeks have with Russia.

The bigger takeaway is that in a multipolar world where borders are no longer sacrosanct, places like Oinousses will become more detached from the West. Oinousses' big neighbor is Türkiye, not Russia. That is the worry here. The imbalance between Greece and Türkiye in populations and military might means that what happens in Türkiye is going to ripple across to islands like Oinousses. That could be good or bad. This island hangs heavy over my identity, as it does all Oinoussens. Oinousses commands respect. It is a frontier island whose skies are buzzed often by Turkish jet fighters. "If the Turks come here, we will fight," Oinoussens like to say. That might sound like an exaggeration, but it's worth asking, what do the borderlands of the European Union and NATO look like in a decade, as the West fractures and revisionist powers get more comfortable—with US indifference—dominating their smaller neighbors?

One trend that will gain momentum is Greece's quest for Eastern allies. That is why it turned to Egypt to counter Türkiye and why Israel's influence here is expanding dramatically. At the same time, Greece will become more valuable to Western European countries, who looked down on it during the financial crisis. Greece is their frontline against migration.

What about Oinousses? These momentous changes could bypass it altogether, leaving the old sea captains and young sailing cadets here to bask in their island bliss. Like good Levantines, Oinoussens have benefited financially from the wars unleashed in Eastern Europe and the Middle East, profiting from higher shipping rates.

Oinousses scoffs at tourists. It doesn't need or want them. The island is renowned for its powerful and wealthy Greek shipping families. My grandfather's seafaring tales weren't far off. Oinoussens made a living plying their trade across the Near East. Oinousses and its big brother island, Chios, benefited from their geography. They sat on the trade route connecting the Black Sea and the Mediterranean. Together with Chios, and specifically the village of Kardamyla, these two islands control about ten per cent of the world's shipping.[1] Oinoussens who don't own vessels have traditionally been the captains of them. However, most ships are crewed by Filipinos and South Asians nowadays, not Greeks.

Oinousses' shipping titans decamped to London and New York generations ago. But some of these families come back in the summer. They hold court in their grand villas, and you can hear their kids' posh boarding school accents at Bilali, the island's only beach bar. So, while remote, Oinousses is very much wired into the global economy. That is the trick that other Greek borderlands need to copy. In an interconnected, hard-to-govern world of diffuse and unequal wealth, tapping into dynamic trade and the global rich matters. Ship owners aren't known to be sticklers for where they are domiciled, but they call Oinousses home. The bar is set very low for Greece's borderlands to succeed.

The protector of Oinousses is the patron of sailors, Saint Nicholas. The soft, baby-blue church of Agios Nikolaos is adjacent to the only grocery store on the island, which my dad's great-uncle owned. The summers I am able to get back to remote Oinousses (the island has no airport and the ferry connection is from Chios), I sip Turkish coffee and listen to the Orthodox chanting at midday as it echoes through the hilltop town. Those ancient cries seem louder to my ears on Oinousses than anywhere else in Greece. Of course, I am biased. But here, I reflect on the words of Egyptian-born Greek businessman and diplomat, Constantine Rodocanachi:

> To the ear, the basilica and the mosque are closely mingled and, the music being the essence of the soul, this union in melody is perhaps the reason why the Greek feels himself more at home in the Moslem Orient than elsewhere, though here he is surrounded by his enemies of several centuries of conflict.[2]

Greece has no easy answer to the migration crisis, but its Orthodox religion and Eastern values will allow it to weather the turmoil better than its Western European counterparts, even as it sits on the frontlines. That sounds paradoxical, but remember Zografion. Greeks know who they are. This helps in a shrinking, populist world.

Chios was one of the epicenters of the 2015 migrant crisis. As many as 2,000 migrants washed ashore there per day during the peak. Those numbers have dramatically decreased, but will not stop. If Türkiye stops policing its shores, they will rise quickly.

SEA CAPTAINS ON THE EDGE OF ASIA

In 2024, more than 54,000 migrants came via the sea to Greece. Chios at the time of writing hosts around 1,200 migrants.

The migration crisis was not the main focus of my travels. So much has been written about it that I did not want to condense Greece's place in the new Near East down to migration. I feel that Rodocanachi's colorful observation holds a timeless truth about Islam and Orthodox Christianity that has been buried in conversations about migration, but is more relevant now because of the geopolitical changes sweeping the region. Migration is just one symptom of Greece's reabsorption into the Near East, a region which it never really left. People are on the move here. I find the overlooked but consequential trend of middle-class and upper-middle-class people from Türkiye, Israel and the Arab world moving to Athens and to a lesser extent Thessaloniki fascinating.

I have tried to show how Greece belongs in the Near East because of its culture, history and religion. Living in Greece as the United States retreats from Europe has been incredible, because Greece was the first protectorate fashioned out of the wider Middle East by Western powers and the first country of post-war American intervention.

Oinousses was created out of the ashes of Middle Eastern war. Many families, like my cousins, trace their ancestors back to Greeks who washed ashore here fleeing Atatürk's army in 1922. The island was first settled by shepherds from Kardamyla, who left Chios after the Turkish massacre a century earlier.

My earliest understanding of Middle Eastern conflict was shaped by a cheap reproduction print my *pappous*, an amateur painter, had of Eugene Delacroix's *The Massacre at Chios*. The painting, which captured the Ottomans' devastation of Chios, was released in 1824. It galvanized public support for Western intervention against the Ottomans. The image of naked white women and a turbaned man wielding a sword was burned into

313

my seven-year-old's memory. My *pappous* would point to it and say, "That's where we are from." That print made him pretty cool; no other kids' grandfathers I knew had that kind of art laying around. For good or bad, that sense of adventure laid the seeds for me to come back to the Eastern Mediterranean.

The irony for Chios, as historian Philip Mansel pointed out, is that "the Greek island which least wanted independence suffered most because of it." Mansel called Chios "the first Levantine paradise to be destroyed" by nineteenth-century nationalism.[3]

When the Greek Revolution erupted, Chios was one of the richest and freest islands in the Ottoman Empire. French statesman and writer François-Rene de Chateaubriand, who dropped anchor there in 1806, called Chios, "a fairy region" of ringing church bells, incredibly fertile hills and a port, "thronged with Greeks, Franks, and Turks."[4]

For all these reasons, Chians rebuffed pleas from their fellow Greeks to join the revolt. Chios was dragged into the war after it was invaded by Greeks from the neighboring island of Samos. The Samians pillaged the wealthy island and shipped the spoils back home. It made no difference to the Ottomans that the Chians had not welcomed their neighbors. In retaliation, Sultan Mahmud II ordered his army to lay waste to Chios. At least 25,000 people were slaughtered by the Ottomans and 50,000 more, mainly women and children, were enslaved.[5]

Before the massacre, the sultan had granted Chios a high level of autonomy because of the cultivation of mastic. This sticky resin is extracted from stubby trees that only grow in southern Chios. If you find yourself driving through Chios' parched southern hills one day, the trees are easy to spot because of a distinctive white powder, a calcium carbonate mixture, under their trunks. The powder provides a clean surface for the mastic resin to fall on before it is collected.

Today, the twenty-four *mastichochoria*, or mastic villages, are gorgeous honeycombs of bougainvillea-scented alleys and stone houses connected by passageways. In the summer, they are filled with Greek Americans who return home. When Chios passed from Byzantine to Genoese rule in the fourteenth century, the villages were exploited by the Maona, a mercantile company headed by the Giustiniani family. As one historian noted, the Genoese rule was "harsh and humiliating" for local Greeks, which is why they welcomed the Ottomans in 1566.[6]

By then, mastic had already been popularized as a luxury ingredient across the wider Middle East. It was listed in the medieval Arabic cookbook *Kitab al-Tabikh*. Mastic spread throughout the region because of Chios' enviable location on the trade routes. The sultan's harem developed a ravenous appetite for mastic gum, so much so that the *mastichochoria* for a time were placed directly under the control of the sultan's mother, the valide sultan. Today, mastic is an essential ingredient in Arabic and Turkish cuisine. It is added to sweets like baklava and meat marinades; and it is used to flavor coffee. If you have ever tasted Turkish ice cream, *dondurma*, or its Arab equivalent, *booza*, mastic is what contributes to their stretchy texture.[7]

After I left medical school, I spent a week on Oinousses before moving to Jordan. That was the freest I ever felt in my life. Like my Oinoussen ancestors who took to the seas, I had no set path ahead of me. There is no feeling quite like embarking on a journey from an Aegean island. It is all the easier to savor if you are privileged enough to call that island your family's home. Arriving in dusty Amman, I thought I had left my ancestor's homeland behind me. I was wrong. Jordanians didn't know Oinousses, but they all knew Chios. One of my first weeks in Amman, a group of Jordanian friends took me to Bekdash Ice Cream (a sister shop of the original in Damascus, Syria) to taste *booza* for the first time. They were thrilled to teach me something about my

THE NEW BYZANTINES

homeland. That's when I started to realize that Greece is closer to the Middle East than to the West, both culturally and, as it is turning out, geopolitically.

"The first thing we do is check that the mastic in our ice cream is from Chios," the owner of Bekdash told me years later, after I became a regular customer. One mastic retailer based in Dubai but originally from Syria told me he loved Chios because it "looked and felt" like his homeland. There is a hard-to-pin-down continuum between Greece and the Middle East that exists in the senses. I hear it expressed in so many encounters like that. I have tried to communicate them during my travels.

The ancient mastic trade across the East endured the collapse of empires, the rise of new borders, and wars. Today, Chios exports around $40 million worth of mastic a year, mostly to the Arab world. That is a forgettable number in the grand sweep of things, but meaningful for an island of 50,000 people. Of course, the mastic trade can only get you so far. I emphasize it because it represents Greece's ties to the East, which can show up in the unlikeliest of places. This is the trend that will dominate Greece and Europe's future.

The Byzantines are back.

NOTES

1. DANCING IN PIRAEUS

1. Feargus O'Sullivan, "Behind the Accidentally Resilient Design of Athens Apartments," Bloomberg.com, 15 July 2020, https://www.bloomberg.com/news/features/2020-07-15/the-design-history-of-athens-iconic-apartments?sref=p1whY86y (accessed 10 October 2024).
2. Sean Mathews, "Greek Armenians Hold Rally in Athens: 'We are Like Brothers and Sisters,'" GreekReporter.com, 1 October 2020, https://greekreporter.com/2020/10/01/greek-armenians-hold-rally-in-athens-we-are-like-brothers-and-sisters/ (accessed 12 December 2024).
3. Nikos Roussanoglou, "Piraeus continues to lead realty rate rise," eKathimerini.com, 7 February 2024, https://www.ekathimerini.com/economy/real-estate/1242899/piraeus-continues-to-lead-realty-rate-rise/ (accessed 1 January 2025).
4. Anon., "From Brain Drain to 'Rebrain': Greek Labor Ministry Launches New Job Website," Tovima.com, 8 November 2023, https://www.tovima.com/finance/from-brain-drain-to-rebrain-greek-labor-ministry-launches-new-job-website/ (accessed 1 January 2025).
5. Patrick Leigh Fermor, *The Broken Road: From the Iron Gates to Mount Athos*, New York: The New York Review of Books, 2013, p. 245.
6. Ibid.
7. David Holden, *Greece Without Columns*, New York: J.B. Lippencott Company, 1972, p. 34.

8. Tasos Kokkinidis, "Eighty Percent of Greek Properties Bought with Cash," GreekReporter.com, 14 January 2019, https://greekreporter.com/2019/01/14/eighty-per cent-of-greek-properties-bought-with-cash/ (accessed 1 January 2025).
9. Anon., "Greece Tops Europe in Rent Payment Struggles," Tovima.com, 18 October 2024, https://www.tovima.com/finance/greece-tops-europe-in-rent-payment-struggles/ (accessed 1 January 2024).
10. Fernand Braudel, *The Mediterranean and the Mediterranean World In The Age Of Philip II, Volume I*, London: University of California Press, 1995, p. 278.
11. David Gilmour, "The Unregarded Prophet: Lord Curzon and the Palestine Question," *Journal of Palestine Studies*, Vol 25, No. 3, 1996, pp. 60–68.
12. George Nathaniel Curzon, *Frontiers*, Oxford: Clarendon Press, 1907, p. 14.
13. Laurence Barton Grafftey-Smith, *Bright Levant*, London: John Murray, 1970, p. 1.
14. Philip Mansel, *Levant: Splendour and Catastrophe on the Mediterranean*, New Haven: Yale University Press, 2011, pp. 1–5.
15. Ibid., pp. 10–20.
16. Grafftey-Smith, *Levant*, p. 34.
17. Mansel, *Splendour and Catastrophe*, pp. 137–39.
18. Grafftey-Smith, *Levant*, p. 32.
19. Lawrence Durrell, *Bitter Lemons*, London: Faber and Faber, 1957, p. 121.
20. C. M. Woodhouse, *Modern Greece: A Short History*, London: Faber and Faber, 1998, p. 62.
21. Ibid., p. 90.
22. Patrick Leigh Fermor, *The Broken Road: From The Iron Gates To Mount Athos*, 2013, New York, The New York Review of Books, 47.
23. Robert Byron, *The Byzantine Achievement*, 1929, London, George Routledge, 45.
24. Ibid., 16.
25. Mark Mazower, *The Greek Revolution: 1821 and the making of modern Greece*, London: Penguin Random House, 2021, pp. xxviii–xxix.
26. Sean Mathews, "Athens reaches out to Syria via Greek Orthodox

community," Al-Monitor.com, 20 October 2020, https://www.al-monitor.com/originals/2020/10/greece-renew-relations-syria-assad-christians-minority.html (accessed 8 August 2024).

2. EPIRUS: PASHAS, COMMUNISTS AND MERCHANTS

1. David Holden, *Greece Without Columns*, Philadelphia and New York: J.B. Lippencott Company, 1972, p. 28.
2. Ibid.
3. Ibid., p. 103.
4. Edi Gemi and Bledar Feta, "Migration Developments in Greece in 2023," Hellenic Foundation for European and Foreign Policy, 2024, https://www.eliamep.gr/wp-content/uploads/2024/07/Working-paper-128-SOPEMI-.pdf (accessed 10 February 2025).
5. Fernand Braudel, *The Mediterranean and the Mediterranean World in the Age of Philip II*, Volume II, London, University of California Press, 1995, p. 776.
6. Ibid., Vol I, p. 40.
7. Quentin and Eugenia Russell, *Ali Pasha, Lion of Ioannina: The Remarkable Life of the Balkan Napoleon*, South Yorkshire, Pen & Sword Books, 2017, pp. 15–18.
8. Ibid., p. 38.
9. Ibid., p. 46.
10. Ibid., pp. 53–60.
11. David Mason, "Lord Byron—Seven Takes," *The Hudson Review*, 2024, https://hudsonreview.com/2024/02/lord-byron-seven-takes/#:~:text=His%20first%20question%20was%20why,Ali%20Pacha%20present%20to%20you (accessed 10 February 2025).
12. Russell, *Lion of Ioannina*, p. 21.
13. Ibid., p. 38.
14. Mark Mazower, *The Greek Revolution: 1821 and the making of modern Greece*, London: Penguin Random House, 2021, pp. 43–50.
15. Ibid., pp. 115–119.
16. Nikos Kazantzakis, *Freedom and Death*, London: Faber and Faber, 1956, p. 27.
17. Ibid., p. 136.

18. Ibid., p. 36.
19. Traian Stoianovich, "The Conquering Balkan Orthodox Merchant," *Journal of Economic History*, Vol. 20, No. 2, 1960.
20. Ibid., pp. 234–313.
21. Ibid., p. 241.
22. Ibid., p. 238.
23. Tim Judah, "Greece's Ticking Demographic Time Bomb," Balkan insight.com, 8 September 2022, https://balkaninsight.com/2022/09/08/greeces-ticking-demographic-time-bomb/ (accessed 10 February 2025).
24. Anon., "Greece to spend 20 bln euros on lifting low birth rate," eKathimerini.com, 2 October 2024, https://www.ekathimerini.com/economy/1249927/greece-to-spend-20-bln-euros-on-lifting-low-birth-rate/ (accessed 10 February 2025).
25. C.M. Woodhouse, *The Struggle For Greece: 1941–1949*, New York: Beekman-Esanu, 1979, p. 161.
26. Ibid., p. 163.
27. Ibid., pp. 148–9.
28. Roderick Beaton, *Greece: Biography of a Modern Nation*, London: Penguin Books, 2020, p. 291.
29. Ibid., p. 292.
30. Woodhouse, *Struggle for Greece*, p. 235.
31. Suzy Hansen, *Notes On A Foreign Country: An American Abroad In A Post-American World*, New York: Farrar, Straus and Giroux, 2018, p. 145.
32. Woodhouse, *Struggle for Greece*, 233.
33. Anon., "World: Stalin Still Lives," *Time Magazine*, 25 May 1962.

3. PEARL OF THE AEGEAN: ORIENTALISTS AND OLIGARCHS

1. Helen Cooper and Eric Schmitt, "U.S. Spycraft and Stealthy Diplomacy Expose Russian Subversion in a Key Balkans Vote," *New York Times*, 9 October 2018, https://www.nytimes.com/2018/10/09/us/politics/russia-macedonia-greece.html (accessed 8 August 2024).
2. Ruby Gropas and Anna Triandafyllidou, "Immigrant and Political Life

in Greece: Between political patronage and the search for inclusion," Hellenic Foundation for European and Foreign Policy, April 2009, https://migrant-integration.ec.europa.eu/sites/default/files/2011-07/docl_21751_14107470.pdf (accessed 14 July 2024).
3. James Montague, "Macedonia's ultra-important referendum," Politico.com, 29 September 2018, https://www.politico.eu/article/macedonias-ultra-important-referendum-greece-footbal-thessaloniki-ivan-savvidis/ (accessed 11 February 2025).
4. Ioanna Zikakou, "PAOK FC Owner Repays Club's €10.8 Mln Debt to Greek State," GreekReporter.com, 13 May 2015, https://greekreporter.com/2015/05/13/paok-fc-owner-repays-e10-8-mln-debt-to-greek-state/ (accessed 11 February 2025).
5. Vassilis Nedos, "US has its eye on Greek Ports," Ekathimerini, 19 May 2025, https://www.ekathimerini.com/economy/1270027/us-has-its-eye-on-greek-ports/ (accessed 27 May 2025).
6. John Psaropoulos, "Russian anger builds as Greece prepares a military deal with Ukraine," "Hellenica," Substack, 20 July 2024, https://johntpsaropoulos.substack.com/p/russian-anger-builds-as-greece-prepares?r=17bt7m&utm_campaign=post&utm_medium=web&triedRedirect=true (accessed 11 February 2025).
7. Vassilis Nedos, "Greece decides to expel Russian diplomats," ekathimerini.com, 11 July 2018, https://www.ekathimerini.com/news/230551/greece-decides-to-expel-russian-diplomats/ (accessed 11 June 2024).
8. Cooper and Schmitt, "U.S. Spycraft and Stealthy Diplomacy Expose Russian Subversion."
9. Pierre Loti, *Aziyade*, Paris, 1879–2016, North Star Ed, p. 1.
10. Ibid., p. 8.
11. Mark Mazower, *Salonica, City of Ghosts: Christians, Muslims and Jews, 1430–1950,* New York: Alfred Knopf, 2005, p. 35.
12. Ibid., pp. 46–7.
13. Ibid., p. 49.
14. Iason Athanasiadis, "From Rimland to Rimland," 30 April 2024, lab.imedd.org, https://lab.imedd.org/en/from-rimland-to-rimland-no-map/ (accessed 25 February 2025).

15. Roderick Beaton, *Greece: Biography of a Modern Nation*, London: Penguin Books, 2020, p. 181.
16. Zulfu Livanli, *On The Back Of The Tiger*, New York: Other Press, 2022, p. 23.
17. Anon., "Muslims pray in Thessaloniki mosque, but for one day only," ekathimerini.com, 1 April 2013, https://www.ekathimerini.com/news/149946/muslims-pray-in-thessaloniki-mosque-but-for-one-day-only/ (accessed 7 July 2024).
18. Mazower, *Salonica, City of Ghosts*, p. 211.
19. Anon., "Number of Turkish Travelers Visiting Greece Soars in 2023," news.gtp.gr, 13 June 2024, https://news.gtp.gr/2024/06/13/number-of-turkish-travelers-visiting-greece-soars-in-2023/ (accessed 1 August 2024).
20. Michael Llewellyn-Smith, *Ionian Vision: Greece in Asia Minor 1919–1922*, London: Hurst, 2022, p. 21.
21. Ibid., 62–3.
22. A. Goff and Hugh A. Fawcett, *Macedonia: A Plea For the Primitive*, London, 1921, John Lane, 14.
23. Ibid., 157.
24. Harold Nicolson, *Peacemaking 1919*, London: University Paperbacks, 1933, p. 342.
25. Llewellyn-Smith, *Ionian Vision*, p. 72.
26. Ibid., p. 176.
27. Beaton, *Biography of a Modern Nation*, p. 224.

4. THE LAST PASHA OF KAVALA

1. John Foster Fraser, *Pictures From The Balkans*, London: Cassell, 1906, p. 168.
2. Khaled Fahmy, *All the Pasha's Men: Mehmed Ali, his Army and the Making of Modern Egypt*, Cairo: American University of Cairo Press, 1997, p. 7.
3. Ibid., 52.
4. C.M. Woodhouse, *Modern Greece: A Short History*, London, Faber and Faber: 1998, p. 108.
5. John Freely, *The Grand Turk: Sultan Mehmet II - Conqueror Of*

Constantinople And Master Of An Empire, New York: The Overlook Press, 2009, p. 26.
6. Ibid., 48.
7. Mark Mazower, *The Greek Revolution: 1821 and the making of modern Greece*, London: Penguin Random House, 2021, p. 123.
8. Ibid., pp. 236–7.
9. Fahmy, *All the Pasha's Men*, 53.
10. Philip Mansel, *Levant: Splendour and Catastrophe on the Mediterranean*, New Haven: Yale University Press, 2011, p. 49.
11. Ibid., p. 50.
12. Alexander Kitroeff, *The Greeks and the Making of Modern Egypt*, Cairo: American University of Cairo Press, 2019, p. 31.
13. Nikos Kazantzakis, *Zorba the Greek*, New York: Simon and Schuster, 1953, p. 226.
14. Lawrence Durrell, *Justine*, New York: E.P Dutton & Co., 1957, p. 162.
15. A. Goff and Hugh A. Fawcett, *Macedonia: A Plea For the Primitive*, London: John Lane, 1921, pp. 221–2.
16. Velika Ivkovska, *An Ottoman Era Town in The Balkans Kavala*, New York: Routledge, 2020, p. 105.

5. EGYPT: GREECE'S ALLY OR A TICKING TIME BOMB?

1. Taha Hussein, *The Future of Culture in Egypt*, Washington: American Council of Learned Societies, 1954, p. 4.
2. John Eliot Bowen, "The Conflict of East and West in Egypt," *Political Science Quarterly*, Vol. 1, No. 2, 1886, pp. 295–335.
3. Mona Makram-Ebeid, "Political Opposition in Egypt: Democratic Myth or Reality?" *Middle East Journal* 43, No. 3, 1989, pp. 423–36.
4. Alexander Kitroeff, *The Greeks and the Making of Modern Egypt*, Cairo: American University of Cairo Press, 2019, p. 89.
5. Sondos Assem, "Egypt announces $35bn deal with UAE to buy premium Mediterranean area," middleeasteye.com, 23 February 2024, https://www.middleeasteye.net/news/egypt-announces-massive-35-billion-deal-uae-develop-ras-el-hekma-north-coast (accessed 23 February 2024).

6. Jason Horowitz, "Greek Coast Guard Under Scrutiny for Response to Migrant Mass Drowning," *New York Times*, 19 June 2023.
7. Maged Mandour, "How Europe is profiting at the expense of Egypt's poor," middleeasteye.com, 25 March 2024, https://www.middleeasteye.net/opinion/egypt-europe-profiting-expense-poor-how (accessed 1 April 2024).
8. Sean Mathews, "Türkiye looks to pull ahead of EastMed rivals in Libya," Al-Monitor.com, 23 April 2021.
9. Ahmed Shams, "Egypt: Greek diplomats worked with Cairo to block EU criticism of Sisi," middleeasteye.org, 7 March 2022, https://www.middleeasteye.net/news/egypt-eu-criticism-sisi-blocked-greece-diplomats-worked (accessed 12 February 2025).
10. Patrick Kingsley, "Decimated Muslim Brotherhood Still Inspires Fear. Its Members Wonder Why," *New York Times*, 15 July 2017.
11. Sean Mathews, "Turkish-Greek talks, all talk?" al-monitor.com, 19 January 2021.
12. Sean Mathews, "Greece warns of Ukraine-style war with Türkiye in East Mediterranean," middleeasteye.org, 7 September 2022, https://www.middleeasteye.net/news/greece-warns-ukraine-war-eastmed (accessed 20 January 2025).
13. Michael Llewellyn-Smith, *Ionian Vision: Greece in Asia Minor 1919–1922*, London: Hurst, 2022, p. 78.
14. Kareem Fahim, "Amid Mediterranean tensions, retired Turkish admiral grabs the spotlight touting supremacy at sea," Washington Post, 27 September 2020.
15. David Kirkpatrick, "A Police State With an Islamist Twist: Inside Hifter's Libya," *New York Times*, 20 February 2020.
16. Sean Mathews, "Türkiye looks to pull ahead of EastMed rivals in Libya," Al-Monitor, https://www.al-monitor.com/originals/2021/04/turkey-looks-pull-ahead-eastmed-rivals-libya (accessed 28 July 2025).
17. Anon., "'I have to build a new life here', Palestinians start again in Cairo's 'Little Gaza' after fleeing Israel's war," TheNewArab.com, 5 November 2024, https://www.newarab.com/features/palestinians-build-new-lives-cairos-little-gaza (accessed 29 May 2025).
18. Anon., "An Egypt firm is making $2m a day from Palestinians fleeing

Israel's war on Gaza," middleeasteye.org, 1 May 2024, https://www.middleeasteye.net/news/egypt-firm-palestinians-fleeing-war-gaza (accessed 29 May 2025).
19. David Kirkpatrick, "Egyptians Say Military Discourages an Open Economy," *New York Times*, 17 February 2011.
20. Andrew England, "Egypt and the IMF: will Sisi take the economy out of the military's hands?" *Financial Times*, 31 October 2022.
21. Carlotta Gall, "Türkiye Emerges as a Big Winner in the Wake of al-Assad's Ouster," *New York Times*, 13 December 2024.
22. Christian Jakob and Stavros Malichudis, "Egypt: The EU's unexpected ally against migration," Heinrich Boll Foundation, 20 January 2025, https://gr.boell.org/en/2025/01/16/aigyptos-o-aprosdokitos-symmahos-tis-ee-kata-tis-metanasteysis (accessed 12 February 2025).
23. Anthee Carassava, "Greece Alarmed by Rising Tides of Migrants," Voice of America, 17 March 2024, https://www.voanews.com/a/greece-alarmed-by-rising-tides-of-migrants-/7531155.html (accessed 12 February 2025).

6. CAIRO: BEER IN THE GREEK CLUB

1. Anthony Shadid, *House of Stone: A Memoir of Home, Family, and a Lost Middle East*, Boston: Houghton Mifflin Harcourt, 2012.
2. Fernand Braudel, *The Mediterranean and the Mediterranean World in the Age of Philip II*, Volume I, London: University of California Press, 1995, p. 170.
3. Olivia Manning, *Fortunes of War: The Balkan Trilogy*, New York: New York Review of Books, 2010, p. 202.
4. Waugh Gali, *Beer in the Snooker Club*, London, Serpent's Tail, 1987, p. 17.
5. Ibid., 52.
6. Osama Gaweesh, "Egypt: Sisi fears a popular uprising after the fall of Assad in Syria," 25 December 2024, middleeasteye.com, https://www.middleeasteye.net/news/egypt-sisi-fears-uprising-after-assad-fall-syria (accessed 13 February 2025).
7. Declan Walsh, "A Decade On, Silence Fills Egypt's Field of Broken Dreams," *New York Times*, 23 January 2021.

8. Declan Walsh and Vivian Yee, "A New Capital Worthy of the Pharaohs Rises in Egypt, but at What Price?" *New York Times*, 8 October 2023.
9. Heba Saleh, "Egypt's economic woe spreads across all classes," *Financial Times*, 16 February 2023.
10. Stratis Tsirkas, *Drifting Cities*, Athens: Kedros Publishers, 1995, p. 605.
11. Lawrence Durrell, *The Alexandria Quartet*, London: Faber and Faber, 1968, p. 17.
12. Tsirkas, *Drifting Cities*, p. 341.
13. Ibid., p. 273.
14. Alexander Kitroeff, *The Greeks and the Making of Modern Egypt*, Cairo: American University of Cairo Press, 2019, pp. 79–81.
15. Ibid., pp. 86–8, 174.
16. Tsirkas, *Drifting Cities*, p. 573.
17. Ibid., p. 273
18. Ibid., *Greeks and the Making of Modern Egypt*, p. 56.
19. Ibid., p. 181.
20. Anon., "Egypt Feels the Economic Pinch," *New York Herald Tribune*, 28 December 1965, https://archive.nytimes.com/iht-retrospective.blogs.nytimes.com/2015/12/27/1965-egypt-feels-the-economic-pinch/ (accessed 14 February 2025).
21. Alex Rowell, "Hoping to Channel Nasser, Egypt's Sisi Provokes a Backlash," newlinesmag.com, 3 October 2023, https://newlinesmag.com/spotlight/hoping-to-channel-nasser-egypts-sisi-provokes-a-backlash/ (accessed 14 February 2025).
22. Heba Saleh, "Egypt secures $8bn IMF deal after removing currency controls," *Financial Times*, 6 March 2024.

7. PRIESTS AND CRYPTO-CHRISTIANS: INTRIGUE IN JERUSALEM

1. Sean Mathews, "In Greece, Israelis find cheap property, nightlife and political refuge," middleeasteye.net, 8 May 2023, https://www.middleeasteye.net/news/greece-israel-property-real-estate-political-refuge (accessed 18 February 2025).

2. David Holden, *Greece Without Columns*, Philadelphia and New York: J.B. Lippencott, 1972, p. 164.
3. Ibid., p. 62.
4. Daniel Estrin, "Greek Orthodox Church Sells Land In Israel, Worrying Both Israelis And Palestinians," npr.com, 2 December 2017, https://www.npr.org/sections/parallels/2017/12/02/565464499/greek-orthodox-church-sells-land-in-israel-worrying-both-israelis-and-palestinia, (accessed 18 February 2025).
5. Nir Hasson, "Greek Church Says It Has Evidence of Corruption in Settler Takeover of Jerusalem Properties," haaretz.com, 5 August 2019, https://www.haaretz.com/israel-news/2019-08-05/ty-article/.premium/greek-church-says-has-evidence-of-corruption-in-settler-takeover-of-jlem-properties/0000017f-db0c-ddf3-af7f-ff2d966e0000 (accessed 18 February 2025).
6. Nir Hasson, "'You Want a Girl? How Many?': Tapes Reveal How Right-wing Group Tried to Make East Jerusalem Jewish," haaretz.com, 7 January 2018, https://www.haaretz.com/israel-news/2018-01-07/ty-article/.premium/tapes-reveal-how-right-wing-group-tried-to-make-east-jerusalem-jewish/0000017f-e573-da9b-a1ff-ed7fc2be0000 (accessed 18 February 2025).
7. Matt Rees, "An Unorthodox deal," time.com, 29 May 2005, https://time.com/archive/6672965/an-unorthodox-deal/ (accessed 18 February 2025).
8. Barak Ravid and Meron Rapoport, "Panel: Recognize Theofilis as Rightful Greek Patriarch," haaretz.com, 29 October 2007, https://www.haaretz.com/2007-10-29/ty-article/panel-recognize-theofilis-as-rightful-greek-patriarch/0000017f-db87-db5a-a57f-dbef0af40000 (accessed 18 February 2025).
9. Jihad Abu Raya, "The most disputed land on earth: How Greek Orthodox church sold off Palestinian plots," middleeasteye.net, 6 December 2017, https://www.middleeasteye.net/big-story/most-disputed-land-earth-how-greek-orthodox-church-sold-palestinian-plots (accessed 18 February 2025).
10. Joseph Massad, "Palestinian Orthodox Christians struggle against two colonialisms," middleeasteye.net, 2 May 2022, https://www.

middleeasteye.net/opinion/palestinian-orthodox-christians-struggle-two-colonialisms (accessed 18 February 2025).
11. Anon., "Putin aide says Jerusalem Old City property dispute is at top of Russian agenda," timesofisrael.com, 19 April 2022.
12. George Grylls, "Settlers 'using the war' to target Christian homes in the West Bank," *The Times*, 22 October 2024, https://www.thetimes.com/world/middle-east/israel-hamas-war/article/target-christians-west-bank-gaza-israel-r9m2lmmqv (accessed 20 February 2025).
13. Canaan Lidor, "Russian immigration streams in as Israel predicts uptick in Western newcomers," timesofisrael.com, 21 May 2024, https://www.timesofisrael.com/russian-immigration-streams-in-as-israel-predicts-uptick-in-western-newcomers/ (accessed 19 February 2025).
14. Judah Ari Gross, "Data shows most recent immigrants from former Soviet Union aren't considered Jewish," timesofisrael.com, 17 November 2022, https://www.timesofisrael.com/data-shows-major-drop-in-immigrants-from-former-soviet-union-considered-jewish/ (accessed 18 February 2025).
15. Nir Hasson, "New Details Emerge on Greek Orthodox Church's Massive Asset Sell-off in Israel—and the Mystery Only Deepens," haaretz.com, 27 October 2017, https://www.haaretz.com/israel-news/2017-10-27/ty-article/new-details-emerge-on-greek-orthodox-churchs-fire-sale-in-israel/0000017f-dbaa-db5a-a57f-dbea1af00000 (accessed 18 February 2025).
16. Ibid.
17. P.J. Vatikiotis, *Among Arabs and Jews: A Personal Experience 1936–1990*, London: Weidenfield and Nicolson, 1991, p. 21.
18. Ibid., p. 27.
19. Ibid., p. 79.
20. Ibid., pp. 83–4.
21. Constantine Zurayk, *The Meaning of the Disaster*, Beirut: Khayat's College Book Cooperative, 1956, p. 34.
22. Vatikiotis, *Among Arabs and Jews*, p. 105.
23. Ibid., p. 103.
24. Abdel Raouf Arnaout, "Jerusalem's Christian population sees steep decline: Church leader," aa.com.tr, 25 March 2020, https://www.

aa.com.tr/en/middle-east/jerusalem-s-christian-population-sees-steep-decline-church-leader/2545814 (accessed 19 February 2025).
25. Stratis Tsirkas, *Drifting Cities*, Athens: Kedros Publishers, 1995, p. 40.

8. THE ISRAEL–GREECE ALLIANCE

1. Peter Evans, *Ari: The Life and Times of Aristotle Socrates Onassis*, New York: Summit Books, 1986, p. 55.
2. Thomas W. Lippman, *Crude Oil, Crude Money: Aristotle Onassis, Saudi Arabia, and the CIA*, Santa Barbara: Praeger, 2019, pp. 114–15.
3. Ibid., p. 163.
4. Sean Mathews, "Stock prices of shipping companies are soaring because of Houthi attacks," middleeasteye.net, 22 December 2023, https://www.middleeasteye.net/news/israel-palestine-war-houthis-attacks-red-sea-ships-stock-prices-soaring (accessed 19 February 2025).
5. Anon, "Arafat in Greece in snub to Arabs," *New York Times*, 2 September 1982.
6. Ibid.
7. Paul Anastasi, "Greece disregards a deal with Italy," *New York Times*, 7 December 1988.
8. Eitay Mack, "The suppressed history of Israel's support for the brutal Greek junta," 972mag.com, 28 April 2023, https://www.972mag.com/israel-support-greece-junta/ (accessed 19 February 2025).
9. Leonidas Kallivretakis, "Greek-American relations in the Yom Kippur War concurrence," *The Historical Review*, Vol 11, 2014, pp. 105–126.
10. Ibid., p. 120.
11. Sean Mathews, "'Unprecedented': Why Hezbollah threatened to attack Cyprus," middleeasteye.net, 19 June 2024, https://www.middleeasteye.net/news/israel-palestine-war-why-hezbollah-threatened-attack-cyprus, 19 February 2025.
12. Anon., "PM Netanyahu's interview with Kathimerini (Greece)," Embassy of Israel in Cyprus, 18 June 2017.
13. Marc Champion, "Raid Further Strains Türkiye's Israel Ties," *Wall Street Journal*, 1 June 2010.

14. Barak Ravid, "Netanyahu's Big Fat Greek Wedding," haaretz.com, 1 July 2011, https://www.haaretz.com/2011-07-01/ty-article/netanyahus-big-fat-greek-wedding/0000017f-db32-df9c-a17f-ff3ae3e50000 (accessed 19 February 2025).
15. Dan Arbell, "The US-Türkiye-Israel Triangle," Analysis Paper No. 34, 2014, Brookings Institute.
16. Anon, "Majority of Americans hold unfavourable view of Israel, Pew poll finds," middleeasteye.org, 9 April 2025, https://www.middleeasteye.net/news/majority-americans-hold-unfavourable-view-israel-pew-poll-finds (accessed 4 June 2025).
17. Sean Mathews, "Sunburned tourists and fighter jets: The Israel-Greece alliance," aljazeera.com, 7 April 2021, https://www.aljazeera.com/news/2021/4/7/sunburned-tourists-and-fighter-jets-the-greek-israeli-alliance (accessed 19 February 2025).
18. Sean Mathews, "UAE joins Greek, Egyptian naval exercise in Eastern Mediterranean," almonitor.com, 1 December 2020, https://www.al-monitor.com/originals/2020/12/uae-greece-defense-agreement-turkey-eastern-mediterranean.html (accessed 29 July 2025).
19. Mathews, "Sunburned tourists and fighter jets."
20. Vassilis Nedos, "Anti-drone umbrella over the islands," ekathimerini.com, 1 July 2022, https://www.ekathimerini.com/news/1188019/anti-drone-umbrella-over-the-islands/ (accessed 20 February 2025).
21. Mathews, "In Greece, Israelis find cheap property, nightlife and political refuge."
22. Nektaria Stamouli, "Greece leaves spy services unchecked on Predator hacks," politico.eu, 7 August 2024, https://www.politico.eu/article/greek-spyware-predatorgate-government-court-report-telephone/ (accessed 20 February 2025).
23. Crofton Black, Tasos Telloglu, Eliza Triantafillou and Omer Benjakob, "Flight of the Predator: Jet Linked to Israeli Spyware Tycoon Brings Surveillance Tech From EU to Notorious Sudanese Militia," haaretz.com, 30 November 2022, https://www.haaretz.com/israel-news/security-aviation/2022-11-30/ty-article-magazine/.premium/jet-linked-to-israeli-spyware-tycoon-brings-spy-tech-from-eu-to-notorious-sudanese-militia/00000184-a9f4-dd96-ad8c-ebfcd8330000 (accessed 20 February 2025).

9. THRACE: GREEK MINARETS

1. Patrick Leigh Fermor, *The Broken Road: From the Iron Gates to Mount Athos*, New York: The New York Review of Books, 2013, p. 33.
2. Konstantinos Tsitselikis, *Old and New Islam in Greece*, Leiden, Boston: Martinus Nijhoff, 2012, p. 135.
3. Ibid., pp. 112–13.
4. Ibid., pp. 112, 133–5.
5. Anon, "Ethnic Turks and Greeks Reportedly Clash," *New York Times*, 30 January 1990.
6. Tsitselikis, *Old and New Islam*, p. 137.
7. Michael Llewellyn-Smith, *Ionian Vision: Greece in Asia Minor 1919–1922*, London: Hurst, 2022, pp. 209–301.
8. Matina Stevis-Gridneff and Carlotta Gall, "Erdoğan Says, 'We Opened the Doors,' and Clashes Erupt as Migrants Head for Europe," *New York Times*, 29 February 2020.
9. Sean Mathews, "The survivors of Lausanne: Intrigue and rivalry in Western Thrace," middleeasteye.com, 28 January 2023, https://www.middleeasteye.net/news/western-thrace-lausanne-survivors-intrigue-rivalry (accessed 14 February 2025).
10. Tsitselikis, *Old and New Islam*, 143.
11. Llewellyn-Smith, *Ionian Vision*, p. 303.
12. Tsitselikis, *Old and New Islam*, p. 173.
13. Talha Ozturk, "N. Macedonia purchases 18 howitzers from Türkiye," Anadolu Ajansı, 13 January 2023, https://www.aa.com.tr/en/europe/n-macedonia-purchases-18-howitzers-from-turkiye/2787125 (accessed 14 February 2025).
14. Sean Mathews, "The survivors of Lausanne."
15. Ibid.
16. Stuart Elliott, "Greece-Bulgaria gas link operator to press on with expansion to 5 Bcm/year," spglobal.com, 7 August 2024, https://www.spglobal.com/commodity-insights/en/news-research/latest-news/natural-gas/080724-greece-bulgaria-gas-link-operator-to-press-on-with-expansion-to-5-bcmyear (accessed 14 February 2025).
17. Martin Vladimirov, "Closing the backdoor: The new TurkStream is here. Can the West stop it?" Politico, 30 August 2024, https://

www.politico.eu/article/turkstream-putin-Erdoğan-gas-pipeline-gazprom-eu-sanctions/ (accessed 14 February 2025).
18. Anon., "Russian gas deliveries via TurkStream set new record," turkiyetoday.com, 12 February 2025, https://www.turkiyetoday.com/business/russian-gas-deliveries-via-turkstream-set-new-record-118255/ (accessed 28 February 2025).
19. Anton Troinaovski, Jeanna Smialek, Melissa Eddy, "Europe Wants to Banish Russian Gas. The U.S. May Have Other Plans," *New York Times*, 5 June 2025.
20. Sean Mathews, "The survivors of Lausanne."
21. Ibid.
22. Patrick Leigh Fermor, *Roumeli: Travels in Northern Greece*, New York: New York Review of Books, 1966, p. 7.
23. Nektaria Stamouli, "Greece draws in the US—and edges out Russia," Politico, 9 February 2022, https://www.politico.eu/article/greece-us-russia-military-energy-relation/ (accessed 15 February 2025).
24. Anon., "Moscow dismay over Alexandroupoli," ekathimerini.com, 11 December 2021, https://www.ekathimerini.com/news/1173574/moscow-dismay-over-alexandroupoli/ (accessed 15 February 2025).
25. Manolis Kostidis, "Rafales, Alexandroupoli base irk Erdoğan," ekathimerini.com, 2 November 2021, https://www.ekathimerini.com/news/1170925/rafales-alexandroupoli-base-irk-Erdoğan/ (accessed 15 February 2025).

10. ISTANBUL: THE OLD BYZANTINES

1. Traian Stoianovich, "The Conquering Balkan Orthodox Merchant," *Journal of Economic History*, Vol. 20, No. 2, 1960, 234–313.
2. Edmondo De Amicis, *Constantinople*, Vol II., Philadelphia: Henry T. Coates & Co., 1896, pp. 98, 104.
3. Kemal Karpat, "Ottoman Population Records and the Census of 1881/82–1893," *International Journal of Middle East Studies*, Vol. 9, No. 3, 1978, 237–74.
4. Author interview, Giannis Demirtzoglou, Zografion President, 18 September 2024.
5. Speros Vryonis, *The Mechanism of Catastrophe: The Turkish Pogrom of*

September 6–7, 1955, and the Destruction of the Greek Community of Istanbul, New York: greekworks.com, 2005, pp. 51–2.
6. Nektaria Anastasiadou, *A Recipe for Daphne*, New York: University of Cairo Press, 2020, p. 113.
7. Vryonis, *The Mechanism of Catastrophe*, pp. 74–94.
8. Ishaan Tharoor, "The execution of a former Turkish leader that still haunts Erdoğan," *Washington Post*, 30 July 2016.
9. Jay Walz, "Turks expelling Istanbul Greeks; Community's Plight Worsens During Cyprus Crisis," *New York Times*, 9 August 1964.
10. Patrick Leigh Fermor, *Roumeli: Travels in Northern Greece*, New York: New York Review Books Classics, 2006, p. 113.
11. Ibid., pp. 114–16.
12. Elif Shafak, *The Bastard of Istanbul*, London: Penguin, 2007, p. 178.
13. Nektaria Anastasiadou, Στα Πόδια Της Αιώνιας Ἀνοιξης [At the foot of the Eternal Spring], Athens: Ekdoseis Papadopoulos, 2023, p. 165.

11. MEZE IN KADIKÖY

1. Recep Tayyip Erdoğan, "Why the EU Needs Turkey," *Insight Turkey*, Vol. 6, No. 3, 2024, pp. 7–15.
2. Uwe Hessler, "Schroder Hails Erdoğan as a 'Great Reformer,'" dw.com, 10 April 2004, https://www.dw.com/en/schr%C3%B6der-hails-Erdoğan-as-a-great-reformer/a-1346679 (accessed 16 February 2025).
3. Jaakko Laakso, "Colonisation by Turkish settlers of the occupied part of Cyprus," May 2003, European Union, Committee on Migration, Refugees and Demography.
4. Sewell Chan, "Cyprus: Why One of the World's Most Intractable Conflicts Continues," *New York Times*, 7 November 2016.
5. Hugh Pope, "Time for EU-Turkey 'Urgency,'" *Wall Street Journal*, 16 December 2008.
6. David Holden, *Greece Without Columns*, Philadelphia and New York: J.B. Lippencott Company, 1972, p. 78.
7. Uri Friedman, "The Thinnest-Skinned President in the World," *The Atlantic*, 26 April 2016, https://www.theatlantic.com/international/

archive/2016/04/turkey-germany-Erdoğan-bohmermann/479814/ (accessed 16 February 2025).

8. Laura Pitel, "Erdoğan recasts failed coup's place in Turkish history," *Financial Times*, 16 July 2017.
9. De Amicis, *Constantinople*, 105.
10. Mark Lowen, "Istanbul mayoral vote: Is 'disastrous' loss beginning of Erdoğan's end?", BBC, 24 June 2019, https://www.bbc.com/news/world-europe-48744733 (accessed 16 February 2025).
11. Carlotta Gall, "How a Message of Unity and Mistakes by Erdoğan Tipped the Istanbul Election," *New York Times*, 26 June 2019.
12. Anon., "Istanbul mayor supports Hagia Sophia conversion move 'as long as it benefits Turkey,'" hurriyetdailynews.com, 13 July 2020, https://www.hurriyetdailynews.com/istanbul-mayor-supports-hagia-sophia-conversion-move-as-long-as-it-benefits-turkey-156527 (accessed 16 February 2025).
13. Edmondo De Amicis, *Constantinople*, Vol II., Philadelphia, Henry T. Coates & Co., 1896, pp. 98, 260.
14. Nevzat Devranoglu and Orhan Corkun, "Exclusive: Turkey defers $600 million Russian energy payment under deal-sources," reuters.com, 10 May 2023, https://www.reuters.com/business/energy/turkey-defers-600-mln-russian-energy-payment-sources-2023-05-10/ (accessed 16 February 2025).
15. Anon, "Russia, Turkey Discuss Gas Swap to Pay for Nuclear Plant," bloomberg.com, 11 February 2025, https://www.bloomberg.com/news/articles/2025-02-11/russia-turkey-discuss-gas-swap-to-pay-for-akkuyu-nuclear-plant?sref=p1whY86y (accessed 16 February 2025).

EPILOGUE: SEA CAPTAINS ON THE EDGE OF ASIA

1. Harry Papachristou, "Feasting and folklore light up navigator forum on Aegean Islands," tradewindsnews.com, 20 October 2022, https://www.tradewindsnews.com/people/feasting-and-folklore-light-up-navigator-forum-on-aegean-islands/2-1-1338171 (accessed 21 February 2025).

2. C.P. Rodocanachi, *Forever Ulysses*, New York: Viking Press, 1938, p. 84.
3. Philip Mansel, *Levant: Splendour and Catastrophe in the Mediterranean*, London: John Murray, 2010, p. 50.
4. Francois Rene Chateaubriand, *Travels in Greece, Palestine, Egypt, and Barbary, during the years 1806 and 1807*, London: Henry Colburn, 1812, p. 291.
5. John Contoudis, *Chios: A History*, River Vale: Cosmos Publishing, 2009, pp. 107–18.
6. Ibid., p. 71.
7. Sean Mathews, "Chios, the Greek island fuelling the Arab world's sweet tooth," middleeasteye.net, 8 September 2023, https://www.middleeasteye.net/news/chios-greek-island-powering-arab-worlds-mastic-addiction (accessed 23 February 2025).

SELECTED BIBLIOGRAPHY

Beaton, Roderick, *Greece: Biography of a Modern Nation*, London: Penguin Random House, 2019.

Braudel, Fernand, *The Mediterranean and the Mediterranean World in the age of Philip II*, Berkeley: University of California Press, 1995.

Chateaubriand, François-Rene de, *Travels in Greece, Palestine, Egypt, and Barbary, during the years 1806 and 1807,* London: Henry Colburn, 1812.

Contoudis, John, *Chios: A History*, River Vale: Cosmos Publishing, 2012.

Curzon, George Nathaniel, *Frontiers*, Oxford: Clarendon Press, 1907.

Dalrymple, William, *From the Holy Mountain*, London: Harper Collins, 1997.

Fermor, Patrick Leigh, *Roumeli: Travels in Northern Greece*, New York, Harper & Row, 1966.

——, *The Broken Road: From the Iron Gates to Mount Athos*, New York, New York Review of Books, 2013.

Freely, John, *The Grand Turk: Sultan Mehmet II—Conqueror of Constantinople and Master of an Empire*, New York: The Overlook Press, 2009.

Grafftey-Smith, Laurence Barton, *Bright Levant*, London: John Murray, 1970.

Hansen, Suzy, *Notes on a Foreign Country: An American Abroad in a Post-American World*, New York: Farrar, Strauss and Giroux, 2017.

Holden, David, *Greece Without Columns*, New York: JB Lippincott, 1972.

Llewellyn-Smith, Michael, *Ioanian Vision: Greece in Asia Minor 1919–1922*, London: Hurst, 2022.

Kazantzakis, Nikos, *Zorba the Greek*, London: John Lehmann Ltd., 1952.

———, *Freedom and Death*, London: Faber and Faber, 1956.

Kitroeff, Alexander, *The Greeks and the Making of Modern Egypt*, Cairo: The American University of Cairo Press, 2019.

Mansel, Philip, *Levant: Splendour and Catastrophe on the Mediterranean*, New Haven: Yale University Press, 2011.

Mazower, Mark, *Salonica, City of Ghosts: Christians, Muslims and Jews, 1430–1950*, New York, Knopf: 2005.

———, *The Greek Revolution: 1821 and the Making of Modern Europe*, London; Allen Lane, 2021.

Russel, Eugenia and Quentin, *Ali Pasha: The Lion of Ioannina: The Remarkable Life of the Balkan Napoleon*, Barnsley, Pen & Sword Military, 2017.

Tsirkas, Stratis, *Drifting Cities*, Athens: Kedros, 1995.

Woodhouse, C.M., *Modern Greece: A Short History*, London: Faber and Faber, 1977.

———, *The Struggle For Greece: 1941–1949*, New York: Beekman Esanu, 1979.

ACKNOWLEDGEMENTS

I want to thank my parents for a lifetime of unparalleled love, support and selflessness. My mom engendered my brother and I with a love of travel and has paid dearly for it because of the Christmases, Easters and Thanksgivings we have missed. She is my most committed reader and rock. My dad gave me my love for history and pride in my Greek roots. He encouraged every adventure and raised Mark and I to think outside the box. Mark, this book is dedicated to you. We have been through so much together, including some of the adventures in these pages. I know there are more to come. I love you brother.

This book would not have happened without Robert Dudley, my agent, who never gave up on my proposal. Michael Dwyer at Hurst Publishers took a chance on this book and I am forever grateful to him. I must thank Alice Clarke, my wonderful editor, for her keen eye, too.

Some of the travels and encounters in this book go back five years. They picked up pace after a Middle East war started on 7 October 2023. This was the worst moment for a full-time journalist to write a book, which I did across four continents. I am deeply indebted to Middle East Eye for the trust, patience, support and precious time they afforded me to write to this book.

ACKNOWLEDGEMENTS

I especially have to thank Ali Amir, editor-in-chief David Hearst, Shaheryar Mirza and Faisal Edroos. Faisal, thanks for your editing and support for this adventure.

The people inside and outside of this book are even more important than the places to which I traveled. To start, I have to thank three brilliant diplomats and dear friends: Foivos Georgakakis, Evangelos Kalpadakis, and Eleni Petroula. Eleni was selfless with her help.

Many others contributed to making this book a reality, including: Stratos Efthymiou, Andreas Stamatiou, Nikos Papadopoulos, Dimitrios Angelosopoulos, and Vasilis Tolis, to name a few. Giannis Boutaris welcomed me in Thessaloniki. Anna Missirian hosted me at Imaret and Kavala. Omniya Abdel Barr showed me the wonders of medieval Cairo, and Valia was my sidekick in Jerusalem when Mark was at the embassy. Minas Vasiliadis and Nektaria Anastasiadou were indispensable guides in Istanbul. The Gkoumas family welcomed me first to Oinousses.

David Kirkpatrick provided the initial motivation for this book over a coffee in New York City. Summer Said read the chapters on Egypt and gave invaluable advice. Friends in Athens were a wellspring of support. Thanos Davelis' passion for Greece is inspiring. George Meneshian read many chapters, edited them and encouraged me at every turn. Cameron Bell was always there to read and give insightful feedback. Iason Athanasiadis is one of the sharpest journalists I know. His work is an inspiration and my reporting would not be possible without him.

Petros Kasfikis helped me in Washington, DC. Chris Bowe came out of retirement to read several chapters. Michael Vatikiotis gave several helpful suggestions.

One person endured more of the stresses of this project than anyone else. She put up with all the long interviews, trips and messy piles of books, my love and muse, Athena. I love you.

This list is not exhaustive. If I have forgotten anyone, I am sorry. Thank you.

INDEX

Abdul Hamid II, Ottoman Sultan, 85–6, 252
Abdullah II, King of Jordan, 185, 294
Abdulmejid I, Ottoman Sultan, 295
Abdulmejid II, Ottoman Sultan, 295
Abraham Accords (2020), 180
Abramovich, Roman, 69
Abu Dhabi, United Arab Emirates, 127
Abu Nidal, 214
Adrianople, 256
Aegean Sea, 47, 61, 67, 85, 95, 128, 140–42, 286, 304
Blue Homeland doctrine, 143–4, 227, 304, 306
Afghanistan, 293
agriculture, 73, 231
Ahmet, Ilhan, 250–51
Airbnb, 2, 24, 89, 107, 238
Akkuyu Nuclear Power Plant, 302
AKP (*Adalet ve Kalkınma Partisi*), 285–304
Akrotiri, Cyprus, 216
Alaca Imaret mosque, Thessaloniki, 90
Alan Kogioy, Komotini, 249
Albania, 41–2, 43, 45, 60, 81, 106, 114, 230, 243
Albanian language, 271
Aleppo, Syria, 3, 21
Alevis, 231
Alexander the Great, 75, 79, 92, 115
Alexander II, Emperor of Russia, 257
Alexander's Courtyard, Jerusalem, 188
Alexandretta, 270
Alexandria, Egypt, 3, 7, 9, 18, 25, 26, 34, 115, 119, 164–5
Alexandria Quartet (Durrell), 79, 164–5, 181
Alexandroupoli, Thrace, 74, 247, 256–9, 297, 310

INDEX

Algeria, 124
Ali Pasha, 43–7, 114, 126
Allatini family, 84–5
Allenby, Edmund, 1st Viscount, 166, 202
Ambler, Eric, 111
American University of Cairo, 203
de Amicis, Edmondo, 262, 297, 299
Amman, Jordan, 11, 315
Among Arabs and Jews (Vatikiotis), 200–201
anarchists, 15, 17
Anastasiadou, Nektaria, 267, 278–83
Andrić, Ivo, 48
Androulakis, Nikos, 225
Annan, Kofi, 287
Ano Poli, Thessaloniki, 67, 92, 98, 104, 107
Antakya, Türkiye, 270
antidoron, 264
Antioch, 12, 188, 270
Antiochian Christians, 270
antiparochi, 2–3
Apoyevmatini, 289–93
Aqaba, Jordan, 4
al-Aqsa compound, Jerusalem, 184, 195
Arab Legion, 207
Arab Revolt (1916–18), 99, 100
Arab Spring (2010–11), 138, 139, 153, 162–3, 219, 288
Arab-Israeli War (1948–9), 194, 203–4, 207
Arabic, 4, 11, 12, 134, 271

Arafat, Yasser, 192, 213
arak, 11, 303
Aramco, 248
Argiros, Konstantinos, 9
Aristotelous Square, Thessaloniki, 83–4
armatoles, 43, 56
Armenian Apostolic Church, 209
Armenians, 2, 3–6, 23, 71, 86, 100, 231, 232, 250, 267, 273
 genocide (1915–17), 2, 3, 68, 220
 Greco-Turkish War (1919–22), 103
Army of the Orient, 97–9
Arnona, Jerusalem, 179–80, 193–4
Aromanian, 91
Art Deco, 135, 157, 162, 168
Arvanitakis, Georgios, 166
Asafoglu, Cigdem, 250
Aslan Pasha mosque, Ioannina, 38, 49
al-Assad, Bashar, 35, 72, 162, 182, 193, 214, 222, 288, 302
al-Assad, Hafez, 3–4
At the Foot of the Eternal Spring (Anastasiadou), 278, 281
Atatürk, Mustafa Kemal, 92–5, 101–2, 234, 267, 268, 283, 294, 295, 301
Athanassoulis, Angelo, 170–73, 176
Athens, Greece, 1–9, 53
 Christian refugees in, 2–4
 Civil War period (1946–9), 60

INDEX

Ellinikon Project, 6–7
  Islam in, 237
  Israelis in, 180–81
  Kolonaki, 7, 17, 26
  Neos Kosmos, 1–4, 11, 12
  Omonia Square, 224
  Piraeus, 5–10, 11, 26, 78–9,
    105, 181, 310
  polykatoikias, 1–3
  property market, 6–7, 16–18,
    154–5, 180–81, 224, 313
  tourism in, 2, 24, 53
'Athina Mou' (Argiros), 9
Athonos Market, Thessaloniki,
  84
Australia, 169
Austria-Hungary (1867–1918),
  95, 99, 205
Austrian Hospice, Jerusalem, 205
Azerbaijan, 5, 247, 248
Aziyadé (Loti), 78

Bahai, 200
baklava, 11
Balenciaga, 93
Balfour, Arthur James, 99
Balik Bazaar, Istanbul, 279
Balkan Wars (1912–13), 81, 107,
  116, 127, 128, 241
bandits, 43, 46
al-Banna, Hassan, 139
Baqa, Jerusalem, 206
Bartholomew, Patriarch of
  Constantinople, 186, 274
Basil II, Byzantine Emperor, 29
Bastard of Istanbul, The (Shafak),
  278

Batman bar, Athens, 5
Battle of Dobro Pole (1918), 99
Battle of Gallipoli (1915–16),
  101
Battle of Lepanto (1571), 63
Battle of Navarino (1827), 34,
  104, 125
Battle of the Pyramids (1798),
  113
Bauhaus, 17, 157
bawabs, 160
Bayezid II, Ottoman Sultan, 80
Bayraktar, Selçuk, 294–5
Bayraktar TB2 drones, 243,
  294–5, 302
Beaton, Roderick, 86
Bebek, Istanbul, 301
Beer in the Snooker Club (Ghali),
  161
Begin, Menachem, 200
Beirut, Lebanon, 3, 9, 18, 21,
  23, 83, 118, 119, 239
Beit Hanina, Jerusalem, 190–91
Bekdash Ice Cream, 315–16
Bektashism, 43
Belgrade, Serbia, 83
belly dancing, 8, 10, 28, 159, 281
Belterra Investments, 72
Benaki family, 24–5, 164
Benaki Museum, Athens, 24–6
Benakis, Antonis, 24–6, 115
Benakis, Emmanuel, 25
Bethlehem, Palestine, 184, 189,
  194, 196
Beyazit II, Ottoman Sultan, 121
Beyoğlu, Istanbul, 261–73, 288
Biden, Joseph, 258

Bin Laden group, 202
birthrates, 53–4, 238–9
Bit Bazaar, Thessaloniki, 103–7
Bitter Lemons (Durrell), 29
Black Sea, 68, 91, 102
Blue Homeland doctrine, 143–4, 227, 304, 306
Boghos Nubar Pasha, 100
Bolshevik Revolution (1917), 188
booza, 315
börekcisi, 293
Bosnia, 46, 244
Bosporus, 30, 37, 102, 230, 258, 262, 280
bougatsa, 251
Boutaris, Giannis, 78, 87–94, 106, 107, 108–9
bouzouki, 9, 81, 84
Brankovic, Mara, 121
Braudel, Fernand, 18, 43, 158
Bridge on the Drina, The (Andrić), 48
Bright Levant (Grafftey-Smith), 22, 24, 26
British Empire, 22, 60, 61, 62, 63, 99–100, 112
    Egypt, 25, 57, 100, 134, 135–6, 166
    India, 20, 60, 112, 134, 154
    Palestine, 20, 60, 81, 99–100, 186, 194, 200
Brotherhood of the Holy Sepulchre, 186
Brouzis, Panayiotis, 308
Bulgaria, 1, 127–8, 230

Balkan Wars (1912–13), 116, 127, 128, 241
First World War (1914–18), 96, 97, 99, 128
Greek Civil War (1946–9), 62
IGB pipeline, 247, 248
independence (1908), 86
North Macedonia, relations with, 77
Ottoman period, 244
People's Republic (1946–90), 60, 62, 234
Second World War (1939–45), 55, 128
Bulgarian Orthodox Church, 265, 271
Bulgarians, 29, 81, 82, 83, 85, 106, 108, 109, 117, 130
Bureau of European Affairs, 21
Bureau of Near Eastern Affairs, 21
Bush, George Walker, 185
Byron, George Gordon, 6th Baron, 43, 45, 123
Byron, Robert, 31–2, 276
Byzantine Achievement, The (Byron), 31–2
Byzantine Empire (330–1453), 12, 28–32, 33, 108, 208, 261, 276, 277, 279, 282
    Christianity in, 187, 264, 271, 291
    Christoupolis, 112
    Crusader invasion (1204), 29–30, 120
    double eagle emblem, 70
    Greco-Turkish War and, 102

INDEX

Greek War of Independence and, 96
Ioannina, 40, 49–50
Jews in, 80
Ottoman conquest, 30, 40, 49–51, 79, 80, 112, 119–21, 240, 262, 271, 282–3, 291
Thessaloniki and, 79, 80, 83, 84, 109
Thrace, 232
Young Turk Revolution and, 86

Caesarea, Israel, 193
Cairo, Egypt, 21, 29, 39, 57, 79, 118, 133–55, 157–77
coronavirus pandemic in, 158–9, 161, 162
Estoril, 151–2
Greek Club, 169–77, 205
Greeks in, 154–5, 164–77
Mogamma Complex, 163
New Administrative Capital, 163
prostitution in, 160–61
Second World War (1939–45), 158, 159
Tahrir Square, 162–3
Talaat Harb Square, 171
Zamalek, 154, 159
Caliphate, 22, 32, 295
cannabis, 41–2
Cape of Good Hope, 212–13
Capitulations, 22–3, 136, 166, 167
Casablanca, Morocco, 84

Catherine II, Empress of Russia, 44, 68
Catherine's Courtyard, Jerusalem, 188
Catholicism, 12, 209, 264, 265, 271
Catinis, Charles, 34–5
Cavallis, Christos, 173–4, 176, 177
çay, 293
Cemal Pasha, 87
Central Intelligence Agency (CIA), 143, 212, 215
de Chateaubriand, François-Rene, 314
Chatzimichail, Konstantinos, 258–9
Chatzivasileiou, Tasos, 242
Chelebi, Evliya, 80
Chemins de fer Orientaux, 256
Chermantas, Dimitri, 202–3
Chermantas, George, 202
'Childe Harold's Pilgrimage' (Byron), 44
China, 6, 18, 20, 78–9, 181, 204, 302, 310
Chios, 22, 25, 125, 141, 286, 311, 313–16
CHP (*Cumhuriyet Halk Partisi*), 93, 266, 267, 268, 269, 292, 298–304
Christian refugees, 2–4, 82
Christianity, 11, 12–14, 19
Antiochian Christians, 270
in Bulgaria, 265, 271
in Byzantine Empire, 187, 264, 271, 291

345

INDEX

Catholicism, 12, 209, 264, 265, 271
Crusades, 29–30, 120, 187, 209
Easter, 13, 210
  in Egypt, 131, 134, 136, 154, 160, 161, 174, 181
  in First World War, 96–7
  in Greco-Turkish War, 32, 82, 101, 102–3
  in Greek War of Independence, 123
  incantations, 42–3
  invocations, 13
  in Israel/Palestine, 183, 184–99, 207–10, 223, 228
  names and, 13–14
  in Ottoman Empire, 23, 33, 43, 46, 47, 50–51, 80, 85, 86, 120, 265, 273, 291
  in Russia, 12, 33, 63, 187–8, 189
  in Türkiye, 95, 103, 263–83
  in United States, 208–9
Church of the Holy Sepulchre, Jerusalem, 189, 207, 209, 210
Churchill, Winston, 56, 57, 58–9
Cihangir, Istanbul, 269, 283, 296
Circassians, 48
Citadel of Saladin, Cairo, 135
Clemenceau, Georges, 99
CMA GGM, 72
coffee, 3, 6, 7, 11, 24, 51, 103, 234, 251, 312
Cohanim, Ateret, 185
Cold War (1947–91), 15, 20, 58–63, 128, 234
communism, 15, 41, 56–63, 88, 128, 190, 215, 220, 234, 268, 309
Communist Party of Greece, 56–63, 88, 190, 220
Consolidated Contractors Company, 201–2
Constantine, Roman Emperor, 264
Constantine I, King of Greece, 97, 98
Constantine XI, Byzantine Emperor, 121
Constantinople, 12, 28, 29, 34, 50–51, 70, 102, 264
  Crusader sacking (1204), 29–30, 120
  Greek community, 30, 33, 232–3, 235, 261, 265
  Ottoman conquest (1453), 30, 80, 240, 262, 282–3
Convention of London (1840), 129
Coptic Christians, 131, 134, 136, 154, 160, 161, 174, 181, 209, 244
Corfu, 38, 40, 41
coronavirus pandemic (2019–23), 65, 158–63
corruption, 5, 41–2, 89
COSCO, 6, 78–9, 181
cosmopolitanism, 187, 236, 278
  in Egypt, 25, 26, 165, 168, 239
  in Istanbul, 267, 271, 273
  in Kavala, 126, 127

INDEX

in Ottoman Empire, 86, 103, 116, 126, 263, 275
in Palestine, 188, 196, 200, 206
in Thessaloniki, 71, 86, 88, 106–7, 239
in Thrace, 231–2, 236, 239, 249–50
cost of living
Egypt, 153, 170, 176
Greece, 9, 16, 53, 94, 109
Türkiye, 94, 293, 298
Crete, 22, 40, 48, 49, 56, 96, 120, 144, 202, 221, 238, 297
crossroads of civilizations, 229, 310
Crusades
First (1096–99), 187
Fourth (1202–4), 29–30, 120
Siege of Jerusalem (1187), 209
cuisine, 83, 239, 251, 252, 255, 263, 303, 315
culture wars, 8, 68, 272
Curzon, George, 1st Marquess, 20
Cycladic Islands, 25, 33, 39
Cyprus, 18, 64, 120, 142, 144, 181, 216, 221, 235, 269, 286–7
Annan Plan (2004), 286–7
Turkish invasion (1974), 7, 111, 224, 242, 265, 287

Dahab, Egypt, 177
Dalrymple, William, 45
Damascus, Syria, 3, 29, 34–5
Dar al-Islam, 113
Darfur, 47
Dassin, Jules, 112
Davos Summit (2009), 217
Dedeagach, 257
Delacroix, Eugene, 313
Delta, Penelope, 26
Demetrius, Saint, 70
Demirtzoglou, Giannis, 271–2
democracy, 33, 42, 59, 63, 64, 208, 236
Democratic Reform Current, 190
demographic decline, 53–4, 238–9
Dermaris, Nikolas, 53
Despotate of Epirus (1205–1479), 50
Diab, Amr, 159
Diafonidou, Eleni, 231–3, 245
diaspora, 8–9, 33, 51
Dilian, Tal, 225
Diliani, Dimitri, 190–93
Doctors Without Borders, 223
Dodecanese Islands, 101
Dokki, Cairo, 152
dolma, 303
Dolmabahçe Palace, Istanbul, 295
dondurma, 261, 315
Donskoy Tabak, 69
dragomans, 274–5
Drifting Cities (Tsirkas), 164–5, 167, 207, 209
Drone Dome, 222
drones, 222, 243, 294–5

347

INDEX

Dubai, United Arab Emirates, 6, 40, 127, 136, 173, 238, 316
Durrell, Lawrence, 29, 79, 111, 130, 165, 181, 205, 224, 276
Dussaud brothers, 257

EAM, 56, 57–8
Easter, 13, 210
Edirne, Turkey, 254, 256
Edison, 248
Egnatia Odos, 230, 247
Egypt, 3, 11, 19, 21, 26, 28, 31, 39, 46, 112–17, 131, 133–55, 157–77, 311
   alcohol in, 169–70, 173
   British rule (1882–1956), 25, 57, 100, 134, 135–6, 166
   Copts, 131, 134, 136, 154, 160, 161, 174, 181, 209, 244
   coronavirus pandemic in, 158–63
   cost of living, 153, 170, 176
   coup d'état (2013), 138–9
   currency devaluation (2016), 174
   economic crisis (2023–4), 150, 153–4, 170, 174–7
   French War (1798–1801), 112–13
   Gaza War (2023–), 148–9
   Greeks in, 154–5, 164–77, 211
   independence (1956), 136
   infitah (1974), 149
   Israel, relations with, 146–9, 214, 219
   Libya, relations with, 143, 145, 150
   migration crisis, 137–8, 164
   Muhammad Ali dynasty (1805–1953), 112–17, 122, 126, 129, 133, 134, 135, 164, 166
   Nasser government (1954–70), 25, 129, 146, 149, 161, 162, 168–70, 171, 212
   Palestine War (1948–9), 194
   Paris Peace Conference (1919), 100, 135
   Red Sea crisis (2023–), 146
   Revolution (1952), 129, 159, 168
   Revolution (2011), 139, 162–3
   Sadat assassination (1981), 147
   Sadat government (1970–81), 146–7
   Second World War (1939–45), 158, 159
   secularism in, 115, 135, 138, 139
   sex in, 160–61, 165, 179
   Sisi government (2013–), 138–9, 145, 146, 149–53, 162–3, 170, 174–7
   Six-Day War (1967), 146, 194, 199
   Suez Canal, 134, 135, 136, 146, 161, 168, 212
   Suez Crisis (1956), 136, 161–2, 168, 212

INDEX

Syria, relations with, 150
Türkiye, relations with, 138–9, 144, 145, 151
Yom Kippur War (1973), 146
'Egyptian Girl', 10
Egyptians, 6, 31, 131
Eid, 90
Eirinaios I, Patriarch of Jerusalem, 185–6, 190, 191
ELAS, 56, 57–63
Elbit Systems, 222
elections 2023 parliamentary election, 15
Ellinikon Project, 6–7
emigration, *see* migration
EMPROS, 231
end-of-times prophecies, 208
energy, 53, 73, 247–9, 302
  natural gas, 53, 64–5, 140, 142, 144, 247–9, 298, 303
Enlightenment (c. 1637–1789), 33, 37, 124
entrepôts, 18
entrepreneurialism, 23
Enver Pasha, 85, 87
Epirus, 37–54, 95
  Albanians in, 41–2
  corruption in, 41, 42
  Greek War of Independence (1821–32), 46–7
  merchant class in, 46, 50–51
  Ottoman period, 43–51
  Second World War (1939–45), 55–8
  tech industry in, 51–3
Episcopal Church, 190
Erbakan, Necmettin, 294

Erdoğan, Recep Tayyip, 5, 91, 94, 108–9, 138–41, 181, 221, 243, 282–3, 285–304
  Albania visit (2024), 244
  Blue Homeland doctrine (2006), 143–4, 227, 304
  coup attempt (2016), 93, 295–6
  EEZs dispute, 140–42, 221, 223
  Egypt, relations with, 138–40, 144–5, 151, 152
  EU candidacy and, 286–9
  Greece visit (2017), 246
  Hagia Sophia conversion (2020), 90–91, 108, 266, 282–3, 299
  Israel, relations with, 193, 217, 219, 221, 227
  Menderes, admiration of, 268–9
  Nagorno Karabakh conflict and, 5
  Rum and, 285–304
  Syria, relations with, 4, 193
  Thrace migrant crisis (2020), 241
Estoril, Cairo, 151–2
Ethiopian Orthodox Church, 209
ethnic cleansing
  Gaza (2023–), 147–8, 192, 223, 226–7
  Greece-Turkey (1923), 2, 81, 98, 103, 104–5, 107, 127, 130, 232, 265
Ethnos, 70

European Court of Human
    Rights, 251
European Union (EU), 5, 12, 19,
    27, 42, 54, 65, 82, 94, 109,
    137, 230, 277, 297, 309–11
    agricultural policies, 231
    Bulgaria and, 128
    Egypt, relations with, 138
    far right politics in, 237
    Greek financial crisis (2009–
        18), 15, 218
    Israel, relations with, 218–19
    natural gas imports, 248, 249
    Next Generation program, 65
    North Macedonian
        candidacy, 75, 77
    Russo-Ukrainian War, 248,
        249, 302
    Thrace and, 237, 241, 254,
        256
    Turkish candidacy and, 286–9
    Ukrainian candidacy, 255
    United States, relations with,
        64
Evangelical Christianity, 208–9
Evosmos, Thessaloniki, 70–71
Evros River, 241, 262
Exarcheia, Athens, 17, 31, 224
Exclusive Economic Zones
    (EEZs), 140–42, 221, 223

Faisal I, King of Iraq, 100
Farouk, King of Egypt, 122, 129,
    134, 159, 168
Fascist Italy (1922–43), 55
Fatah, 190, 192
fellahin, 26, 114

Ferdinand, King of Spain, 80
fertilizer, 73, 231
feta cheese, 256
15 July Bridge, Istanbul,
    295–6
Filiki Eteria, 46, 274
financial crisis (2009–18), 8,
    14–15, 16, 65, 69, 73, 176,
    218, 219, 305
Finland, 77
First World War (1914–18), 2,
    20, 28, 87, 95–9, 128, 202
Floating Storage Regasification
    Unit, 247
football, 70–72
Fortunes of War, The (Manning),
    158
France
    Algerian War (1954–62),
        124
    Capitulations, 22
    Cretan State peacekeeping
        (1898–1913), 49
    First World War (1914–18),
        95, 97, 99
    Greek War of Independence
        (1821–32), 34, 73, 123,
        124, 125
    immigration, 31
    Napoleonic Wars (1803–15),
        45, 122
    Ottoman War (1798–1801),
        112–13
    Paris Peace Conference
        (1919), 99, 101
    Suez Crisis (1956), 168
Frankfurt, Germany, 237

INDEX

Fraser, John, 111
Freedom and Death (Kazantzakis), 48
French language, 81, 134
Friendly Society, 46
Friendship, Equality, and Peace Party, 250, 255
Frontiers, 20
Future of Culture in Egypt, The (Hussein), 133–4

Gallant, Yoav, 223
Gallipoli campaign (1915–16), 101
gay pride parades, 89
Gaza, Palestine, 194
   Freedom Flotilla, 217–18
   Israeli War (2008–9), 217, 221
   Israeli War (2023–), see Gaza War
Gaza War (2023–), 4, 124, 128, 179, 181, 192, 214–15, 216
   Alexandroupoli and, 258
   Cyprus and, 216
   Egypt and, 147–9
   ethnic cleansing, 147–8, 192, 223, 226–7
   Houthis and, 146, 213, 216
   ICC arrest warrants (2024), 63, 223
   Saudi Arabia and, 215
   Türkiye and, 107, 306
Gaziantep, Türkiye, 3
Gazprom, 249
Gennadius II, Patriarch of Constantinople, 121

Genoa, Republic of (1099–1797), 22, 50, 315
George, Saint, 247
Georgia, 46, 68, 71
Germany
   Federal Republic (1949–), 237
   Second Reich (1871–1918), 87, 95
   Third Reich (1933–45), 55–8, 81
Ghali, Waguih, 161, 173
Gianaclis wine, 169–70
Giustiniani family, 315
Givat Hamatos, Palestine, 196
globalization, 136, 275, 276
Glyfada, Athens, 136
Gokalp, Ziya, 294
Golan Heights, 42
golden visas, 9, 18, 93
Grafftey-Smith, Laurence, 22, 24, 26
Greco-Turkish War (1919–22), 32, 82, 101–3, 241, 243, 313
Greece
   Junta (1967–74), 10, 215
   Kingdom, First (1832–1924), see Kingdom of Greece, First
   Kingdom, Second (1935–73), 10, 55–63, 128
   Ottoman period (1371–1832), see Ottoman Empire
   Republic, Third (1974–), see Greek Republic, Third
Greece Without Columns (Holden), 38–9, 291
Greek Civil War (1946–9), 58–63

351

INDEX

Greek Club, Cairo, 169–77, 205
Greek Colony, Jerusalem, 209
Greek language, 12, 81, 270, 271, 281
Greek Orthodox Church, *see* Orthodox Christianity
Greek Republic, Third (1974–)
  coronavirus crisis (2020–21), 65, 158
  cost of living, 9, 16, 53, 94, 109, 176
  Cyprus crisis (1974), 7, 111, 224, 242, 265, 287
  demographic decline in, 53–4, 238–9
  diaspora, 8–9, 51
  emigration, 8–9, 33, 51
  energy costs, 53, 73
  EU membership, 5, 12, 15, 19, 27, 42, 54, 75
  financial crisis (2009–18), 8, 14–15, 16, 65, 69, 73, 176, 218, 219, 305
  immigration, 2–4, 15, 18, 27, 31, 137, 179, 241, 312–13
  Komotini riot (1990), 236
  Limnos–Kemal Reis collision (2020), 227
  Messenia boat disaster (2023), 137
  NATO membership, 6, 12, 16, 19, 54–5, 62, 74–7, 108, 137
  property market, *see* property market
  tech industry, 51–3
  tourism, 2, 8–9, 16–18, 24, 38, 40, 62, 65, 89, 238–40, 280, 311
  Treaty of Friendship (1930), 267, 269
  wealth inequality, 7
Greek War of Independence (1821–32), 24, 30, 33–4, 46–7, 95, 122–5, 166, 274, 313–14
Güler, Ara, 297

Haaretz, 218
Haddad, Wadie, 204
Haftar, Khalifa, 143
Hagia Sophia, Istanbul, 90–91, 108, 266, 282–3, 299
Haifa, Israel, 81, 200
Haj prefix, 13–14
Halil Bey Mosque, Kavala, 130
Halkidiki, 106
Hamas, 128, 146, 147, 148, 181, 191, 192, 195, 216, 217, 306
harems, 45, 78, 86, 121, 134
Hashemites, 186, 194
Hass Murat Pasha, 121
Hatay, 270
Haussmannian architecture, 135, 157, 171
Hay'at Tahrir al-Sham's (HTS), 3, 35, 150, 192, 193, 214, 222, 226, 288, 302
Hayworth, Rita, 168
Hebrard, Ernest, 83
Helen, Saint, 264
Heliopolis, Cairo, 145, 172
Hellenic identity, 277–8

INDEX

Hellenic Popular Mobilization
  Army (ELAS), 56, 57–63
Herzog, Peter, 126
Hezbollah, 148, 182, 214, 216,
  222
hijab, 237, 274, 299
de Hirsch, Maurice, 256
Hitler, Adolf, 55, 56
Holden, David, 11, 38–9, 182,
  276, 291
Holocaust (1941–5), 81
Holy Fire ceremony, 210
Holy League (1571), 63
House of Islam, 113
House of War, 113
Houthis, 146, 213, 216
howitzer canons, 243
Huma Hatun, 121
Human Rights Watch, 223
Hungary, 288
Hunker Begendi, 239
Hussein, Saddam, 213
Hussein, Taha, 133–4, 136
huzun, 262, 297, 306
Hydra, 125, 200

Ibn Saud, 116
Ibrahim Pasha, 122, 124, 125
ice cream, 261, 315–16
IGB pipeline, 247, 248
İmamoğlu, Ekrem, 298–300, 304
Imaret, Kavala, 117–21, 125,
  129–30, 131, 251
Imbros, 232, 285
IMEC corridor, 77–8, 183
immigration, *see* migration
Immobilia Building, Cairo, 168

Imperial Orthodox Palestine
  Society, 74, 187
incantations, 42–3
India, 60, 63, 77–8, 112, 127,
  129, 134, 154, 183
IMEC corridor, 77–8, 183
infitah, 149
İnönü, İsmet, 267, 269
Intellexa, 225
International Court of Justice
  (ICJ), 195
International Criminal Court
  (ICC), 63, 223
International Monetary Fund
  (IMF), 15, 174–5
invocations, 13
Ioannina, Epirus,, 37–54, 81
  Greek War of Independence
    (1821–32), 46–7
  merchant class in, 46,
    50–51
  tech industry in, 51–3
Ionian Islands, 120
Ionian Vision (Llewellyn-Smith),
  100
Iran, 146, 182, 200, 214, 221,
  222, 305
Iraq, 194, 204, 213, 229, 294
Irgun, 200
Isa, Selim, 251
İşçi, Onur, 298–304
Islam, 12, 13, 15, 20, 31, 42, 43,
  46, 49, 69, 80, 81, 86
  in Egypt, 138–9, 144, 147,
    149, 151, 152
  in Kavala, 117, 130, 131
  in Kingdom of Greece, 98

in Thessaloniki, 79, 80, 81, 90, 98
in Thrace, 119, 230, 231, 232–8, 241–7, 250–56, 278
in Türkiye, 93, 94, 95, 138–9, 243, 273–4, 282–3, 292, 294, 298–9
Wahhabism, 115–16, 122, 204
Young Turks and, 87
Islamism, 93, 94, 95, 138–9, 147
in Egypt, 27, 138–9, 144, 147, 149, 151, 152
in Libya, 143
in Palestine, 183, 191, 192
in Syria, 3, 35, 150
in Türkiye, 93, 95, 95, 243, 273, 282–3, 292, 294, 306
Israel, 7, 19, 21, 28, 63, 64, 77, 107, 128–9, 136, 179–210, 211–28, 297, 311
Abraham Accords (2020), 180
Christianity in, 184–99, 206–10, 223, 228
Egypt, relations with, 146–9, 214, 219
establishment (1948), 194, 203–4, 207
Gaza War (2008–9), 217, 221
Gaza War (2023–), *see* Gaza War
Gulf States, relations with, 214–15
ICC arrest warrants (2024), 63, 223

Lebanon conflict (2023–), 181, 182, 214, 216
Leviathan gas field, 142
Mavi Marmara incident (2010), 217
natural gas industry, 142, 144
October 7 attacks (2023), 129, 146, 147, 180, 181, 192, 195
Oslo Peace Process (1993–5), 183, 192
Petra Hotel affair (2004), 185–6, 190, 191, 206
Red Sea crisis (2023–), 146, 213, 216
revisionism, 64, 136, 227
Russian migration to, 189
Saudi Arabia, relations with, 214, 215
secularism in, 18, 181, 203, 227
Six-Day War (1967), 146, 194, 199
Suez Crisis (1956), 161–2
Syria conflict (2024), 181, 193, 222
Türkiye, relations with, 193, 217, 219, 227
United States, relations with, 214, 215, 219–20, 227–8, 301
Yom Kippur War (1973), 146, 215–16
Zionism, 20, 81, 99–100, 180, 194, 200–201, 203, 211

INDEX

Israelis, 4, 6, 18, 81, 82, 106, 108, 109, 180–81, 224, 227
  property market and, 4, 6, 18, 81, 82, 180–81, 224–5, 227
Istanbul, Türkiye, 9, 21, 93, 94–5, 230, 232, 240–41, 261–83, 285–306
  cosmopolitanism in, 271, 273
  coup attempt (2016), 93, 295–6
  Dolmabahçe Palace, 295
  15 July Bridge, 295–6
  Greek community, *see* Rum
  Hagia Sophia conversion (2020), 90–91, 108, 266, 299
  İmamoğlu mayoralty (2019–), 298–9
  Panagia Greek Orthodox Church, 261, 263–5
  White Palace, 295
  White Turks, 301
  Zografion Lyceum, 261, 265–6, 270–73, 312
İstiklal Street, Istanbul, 261, 263, 265
Italy
  Cretan State peacekeeping (1898–1913), 49
  Fascist period (1922–43), 55
  Great Synagogue of Rome attack (1982), 214
  Paris Peace Conference (1919), 99, 101
  Turkish War (1911–12), 92
Izmir, Türkiye, 9, 102

Jacob, Saint, 199
Jaffa Gate, Jerusalem, 205–6
Jaffa, Israel, 193, 206
Janissaries, 80
Jerusalem, 12, 14, 29, 79, 165, 166, 179–210
  al-Aqsa compound, 184, 195
  Greek Orthodox Church in, 184–99, 223
  Jewish settlers in, 183–6, 190–91, 195–6, 198–9, 205–6, 223
  King David Hotel bombing (1946), 200
  Petra Hotel affair (2004), 185–6, 190, 191, 206
  Russian Orthodox Church in, 187–90
Jesus, 207–8, 264
Jews, 23, 25, 32, 80–81, 85, 88, 126, 134, 267, 273
Jordan, 4, 11, 21, 144, 185, 186, 194, 207, 214, 315
Junta (1967–74), 10, 215
Justice and Development Party (AKP), 285–304
Justine (Durrell), 130
Justinian, Byzantine Emperor, 282

kabadayı, 293
Kadir Kas University, 298
Kadıköy, Idanbul, 304
kafenios, 5
kágkouras, 24, 71
Kalpadakis, Evangelos, 26–7
Kantakouzene, Irene, 121

355

INDEX

Kapani Market, Thessaloniki, 84
Kapustin, Antonin, 187
Kardamyla, Chios, 311, 313
Kasampisa, Istanbul, 262, 293
Kastellorizo, 142, 144
Katamon, Jerusalem, 206
Kathimerini, 217
Kavala, Macedonia, 74, 111–31, 137, 202, 230
  Bulgaria and, 128
  cosmopolitanism, 126, 127
  Imaret, 117–21, 125, 129–30, 131
  Ottoman period, 111–20, 125
  property market, 127
  tourism in, 117, 130
Kazantzakis, Nikos, 48, 59, 128
Kefalonia, 9
Khurshid Pasha, 46–7
Kifisia, Athens, 136
King David Hotel bombing (1946), 200
Kingdom of Greece, First (1832–1924), 15, 34, 47, 63, 73
  Crete annexation (1913), 49
  First World War (1914–18), 95–9
  National Schism (1914–17), 97
  Paris Peace Conference (1919), 99
  population exchange (1923), 2, 81, 98, 103, 104–5, 107, 130, 232–3, 265, 278
  Thessaloniki annexation (1912), 81, 107
  Treaty of Lausanne (1923), 103, 232, 233, 235, 241, 246, 265
  Treaty of Sèvres (1920), 101
  Turkish War (1919–22), 32, 82, 101–3, 241, 243, 313
Kingdom of Greece, Second (1935–73), 10
  Civil War (1946–9), 58–63
  Metaxas dictatorship (1936–41), 10, 55
  Second World War (1939–45), 55–8, 81, 128
Kitab al-Tabikh, 315
Kitroeff, Alexander, 166, 168
klephts, 43, 46
Knesset, Israel, 184, 190
kodjabashis, 120
Kolokotronis, Theodoros, 47
Kolonaki, Athens, 7, 17, 26
kombologia, 6, 41, 131
komboskini, 308
Komotini, Thrace, 236, 239, 246–52, 255
Konya, Anatolia, 112, 129
Kosovo, 244
Koukaki, Athens, 24
koulouri, 293
Koutlas, Tassos, 51–2
Kurds, 100, 286, 294, 301

Ladino, 80, 81
lahmacun, 251
Lawrence, Thomas Edward, 99, 118
le Carré, John, 219
Lebanon, 3–4, 6, 8, 9, 11, 12, 18, 21, 23, 194, 229

INDEX

Civil War (1975–90), 3–4, 213
Israel–Hezbollah conflict (2023–), 181, 182, 214, 216, 222
Leigh Fermor, Patrick, 10, 28, 30, 45, 57, 154, 201, 257, 277
Lerman, Eran, 218–19
Lesbos, 141, 286
Lesky, Jerusalem, 209–10
de Lesseps, Ferdinand, 134
Levant, 22–4, 118, 158, 213, 215, 239, 272–6
Levant Lunatics, 45
Leviathan gas field, 142
Lewis, Bernard, 204
Libya, 127, 138, 143, 145, 213, 294
Light of Day, The (Ambler), 112
Limassol, Cyprus, 18
Liquified Natural Gas (LNG), 53, 64–5, 140, 142, 144, 247–9, 298, 303
Little Drummer Girl, The (le Carré), 219
Livaneli, Zulfu, 86
Llewellyn-Smith, Michael, 100
Lloyd George, David, 96, 99
lokantas, 262
London School of Economics, 219
London, England, 8, 22, 311
Loti, Pierre, 78–9, 80, 81, 97
Louis-Dreyfus, 72
Luciana restaurant, Jerusalem, 218

Luddite movement (c. 1811–16), 45
Lyon, France, 51

Macedonia, 59, 69, 74–8, 83, 91, 95, 119
Macedonia: A Plea for the Primitive (Fawcett and Goff), 98, 107, 130, 239
Madagascar, 225
Mahmud II, Ottoman Sultan, 115, 314
mahraganat, 159
Makedonia Palace, Thessaloniki, 72
Makronisos, 61
Mamilla Mall, Jerusalem, 218, 227
Mamluks, 113–14
Manganis, George, 24–6
mangas, 87, 293
Mani peninsula, 47
Mansel, Philip, 314
Manuel II, Byzantine Emperor, 79
Maona, 315
Markovitis, Nikos, 285, 293–6, 305
Marousi, Athens, 201
Marrakech, Morocco, 84
marriage, 121, 161, 174, 179, 201–2, 269, 270, 280
Marshall Plan (1948), 62, 268, 309
Massacre at Chios, The (Delacroix), 313
mastichochoria, 315

INDEX

Matarangas, Byron, 305
Mathaios, Michail, 307
Mavi Marmara, 217
Mavi Vatan, 143–4, 227, 304, 306
Mavromichalis, Petros, 47
McCarthyism, 204
Mecca, 38, 114, 116, 131
medical tourism, 9
Medina, 116
Mega Channel, 70
Megali Idea, 96, 201
megirefta, 263
Mehmed II, Ottoman Sultan, 30, 50, 121, 262, 282, 291
Melachrinoudis, Giannis, 169
Menderes, Adnan, 268–9
Meneshian, George, 5–6
Meneshian, Tasos, 3–4, 21, 230
Mesih Pasha, 121
Mesolonghi, 124
Metaxas, Ioannis, 10, 55
Metsovo, 126
Michaelidis, Evgenios, 166
middle class, 18, 82
  in Egypt, 136, 153, 154, 165, 170
  in Greece, 16, 31, 52, 224, 265
  in Palestine, 190
  in Türkiye, 286, 293, 304
Middle East, 1, 3, 4, 5, 7, 12, 18–21, 26, 37–8, 54, 92, 137, 183, 236, 278, 280
  corruption and, 89
  democracy in, 298
  rebetiko and, 10

  religion and, 13
migration, 2–4, 8–9, 15, 18, 27, 31, 33, 164
  Egyptian Greeks, 164, 169–70
  European crisis, 15, 137–8, 164, 179, 312–13
  Greek diaspora, 8–9, 33, 51
  to Israel, 189, 227–8
  Thrace crisis (2020), 241
millets, 32, 187, 233, 270
Mishkenot Sha'ananim, Jerusalem, 197–8
'Misirlou', 10
Misiroglou, Thouli, 71, 83
Missirian, Anna, 117–21, 126–30, 230, 276
Mitsotakis, Konstantinos, 216, 236
Mitsotakis, Kyriakos, 28, 225, 259
mixed marriages, 121, 174, 201–2, 269, 270, 280
Mogamma Complex, Cairo, 163
Mohammad Bin Salman, Saudi Crown Prince, 116, 215, 294
Mohammed Ali Research Center, 126
Moldova, 33
Montefiore, Moses, 197–8
Montenegro, 257
Montreux Convention (1936), 258
Moon Deck, Zamalek, 159
Morocco, 84
Morsi, Mohammad, 138–9, 144
Mount Athos, 70, 90

358

INDEX

Mount Zion, Jerusalem, 197–8, 223, 228
Mubarak, Hosni, 117, 139, 149, 163
muftis, 252–3
Muhammad Ali Pasha, 112–17, 122–7, 129, 131, 164, 166
multipolarity, 44, 109, 126, 144, 278, 288, 310
Murad II, Ottoman Sultan, 67, 79, 121
Museum of Contemporary Art, Thessaloniki, 71
Muslim Brotherhood, 27, 138–9, 149, 152, 192, 195, 219, 294
Mussolini, Benito, 55
Mustafa Mustafa, 245
Mykonos, 9, 40, 118

Nagorno Karabakh, 5
Naguib, Mohammad, 168
names, 13–14
Naoussa, 91
napalm, 60
Napoleon I, Emperor of the French, 44, 112–13, 122, 279
Napoleonic Wars (1803–15), 45, 122
*nargile*s, 5, 39, 162, 239, 252, 277, 308
Nasrallah, Hassan, 216
Nasser, Gamal Abdel, 25, 129, 146, 149, 161, 162, 168–70, 171, 212
Nasser, Khalid Abdel, 171–2
Natech, 52
National Gardens, Athens, 24

National Liberation Front (EAM), 56, 57–8
National Republican Greek League, 56
National Schism (1914–17), 97
natural gas, 53, 64–5, 140, 142, 144, 247–9, 298, 303
Navrozoglu, Thanasis, 52
Nazi Germany (1933–45), 55–8, 81, 128
Near East, 21–4, 27, 28, 35, 41, 53, 62–3, 158, 172, 204–5, 223, 276, 280
 democracy and, 64, 236
 Egypt and, 136, 143
 Israel and, 222
 migration and, 31, 133, 164, 187, 271, 312–13
 multipolarity, 44, 109, 126, 144, 278
 Russia and, 65, 73–4
 Thessaloniki and, 79, 82–3, 87, 104, 106, 109
 Türkiye and, 141
Nelson, Horatio, 113
neo-Ottomanism, 93, 204
neoliberalism, 15, 149
Neos Kosmos, Athens, 1–4, 11, 12
Netanyahu, Benjamin, 63, 181, 217, 218, 219, 223, 294
New York, United States, 8, 10–11, 264, 308–9, 311
Newtown, Wayne, 207
Nicholas, Saint, 312
Nicolson, Harold, 99
Nobel Peace Prize, 267

INDEX

Noble Dina, 221
Nord Stream, 249
North Atlantic Treaty Organization (NATO), 6, 12, 16, 19, 54–5, 74–7, 137, 221, 250, 309–11
  Russia and, 74–7, 182
  Thrace and, 230, 254, 256
  Türkiye and, 62, 108–9, 140, 193, 268
  United States and, 6, 54, 62, 64, 108, 141, 222
North Macedonia, 74–8, 83, 91, 109, 187, 243, 244
Notaras, Lucas, 120

October 7 attacks (2023), 129, 146, 147, 180, 181, 192, 195
Odessa, Ukraine, 46
oil, 211
Oinousses, 307–16
olive oil, 256
Olivia Manning, 158
Omonia Square, Athens, 224
On the Back of the Tiger (Livaneli), 86
Onassis, Aristotle, 211–12
Open TV, 70
Operation Nickel Grass (1973), 215
Orbán, Viktor, 288
Orbiter 3 UAVs, 222
Organized Crime and Corruption Reporting Project, 75
Orient Express, 256
Orientalism, 45, 78, 204
Orientalism (Said), 78

Orlando, Vittorio Emanuele, 99
Orthodox Christianity, 11, 12–14, 24, 28, 31, 33, 64, 70, 71, 90
  in Albanian communities, 41
  in Arab communities, 270
  in Bulgaria, 265, 271
  in First World War, 96–7
  in Greco-Turkish War, 32, 82, 101, 102–3
  in Greek War of Independence, 123
  in Israel/Palestine, 183, 184–99, 207–10, 223, 228
  in Ottoman Empire, 23, 33, 43, 46, 47, 50–51, 80, 85, 86, 120, 265, 273
  in Russia, 12, 33, 63, 187–8, 189
  in Türkiye, 95, 103, 263
Oslo Peace Process (1993–5), 183, 192
Osman Hamdi Bey, 112
Osman Sait Bey, 87
Othman, house of, 29
Otto, King of Greece, 34
Ottoman Empire (1299–1923), 2, 3, 9, 15, 22–3, 24, 30–34, 244
  Arabian rebellion (1811–12), 115–16
  Armenian genocide (1915–17), 2, 3, 68, 220
  Balkan Wars (1912–13), 81, 107, 116, 128, 241
  Capitulations, 22–3, 136, 166, 167

INDEX

Christianity in, 23, 33, 43, 46, 47, 50–51, 80, 85, 86, 120, 265, 273, 291
cosmopolitanism, 86, 103, 116, 126, 263, 275
Crete, 48, 49, 96
Egypt, 112–17, 122, 126, 129
Egyptian War (1831–3), 129
Epirus, 40, 42, 43–51
First World War (1914–18), 95–9
French War (1798–1801), 112–13
Greek War (1919–22), 32, 82, 101–3, 241, 243, 313
Greek War of Independence (1821–32), 24, 30, 33–4, 46–7, 95, 122–5, 166, 274, 313–14
Holy League War (1571), 63
Italian War (1911–12), 92
Jerusalem, 185, 187, 197, 209
Kavala, 111–20, 125
merchant class, 46, 50–51
millets, 32, 187, 233, 270
Paris Peace Conference (1919), 99
Pontic Greek genocide (1914–23), 68, 91
Russian War (1877–8), 257
Salonica, 67, 78, 79–81, 83, 93, 104, 106, 107–8
Tanzimat reforms (1839–76), 83, 86
Thrace, 240, 247, 252, 256–7

tourism in, 45, 80, 111
Treaty of Kutchuk Kainardji (1774), 44
Treaty of Moscow (1921), 102
Treaty of Sèvres (1920), 101
Young Turk Revolution (1908), 85–7
Ottomanism, 85–7
ouzo, 5, 11, 84, 94

Palestine, 4, 20, 60, 81, 99, 183–210, 211, 223
Arab-Israeli War (1948–9), 194, 203–4, 207
British Mandate (1920–48), 20, 60, 81, 99–100, 186, 194, 200
Christianity in, 184–99, 207–10
First World War (1914–18), 202
Gaza, *see* Gaza
Nakba (1948), 203–4
Oslo Peace Process (1993–5), 183, 192
Petra Hotel affair (2004), 185–6, 190, 206
Six-Day War (1967), 146, 194, 199
UN partition plan (1947), 194, 211
West Bank, 149, 183, 188, 192, 194, 195–6, 219, 223, 227
Yom Kippur War (1973), 146, 215–16

INDEX

Palestine Liberation Organization (PLO), 204, 213
Palestinian Authority, 192
Palikares, 24
Pamuk, Orhan, 262, 297
Panagia, Kavala, 112
Panagia Greek Orthodox Church, Istanbul, 261, 263–5
Pangrati, Athens, 224
PAOK FC, 70–72, 73
Papandreou, Andreas, 140, 213–14, 217
Papandreou, George, 217, 219
Paris Exposition (1867), 135
Paris Peace Conference (1919), 99–101, 135
Paros, 40
Pascha, 13
PASOK, 69, 213, 225, 250
Paul the Apostle, 79
Peacemaking 1919 (Nicolson), 99
Percentages Agreement (1944), 59
Peres, Shimon, 217
Peskov, Dmitry, 257
Petra Hotel affair (2004), 185–6, 190
Pfizer, 109
Phanar, Constantinople, 30
Phanariot Greeks, 30, 33, 274
Philip II, King of Macedonia, 75
Pindus mountains, 37, 39, 43
Piraeus, Athens, 5–10, 11, 26, 60, 78–9, 105, 181, 310
Plaka, Athens, 24

Platia Eleftherias, Thessaloniki, 85
Plato, 28, 123, 277
Platon Antiques, Thessaloniki, 103–8
Pleteno Koinsep, Xanthi, 234
Politi, Villy, 154–5
Politika, 281
Polk, George, 61
polykatoikias, 1–3, 5, 67
Pomakochoria, 233
Pomaks, 232, 234–8, 242
Pontic Greeks, 68–9, 71, 76, 91
pop music, 8, 131
population exchange (1923), 2, 81, 98, 103, 104–5, 107, 127, 130, 232–3, 265, 278
populism, 14, 68, 76, 91, 93, 108, 109, 217, 282–3
prayer beads, 68, 247, 252
Predator spyware, 225
Prespa Agreement (2018), 75–8, 109
property market, 6–7, 16–18, 81–2, 107, 127, 313
    Egyptians and, 6, 154–5
    Israelis and, 4, 6, 18, 81, 82, 180–81, 224–5, 227
prostitution, 87, 160–61, 269
Protestantism, 12
punk music, 278
Pushkin Café, Moscow, 217
Putin, Vladimir, 65, 68, 72, 73, 76, 188

Qaddafi, Muammar, 143, 213
Qatar, 182, 248, 256

INDEX

Quinn, Anthony, 48

Rafael Systems, 222
raki, 95, 302–3
Ramadan, 90
rayah, 120
rebetiko, 9–10, 87, 308
Recanati, Abraham, 81
Recipe for Daphne, A (Anastasiadou), 267, 280–81
remittances, 62
Republic of Thrace (1913), 241
Republican People's Party (CHP), 93, 266, 267, 268, 269, 292, 298–304
revisionism, 20, 35, 64
   Israel, 64, 136, 227
   North Macedonia, 76
   Türkiye, 19, 27, 49, 64, 136, 138, 140–44, 217, 221, 223, 227
Revithoussa, 248
Rhodes, 22, 40, 141, 144, 201
Rhodopi mountains, 230, 235, 237
Rizopoulos, Spiros, 41–2
Road to Oxiana, The (Byron), 32
Rodocanachi, Constantine, 312–13
Roma, 231, 242, 246
Romaic identity, 277–8
   Roman Catholicism, 12, 209, 264, 265, 271
Romania, 57, 60, 158, 230, 257, 274, 300
Romanticism, 123
Rome, Italy, 214

romeiko, 33, 46
ROSATOM, 302
Rostov-on-Don, Russia, 69
Royal Air Force (RAF), 216
Rum, 30, 33, 232–3, 235, 261, 265–83, 285–306
   demographic decline, 265–6, 289
   Erdoğan and, 285–304
   expulsion (1964–5), 235
   pogrom (1955), 233, 235, 267–9
   property rights, 288
   Zografion Lyceum, 261, 265–6, 270–73, 312
Rumelia, 121
Russian Civil War (1917–23), 87
Russian Empire (1721–1917), 34, 44, 61, 63, 204
   Cretan State peacekeeping (1898–1913), 49
   First World War (1914–17), 95
   Greek War of Independence (1821–32), 34, 73, 125
   Holy Land and, 187
   Ottoman War (1877–8), 257
   Pontians in, 68
   Revolution (1917), 188
   Treaty of Kutchuk Kainardji (1774), 44
Russian Federation (1991–), 19, 20, 33, 61, 65, 68–9, 72–77, 181–2, 310
   Alexandroupoli and, 257–9
   Imperial Orthodox Palestine Society, 74–6, 187

Jerusalem property and, 188
Libya, relations with, 143
NATO and, 74–7, 182
natural gas industry, 247–9, 303
ROSATOM, 302
Syrian War (2015–24), 72, 182, 302
Türkiye, relations with, 72, 301–4
Ukraine War (2014–), *see* Russo-Ukrainian War
Russian Orthodox Church, 12, 33, 63, 187–90
Russo-Ukrainian War (2014–), 4, 49, 54, 65, 73, 141, 148, 181, 242, 298
Alexandroupoli and, 258–9
Crimea invasion (2014), 54
Egypt and, 175
emigration and, 189
NATO and, 62, 77
natural gas and, 53, 64–5, 148, 247–9
Savvidis sanctions (2023), 72–3
shipping and, 23
Thrace and, 232
Türkiye and, 288, 295, 301–2

sachnisi, 38, 92, 240, 293
al-Sadat, Anwar, 146–7
al-Sadat, Mohammad Anwar, 145–51
Said Pasha, 134
Said, Edward, 78, 204

Saladin, Sultan of Egypt and Syria, 209
Salafism, 143
Salonica, *see* Thessaloniki
Samaras Café, Jerusalem, 206, 207
Samos, 141, 286, 314
Santorini, 19, 118
Sarrail, Maurice Paul, 97
al-Saud, Abdullah bin Saud, 115
Saudi Arabia, 20, 31, 116, 117, 151, 211–12, 214, 215, 256
Savvidis, Ivan, 68–78, 91, 259, 310
Schengen Zone, 128
Second World War (1939–45), 28, 55–8, 81, 128, 158, 159, 267
secularism, 272
in Egypt, 115, 135, 138, 139
in Israel, 18, 181, 203, 227
in Palestine, 183, 190, 192
in Türkiye, 93, 94–5, 140, 220, 243, 266, 268, 292, 294, 298–304
Seidemann, Danny, 194–6
Selim III, Ottoman Sultan, 112
Sephardic Jews, 80
September 11 attacks (2001), 20, 117
Septemvriana pogrom (1955), 233, 235, 267–9
Serbia, 50, 83, 99, 229, 257
Sergei Courtyard, Jerusalem, 188
sesame pastry rings, 293
Sève, Joseph Anthelme, 122, 125

INDEX

sex, 160–61, 165, 179
Shadid, Anthony, 158
Shafak, Elif, 278
al-Sharaa, Ahmed, 193
Sharia law, 233
Sheikh Zayed City, Cairo, 136
shipping, 6, 23, 62, 68–78, 85, 211–12, 311
simit, 293
Sipahi, 247
el-Sisi, Abdel Fattah, 138–9, 145, 146, 149–53, 162–3, 170, 174–7
Six-Day War (1967), 146, 194, 199
Skopje, North Macedonia, 76
Skripal, Sergei, 74
slavery, 45, 46, 48, 79, 80, 113, 122, 124–5
Slavic languages, 81, 234, 271
Smyrna, 9, 18, 23, 34, 91, 101, 102–3, 308
socialism, 15, 18, 25, 69, 167, 168
Socrates, 28
Soliman Pasha, 122, 125
Somalia, 33
Souda Bay, Crete, 297
Souliotes, 44
South Africa, 169
Soviet Union (1922–91), 39, 68
    Cold War (1947–91), 15, 20, 58–9
    dissolution (1991), 68, 189, 190
    Greek Civil War (1946–9), 58–9, 62

    Israeli land purchase (1964), 188
    Percentages Agreement (1944), 59
    Second World War (1939–45), 55, 57, 59
    Treaty of Moscow (1921), 102
    Yom Kippur War (1973), 215–16
Spain, 80
Special Operations Executive (SOE), 57
Spetses, 125
Spitogatos, 94
sprezzatura, 24
Stalin, Joseph, 58–9, 60, 62, 63, 72, 182
Stark, Freya, 118
Stergiadis, Aristeidis, 102
Stoianovich, Traian, 49, 50, 262
Strymonas river, 119
sucuk lokum, 252
Sudan, 127, 145, 148, 226
Suez Canal, 134, 135, 136, 146, 161, 168, 212
Suez Crisis (1956), 136, 161, 168, 212
Sufism, 43
suicide, 15
Suleiman I, Ottoman Sultan, 22, 197
Suleymaniye Mosque, Istanbul, 282
Sunday Times, The, 39
Sweden, 76, 100, 107
Syntagma Square, Athens, 5

INDEX

Syria, 3–4, 21, 26, 28, 34–5, 42–3, 182, 293
  Civil War (2011–), 47, 72, 294
  Egyptian–Ottoman War (1831–3), 129
  French War (1798–1801), 113
  HTS takeover (2024), 3, 35, 150, 182, 192, 214, 222, 226, 288, 302
  Iran, relations with, 214, 222
  Israel, relations with, 181, 193, 222
  Ottoman period (1516–1918), 23, 46, 113, 123
  Palestine War (1948–9), 194
  Russia, relations with, 72, 182, 302
  Türkiye, relations with, 5, 150–51, 182, 192, 226, 288
Syrian Orthodox Church, 209
Syriza, 27, 28, 73, 138, 220–21, 245, 250
Syros, 25

Tahrir Square, Cairo, 162–3
Taksim Square, Istanbul, 293
Talaat Harb Square, Cairo, 171
Talat Pasha, 87
Tanzimat reforms (1839–76), 83, 86
Tarlabaşı, Istanbul, 293–7
taxi drivers, 24
Taymur, Mahmud, 114
Teenager Immigrant, The (Brouzis), 308

Tel Aviv, Israel, 21, 179, 181
Tenedos, 232
Tepelene, Albania, 43
Thasos, 116
Theophilos III, Patriarch of Jerusalem, 186, 193
Theros, Patrick, 21
Thessaloniki, Greece, 9, 23, 34, 41, 47, 52, 67–109, 176, 313
  Aristotelous Square, 83–4
  Atatürk's childhood in, 92–5, 101, 268
  Bit Bazaar, 103–7
  Byzantine period, 79
  cosmopolitanism, 71, 86, 88, 106–7
  cost of living in, 94, 109
  cuisine, 83
  founding (315 BCE), 79
  gay pride parade, 89
  Greek annexation (1912), 81, 107
  Jewish community, 80–81, 88
  mosques, 79, 90
  National Schism (1914–17), 97
  Ottoman period, 67, 78, 79–81, 83, 85–7, 93, 104, 106, 107–8
  PAOK FC, 70–72, 73
  port, 68–78, 107
  property market, 82, 89, 107, 313
  service-sector economy, 93
  tourism in, 88, 90, 92–5, 106–7
  Turks in, 93–5, 106, 107

INDEX

Venetian period, 79
Young Turk Revolution (1908), 85–7
Thrace, 69, 101, 119, 229–59
  Alexandroupoli, 74, 247, 256–9, 310
  cosmopolitanism, 231–2, 236, 239–40, 249–50
  cuisine, 239, 251, 252, 255
  Islam in, 119, 230, 231, 232–8, 241–7, 250–56, 278
  migrant crisis (2020), 241
  natural gas industry in, 247–9
  Ottoman period, 240, 247, 252, 256–7
  Pomaks in, 234–8
  Republic of Thrace (1913), 241
  tourism in, 238–40
Thubron, Colin, 45
Thucydides, 119
Tirana, Albania, 45, 244
Tito, Josip Broz, 59
tobacco, 69, 70, 85, 118, 125, 126, 165–6, 231
Tobruk, Libya, 92
topik, 303
Topkapi (1964 film), 112
Tortoise Trainer, The (Osman Hamdi), 112
Tositsas, Michalis, 126
Toumba, Thessaloniki, 70
tourism, 2, 8–9, 16, 17–18, 24, 38, 40, 62, 65, 238, 280, 286, 311
  in Kavala, 117, 130
  in Ottoman period, 45, 80, 111
  in Thessaloniki, 88, 90, 92–5, 106–7
  in Thrace, 238–40
Trampa, Mustafa, 253
Trans Adriatic Pipeline (TAP), 247
Treaty of Friendship (1930), 267, 269
Treaty of Kutchuk Kainardji (1774), 44
Treaty of Lausanne (1923), 103, 232, 233, 235, 241, 246, 265
Treaty of Moscow (1921), 102
Treaty of Sèvres (1920), 101
Truman, Harry S., 60, 309
Trump, Donald, 76, 222, 249, 303
tsipouradika, 38, 42
Tsipouro, 39
Tsipras, Alexis, 27, 28, 138, 220
Tsirkas, Stratis, 164–5, 167, 207, 209
Tsoukka, Phthiotis, 308
Turkish coffee, 3, 6, 7, 11, 103, 234, 251, 312
Turkish delight, 252
Turkish language, 81, 236, 245, 270
Turkish Union of Xanthi, 251
Turkish Youth Union of Komotini, 251–2
Türkiye, 6, 11, 18, 19, 20, 21, 27, 28, 64, 69, 108, 136, 138–44, 181, 203, 217, 261–306
  Alexandroupoli and, 257

367

INDEX

Azerbaijan, relations with, 5, 248
Blue Homeland doctrine (2006), 143–4, 227, 304, 306
Bosporus closure (2022), 258
cost of living in, 94, 293, 298
coup attempt (2016), 93, 295–6
crossroads, 229
Cyprus invasion (1974), 7, 111, 224, 242, 265, 287
drone exports, 243, 294–5, 302
EEZs dispute, 140–42, 221, 223
Egypt, relations with, 138–9, 144, 145, 151
EU candidacy, 286–9
Greek community, *see* Rum
Hagia Sophia conversion (2020), 90–91, 108, 282–3
Islam in, 93, 94, 95, 138–9, 243, 273–4, 282–3, 292, 294, 298–9, 306
Israel, relations with, 193, 217, 219, 221, 227
Kurds, 286, 294, 301
Libya, relations with, 143–4
Limnos–Kemal Reis collision (2020), 227
NATO membership, 62, 108–9, 140, 193, 268
natural gas industry, 247, 248, 303
neo-Ottomanism, 93, 204
population exchange (1923), 2, 81, 98, 103, 104–5, 107, 130, 232–3, 265, 278
revisionism, 19, 27, 49, 64, 136, 138, 140–44, 217, 221, 223, 227
Russia, relations with, 72, 301–4
Russo-Ukrainian War (2022–), 288, 295, 301–2
secularism in, 93, 94–5, 140, 220, 243, 266, 268, 292, 294, 298–301
Septemvriana pogrom (1955), 233, 235, 267–9
Syria, relations with, 5, 150–51, 182, 192, 226, 288
Thrace, relations with, 241–6
tourists from, 92–5, 117, 239, 304
Treaty of Friendship (1930), 267
Treaty of Lausanne (1923), 103, 232, 233, 235, 241, 246, 265
United States, relations with, 140–41, 220
White Turks, 301
Yom Kippur War (1973), 215–16
Turkolimano, Piraeus, 7
TurkStream, 248–9
tzigerosarmas, 255

Uber, 24
Ukraine
EU candidacy, 255

INDEX

Israel, migration to, 189–90
NATO candidacy, 62, 77
Predator spyware and, 226
prostitution in, 161
reconstruction planning, 298, 302
Russian War (2014–), *see* Russo-Ukrainian War
Savvidis sanctions (2023), 72–3
unemployment, 14, 15
United Arab Emirates, 6, 31, 40, 63, 64, 127, 145, 173, 175, 229
  Egypt, relations with, 136
  Israel, relations with, 180, 214, 221
  Libya, relations with, 143
  Syria, relations with, 150
United Kingdom, 9, 22, 28–9, 34, 63, 73
  Cretan State peacekeeping (1898–1913), 49
  Egypt, rule of (1882–1956), 25, 57, 100, 134, 135, 166
  First World War (1914–18), 95, 97, 99
  Greco-Turkish War (1919–22), 102, 241
  Greek Civil War (1946–9), 58–9, 62, 63
  Greek War of Independence (1821–32), 34, 123, 124, 125
  Levant Lunatics, 45
  Luddite movement (c. 1811–16), 45

Palestine Mandate (1920–48), 20, 60, 81, 99–100, 186, 194, 200
Paris Peace Conference (1919), 99–101, 135
Percentages Agreement (1944), 59
RAF Akrotiri, 216
Second World War (1939–45), 56–8
Skripal poisoning (2018), 74
Suez Crisis (1956), 136, 168
United Nations (UN), 138, 274
  Convention on the Law of the Sea (UNCLOS), 140
  ICJ Israel ruling (2024), 195, 223
  Palestine partition plan (1947), 194, 211
United Russia, 69, 76
United States, 6, 8, 9, 20, 27, 28, 44, 108, 181–2, 297, 301, 309–10
  Alexandroupoli and, 257–9
  Cold War (1947–91), 15, 20, 58, 59–63
  Egypt, relations with, 150
  Gaza War (2023–), 147
  Greek Civil War (1946–9), 58, 59–63
  IMEC corridor, 77–8, 183
  Israel, relations with, 214, 215, 219–20, 227–8, 301
  Marshall Plan (1948), 62, 268, 309
  NATO membership, 6, 54, 62, 64, 108, 141, 222

INDEX

natural gas industry, 247–9, 298, 303
Paris Peace Conference (1919), 99
Russo-Ukrainian War (2022–), 247–9, 301
Saudi Arabia, relations with, 211–12
slavery in, 124–5
State Department, 21, 27, 212, 215
Truman Doctrine (1947), 60
Türkiye, relations with, 140–41, 220
War On Terror (2001–), 20, 117
University of Ioannina, 52
University of Pennsylvania, 160, 191
Üsküdar, Istanbul, 280, 306
Usmanov, Alisher, 69
Usta, Omer, 255

vacation loans, 14
Vandi, Despina, 8
Vasiliadis, Minas, 289–93, 301
Vasilissis Sofias Avenue, Athens, 24
Vassiliki, Kyra, 46
Vassilisis Olgas Avenue, Thessaloniki, 84–5
Vatikiotis, Panayiotis Jerasimof, 200–201, 202, 203, 204
Vavatsis, Andreas, 105–8
Venice, Republic of (697–1797), 22, 40, 44, 50, 52, 79, 120

Venizelos, Elefterious, 96–8, 99, 135, 183, 267
Via Egnatia, 230
Vienna, Austria, 51, 256
Villa Allatini, Thessaloniki, 85–6
Villa Tara, Zamalek, 154
Vingas, Lakis, 266, 274
Vingas, Yvonne, 274–7, 282
Virgin Islands, 194
Vlachs, 91
volta, 38

Wafd, 135
wages, 16
Wahhabism, 115–16, 117, 122, 204
Wallachia, 33
*waqf*s, 116–17, 251–2
War On Terror (2001–), 20, 117
wealth inequality, 7
Weizmann, Chaim, 100
West Bank, Palestine, 149, 183, 188, 192, 194, 195–6, 219, 223, 227
White Palace, Istanbul, 295
White Turks, 301
Wilson, Woodrow, 99
'woke' culture, 8, 68
Woodhouse, Christopher Montague, 5th Baron, 56, 58, 60, 61
work–life balance, 8
World Bank, 153

Xanthi, Thrace, 230–47, 249, 251, 252, 253–4, 256

INDEX

'Ya Habibi' (Vandi), 8
Yalta Conference (1945), 59
Yemen, 127, 146
Yeni Mosque, Komotini, 247, 252
Yeni Mosque, Thessaloniki, 90
Yesil Mavi, Istanbul, 280, 295
Yom Kippur War (1973), 146, 215
Young Turk Revolution (1908), 85–7
Ypsilantis, Alexandros, 33, 274
Yugoslavia (1918–92), 1, 60, 62, 69, 74, 236, 243

Zaev, Zoran, 75, 78, 92

Zaghlou, Saad, 100, 135, 166
Zagorochoria, 39
Zamalek, Cairo, 154, 159
Zeibekiko, 9
Zionism, 20, 81, 99–100, 180, 194, 200–201, 203, 211
Ziraat Bank, 252
Zografion Lyceum, Istanbul, 261, 265–6, 270–73, 312
Zohr gas field, 142
Zorba the Greek (Kazantzakis), 48, 128
Zumwalt, Elmo, 215–16
Zurayk, Constantine, 203–4